STUDIES IN FOLKLORE

edited by RICHARD M. DORSON

2

D1738269

Analytic Essays in Folklore

by

ALAN DUNDES

University of California
Berkely, California

1975
MOUTON
THE HAGUE · PARIS

ISBN 90 279 3231 X

To my wife Carolyn who shared the excitement of
researching and writing these essays

ACKNOWLEDGMENTS

For permission to reprint the essays in this volume, I wish to thank the follow-
ing publishers and societies: American Anthropological Association, American
Folklore Society, The University of California Press, The Catholic University
of America Press, the Folklore Institute of Indiana University, The Edward C.
Hegeler Foundation, the Kroeber Anthropological Society, Eleanor and Leonard
Manheim, the National Psychological Association for Psychoanalysis, Inc., The
University of New Mexico Press, the New York Folklore Society, Prentice-Hall,
Inc., the Tennessee Folklore Society, and Dr. George B.Wilbur.

FOREWORD

"Why collect folklore?" is a question the folklorist repeatedly encounters from puzzled and not necessarily unsympathetic colleagues in established disciplines. They wonder aloud what contribution of import will result from this ceaseless accumulation of texts and their identification with hieroglyphic letters and numbers. No better response can be made to this bafflement than to place in an inquisitor's hands the present selection of his essays by Alan Dundes, who obtained his doctorate in folklore at Indiana University in 1962 and became a full professor at the University of California in Berkeley in the anthropology department at the age of thirty-three. For Dundes is first and foremost a theorist, an analyst, a bold speculator about the meaning of the materials of folklore to their human conveyors. While in my classes in folklore I insisted on the student documenting each textual item of folklore with informant data, Dundes, once a student in those classes, went one better on becoming the instructor and required that his student collectors in addition interpret the meaning of the recorded text. His quest for meanings has led him to seek context along with text, metafolklore as well as folklore, and thereby to reorient the conception of fieldwork; interpretations of tradition bearers should carry at least as much weight as those of investigators.

The special achievement of Dundes, who has already contributed so substantially to folklore studies in the twelve years of his professional career to date, becomes clearer when seen against other folklore scholarship. Characteristically the monuments in our discipline have taken the forms of handbooks, indexes, monographs, collections, dictionaries, encyclopedias, bibliographies. Compilation, codification, annotation are the watchwords. What is often lacking in the mountainous literature of folkloristics is the play of the inquiring mind over the materials. Andrew Lang had the gift, but we can think of few volumes to place alongside those provocative essays he pooled into Custom and Myth in 1884. Alan Dundes also possesses the gift for creative scrutiny of the folklore genres. He pulls them apart structurally, probes into them psychologically, extends them culturally to such matters as elephant jokes and bathroom inscriptions. To the lexicon of the folklorist he has added linguistic terms such as "etic" and "emic" units, morphological concepts such as "lack" and "lack liquidated", typologies of collectors such as "anal retentive" and "anal ejective". His examinations of familiar folklore sayings, beliefs, and daily habits have revealed the present anxieties and future aspirations of Americans caught in the system, and their tendency to divide all life's activities into three parts. In one scintillating article after another he has shown, or suggested, the ways in which folklore reflects our conscious and unconscious thoughts.

The success of a discipline depends upon the quality of the minds it attracts. In attracting Alan Dundes, a brilliant speaker, teacher, and scholar, folklore has again proved its mettle.

Richard M. Dorson
Indiana University

CONTENTS

X

PREFACE

The following essays appeared originally in diverse journals and reflect my principal research interests, which, generally speaking, focus upon the analysis of folklore. For too many years, the discipline of folklore has overemphasized collecting and classifying its materials to the point where questions of analysis have inevitably been postponed.

The reader may disagree with the types of analysis I use, namely, structural analysis as a means of rigorously describing the nature of folkloristic data, and psychoanalytic insights I have attempted to apply to folklore so as to bring unconscious content into consciousness. I am well aware that neither structural analysis nor psychoanalysis are widely accepted by American folklorists. But even if the reader does not share my theoretical biases, I would hope that he would at least admit that the field of folklore is in dire need of new analytic methods. The relatively few considerations of folklore theory which exist in the literature prove upon examination to be little more than rehashes of the nineteenth century concern with historical reconstruction, typically by using a form of the comparative method.

The present set of essays is somewhat arbitrarily divided into four sections. A section on folklore theory and method is followed by a series of essays devoted to structural analysis. A third section provides examples of the application of psychoanalytic theory to different types of folklore while the concluding essays are intended to suggest how a student of American culture might profitably use folklore as source material. The section divisions are not hard and fast. The psychoanalytic bias, for example, is found throughout the volume.

Ultimately, theoretical notions, structural analytic techniques, and applications of psychoanalytic theory are only useful to the extent that they aid in illuminating the nature of man. Folklorists should study folklore, not for its own sake (though it is fascinating), but because folkore offers a unique picture of folk. In folklore, one finds a people's own unselfconscious picture of themselves. Folklore as autobiographical ethnography permits the folklorist to see a people from the inside-out rather than from the outside-in. Regarding folklore as a source of native cognitive categories and of worldview paradigms is surely a far cry from the nineteenth century concept of folklore as consisting exclusively of quaint antiquities and fragmentary survivals. The shift from considering folklore as something dead and static to something alive and dynamic has been a dramatic one. Folklore can no longer be defined in terms of meaningless survivals. Rather folkore is a rich and meaningful source for the study of cognition and values. Once this is accepted, then it is likely that the discipline of folklore will become of increasing importance in academic circles. Through the study of folklore, we should be better able to understand others as well as ourselves.

SECTION ONE

FOLKLORE THEORY AND METHOD

THE AMERICAN CONCEPT OF FOLKLORE

It is probably unwise to speak of "the" concept of American folklore as if there were just one. In the past, and even in the present, there has been considerable disagreement among folklorists as to the nature of folklore. One is tempted to suggest that there have been almost as many American concepts of folklore as there have been American folklorists. Thus "the American concept of folklore" can really only be discussed as "some American concepts of folklore".

By "American" I refer to North American and more specifically to the United States of America. The peoples of Latin America also consider themselves "Americans" and folklorists in Latin America have been extremely active in the last few decades, particularly with respect to formulating "concepts" of folklore. [*1] However, the various understandings of folklore held by Latin American folklorists differ quite radically from those championed by North American folklorists and they will not be treated here.

In discussing the American concept of folklore, I shall confine myself to the American folklorists' concepts of folklore, inasmuch as a less specific topic would have to include the views of the general public. The public at large tends to think of folklore as a synonym for error, fallacy, or historical inaccuracy. One hears, for example, the phrase "That's folklore", meaning 'That is not true', and while this does not help the image of the professional folklorist - he is implicitly relegated to the role of a full-time student of error - it need not concern us here.

A problem which arises in considering American concepts of folklore is the fact that the term "folklore" in American usage refers to both the materials (e. g. folktales and folksongs) under study and the study itself. Consequently, an American folklorist's concept of folklore may include his definition of the materials of folklore (and not all contemporary American folklorists share the same definition by any means) as well as his notion of the theories and methods of a discipline called folklore (and once again there are serious differences of opinion as to what theoretical aims and methodological techniques should be employed). I shall attempt to survey both American concepts of folklore in the sense of the materials of folklore and of folklore as a disciplinary study of these materials.

Perhaps the easiest way to describe the American concept of what the materials of folklore are is to divide the word folklore into "folk" and "lore". What is the American concept of "folk"? What is the American concept of "lore"? In order to answer these questions, one may begin by examining the

Reprinted from Journal of the Folklore Institute, 3 (1966), 226-49.

American concepts of these two words in 1888, the year the American Folklore Society was founded and the Journal of American Folklore commenced publication. Many of the notions held at that time substantially influenced the development of subsequent American studies in folklore. (Folklorists not only enjoy
studying tradition but they themselves often tend to be bound by tradition in their
studies. Just as the materials of folklore pass from generation to generation, so
also do the theories and methods of students of these materials pass from generation to generation of folklore scholars. Thus one finds that many of the twentieth-
century American folklorists' concepts of folklore are actually nineteenth-century
concepts in disguise.)

William Wells Newell, in the lead article in the first issue of the Journal of
American Folklore, an article entitled "On the Field and Work of a Journal of
American Folk-Lore", stated that the journal was designed "for the collection
of the fast-vanishing remains of Folk-Lore in America", namely:

(a) Relics of old English folk-lore (ballads, tales, superstitions, dialect,
    etc.)
(b) Lore of Negroes in the southern States of the Union
(c) Lore of the Indian tribes of North America (myths, tales, etc.)
(d) Lore of French Canada, Mexico, etc.

It is clear from this that Newell echoed the European concept of folklore as
survivals from a time long past. Notice that Newell did not include the possibility of any folklore arising anew in the United States, that is, any indigenous
American folklore. However, Newell faced a conceptual problem in defining
folklore, a problem caused by the presence of American Indians. (It might be
noted in passing that the American folklorist's work with American Indian folklore has had important influences upon the direction of American folklore theory.) Folklore in the strict sense was used by Newell to refer to unwritten
popular traditions of civilized countries (Newell 1888c). Thus by definition
the American Indian, since he was not "civilized" but "savage", in the then
popular tripartite unilinear evolutionary scheme of savagery, barbarism,
and civilization, could not have folklore.

Curiously enough, this distinction still applies in the subdiscipline of folk
music. American students of folk music do not normally include the music of
the American Indian in their studies. This is in marked contrast to American
students of the folktale who do include American Indian tales in their studies.
For Newell, the difficulty was resolved by employing the term "mythology" in
addition to "folklore". In a special note on the subject Newell (1888c:163) explained that mythology referred to the "living system of tales and beliefs which,
in primitive peoples, serves to explain existence". Primitive peoples had mythology; civilized peoples had folklore, which was thought to be survivals from
primitive times. The distinction also suggested that mythology was living while
folklore was dying. That Newell was quite serious in making the distinction is
apparent in his remark that had it not been out of regard for brevity, the Journal
of American Folklore might have been titled the Journal of American Folklore
and Mythology. Among most twentieth-century American folklorists, the distinction is not made. Mythology is usually considered to be a subdivision of folklore.
Nevertheless the name of the institute at the University of California at Los
Angeles (UCLA) is Center for the Study of Comparative Folklore and Mythologys

which implies that folklore and mythology are separate entities.

By 1890, Newell had come to realize that the distinction was a false one and he saw that the term folklore had to be more inclusive. On March 24th of that year, Newell presented a paper entitled "The Study of Folklore" to the New York Academy of Sciences. Newell's concept of folklore as expressed in that address is notable because it is remarkably close to the concept of folklore held by many contemporary American folklorists. Newell (1890) said, "By folk-lore is to be understood oral tradition, - information and belief handed down from generation to generation without the use of writing." He then remarked that since European oral traditions were related to traditions found among savage tribes, it was clearly necessary to extend the term folklore so as to cover the latter. So folklore was used first to include tales, beliefs, and practices now retained among the unlettered peasantry of Europe, and then secondly, in a broader sense, so as to embrace the traditional tales, customs, and usages of uncivilized races. Folklore in this second broader sense, according to Newell, was a part of anthropology and ethnography insofar as it concerned the mental side of primitive life, with special reference to folk narratives in which beliefs and habits were related or accounted for. Newell then concluded by distinguishing two sides to the subject of folklore: the aesthetic or literary, and the scientific aspect.

Newell's conception of folklore as "coextensive with oral tradition" (Newell 1898) led to his applauding R.E. Dennett's study of the folklore of the Fjort. The fact that the English Folklore Society had published a work in which the term "folklore" was used in reference to African (i.e. savage) materials confirmed Newell in his decision to use the term in the wider sense.

Newell's list of "folks" in his lead article in the first volume of the Journal of American Folklore is of interest because, with a few important additions and modifications, they are the folk groups with whom modern American folklorists are most concerned. The emphasis upon English (and Scottish) materials, particularly in the area of the ballad, continues. It is worth noting that Newell made a distinction between English survivals in the United States and survivals from other European countries. Logically, English folklore should be part of what might be termed American immigrant folklore. However, traditionally, probably because the English were among the first to arrive in the New World, they put a priority on themselves and called other later groups "immigrants". In American folklore scholarship, this priority is all too obvious when one compares the much greater attention devoted to studies of English folksongs in America (e.g. the Child ballad in the United States) than to studies of American immigrant folksongs.

The second "folk" in Newell's list refers to the Negro in the southern portion of the United States. The lore of Negroes is still an important area of research in American folklore circles and, interestingly enough, the emphasis upon the lore of southern Negroes has persisted up until very recently. It is only in the last decade that collections have been made from northern Negroes, notably by Dorson (1959a), and only in 1964 was there an intensive study made of northern urban Negroes, (Abrahams 1964). Yet even Dorson claims that American Negro folklore belongs primarily to the plantation culture of the Old South and he goes so far as to say that "Free Negroes living north of the Ohio River possessed no traditions" (1959a:181). The difficulty here is that some American folklorists have considered only the folklore of the rural southern Negro. While Dorson is undoubtedly correct in observing that rural Negroes who move north tend to lose many of their traditions, it does appear that the urban northern Negro does have a folklore of his own, much of it probably recast from white folklore, as Abrahams' study of Negro folklore in Philadelphia, Pennsylvania, abundantly demonstrates (Abrahams 1964).

The lore of the American Indian is still a legitimate subject for the American folklorist. However, the collection and study of American Indian folklore has for the most part been left to anthropological folklorists. Comparatively few literary folklorists have worked extensively with American Indian materials. (Stith Thompson is probably the most notable exception). In t he division of "folks" between anthropological and literary American folklorists, it is the Negro who has provided the common ground. Literary folklorists are con- cerned with European-derived folklore and Negro folklore; anthropological folklorists study Asian-derived (i. e. American Indian) folklore and Negro folklore. One reason for this may be the fact that American Negro folklore is a combination of European and African elements. Thus the literary folklorist interested in European folklore and the anthropological folklorist interested in African folklore both find important sources in the rich American Negro oral traditions.

The fourth folk category of Newell's outline, the lore of French Canada and Mexico, has only recently begun to branch out into the field of American immi- grant folklore. Because there have been so many waves of immigration to the United States, from so many different parts of the world, it is possible to col- lect the folklore of almost any European or Asian country within the confines of the United States. Once again, Newell urged in 1895 that immigrant folklore be collected and he expressed the hope that local or regional folklore societies would undertake this task (Newell 1895). Nevertheless, the American immi- grant as a folk source remained largely untapped for some time, as Stith Thompson (1938) observed. Only in the last twenty years has this folk begun to be seriously studied (Dorson 1959a).

American immigrant folklore probably offers the greatest challenge to the American folklorist, and it is important to realize that study of this type of folklore is bound to result in changes in American concepts of folklore. This is because American immigrant folklore is alive. Whereas the nineteenth-century American concept of folklore was limited to dead or dying survivals - relics of Old English lore, southern Negro animal tales, the last remains of a moribund American Indian tradition - the twentieth-century American concept of folklore includes vital and dynamic traditions, ranging from the lore of schoolchildren to the songs of social protest of labor unions and American Negro civil rights workers. American immigrant groups often live in a formally or informally bounded geographic area. They frequently form a community, or perhaps a small community within a larger community. Many immigrant groups are held together by a church (e. g. the Greek Orthodox Church), or by an official organ- ization or association (e. g. the German-American Club). Members of these groups hold weekly or monthly meetings at which original native languages are spoken and folklore transmitted. Sometimes these immigrants become quite nationalistic, much more so than they were at home "in the old country". They may become nostalgic about their country of origin. Even their children may be influenced. Second- or third-generation immigrants may take an active interest in the country of their parents' origin; they may study their parents' language in college; and they may eventually try to visit the "home" country. The opportunities for studying the differences in the folklore among the different generations of American immigrants are great.

The American concept of folk is not, however, limited to English, Negro, American Indian, and immigrant groups. Nor does the modern folklorist limit the concept of folk to peasants, or to rural, or to uneducated peoples, as is still the case in many European folklore cricles. For the contemporary American folklorist in the 1960's, the term "folk" can refer to <u>any group of people whatsoever</u> who share at least one common factor. It does not really matter what that linking or isolating factor is - it could be a common occupation, a common language, or common religion - but what is important is that a group formed for whatever reason will have some traditions which it calls its own. In theory, a group must consist of at least two persons, but obviously most groups consist of many more than that number. A member of the group may not know all the other members of that group, but he probably will know the common core of traditions belonging to it, traditions which give the group a sense of group identity. The group could be lumberjacks, railroadmen, or coal miners; or Catholics, Protestants, or Jews. The members of a country, a state or region, a city or village, a household or family, are all members of groups, and thus there is national, regional, village, and family folklore. It is this broad conception of "folk" which explains why the American folklorist can be interested in collecting American Indian tales one day, and the games of primary school children the next. Universities, colleges, and schools are groups, too, and they have their own traditions. There are, for example, numerous college legends, songs, pranks, and customs (Dorson 1959a:254-67). Even folklorists themselves are a group and must in the strict theoretical sense be considered a "folk" with its own in-group jokes and rituals. Clearly any one individual is a member of a number of different folk units. A Negro steelworker living in Pittsburgh, Pennsylvania, might serve as an informant for Negro folklore, for traditions of the city of Pittsburgh, and for folklore of the state of Pennsylvania. One can see, therefore, that Newell's conception of the folk as essentially a unit of ethnic or national identity has been considerably broadened so as to include a host of folk groups based upon other shared factors.

Having considered the American concept of folk, one may turn to the American concept of lore. Newell's identification of lore with oral tradition is characteristic. Folklore is usually said to be oral or in "oral tradition". There are two difficulties with this criterion: (1) not everything which is transmitted orally is folklore (in cultures without writing everything is transmitted orally); and (2) some forms of folklore are not, strictly speaking, transmitted orally. Examples of this last are games and folk art, on the one hand, and such written forms as epitaphs, traditional letters (e.g. letters to heaven), and bathroom writings (graffiti), on the other. Despite these difficulties, many American folklorists continue to use the criterion of oral transmission (Utley 1961).

Another common criterion is that the lore is spontaneous or, rather unconsciously produced. Materials which are consciously contrived and altered are probably not folklore. Self-consciously produced materials would be literary or popular rather than folk (such as Brahms' Lieder, or composed commercial songs sung in a nightclub). Sometimes, original folklore materials are borrowed by individual writers who consciously reshape and rewrite them. The results should be called "art based on folklore", but occasionally the molders refer to their productions as "folklore". This has aroused the ire of professional folklorists inasmuch as these edited and frequently bowdlerized materials are often quite different in style and content from the original folk forms. Richard Dorson calls such materials "fakelore", arguing that these materials are not authentic products of the traditional folk process. However, there is an important theoretical issue involved. The question is: what happens when an unconscious or un-selfconscious process becomes a conscious one?

The conscious manipulation or changing of folk materials is certainly not a phenomenon peculiar to the United States. As a matter of fact, it is interesting to compare the motivations for the manipulation of folklore in the United States and in the Soviet Union. In the United States, a popularizer may use a dozen versions of a song, lifting one or two stanzas from each to make a "new" version of the folksong. These "composite texts", as they are called, should not be considered true folk materials, inasmuch as they have never been in oral tradition and have never actually been sung by any member of the folk. (However, such a text could go into oral tradition and be accepted by a folk group, in which case fakelore would become folklore!) The reason for this conscious composition is partially aesthetic, but ultimately capitalistic. The popularizer is not interested in scholarship, but in selling many copies of his book of "folklore". In contrast, one finds in the Soviet Union (and also in China), that folklore is consciously altered for quite another reason. The goal is not financial profit, but ideological propaganda. Folklore is supposed to demonstrate the validity and correctness of a particular political point of view (Dorson 1963b).

In the United States, the falsification of folklore serves the purposes of capitalism while in the Soviet Union and China, its distortion serves the purposes of dialectical materialism. One assumes that the scholarly folklorists in both the United States and the Soviet Union deplore this exploitation of folklore. But whether folklorists like it or not, the evolution of man is moving in a direction towards more, rather than less, consciousness and awareness of culture. This may even be a good thing. In the treatment of mental illness, cures are sometimes effected by making the unconscious conscious. Consciousness affords, if not requires, control. Man is no longer the mere passive end product of an evolutionary process. With increased knowledge of the process, man obtains the opportunity to influence the process. More and more, man controls the direction and degree of his own evolution. Within this theoretical framework, it becomes obvious that the conscious manipulation of folklore is not really so extraordinary. Rather it is part of a growing tendency among peoples with complex cultures to actively mold their cultures, instead of simply being passively molded by them. Eventually, the American concept of folklore will have to take account of this self-conscious interference with the folk process.

Another striking example of the conscious interference with folklore is the revival. Folklore revivals are quite distinct from folklore survivals. A survival, by definition, is marked by a continuity of tradition. It is the result of an unbroken historical chain through time. A revival, however, may well follow a break in tradition. It may even occur after the item has, for all practical purposes, died out. The point is that the folklore revival is a conscious and artificial phenomenon. The survival, in contrast, survives with no conscious assistance. Most American folklorists tend to look askance at folklore revivals, considering them to be somehow spurious. Yet folk dance groups which meet to learn and perform folk dances, as well as folksingers who resuscitate songs no longer sung, are found throughout the United States.

The comparison of survival and revival should not be misconstrued to mean that American folklorists think of folklore as surviving in the fashion of Newell. Yet, in fairness, it must be noted that some American folklorists do conceive of folklore as consisting of survivals (Maranda 1963). In one case, folklore was said to be a survival which did not survive, that is, folklore was dead. In 1931, Ruth Benedict wrote an article on folklore for the Encyclopaedia of the Social Sciences, in which she claimed that except for some folktales still told in a few rural groups, "folklore has not survived as a living trait in modern civilization", and that "Thus in a strict sense folklore is a dead trait in the modern world" (Benedict 1931). This is not a majority view, and in fact in that same year, Martha Warren Beckwith wrote an excellent survey of the American approach to folklore in which she remarked that "Folklore is not merely a dead survival but a living art. It is constantly taking fresh forms and recreating old ones" (Beckwith 1931). Beckwith did comment, for example, that the college community was a folk group with its own songs and rituals.

American folklorists do not insist on the anonymity of folklore creators. Songs of protest known to be composed by Woody Guthrie, e. g. "So Long, It's Been Good to Know You", are considered to be folksongs, since they are sung by the folk, but the authorship of most folklore is not known.

Probably the most satisfactory way of defining lore is the enumerative list of folklore genres or forms. Newell's partial list - ballads, tales, superstitions, dialect, myths, games, proverbs, and riddles - remains a reasonably accurate indication of what the American folklorist considers the forms of folklore to be. It is true that there have been several recent attempts to restrict the list of genres. William Bascom, for example, suggested the term "verbal art" to distinguish such verbal forms as folktale, proverb, and riddle, from custom and belief. At one point, he said that "Folklore can be defined as verbal art. " (Leach 1949:398). Generally speaking, anthropological folklorists have tended to conceive of folklore as consisting of primarily verbal materials. In the case of folksong, the text is folklore but the tune is not (Bascom 1953a: 285). (It is noteworthy that the older ballad scholars such as Child considered texts apart from their tunes.) Another instance of an anthropological folklorist's bias is Melville Jacobs' use of the term "oral literature" in lieu of the term folklore. This American concept of folklore is even narrower than Bascom's "verbal art". For Jacobs, folklore is oral literature, which consists of myths and tales. Apparently, Jacobs does not even include riddles and proverbs under the term "oral literature".

The reason for the position taken by American anthropological folklorists is that from their perspective, folklore is just one of many aspects of culture.

Music is another (and those who study it are ethnomusicologists rather than folklorists). Art is still another. This concept of folklore contrasts with that held by American literary folklorists who have tended to be influenced more by the all-inclusive European concept of folklore with its subcategories of folk costume, crafts, art, and music. Nevertheless, for literary as well as anthropological folklorists, the European concepts of Volkskunde and folklivsforskning (Maranda 1963:81) embrace too much by including both folklore and ethnography. In the United States, the compromise between the positions of the anthropological and the literary folklorists is that the American concept of folklore emphasizes verbal materials, but also includes folk music. The distinction is usually made between "folk" and "primitive", the distinction being in part a related survival of the older dichotomy of "folklore" and "mythology". Folk music, for example, is found among peoples with writing, whereas primitive music is found among peoples without writing (usually termed "non-literate peoples"). In terms of the American concept of folklore, folk music, folk art, and folk dance are materials which properly come under the purview of a folklorist. Primitive music, primitive art, and primitive dance do not, and they are left to the interested anthropologist. The glaring exception to the "folk-primitive" dichotomy is the folktale. One section of Stith Thompson's standard work, The Folktale, is entitled "The Folktale in a Primitive Culture - North American Indian". There is agreement between anthropological and literary folklorists primarily with respect to verbal materials (e.g. tales, proverbs, and riddles). Verbal materials are folklore, no matter where in the world they are found.

One consequence of the emphasis upon verbal materials is the neglect of nonverbal materials. The folklore of body movement, that is, gestures, folk dance, and even games, is rarely studied by American folklorists. Folk art, another form of nonverbal folklore is similarly infrequently studied. (Notice that the term "nonverbal" itself signals the priority given to verbal materials. Other forms of folklore are lumped together under a label which indicates they are not verbal.)

While many professional folklorists would definitely claim that their concept of folklore did include folk dance, folk art, and folk recipes, few are engaged in research in these areas. In looking through the major American folklore journals: Journal of American Folklore, Journal of the Folklore Institute, Southern Folklore Quarterly, and Western Folklore, one finds very, very few articles devoted to these aspects of folklore. Another striking difference between the American concept of folklore and the various concepts of folklore found in Europe is the omission of festivals. There are a number of American festivals or ritual days, e.g. Christmas, Easter, Halloween, and birthdays, but few folklorists study them. In contrast, the European folklore journals are filled with studies of festivals. The usual argument presented by American folklorists is that folk dance, folk art, and folk festivals are not as important in American culture as they are in most European cultures. And it is a fact that few Americans wear traditional costumes (with the exception of a few groups like the Amish). On the other hand, this does not fully explain why American folklorists have neglected nonverbal folklore. Even in the case of folk arts and crafts, one could find ample material for research among American immigrant groups. Yet, there has been little work in this area and there are unfortunately very few folk museums in the United States. Except for a small number of institutions such as the Farmer's Museum at Cooperstown, New York, one finds nothing really comparable to the European folk museums.

Of course, the American concepts of folklore are not limited by what research possibilities are available in the United States. To most American folklorists, folklore consists of a number of specific cultural items which are usually transmitted from person to person. Verbal and sung items are normally communicated orally; nonverbal items are usually learned by watching and imitating (e.g. games and folk dance). A list of some specific cultural forms might include: myth, legend, folktale, joke, proverb, riddle, superstition, charm, blessing, curse, oath, insult, retort, taunt, tease, tongue-twister, greeting or leave-taking formula, folk speech (e.g. slang), folk etymologies, folk similes (e.g. as white as snow), folk metaphors (e.g. to jump from the frying pan into the fire), names (e.g. nicknames or place names), folk poetry - which runs from lengthy folk epics to children's rhymes such as ball-bouncing rhymes, jump-rope rhymes, finger and toe rhymes, dandling rhymes, counting-out rhymes (to determine who will be "it" in games), and nursery rhymes. There are also such written folk rhymes as autograph book verse, epitaphs, and latrinalia (graffiti). The common nonverbal genres include: folk dance, folk drama, folk art, folk costume, folk festival, games, practical jokes (or pranks), and gestures. Folklore also includes such major forms as folk instrumental music (e.g. fiddle tunes) and folksong (e.g. ballads and lullabies) and such minor ones as mnemonic devices, the comments made after body emissions (e.g. after burps or sneezes), and the sounds made to summon or command animals. This list is hardly exhaustive but it should reveal the general nature of the American concept of lore.

Having examined, albeit cursorily, the American concept of the materials of folklore by considering both "folk" and "lore", I should like to turn briefly to the concept of folklore as a discipline. One difficulty is that the American concept of the discipline of folklore is no more precise than the concept of folklore as materials. Another problem is that the discipline derives so much from the European concepts of folklore that it is hard to distinguish any aspect of the discipline which may properly be considered as original with American folklorists. The question may thus be put: In what ways, if any, does the American concept of the discipline of folklore differ from those held in Europe?

Historically, American folklorists appear, by and large, to have been imitators rather than innovators. The American Folklore Society itself, founded in 1888, was specifically modeled after the English Folk-Lore Society, organized ten years earlier in 1878. Newell, one of the founders of the American Folklore Society, stated explicitly that the rules of the English society "served as the model of those adopted by the American Folk-Lore Society" (Newell 1888b:79). More importantly, European theories and methods of folklore were readily adopted by American folklorists. Thomas F. Crane, a professor at Cornell University, who was perhaps the leading American student of folktales in the late nineteenth century, used for his research model the European comparative method. Crane made his position perfectly clear in one of the first articles in the Journal of American Folklore. In "The Diffusion of Popular

Tales" (1888) Crane gave a short review of the European methods of studying folklore and suggested that these methods be applied to American materials. Earlier, Daniel G.Brinton and John Fiske had borrowed from various European theories, notably solar mythology.*2 Very few important original theoretical works in folklore have been penned by American folklore scholars. One is tempted to question whether any American study in folklore has been as important for folklore theory generally, as such European contributions as Olrik's analysis of epic laws, Von Sydow's notions of active and passive bearers of tradition, Aarne's laws of change, or Malinowski's functionalistic conception of myth as a sociological charter for belief. Most of the discussions of theory and method in American folklore scholarship are essentially rehashes of European concepts (Beckwith 1931 and Dorson 1936b). One gets the impression that not only is much of American folklore - the materials - essentially transplanted European folklore, but many of the theories and methods of studying folklore employed traditionally by American folklorists are likewise European borrowings. Even in the areas of collection and classification, where American scholars have made their mark, one sees the European influence.

Francis James Child, in his prefatory "advertisement" to part I of his celebrated collection, The English and Scottish Popular Ballads, specifically mentions that he "closely followed the plan of Grundtvig's Old Popular Ballads of Denmark" (p. ix). With regard to the collection of Child ballads in the field, one must note that such fieldwork was largely stimulated by the work of an English collector, Cecil Sharp, in the southern Appalachians. The same situation prevails in folktale and riddle classification. Stith Thompson after failing to utilize Aarne's 1910 tale typology for his 1914 Harvard University doctoral dissertation "European Borrowings and Parallels in North American Indian Tales" (or for the 1919 partial publication, European Tales Among the North American Indians) made more than an amende honorable by twice revising Aarne's index (in 1928, and again in 1961). Even the idea of making an index of motifs, as opposed to tale types, had occured to Aarne, Arthur Christensen, and Albert Wesselski before Thompson undertook the arduous assignment (Thompson 1946:422). This is not to minimize the incredible amount of time and scholarship which Thompson has devoted to his world-famous projects, but only to assert that the basic underlying ideas for them came from Europe. In the same fashion, one can remark that Archer Taylor's riddle classification scheme, found in his superb English Riddles from Oral Tradition, is an adaptation of one made first by Robert Lehmann-Nitsche in a collection of Argentinian riddles. Inasmuch as the majority of American folklorists were either trained or heavily influenced by Stith Thompson and Archer Taylor, the European concepts have tended to dominate American folklore scholarship. Some students were encouraged to compile tale type or motif indexes; others were encouraged to apply the European comparative method to American Indian materials.

What are some of the theoretical assumptions underlying the European-derived American concept of folklore? First of all, one must remember that in nineteenth-century Europe, folklore was conceived of as a historical science whose aim was the historical reconstruction of the past. Folklore, according to this view, provided a key to the past. By applying the comparative method, in 1886 refined into the historical-geographic or Finnish method, one could arrive at a hypothetical ur-form of an item of folklore, and in addition show the possible, if not probable, paths of diffusion of the item. In the United States, Child, Newell, Kittredge, Thompson, and Taylor sought to reconstruct past forms of present folklore. American folklorists, like their European precursors, looked backwards. Present folklore was collected primarily to illuminate the historical past. Even the development of one of the principal American contributions to folklore theory, the oral-formulaic theory of Parry and Lord, was motivated by an interest in the past. The extensive fieldwork in Yugoslavia and the detailed analyses of Serbo-Croatian folk epics were undertaken principally because of the hope that an analysis of present-day epic creation would shed light on the epic-making techniques employed in Homer's day. The idea of studying the present to discover the past is entirely in keeping with nineteenth-century historical reconstructionist aims.

The historical bias remains strong in American folklore scholarship. Alexander H. Krappe, an American folklorist greatly influenced by European scholarship, made an unequivocal statement in his The Science of Folklore to the effect that folklore is a historical science (p. xv). More recently, Dorson has argued that "... the only meaningful approach to the folk traditions of the United States must be made against the background of American history" (1959a:5 and 1959b). However, Dorson is more interested in using history to understand the significance of folklore than in limiting the discipline to using folklore to reconstruct history.

American anthropological folklorists under the influence of Franz Boas have also favored a historical approach to folklore. Like their literary colleagues, they have sought to ascertain the distribution and diffusion patterns of particular items of folklore. Nevertheless, the anthropological folklorists have contributed to the American concept of folklore by documenting the fallacy of the older notion that folklore reflects only the past. Boas (1916:393) considered folklore to be a kind of a mirror for a culture and he suggested that a people's folklore was that people's autobiographical ethnography. This meant that although folklore might be a key to the past, it likewise reflected the present culture and thus was also a key to the present. The importance of this shift in the American concept of folklore cannot be exaggerated. If folklore was not limited to dead survivals but included living materials, then the study of folklore did not have to be limited to the search for origins. Instead, the present day functions of folklore could be investigated.

This distinction between folklore as a product of the past and folklore as a reflector of the present has had crucial implications for folklore methodology. If folklore were limited to nonfunctioning survivals from the distant past, then by definition there would be no point in trying to observe folklore in context. For this reason, the past-oriented American folklorist was interested only in collecting texts. Minimal informant data was recorded, for instance, name and age plus the place and date of the recording, but no attempt was made to discover how that item was used or how the informant himself regarded the item. On the other hand, present-oriented American folklorists have become more and more interested in the dynamics of the use of folklore in particular situations. The concern for the recording of folklore in context has led to new requirements and techniques in the collection of folklore (Goldstein 1964; see also Dundes 1966a). For example, how does a racounteur evaluate and interpret the tales he tells? What are his aesthetic principles? If there is "oral literature", then there is bound to be "oral literary criticism". As folklore is transmitted from one generation to another, so also are the traditional attitudes and inter- pretations of folklore communicated in similar fashion even if they are not al- ways formally articulated. Another contextual factor is the set of rules which determines whether or not a particular individual will use a particular item of folklore in a given situation. What makes one proverb appropriate, but another one inappropriate? The rules for the use of folklore, or as it has been termed, "the ethnography of speaking folklore", are just beginning to be seriously stu- died (Arewa and Dundes 1964).

Besides the shifts in the American concepts of folklore from "the past" to "the past and the present", from "survival" to "survival and functioning el- ement", one detects a tendency to move away from the narrow historical ap- proach to folklore towards a broader outlook which includes both historical and psychological perspectives. In American folklore scholarship, there has been enormous resistance to the application of psychological principles to folklore materials. There are at least two reasons for this. First, with the historical bias came an accompanying literal reading of folklore. For Boas, what was in the culture was also in the folklore. Boas did not concern himself with the ma- terials that were in the folklore but not in the culture (Jacobs 1959b). Folklore was not recognized as a socially sanctioned outlet for taboo thoughts and acts. It was not understood that an item of folklore can serve as a vehicle which re- quires an individual to do what he may not be permitted to do in everyday re- ality (e.g. in courtship games, complete strangers may kiss; in games of chase, acts of physical aggression are mandatory). Moreover, Boas did not bother about the apparently irrational content of much of folklore: the cannibal- istic ogres, the magical objects, and the like. Both anthropological and literary folklorists have been united in favoring a historical, literal approach to folk- lore as opposed to a psychological, symbolic approach. If American folklorists speak of psychological approaches, it is only to berate and demean them.

The second and probably the most important reason for the strong hostility towards psychological interpretations of folk materials stems from a super- organic concept of folklore. Both American anthropological folklorists and lit- erary folklorists have shared this concept. For anthropologists, folklore is a part of culture and culture has been conceived to be an autonomous abstract process separate and distinct from the human behavior in which it is manifest- ed. The superorganic is a level of reality sui generis independent of, and not reducible to, the organic, that is to say, man. Thus abstract patterns or prin- ciples have been thought to govern man. For the literary folklorists, folklore has been thought to be ruled by laws which operated independent of individuals. In theory, one could "discover" these laws and their mechanics without refer- ence to the humans who were subject to them. Typically, the superorganic principles are reified and given a "life" of their own. Thus Stith Thompson (1946:426) asks whether motifs combine freely or whether some are isolated, each one "living an independent life as a single-motif tale-type?" This is not merely a matter of phrasing but a serious matter of theoretical principle. Literary folklorists speak of the "life-history" of a tale or song, but not of the "life-history" of the people who tell or sing it. This artificial separation of the lore from the folk is recognized. Thompson speaks of the personal affection an amateur collector may have for his informants and then observes that "The comparative folklorist is disturbed by no such affection. . . . If he is interested in the people who tell the tale or sing the song, such interest is purely incidental. " (1938:2). The study of text without context, of folklore without reference to folk, continues. The logic is that if folklore is a superorganic phenomenon which can be studied without reference to the folk, then there is obviously little need of examining the psychology of that folk. By this reasoning, the study of folklore does not require recourse to analyses of individual psychology (Dundes 1965).

It is encouraging to note that in American anthropology, the importance of the individual and his psychology is now understood. However, the subdiscipline in anthropology is termed "Culture and Personality", which clearly implies that personality is not part of culture but is something separate from it. In the study of folklore, the relationship of individual and social psychology to folklore materials barely has been hypothesized. Yet despite the strong historical-literal tradition and the powerful influence of superorganicism in American folklore scholarship, one can conjecture that the American concept of folklore will in time become eclectic enough to utilize psychological theories (Fischer 1963).

One of the most intriguing psychological approaches to folklore is that employed by psychiatrist Abram Kardiner. Kardiner took Freud's original notion that folklore, like religion, is a projective system derived in part from infantile life (with specific reference to the relationship between infant and parent), and added the necessary element of cultural relativism. In other words, Kardiner saw that as child-parent relationships differed in various culture, so the content of the folklore in these culture would vary (Kardiner 1939 and 1945). More recent studies have compared the results of such psychological tests as the T. A. T. (Thematic Apperception Test) with myths from the same culture. The similarity of themes is striking (Kaplan 1962). The significance for folklorists is that a folktale or a folksong is a "natural" T. A. T. Whereas the psychological test is usually introduced into a culture from without and may or may not test what it is said to test, the folktale or folksong is a projection of personality from within the culture.

In this modern updating of Boas' notion of folklore as a mirror of culture, it is possible to conceive of folklore as providing an invaluable means of seeing a culture from the inside out instead of from the outside in. This includes the corollary notion of folklore as a source of native categories. Each culture has its own system for slicing up objective reality. There may be different logical, linguistic, and semantic categories. Concepts of space, time, number, weight, distance, direction, and many others, vary with each culture. An obvious example is the fact that the color spectrum is divided differently in different cultures. For those interested in understanding how a people live and think, it is essential to discover and describe these native cognitive categories. But it is difficult for the collector to put aside his own native categories. They are so "natural" that it may not occur to him to question their universality. But, in the folklore of a people, native classifications are recorded or alluded to. This means that by collecting and analyzing folklore, one has an excellent opportunity of coming upon these crucial categories.

The American concept of folklore is a discipline appears to be in the process of change. While the European heritage of historical reconstruction and the comparative method remain, there may be some American innovations, coming partly from the historical accident of American anthropologists working with aboriginal folklore materials. Folklore is still a historical science but it is also a social science. With the advent of M. A. 's and Ph. D. 's in folklore at such leading universities as Indiana University, the University of California, and the University of Pennsylvania a new generation of professional folklorists is being born. For these folklorists, there is no difficulty in reconciling the literary and the anthropological approaches to folklore. The possible fruits of a combination of the comparative method with a psychological perspective are such that it is quite likely that the American concepts of folklore will change more drastically in the next several decades than they have in all the years that American folklorists have been studying folklore.

NOTES

*1 See, for example, Ramos (1958), Vega (1960), Carvalho Neto (1956a and 1962), and Morote Best (1950). For a useful survey, see Moedano (1963).

*2 Dorson (1955) includes a critique of these men among the followers of Max Müller; for their original writings, see Brinton (1868) and Fiske (1873).

	M	Tu	W	Th	F
8	Chem. 14 101 Winter		Chem 14		Chem 14
9	German 1 289 Dwinelle	German	German	German	German
10	Econ. Math Wheeler	Math 51A 10 Evans	Econ. Math	Math 51A	Econ. Math
11		Badminton 237 Hearst		Badminton	
12	CS 210 Wheeler	Physics SE	CS		CS
1		Geo. 103 325 ESB			
2		Anthro 2003 LSB	Math 3/Evans	Anthro.	Math 51A 3/Evans
3					
4					

THE DEVOLUTIONARY PREMISE IN FOLKLORE THEORY

There has been far too little progress observed in the development of folkloristics. But this lack of "progress" is not so surprising in view of the unmistakable and consistent bias against progress inherent in the majority of folklore theories. Even a cursory examination of the intellectual history of folklore scholarship reveals a definite unquestioned basic premise that the golden age of folklore occurred in the past, in most cases specifically the far distant past. As a result of the past-oriented Weltanschauung of most folklorists - and it is really with the worldview of folklorists that this essay is concerned - it has always appeared to be logically necessary and highly desirable to engage in historically reconstructing the golden age of folklore. The endless quest for the land of "ur" as in "ur-form", or "archetype" in Finnish Method parlance, continues unabated in conservative folkloristic circles. Inasmuch as the means and direction of folklore methodology are probably inescapably controlled by the nature of the theoretical premises, hitherto largely unexamined, held by professional folklorists, it is absolutely essential that these crucial underlying premises be held up to the light of reason if there is ever to be any appreciably significant change in methods of folklore analysis.

The bias against "progress" in folklore theory may be easily demonstrated by briefly considering some of the numerous examples of degeneration, decay or devolution - the particular term is not the issue - which abound in so much of traditional folklore theory. Perhaps the most obvious instances are those underlying the various folklore transmission theories. Typically, surveys of such theories begin with a detailed consideration of degeneration, perhaps signalling its hallowed position.[*1] The most common devolutionary notion is that folklore decays through time. Another notion is that folklore "runs down" by moving from "higher" to "lower" strata of society. These two notions are by no means mutually exclusive since one can without difficulty imagine that if folklore really moved from "higher" to "lower" strata, it could easily undergo textual deterioration at the same time. Classic examples of these notions include Max Müller's "disease of language" according to which theory of semantic devolution the original names of Vedic and other gods became confused or forgotten as time passed, as well as Hans Naumann's "gesunkenes Kulturgut"[*2] which held that cultural items originating in the upper stratum of society filtered down to the lower stratum which was wrongly thought to be synonymous with the "folk". A logical consequence of this "aristocratic" origin of folklore theory was that folklore consisted largely of reworked remnants that had man-

Reprinted from the Journal of the Folklore Institute, 6 (1969), 5-19.

aged somehow to survive the presumed downward transmission of culture.

It should be remarked that the gesunkenes Kulturgut notion is still very much with us. Folklorist Walter Anderson believed that folktales usually moved from "culturally higher" to "culturally lower" peoples, according to Stith Thompson (1946:438) who echoes the idea, pointing out that American Indians have borrowed European tale types whereas Europeans have not borrowed American Indian tales. Thompson even goes so far as to say that "If the principle is really valid we may ask whether tales must keep running down hill culturally until they are found only in the lower ranges", although he concedes this would be an overstatement of Anderson's position. Nevertheless, Thompson's own devolutionary bias may well have led him to misinterpret the available data regarding a hypothetical archetype for the "Star Husband" tale which he studied using the Finnish method. Like all devolutionary folklorists, he assumes that the original form of the tale must have been the fullest and most complete version. Later, shorter versions are thus assumed to be fragments. The devolutionist normally postulates a movement from complex to simple whereas an evolutionist might argue that the development from simple to complex is equally likely. In any case, Thompson is forced to label some of the shorter versions of Star Husband as confused or fragmentary despite the fact that his "fragmentary" versions demonstrate a common uniform pattern.*3

There are many other striking illustrations of the devolutionary premise in folklore transmission theories. The Grimms argued that folktales were the detritus of myths (Thompson 1946) and just as folktales were assumed to be broken down myths, so it was held that ballads were the detritus of epics or romances (Ortutay 1959:202 and Wilgus 1959:43). But perhaps no more overt statement of the premise can be found than in the conception of "zersingen" in folksong theory. "Zersingen " refers to the "alterations of a destructive nature"*4 which occur as songs are sung. The very act of singing a folksong is thus construed to be a potentially destructive act endangering the continued stability of the song sung.*5 Moreover, just as singing songs is presumed to destroy them, so the telling of folktales is thought to run the risk of ruining them. Retelling a tale allows the forgetfulness of the raconteur to become a factor (Krohn 1926). This is implicit in Walter Anderson's famous superorganic "law of self-correction" (Gesetz der Selbstberichtigung) (cf. Glade 1966). Anderson's idea was that folktale stability was not attributable to the remarkable memories of raconteurs, but was rather the result of an individual's hearing a given tale on many different occasions, perhaps from many different sources. Narratives essentially corrected themselves, argued Anderson, but the very term used indicates the devolutionary bias. Why is it assumed that folktales need to be corrected? Only the unquestioned assumption that folktales become "incorrect" through time can possibly justify the notion that folktales need to "correct themselves" - granting for the sake of argument that tales rather than people do the "correcting".

A critical correlative of the devolutionary premise is the assumption that the oldest, original version of an item of folklore was the best, fullest or most complete one. A change of any kind automatically moved the item from perfection toward imperfection. Partly for this reason, one finds a deep resentment of change and an equally deep-seated resistance to the study of change in folklore. A similar situation prevailed until relatively recently in anthropology where even up to the first several decades of the twentieth century pioneer ethnographers sought to obtain "pure" precontact cultural data. Students of the American Indian, for example, would often write up their field data as if the Indians had never been exposed to or affected by acculturative European influences. Mooney, in collecting Cherokee tales, specifically commented that he did not bother to record what were obviously European borrowings. This made perfect sense in the light of a past-oriented Weltanschauung. If the forms of the past were more valuable, then it logically followed that changes of any kind were by definition potentially destructive in nature. Although anthropologists have learned to accept and study culture change, folklorists generally have tended to continue to look askance at change.

The Hungarian folklorist Ortutay, in probably the most detailed critique of folklore transmission theories, notes that, "Retelling nearly always involves a change" and although there may be an element of creativity involved in making any change, "in its later, final stages ... oral transmission comes to be equivalent to deterioration, to a process of stuttering forgetfulness" (Ortutay 1959:180). The same attitude towards change is expressed by Stith Thompson when in summarizing Walter Anderson's views he says, "The first time a change of detail is made in a story it is undoubtedly a mistake, an error of memory." (1946:437). Deleterious changes could be caused by weakness of memory, unwelcome interpolations, or from contaminations of themes. Note the obvious pejorative connotation of the term "contaminated text", a term which once again reflects the ever present devolutionary premise (cf. Krohn 1926, Thompson 1946, Ortutay 1959, and Bach 1960).

The generally negative attitude towards change has been clearly reflected in folklore methodology. Just as ethnographers carefully sifted through unavoidable details obviously only recently added through acculturative contact in an attempt to discover the pure unadulterated original native culture, so practitioners of the Finnish historic-geographic method sought to work backwards through the unfortunate changes (or, in Thompson's terms, the mistakes and errors) in order to find the pure unadulterated original ur-form. The difficulties of searching for the ur-form, too often presumed to be hopelessly hidden by the destructive, deteriorative effects of oral transmission were considerable, but not always insurmountable. Possibly one of the most ambitious and optimistic efforts was made by students of the Bible engaged in Form Criticism.

Form Criticism, according to Redlich (1939) is a method of study and investigation which deals with the preliterary stage of the Gospel tradition, when the material was handed down orally. It was assumed that Biblical materials before being set down in written tradition "were subject to the usual inevitable fate of oral tradition, such as adaptation, alteration, and addition". However, it was also assumed that there were definite, discernible laws governing the oral transmission process, laws which once discovered might be applied (in reverse) to the written Gospels. By thus working backwards, Form Critics hoped to be able to reconstruct "the narratives as they actually happened and the sayings as they were actually uttered by our Lord" (Redlich 1939:11).

A few folklorists have commented upon the consequences of the devolutionary premise. Von Sydow, for instance, challenged the hypothesis that the original

form of a folktale was necessarily the most complete, most logical version
(Dundes 1965:233), although he confessed this had been his own view when he
began his folktale research. Similarly, Gerould in The Ballad of Tradition
deplores the "unfortunate tendency on the past of scholars to take it for granted
that earlier ballads are likely to be better than later ones ..." (p. 214). Yet
Gerould argues that the process of deterioration is inevitable: "Degeneration
of noble themes and captivating tunes must have gone on ever since ballads became current ..." (p. 185). The implicit nature of the devolutionary premise
is also revealed in the wording of Gerould's consideration of the American
"Old Bangun" versions of "Sir Lionel" (Child #18) when he observes, "The
interesting point about all these versions, it seems to me, is the evidence they
give that changes and even abbreviations do not necessarily imply any structural degeneracy;" (p. 174; emphasis added). More recently, Ortutay has suggested that short elementary forms such as proverbs or jests are "most capable of
resisting the corroding effect of degressive processes" (Ortutay 1959:207).

Despite a few critical comments by folklorists, there does not appear to be
much awareness of the enormous impact of devolutionary ideas upon folklore
theory and methodology. At best, folklorists seem to accept the idea that the
universe of folklore is running down. Even Olrik's so-called epic laws of folklore were presumed to weaken in time. Olrik suggested, for example, that the
law of the number three "gradually succumbs to intellectual demands for
greater realism" (Dundes 1965:134). One possible reason for the lack of awareness may be that folklore has often been associated with evolution rather than
devolution. And the interesting question does arise, how folklorists could remain so utterly committed to a devolutionary worldview at a time when ideas
of evolution and of progress were so much at the fore of European intellectual
thought.

The intellectual history of the idea of progress is reasonably well documented*6 and there can be no doubt that this idea came into prominence at about
the same time that the discipline of folklore began to emerge. Progress meant
more than that the "moderns" were just as good as the "ancients" as had been
argued in the late seventeenth century. Progress meant that the golden age was
not behind us but ahead of us (Barnes 1965). The positivistic ethic of the ultimate perfectibility of man and society had considerable influence upon the
course of most academic disciplines. However, as we shall see, the effect of
the evolutionary idea of progress on the treatment of folklore materials was
largely a negative rather than a positive one.

To be sure, there were some attempts to borrow evolutionary ideas in folklore theory. One of the most striking instances is Hartland's (1890:350) suggestion that narratives all over the world followed a basic evolutionary general
law. Folktales, and specifically incidents in tales, changed with different
stages of civilization in accordance with this law. Speaking of an incident in
the Forbidden Chamber cycle of tales, Hartland (1885) observed, "The incident in this shape is specially characteristic of savage life. As with advancing
civilization the reasoning which has moulded it thus becomes obsolete we may
expect that the incident itself will undergo change into a form more appropriate to the higher stages of culture...." An item of folklore had to become fit
in order to survive. Hartland (1896:III, 156) spoke of the popular mind and how

it "rendered by a process analogous with that of natural selection, which we may call traditional selection, the version that has reached us predominantly over all others". Hartland even suggested that it was traditional selection which tended to "eliminate the ruder and coarser, preserving and refining, not necessarily the more credible, but the more artistic". The idea that traditional selection operated in such a way as to ensure esthetically superior products was of course entirely in keeping with the concept of evolution as progress.

In spite of this isolated example of a positive application of evolutionary "progress" oriented theory to folklore - and there are several others - it is quite evident that the concept of progress per se had a devastatingly negative effect upon folklore theory. The association of folklore with the past, glorious or not, continued. Progress meant leaving the past behind. From this perspective, the noble savage and the equally noble peasant - folkloristically speaking - were destined to lose their folklore as they marched ineluctably towards civilization. Thus it was not a matter of the evolution of folklore; it was more a matter of the evolution out of folklore. This may best be seen in the work of Tylor who in adamantly opposing rigid degenerative theories definitely championed unilinear cultural evolution. At the same time, he forcefully argued the devolution of folklore. There was no inconsistency in this. On the one hand, Tylor states that "notwithstanding the continual interference of degeneration, the main tendency of culture from primaeval up to modern times has been from savagery towards civilization" (1958:21). On the other, Tylor conceived folklore, that is, "survivals", to be "transformed, shifted or mutilated" fragments of culture (p. 17; emphasis added). To put it succinctly, as man evolved, so folklore devolved. Tylor's view of folklore is clear. For example, he suggested that it might be possible to trace the origins of games of chance from ancient divination rituals insofar as such games were "survivals from a branch of savage philosophy, once of high rank though now fallen into merited decay" (p. 78). In an unequivocal statement, Tylor remarks, "The history of survival in cases like those of the folk-lore and occult arts which we have been considering, has for the most part been a history of dwindling and decay. As men's minds change in progressing culture, old customs and opinions fade gradually ...", although Tylor does admit that there are in fact occasional exceptions to this "law" (p. 136). If survivals or folklore were truly dying or dead, then it made a good deal of sense for Tylor to argue that the folklorist's or ethnographer's course should be like that of the anatomist who carried on his studies if possible on dead rather than on living subjects (p. 158). Here we have the ultimate logical consequence of devolution: death. And this is why devolutionary-minded folklorists have devoted themselves by definition to dead materials. The view, still widely held, is that as all the peoples of the world achieve civilized status, there will be less and less folklore left until one day it will disappear altogether. Thus Ruth Benedict could write authoritatively in the Encyclopaedia of Social Sciences in 1931 that "in a strict sense folklore is a dead trait in the modern world" (see Dundes 1966b). Are folklorists doomed to study only the disappearing, the dying, and the dead?

Of course, the gloomy reports of the death of folklore are in part a result of the misguided and narrow concept of the folk as the illiterate in a literate society, that is, the folk as peasant, as vulgus in populo, as isolated rural community.*7 Since the majority of folklorists in Europe and Asia continue to restrict the concept of folk in this way, citing as a matter of fact the definitions of folk society offered by American anthropologists Redfield and Foster for authority, *8 it is easy for them to believe that gradually the folk are dying out. With the devolutionary demise of folk or peasant culture, the deterioration of folklore was a matter of course. Ortutay puts it in these terms: "We suggest that, as long as the oral tradition of the peasantry continued to exist as a uniform system ... degressive and deteriorative processes played a secondary role in the dialectics of oral transmission. " (Ortutay 1959:201). Since unquestionably one of the reasons for the break-up of peasant culture is the advent of industrialization, Communist folklorist Ortutay is able to point the accusing finger of blame at capitalism for destroying peasant (=folk) culture and consequently for destroying folklore (pp. 201, 206). Of course, if folklorists were able to free themselves from so narrow and obsolescent a concept of folk, they could see that there are still numerous active functioning folk groups (e. g. ethnic, religious, occupational, etc.) and that the peasant community is just one of many different types of "folk". In fact, even as this one type of formerly rural homogeneous folk group becomes transformed into urban, heterogeneous, part-time folk groups, new types of folklore are emerging, some of which are actually caused by capitalism as in the creation of folklore from commercial advertisements (Dundes 1963a).

Yet even attempts to repudiate the idea that folklore is dying cannot fully escape the traditional devolutionary bias. Richard Dorson ends his book American Folklore with the statement that "The idea that folklore is dying out is itself a kind of folklore. " (p. 278). On the one hand, Dorson is indicating that this idea is a traditional one, but, in addition, since he obviously doesn't believe that folklore is dying out, the second use of the term folklore has a hint of the idea of folklore as falsehood or fallacy. In any event, the meaning of "folklore" in the phrase "That's folklore" in popular parlance refers to an error. This continued pejorative connotation of the word folklore*9 has a close connection with the devolutionary premise.

If folklore is conceived to be synonymous with ignorance, then it follows that it is a good thing for folklore to be eradicated. With this reasoning, educators and social reformers seek to stamp out superstitions encouraging folk medical practices on the grounds that such practices are either harmful in and of themselves or harmful to the extent that they delay or discourage consultation with practitioners of scientific medicine. In this light, it is not just that folklore is dying out, but rather it is a good thing that folklore is dying out. Moreover since it is regrettable that folklore isn't dying out at an even faster pace, the implication is that men should give the devolutionary process a helping hand.

The education versus folklore (or to put it in other terms: truth versus error) dichotomy is intimately related to the devolutionary premise. In essence, the idea is that the more education, especially the more literacy, the less the illiteracy and thus the less the number of folk and the less the folklore. It is wrongly assumed that literate people have no folklore. This is really the evolutionary progress idea restated. As nonliterate and illiterate man becomes literate, he will tend to lose his folklore. Typical is Gerould's

(1957:244) remark: "Not until the spread of primary education and the conversion of the general public from oral to visual habits, which took place in the
nineteenth century, was folk-song marked for des truction." Much sounder, of
course, is Albert Lord's position: "While the presence of writing in a society
can have an effect on oral tradition, it does not necessarily have an effect at
all."(1960:134-35). It is certainly doubtful whether increased literacy and education have seriously affected the quality and quantity of folk speech or jokes,
at least in American culture. Moreover, if there is any validity to what has been
termed the concept of "postliterate man" (as opposed to preliterate or nonliterate man), referring to the idea that the information communicated by such mass
media as radio, television, and movies depends upon the oral-aural circuit
rather than upon writing or print, then it becomes even more obvious that oral
tradition in so-called civilized societies has not been snuffed out by literacy.

The difference between a future oriented worldview involving progressive
evolution out of folklore and a past oriented worldview reveling romantically in
the glorious folkloristic materials of nationalistic patrimonies seems to be
clear cut. However, it is important to realize that not everyone shares the
future oriented evolutionistic postulate. There are a number of devolutionary
based philosophies of life, philosophies which decry the inroads made by civilization. In such philosophies of cultural primitivism*10 the golden age remains
safely embedded in the past while the evils of civilization do their deadly work,
destroying all that is deemed good and worthwhile. From this perspective, folklore and civilization are still antithetical - just as they were in Tylorian times,
but the critical difference is that folklore is good and civilization is bad, rather
than the other way around. The distinction can also be expressed in terms of
utility. The nineteenth century doctrine of progress included a bias towards
utilitarianism. Evolution and progress meant an increase of useful cultural
items. In this light, folklore as a vestigial remain or relic was defined as essentially useless.*11 With the substitut ion of devolution for evolution in general worldview, there comes the possibility of transvaluing folklore into something useful rather than useless. An example of this may be found in some of
the psychological approaches to folklore.

Freud summarized the devolutionary philosophy of life in Civilization and
Its Discontents - the title itself indicates the bias - when he stated that "our
so-called civilization itself is to blame for a great part of our misery, and we
should be much happier if we were to give it up and go back to primitive conditions". Note also that the Freudian method consisted of clarifying or removing
present neuroses by treating them as survivals from a fuller, more complete
event in the individual's past. The historical reconstruction of the traumatic
ur-form to explain apparently irrational and fragmentary phenomena is cut from
the same methodological cloth as the majority of folklore reconstruction techniques. More revealing perhaps for folkloristics are the actual approaches to
folklore found in the anthroposophical tradition of Rudolf Steiner and his followers as well as in the applications of analytical psychology by Carl Jung and his
followers. For both Steiner and Jung, folklore represented an important vehicle
by means of which individuals could travel backwards through time to gain vital
spiritual benefit. In other words, one of the ways of getting back to nature
(ideal human nature that is) and away from forward marching destructive civi-

lization, was by regaining contact with folklore. Rudolf Steiner's influential lecture "The Interpretation of Fairy Tales", given on December 26, 1908, in Berlin, clearly illustrates the devolutionary nature of civilization as opposed to folklore. Fairy tales, according to Steiner, belong to time immemorial when men still had clairvoyant powers and when men had access to spiritual reality. In modern times, men have wrongly engaged in intellectual pursuits and have gotten out of touch with spiritual reality. Fortunately, by reading and understanding (anthroposophically, of course) fairy tales, modern man can attempt to rediscover his long lost spiritual heritage. In like fashion with only slightly less mystical language does Jung argue that myths and their archetypes "hark back to a prehistoric world with its own spiritual preconceptions".*12 Like Steiner, Jung assumes that the primeval spiritual reality is fundamentally a Christian one, and, like Steiner, he is unalterably opposed to intellectual and rational attempts to explain the content of myth. Perhaps the overt Christian cast of Steiner and Jung's approach to folklore accounts for the placement of the golden age in the past. Fallen from grace and tainted by civilization, man needs to find balm for his injured soul by immersing himself in myths and tales which are presumed to offer the possibility of at least partial spiritual salvation. In this view, it is not folklore but spiritual man which is running the risk of dying out. It is curious how little notice the Steiner and Jung positions have obtained from folklorists, for in truth they are pioneers in the uncharted area of applied folklore. Folklore in their conceptual framework provides a unique source of therapy for the troubled if not sick mind of modern man.

Having delineated the nature of the devolutionary premise, one can see the history of folklore scholarship in a new light. It would appear that each successive methodological innovation has consisted largely of a slightly different application of devolutionary theory. If it is accurate to say that Max Müller's solar mythology yielded to Andrew Lang and company's "anthropological folklore" approach, then one can see that the crucial notion of the "disease of language" was replaced by a notion that fully formed "rational" savage ideas devolved through time to become fragmentary, irrational mental survivals in civilization. Moreover, one might consider that one offshoot of the survival theory was the more specific myth-ritual approach in which games, folkdances, and popular rhymes were presumed to be degenerate derivatives of original myths or even earlier rituals. One thinks, for example, of Lewis Spence's contention that folk rhymes including some nursery rhymes are frequently survivals of myths and ritual, "that is, they represent in a broken-down or corrupted form, the spoken or verbal description of rite" (Spence 1947:2; emphasis added). In addition, if it is accurate to say that the late nineteenth century unilinear cultural evolutionary based doctrine of survivals in turn lost its sway in folklore circles to make way for the Finnish version of the older comparative method, then one can similarly see that the degeneration oriented concept of mutilated, vestigial survivals has been succeeded by a technique whereby multitudinous versions of an item of folklore - versions which are said to suffer from the alleged ravages of performance - are amassed with the hope of reconstructing the perfect, albeit hypothetical, basic form from which these numerous partial realizations must have sprung. The question is thus not whether there is a devolutionary bias or premise in folklore theory and method. There can be no doubt that there is. The question is merely which devolutionary scheme is in vogue at any given point in time.*13

In evaluating the significance of identifying a devolutionary premise in folklore theory, there are several possibilities. One of these is that folklore is in fact devolving and that the various expressions of the devolutionary premise simply attest to this. Another possibility, however, is that the devolutionary premise is a culture bound product of a larger nineteenth century European worldview, a worldview which favored romanticism and primitivism, and which encouraged scholars in many disciplines to look and work backwards, that is, toward the presumed perfect past. If this were the case, then it might be useful to suggest alternative a priori premises so that modern folklorists might be enabled to escape the vise of devolutionary thought. One could, for example, propose a cyclic scheme*14 which assumes that folklore materials could rise phoenix-wise after a period of degeneration. Or one could construct a model in which folklore actually improved or rather evolved in time. Why must we assume, for example, that jokes told in any one age are necessarily inferior in any way to those told in ages past? Is it not within the realm of human possibility that a new version of an old joke might be a finer example of oral style and humor than its precursors? There should be recognition of the fact that change per se is not necessarily negative. Change is neutral; it is neither good nor bad. It may be either; it may be both. In this light, the unity, as Ortutay (1959) referred to it, of "one creation - innumerable variants" need not depend upon the idea that the initial one creation is perfect and the innumerable variants which follow merely imperfect derivatives. The whole idea of one creation giving rise to multiple variants is very likely a manifestation of what the intellectual historian Lovejoy (1957) described under the framework of the great chain of being, a dominant intellectual concept in eighteenth and nineteenth century Europe. The many deriving from the one may certainly be conceived as belonging not to a set in which perfection is necessarily assumed to be logically prior to imperfection, but rather to a set in which members may be ranked genealogically or hierarchically (e.g. in esthetic terms) or even as existential equals.

With a more eclectic theoretical framework, one might say that folklore in general is not devolving or dying out, but only that some genres or some examples of some genres are decreasing in popularity or usage, e.g. the true riddle or ballad in American urban society. By the same token, one might say that folklore in general is not evolving or being born, but only that some genres or some examples of some genres are increasing in popularity or usage and that occasionally new folklore forms are created. One need not, in other words, place the golden age either in the far distant past or in the far distant future. One may merely indicate that folklore is a universal: there has always been folklore and in all likelihood there will always be folklore. As long as humans interact and in the course of so doing employ traditional forms of communition, folklorists will continue to have golden opportunities to study folklore.

NOTES

*1 Ortutay (1959) provides such a survey. See especially pp. 200-07. See also McMillan (1964).

*2 For a convenient summary of Naumann's theory, see Bach (1960:64-69, 435-440) or Hultkrantz (1950:158-59).

*3 For some critical details which suggest that a devolutionary premise can bias hypotheses in historic-geographic studies, see Alan Dundes (ed.)(1965: 449-50, n. 9).

*4 The definition is from Laurits Bødker (1965). The emphasis is added.

*5 For extended discussions of "zersingen", see Renata Dessauer (1928); Goja (1920), an abridged form of which appeared in translation as Goja (1964). "Zersingen" and related phenomena are also discussed by Bach (1960:509-10). Note that if a folklorist truly believed in the reality of "zersingen", he might well exert an all out effort to prevent any further performances of folklore inasmuch as he has assumed that deterioration is an inevitable concomitant or result of performance. One can just imagine folklorists running around begging the folk not to sing folksongs, kindly explaining to them that singing them in time destroys them. This is perhaps analogous to librarians who are so concerned about injuries to and losses of books that they would almost prefer to keep all books safely locked up, away from all potential readers. The difference, of course, is that folklorists could not possibly stop the folk from using folklore - even if they wanted to. Nevertheless, in a way a modified version of "zersingen" philosophy does appear to prevail among those folklorists who express great anxiety about quickly collecting folklore before it disappears, dies out, or suffers further "loss" of meaning.

*6 Some of the standard sources include Baillie (1950), Bury (1955), Ginsberg (1963), and van Doren (1967).

*7 For a useful survey of the various conceptualizations of "folk", see Hultkrantz (1950:126-29).

*8 The point is that there is really no connection between the restricted "folk" of folk society in which "folk" is used simply as a synonym for peasant and the "folk" of folklore. A folk or peasant society is but one example of a "folk" in the folkloristic sense. Any group of people sharing a common linking factor, e.g., an urban group such as a labor union, can and does have folklore. "Folk" is a flexible concept which can refer to a nation as in American folklore or to a single family. The critical issue in defining "folk" is: what groups in fact have traditions?

*9 The negative connotation of "folklore" is by no means limited to the English-speaking world. See, for example, the final comments in Elisée

Legros' valuable Sur les noms et les tendances du folklore.

*10 For an extended discussion of this concept, see Lovejoy and Boas (1935).
Also relevant are Whitney (1924) and Scheffler (1936).

*11 One of the best treatments of "survivals" is Hodgen (1936). See also Voget
(1967).

*12 Jung and Kerenyi (1963:72). Judging from Drake (1967) there appears to
have been little notice taken of Jung's pro-Christian and antirational approach
to myth. Jung claims that Christ exemplifies the archetype of the self and that
in general pure intellectual insight as opposed to "experience" is not enough,
although he admits that he cannot pass on his experience to his public. See
Laszlo (1958:32-36). In any case, when Jung speaks of the "de-Christianization
of our world" and "the Luciferian development of science and technology" (p. 35),
it is an expression of devolutionary worldview. For Steiner's approach to folklore, see his The Interpretation of Fairy Tales, or any of the works cited in
Dundes (1965b).

*13 Once the devolutionary premise has been pointed out, it is easy to find
examples of it. For example, there is Varagnac (1965).

*14 Some of the various cyclic schemes are summarized in Lovejoy and Boas
(1935); see also van Doren (1967).

3

THE STUDY OF FOLKLORE IN LITERATURE AND CULTURE:
IDENTIFICATION AND INTERPRETATION

Many of those outside the discipline of folklore and even some of those within
tend to divide folklorists into literary or anthropological categories. With this
binary division comes a related notion that each group of folklorists has its own
methodology appropriate for its special interests; hence there is thought to be a
method for studying folklore in literature and another method for studying folklore in culture. Looking at this dichotomy from the viewpoint of a professional
folklorist, one can see that it is false; moreover it is a dichotomy whose unfortunate persistence has tended to divide unnecessarily scholars working on
similar if not identical problems. The basic methodology of studying folklore
in literature and studying folklore in culture is almost exactly the same; in
other words, the discipline of folklore has its own methodology applying equally
well to literary and cultural problems.

There are only two basic steps in the study of folklore in literature and in
culture. The first step is objective and empirical; the second is subjective and
speculative. The first might be termed identification and the second interpretation. Identification essentially consists of a search for similarities; interpretation depends upon the delineation of differences. The first task in studying an
item is to show how it is like previously reported items, whereas the second
is to show how it differs from previously reported items - and, hopefully, why
it differs.

Professional folklorists who are usually skilled in the mechanics of identification are apt to criticize literary critics and cultural anthropologists for
failing to properly identify folkloristic materials before commenting upon their
use. And folklorists are quite right to do so. Naive analyses can result from
inadequate or inaccurate identification. Plots of traditional tale types might be
falsely attributed to individual writers; European themes in a European tale
told by American Indians might be mistakenly considered to be aboriginal elements. However, folklorists themselves might be criticized for doing no more
than identifying. Too many studies of folklore in literature consist of little
more than reading novels for the motifs or the proverbs, and no attempt is
made to evaluate how an author has used folkloristic elements and more specifically, how these folklore elements function in the particular literary work as
a whole. Similarly, listing the European tales among the North American Indians does not in itself explain how the borrowed tale functions in its new en-

Reprinted from the Journal of American Folklore 78 (1965), 136-42.

vironment. The concern of folklorists with identification has resulted in sterile study of folklore for folklore's sake and it is precisely this emphasis on text and neglect of context which has estranged so many literary critics and cultural anthropologists. The text-without-context orientation is exemplified by both anthropological and literary folklore scholarship. Folklorists go into the field to return with texts collected without their cultural context; folklorists plunge into literary sources and emerge with dry lists of motifs or proverbs lifted from their literary context. The problem is that for many folklorists identification has become an end in itself instead of a means to the end of interpretation. Identification is only the beginning, only the first step. A folklorist who limits his analysis to identification has stopped before asking any of the really important questions about his material. Until the folklorist is prepared to address himself to some of these questions, he must be resigned to living on the academic fringe in a peripheral discipline. As illustrations of how interprepation must follow initial identification in the study of folklore in context, the following brief discussion of a folktale found in James Joyce's Ulysses and a European tale found among the Prairie Band Potawatomi is offered.

In Joyce's Ulysses, one finds many different kinds of folklore, including tale types, nursery rhymes, tonguetwisters, folksongs, mnemonics, palindromes, and children's games.*1 Joyce's keen interest in folklore is further attested by his depicting one of the minor characters, Haines, as an English folklorist come to Ireland to collect Irish folklore. Of all the examples of folklore in Ulysses, I have selected the riddle Stephen Dedalus asks his class to demonstrate the techniques of identification and interpretation. After reciting the opening formula and first line of a well known riddle for writing, Stephen asks his class this riddle:

The cock crew
The sky was blue:
The bells in heaven
Were striking eleven.
'Tis time for this poor soul
To go to heaven.

The first riddle that Stephen recites in this situation - "Riddle me, riddle me, randy ro / My father gave me seeds to sow" - has been identified by scholars as the first part of riddle number 1063 in Archer Taylor's great compendium, English Riddles from Oral Tradition, and also has received interpretive examination (Weldon Thornton (1964) says, for example, that Stephen's suppression of the last part of the riddle may be an admission of his failure as a writer) - but so far as I know, no one has correctly identified the riddle Stephen puts to his class. Stephen's students are as much in the dark as the literary critics, though he gives them the answer, "the fox burying his grandmother under a hollybush". Work has been done on the problem of identification, since Joyce's frequent allusions to this riddle throughout the book suggest it is obviously important to the interpretation of the book itself.*2 Several scholars have pointed out the similarity of Joyce's riddle with one in P. W. Joyce's English As We Speak It in Ireland:*3

Riddle me, riddle me right
What did I see last night?
The wind blew
The cock crew,
The bells of heaven
Struck eleven.
'Tis time for my poor sowl to go to heaven.
Answer: the fox burying his mother under a holly tree.

P. W. Joyce did not identify the riddle and he even commented upon what he called "the delighful inconsequences of riddle and answer". Yet a trained folklorist knows immediately that the riddle is closely related to a subtype of an international tale type, Aarne-Thompson 955, The Robber Bridegroom. In this subtype, which is very popular in Anglo-American oral tradition, the villainous suitor is frequently named Mr. Fox. Mr. Fox plans to do away with his betrothed and often the frightened girl, hidden in a tree, actually watches Mr. Fox digging her grave-to-be. Later at a large gathering the girl recites the riddle describing the villain's actions and thus unmasks the villain and reveals his nefarious plot. The folklorist can tell from the riddle text alone that there is a reference to the whole folktale, but there is additional evidence that Joyce himself knew the tale. In the memorable Circe chapter, the mob assails Bloom as a disgrace to Christian men, a vile hypocrite, and shouts derisively: "Lynch him! Roast him! He's as bad as Parnell was. Mr. Fox!" (p. 482). This very last allusion is what T. S. Elliot calls an objective correlative in that the mob scene in the folktale is evoked, a scene in which all those present cry out at the evil designs of the wicked Mr. Fox. So much for the identification of Stephen's riddle. What about the interpretation?

All previous interpretations of the significance of the riddle and fox imagery have been made without the benefit of a correct initial identification. William M. Schutte (1957:103), for example, suggests that Stephen thinks of himself as a fox in that the fox as the wily foe of the hounds employs the weapons of silence, exile, and cunning. Schutte also says that the fox must be Stephen who killed his mother without mercy and who cannot stop scratching at the ground where she is buried. *4 However, in terms of the folktale the fox only plans to kill his sweetheart; he does not actually commit the crime. The fox is judged by his thought rather than by his act. In the novel Stephen did not kill his mother, but he judges himself in thought: "I could not save her"; earlier Buck Milligan had spoken of Stephen killing his mother (Ulysses:46). Of even more interest is the fact that in most versions of the tale Mr. Fox's victim is his bride-to-be, whereas in the Joyce variant the fox's victim is a mother. If the mother is equivalent to a sweetheart, then this would be part of the extensive Oedipal aspect of Stephen's character which I have discussed elsewhere. (Dundes 1962c). In this light, Setphen the fox kills his mother instead of marrying her as she expected. If the P. W. Joyce text of the riddle was the source for James Joyce, then Stephen's changing the mother of the original to grandmother in the answer he gives the class also points to Stephen's Oedipal problem, for it is clear that in Stephen's own mind the fox's victim is a mother, not a grandmother.

The folktale source also clarifies the puzzling association of the fox and

Christ. "Christfox" is described as a "runaway in blighted treeforks"(Ulysses: 191). The latter description suggests not only a crucifixion but also the striking scene in the tale when the girl victim, hiding in a tree, looks down upon Mr. Fox digging her grave. The accompanying phrase "women he won to him" could allude to the Bluebeard Mr. Fox plot as well as to Christ and His faithful females. Stephen as "Christfox" is both victim and villain, both innocent and guilty. The point is, however, that unless the reader understands Joyce's skillful use of the riddle from the tale type as an objective correlative, he cannot appreciate the paradox.

One could proceed in similar fashion to identify and interpret other folkloristic elements in Ulysses. For example, one might examine Joyce's ingenious adaption of the riddling question "Where was Moses when the light went out?" (p. 714) - or the impact of Stephen's singing the anti-Semitic ballad "Sir Hugh" or "The Jew's Daughter" (Child 155) at that point in the novel when the Gentile Stephen has been invited to stay the night at the home of the Jew Bloom, who has a marriageable daugther (p. 674-76); but these and other examples would only demonstrate the point made here in the exegesis of the Fox riddle.

So the literary critic without proper knowledge of folklore can go wrong in identification and consequently in interpretation, but so can the anthropologist who knows only the basic tools of his discipline's trade. In April of 1963 I collected a fine example of folklore in culture from William Mzechteno, a 74-year-old Prairie Band Potawatomi in Lawrence, Kansas. Here is the raw story as I transcribed it, with myself identified by the initial D and my informant with the initial M.

M. Well there was once, there was a little boy. There was always a little boy, you know, and he had a name, his name was ah - [pause of six seconds' duration] - P'teejah. His name is P'teejah, and ah -
D. P'teejah?
M. Yeah. And he, he had a little, let's see now - [pause of three seconds' duration] - oh, he had a little tablecloth, you know. He can eat, you know, there's food every time he spreads that tablecloth on the ground or anywheres; he name many food, any kinda food he wants. It'd just appear on the, right on the tablecloth and was eaten. Well, all he had to do to clean up, you know, is just shake; everything was disappear, you know, into thin air. And he was goin' long the road one time, he met a soldier, he had a cap on. Uniform caps, you know, those soldiers wear. And the soldier was hungry. [The boy asked] "You got anything to eat?" [The soldier answered] "Oh, I got this hard bread. " It's all he had. [The boy said] "Let's see that bread", he told him, "oh, that's hard, that's no good, not fit to eat", he told him. He throw it away. [The soldier said] "Mustn't do that, it's all I got to eat. " [The boy said] "I'll give you something better", he told him. He pull out his tablecloth, and spread it on there, on the ground. "You name anything you want, any-thing! So he, ah, he named all he wanted to eat, Soldier, he was real hungry. "So, if you want any of that red water, you can have that too", he told him, whiskey.

D. Red water?

M. Yeah, they call it red water [laughing].

D. Who called it red water?

M. The Indian boy. They called it red water.

D. Yeah?

M. Yeah, 'cause it's red, you know. He didn't call it fire water.

D. This is an Indian boy?

M. Yeah, yeah, And, oh the soldier enjoyed his meal; he filled up, you know, and "Well, I got something to show you," he told me. He [the soldier] took his cap off, you know, and he throwed it on the ground and said, "I want four soldiers." And sure enough, four soldiers, there, well armed, stood there at attention. "It's pretty good", he [the boy] told him, "but you can go hungry with those four soldiers", he told him [laughing]. So, he put on his cap, you know. Course the soldiers disappeared, and he start to go and then the soldier said, "Say, little boy, how you like to trade? I'll give you this cap for that cloth." Naw, he wouldn't trade. "I'd go hungry without it." Oh, he got to thinking, you know. He said, "Well soldiers could get me something to eat", he thought, I guess. So, he traded, fair trade. He kept looking back, the little boy, you know. He had that little cap on. He thought about his table-cloth. He sure hated to lose it. So he, come to his mind, you know, "I'll get it." He took off [laughing] that cap and throwed it on the ground. "Four soldiers", he told 'em. Soldiers come up, you know, stood up right there and [he] says, "See that man goin' over there. He took my tablecloth away from me", he told 'em, "you go and git it [giggling laugh]." So they went [laughing] after that man; he fought 'em like everythin'. "You belong to me", he said, "No [laughing] we belong to him over there", they said. So then he got his tablecloth and the boy got it back. And he had the cap too. That's where.

D. The boy was, you say, an Indian boy?

M. Yeah.

D. But the soldier was a white man.

M. Yeah.

D. So the Indian boy was fooling the white man.

M. Yeah [laughing] he put it on him.

D. In a trade, too.

M. Yeah, it was a fair trade but he was using his noodle [laughing].

D. That's very nice. I didn't know it was an Indian boy.

M. Yeah.

D. I see.

M. Yeah.

D. Well, that's good, that's a fine story.

In order to analyze this tale in terms of Potawatomi culture, one must first identify the tale not as an indigenous Indian story, but as a European tale type. From the detail of the magic food-providing tablecloth (Motif D 1472.1.8), the professional folklorist can easily identify the tale as a version of tale type 569, The Knapsack, the Hat, and the Horn. Moreover, from internal evidence one can without difficulty demonstrate that the tale was borrowed originally from a French source. The Indian boy's name is P'téejah and the long pause before the utterance of the name shows the narrator's praiseworthy concern with getting the name right. P'téejah is a recognizable corruption of the French folktale character of Petit-Jean. As a matter of fact, Franz Boas in his essay "Romance Folk-Lore among American Indians" observed that the name of this French figure had been taken over by a number of American Indian groups (Boas 1940:517. See also Skinner 1927:400-02). Another trace of French culture is the allusion to "red water" which is probably wine although the narrator interpreted it as whiskey. So the tale has been identified: It is a borrowing from a French version of Aarne-Thompson tale type 569 and certainly not an aboriginal tale type. But the statement that it is a European tale does not answer such questions as what have the Potawatomi done with the tale? - how have they changed it and how do these changes tell us something about present-day Potawatomi culture? As a general rule European tales among American Indian groups can be used as indexes of acculturation. If the European tale is little changed, then it is probable that the borrowing Indian culture is waning if not defunct. If on the other hand the European tale is reworked and adapted to fit American Indian rather than European values, then it is more than likely that the American Indian culture in question is still a going concern. What about this Potawatomi tale?

First of all, the hero has been changed from a French character to an Indian boy. The narrator was questioned repeatedly about the identity of P'téejah and each time he insisted that P'téejah was an Indian boy. Secondly, the magic cap which belonged to the white soldier worked magic in American Indian symbolic terms rather than in European. Four soldiers were produced, not three; four is the ritual number of the Potawatomi as of most American Indian groups. Thus the magic soldier-producing hat (Motif D 1475.4) operates in American Indian terms and this in a sense is precisely what the whole tale does. In the tale the soldier offers to make a trade - protection in exchange for food, an exchange not unusual in the light of American colonial history. One senses that the exchange is unfair and that the adult European soldier is tricking the young Indian boy into giving up his only source of food. But in this folktale the Indian boy gets the best of the trade, the "fair trade" proposed by the white man. Although the hero does not appear to have planned his actions in advance, the narrator commented after telling the tale that the boy had "used his noodle", that is, he had out-thought the white man. In this tale of wish fulfillment, the Indian boy has sufficient force to overpower the European soldier antagonist and to regain his original abundance of food.

In the cultural phenomenon which anthropologists term nativistic movements, it is common for the borrowing, dominated culture to dream of taking over the dominating culture's artifacts without the presence of members of that culture.*5 In this tale the Potawatomi has control of European artifacts; it is the Indian who is able to offer the soldier "red water" rather than soldier offering the Indian liquor - it is the Indian boy who uses the white man's object to defeat the white man. One can see even from these few comments why this particular European tale could easily have been accepted by Potawatomi raconteurs and audiences. A few deft changes made it a tale with considerable appeal for most

Potawatomi. One can see from a "mistake" made by the narrator that he identified with the Indian boy. After the soldier finished eating, he told the boy he
had something to show him. At this point, Mr. Mzechteno said "Well, I got
something to show you", he told me. This use of "me" instead of "him" strongly
suggests that the story was in some sense about Mr. Mzechteno and perhaps
other Potawatomi. This detail plus the informant's frequent laughter demonstrate his enjoyment of and involvement with the tale.

The study of Joyce's use of a riddle and the study of a Potawatomi adaptation
of a European tale appear to be distinct, but the methodology employed in both
studies was the same. Identification was equally necessary. Failure to identify
the Mr. Fox riddle in Ulysses could result in one's being unable to appreciate
fully Joyce's use of this folkloristic element and accordingly limiting in a small
way one's comprehension of the novel; failure to identify the Potawatomi tale as
a standard European folktale might have made it difficult to determine just what
changes the Potawatomi had introduced. One might have assumed, for example,
that it was a Potawatomi idea to cast the dupe as a soldier, but in fact the soldier is frequently the dupe in European versions of the tale. But identification
though necessary was only the first step, a prerequisite for interpretation. If
it is true that folklorists too often identify without going on to interpret whereas
literary critics and anthropologists interpret without first properly identifying
folklore, then it seems obvious that some changes are needed. Either folklorists are going to have to educate their literary and anthropological colleagues
in the mechanics of identifying folklore or they will have to undertake some of
the problems of interpretation themselves. Ideally, both alternatives might be
effected so that the study of folklore could become something more than a scholarly series of shreds and patches or a motley medley of beginnings without
ends and ends without proper beginnings.

NOTES

*1 Page references to Ulysses are from the Modern Library edition. For a
sample of Joyce's use of folksongs see Worthington (1956).

*2 Ulysses, 47, 60, 191, 288, 480, 544, 545, 557.

*3 Scholars who have noted this source include Prescott (1952) and Schutte
(1957).

*4 Tindall (1950:23) also remarks on Stephen's identification with the cunning
fox, but he equates the buried grandmother with Stephen's mother, the Church,
and the Poor Old Woman (Ireland).

*5 Sometimes the dominating culture's artifacts may be used as weapons
against it. In this instance the Potawatomi have borrowed a European folktale
and successfully employed it to attack Europeans. For another example of
Potawatomi borrowing of European folktales in which the tales are used as
vehicles for Indian superiority over whites, see Gossen (1964).

4

PROVERBS AND THE ETHNOGRAPHY OF SPEAKING FOLKLORE

(with E. Ojo Arewa)

> "I know the proverbs, but I
> don't know how to apply them."

Introduction

Like other forms of folklore, proverbs may serve as impersonal vehicles for personal communication. A parent may well use a proverb to direct a child's action or thought, but by using a proverb, the parental imperative is externalized and removed somewhat from the individual parent. The guilt or responsibility for directing the child is projected on to the anonymous past, the anonymous folk. A child knows that the proverb used by the scolding parent was not made up by that parent. It is proverb from the cultural past whose voice speaks truth in traditional terms. It is the "One", the "Elders", or the "They" in "They say", who direct. The parent is but the instrument through which the proverb speaks to the audience.

The impersonal power of proverbs is perhaps most apparent in the well-known African judicial processes in which the participants argue with proverbs intended to serve as past precedents for present actions. In European courtrooms, of course, lawyers cite previous cases to support the validity of their arguments. In African legal ritual, an advocate of a cause uses proverbs for the same purpose. Here clearly it is not enough to know the proverbs; it is also necessary to be expert in applying them to new situations. The case usually will be won, not by the man who knows the most proverbs, but by the man who knows best how to apply the proverbs he knows to the problem at hand.

The distinction just made is expressed succinctly in the remark of an Ibo youth, studying at the University of California at Berkeley, which we have quoted as an epigraph: "I know the proverbs, but I don't know how to apply them." He explained that his Western-oriented education in Nigeria had cut him off from the daily use of proverbs. Thus, while he did recall the texts of a great number of proverbs, he was not really certain as to precisely how and when they should be employed in particular situations.

Studying proverbs as communication

The distinction between knowing and applying proverbs is of the utmost importance for folklore field work methodology. Specifically, it makes the difference

Reprinted from <u>American Anthropologist</u> 66. 6, Part 2 (1964), 70-85.

between recording texts and recording the use of texts a critical one. Folklore is used primarily as a means of communication, and it is as communication that it needs to be studied. Yet this is virtually impossible with the common practice of recording just the texts alone, a practice consistent with the mistaken emphasis in folklore upon the lore rather than upon the folk.

In 1929 Roman Jakobson, in a joint essay with P. Bogatyrev, noted that folklore and language were somewhat analogous in that both are collective social phenomena with definite regularities of pattern. This type of conceptual framework permitted and in fact encouraged the study of folklore as a systematic code. If language could be studied structurally, folklore could also be so studied. Although, unlike linguists, folklorists have been slow to study their materials in this way, at least the theoretical possibility of the analysis of folklore as code was cogently stated in 1929, and it has been brought to the fore of anthropological attention by studies by such scholars as Lévi-Strauss and Sebeok.

Jakobson and Bogatyrev had suggested that in folklore there was an analogue to speech (la parole) as well as to language (la langue), inasmuch as there were particular, idiosyncratic, actual texts of folklore utilized by individuals. Recently Hymes (1962) has urged as a general perspective that to the study of linguistic structures must be added the study of the structures of acts of speech. The goal is not simply the delineation of the structure of language as an isolated symbolic system or code, but rather the attempt to discover exactly how language is used in specific situations. Moreover, the conception of the structure of language is extended to include the sequential structure of forms of messages, wherever such linguistic "routines" appear. This approach to the study of language in culture Hymes terms the "ethnography of speaking". In this type of study, one is interested in not only the rules of a language, but also the rules for the use of the language. The question is not only what is a grammatical utterance, but also when does one use one grammatical utterance rather than another. It should be obvious that the notion of the "ethnography of speaking" is extremely relevant to the study of folklore. Applied to proverbs, for example, it would be concerned with precisely the sort of rules that the Ibo youth quoted at the outset had not learned.

In order to study the ethnography of the speaking of folklore (or, ethnography of speaking folklore, more concisely), clearly one cannot be limited to texts. One needs texts in their contexts. One needs to ask not only for proverbs, and for what counts as a proverb, but also for information as to the other components of the situations in which proverbs are used. What are the rules governing who can use proverbs, or particular proverbs, and to whom? Upon what occasions? In what places? With what other persons present or absent? Using what channel (e. g. speech, drumming, etc.)? Do restrictions or prescriptions as to the use of proverbs or a proverb have to do with particular topics? With the specific relationship between speaker and addressee? What exactly are the contributing contextual factors which make the use of proverbs, or of a particular proverb, possible or not possible, appropriate or inappropriate?

Notice that such a study of context is not the same as the more generalized study of functions of folklore. One can say that proverbs sum up a situation, pass judgment, recommend a course of action, or serve as secular past precedents for present action; but to say this does not tell us what the particular

function of a particular proverb used by a particular individual in a particular
setting is. There is merit in prefacing a collection of proverbs (or of any other
form of folklore) with a discussion of the various general functions of the materials (cf. Turner 1960), but this does not substitute for the accurate report-
ing of contextual data.

In a way, it seems to be an absurdly simple request to ask that students of
folklore record the contexts of their texts. Other anthropologists, taking for
granted the call for context that Malinowski issued in Part II of Coral Gardens
and Their Magic (1935), may assume that this is done. But while the accuracy
of the linguistic transcriptions of folklore materials has steadily improved, the
situation with respect to contextual data now is very much like that deplored by
Firth (1926:246) - even the best folklore field workers report only texts. If context is mentioned, it is discussed in general terms, not in terms specific to
given texts. Thus, for example, in an important article on the "dozens", the
characteristic form of verbal dueling among American Negroes (Abrahams
1962), 30 texts are reported and 13 replies, but there is no indication whatso-
ever as to which reply goes with which text; and it is not possible to guess this
sort of relationship. Again, Abrahams (1964:6) has argued that it is vitally important to present with any corpus of lore some analysis of the conflicts which
exist within the culture that uses it. The point is a fine one, but what is needed
even more is collection of the actual use of the lore in specific conflict situations. If, for example, a folklorist wants to study verbal dueling, he should not
limit himself to selected texts of insults together with a general discussion of
the techniques of verbal dueling. He should, if he can, and admittedly it is not
an easy task, present an accurate transcription of a verbal duel. The sequence
(cf. Miller 1952) and the intensity of a series of insults represent data essential for an ethnography of speaking folklore. To report data in this way clearly
would not preclude the usual presentation of texts and the standard generalized
analysis of the materials and their functions. Without such faithful recording
of actual events, however, future analysts are deprived of an opportunity to
see how folklore works.

With particular regard to proverbs, the techniques or "rules" for applying
them cannot be studied unless actual instances of individuals applying proverbs
to life situations are recorded. In the absence of ideal circumstances, which
would consist of recording a representative variety of such instances, together
with interviewing informants as to their judgments of such instances, informants can at least be asked to construct what they consider to be the typical
and appropriate contexts or situations for individual proverbs, and to recall
such instances as they can. If a person does know how to apply the proverbs,
the chances are good that he can report and envision situations in which the
proverbs have been or could be appropriately used. Herskovits used this technique effectively (without explicitly explaining the technique at the time) in his
work with Kru proverbs (1930) and was so pleased with the results that he was
later led to propose the construction of hypothetical situations by informants
as a generally useful methodological device for all types of ethnographic field
work (1950).

In principle, the more varied the contexts of a particular proverb that can be
recorded, the more likely it is that the proverb and its significance in the cul-

ture from which it comes will be understood. By the same token, one should record the informants' associations and comments with regard to the folkloristic materials. If there is oral literature, then there is oral literary criticism, that is, native, as opposed to exogenous, literary criticism. The shelves of folklorists are filled with explanations of what folklore means and what its value is, but few of these explanations and valuations come from the folk. Native literary criticism, which could be considered as an aspect of "ethno-literature", the latter being parallel to ethnobotany, ethnozoology, etc. , does not eliminate the need for analytical literary criticism, but it certainly should be recorded as part of the ethnographic context of folklore, both for its own interest, and because undoubtedly native interpretations and valuations of proverbs influence the decision to employ a particular one in a particular situation. Recording the text of a proverb and the situations in which it occurs may provide sufficient data for correlating the two, but if the goal is the delineation of the rules for using folklore in a given culture, then collection of the interpretation(s) of a proverb by members of the culture is equally essential.

Like other short forms of folklore, such as riddles and jokes, proverbs could easily and profitably be made the subject of an ethnography of speaking folklore. For one thing, proverbs are readily used in situations in which there is close interpersonal contact, often serving to release tensions related to that contact.

Unfortunately, as we have noticed, most proverb collections consist of bare texts. Sometimes even the versions in the original language are absent. Often the meanings are not only unclear, but misrepresented inasmuch as the collector has succumbed to the worst kind of ethnocentrism, explaining a proverb in one culture by citation of a supposedly equivalent proverb from his own. This all-too-common tendency to translate a native culture's folklore into the collector's own makes most collections of proverbs of extremely limited value to serious students. Few collections are of the caliber of those made by Firth, Herskovits, Herzog, and Messenger.

Working in limited time and apart from Yoruba society, it has not been possible for us to complete a study observing all the canons specified above. A selection of Yoruba proverbs, however, can illustrate the useful information regarding context that is quite easy to obtain, even in less than ideal circumstances. One of the most important of the many uses of Yoruba proverbs is in the training of children, and twelve examples are chosen from that sphere. The relationship between use of proverbs and channel is discussed in a separate section. The Yoruba text of each proverb is given with literal translation in an appendix.

Some Yoruba proverbs of child training

(1) One should not say in jest that his mother is fainting.

One important aspect of Yoruba child training has to do with teaching the child the proper sets of relationships to be maintained between himself and his parents, his siblings, members of his lineage, and unrelated elders. The nature of these relationships, at least in terms of ideal culture, is more often

than not communicated to the child by means of proverbs. Children are expected to be obedient and subordinate to parents. The proverb "One should not say
in jest that his mother is fainting" is one that a parent may use to let a child
know that there are certain topics which should not be made the subjects of
jokes. The proverb is usually cited immediately after a child has said something he should not have said. Among the topics a child should avoid in jokes
are the important personal events in his parents' life. If, for example, a father
had quarreled with his wife at some previous time, his child is not supposed to
refer to this quarrel or discuss it with anyone. Even if one of the parents alludes to the quarrel in the presence of the child, the child is still not allowed
to indicate that he has knowledge of the quarrel. If the child later on becomes
angry with one of his parents, he must still refrain from mentioning the event.
If the child did ever refer to the quarrel, he might well receive the proverb as
a reprimand. As with all proverbs, there are other possible contexts for this
one. For example, if a friend joked to another by saying, "I heard you are
planning to assassinate the head chief of your village", the other might reply
with the proverb to convey the thought that there are some things which must
not be joked about. In this event, the proverb would be used only if the person
citing it believed that the original comment was intended as a joke. Literally,
the proverb refers to fainting which is interpreted in Yoruba culture as a significant passage from the normal state of life to another state. Such a passage
is serious business and it is one of those things one does not treat lightly. Figuratively, the proverb could refer to any event of the family's history which
brought shame to the family. For example, if a child's parents were in debt,
this would be a taboo topic for jokes. Thus, in a child-training context, the proverb helps teach the child at an early age to discriminate between those messages he should and those he should not utter regarding his parents, a distinction
which would be of particular interest to someone doing an ethnography of speaking, or a sociolinguistic stody correlating speaker and topic.

(2) Untrained and intractable children would be corrected by outsiders.
(3) If a man beats his child with his right hand, he should draw him to himself
    with his left.

The role of the proverb as an agent of communication is even more apparent in
an actual case in which the parents of a child disagreed as to the amount of indulgence the child should be given. The mother, who felt that her child should
be given more rather than less indulgence, told her husband that the child was
young and foolish, and that because of this he should be given much indulgence.
The husband remained silent for a few seconds and then replied with the proverb: "Untrained and intractable children would be corrected by outsiders;" At
this point, the wife responded by saying, "If a man beats his child with his
right hand, he should draw him to himself with his left;" In the first proverb,
one finds expressed several important cultural values concerning the education
of children. The parents' obligation to give proper and adequate training to
their child is conveyed by the word "untrained" (àbìtkóó). The child's duty to
obey the instructions of his parents is suggested by the word "intractable"
(àkótgbó). If the parent or the child fails to fulfill his or her respective obli-

gations, the community at large might take action, which would be a socially overt recognition or indication of such failure. However, the second proverb frames the cultural expectation that while parents must take active steps to discipline their child effectively, they should also feel and demonstrate parental love for the child. That is what is meant by beating a child with the right hand and drawing him close with the left.

(4) The chameleon has produced its child; the child is expected to know how to dance.

In some instances, a child's parents might have given what they considered to be good training, but nevertheless the child may have turned out to be unmanageable. In such a situation, the parents would no doubt be unhappy, but in order to assure themselves and others thay they had done their part, they might say to one another, to the child, or possibly to an outsider, "The chameleon has produced its child; the child is expected to know how to dance." This means that the parents have fulfilled their obligations in bringing the child into the world and rearing him. It is the child's responsibility to use his opportunities and abilities to the fullest extent. The proverb might be used in a situation like the following. If a child told a friend of his parents that he was foolish, the friend would be annoyed inasmuch as a child is supposed to respect all those who are his elders. The friend would almost certainly tell the parents about the incident. (It is unlikely that the child would have uttered the insult in the presence of his parents.) The parents would assure their friend that appropriate disciplinary action would be taken. Later they might address the chameleon proverb to the offending child to tell him how displeased they were with his conduct and to remind him that his behavior at that point was his, not their, responsibility.

(5) Do not be like me; a thief's child takes after its parents.
(6) The offspring of an elephant cannot become a dwarf; the offspring of an elephant is like the elephant.

Yoruba parents do have responsibility with respect to their own behavior in the child training context. They are expected to do more than simply bring up their child in accordance with cultural norms. They are supposed to be good examples for the child. As evidence for this, there is a proverb which a parent might cite whenever he felt the other parent fell short of being a good example for their child. The proverb would be used to inform the guilty spouse of his mistake. In the proverb "Do not be like me; a thief's child takes after its parents", there is an explicit indication of the importance attached to parental example in the education of a Yoruba child. Suppose a father who quarrels with his siblings strikes them when he gets angry. The child sees this and later when he becomes angry with one of his brothers or sisters, he hits him. The father, observing the child's behavior, is upset and he admonishes the boy not to do such things. When the father complains to the mother about the boy's actions, she might reply (not in front of the child) with the proverb to communicate the idea that if he is disturbed about what the child is doing, he should remember that he himself is the model for the child. This proverb is not limited in its use to indicating only the effects of bad parental example. It may also be used to show the effects of good parental example on the child. Essentially the proverb is an expression of the strong Yoruba belief that the parental influence to which a child has been exposed has a great deal to do with the type of person he ultimately becomes. The same concept is somewhat differently expressed in the proverb: "The offspring of an elephant cannot become a dwarf; the offspring of an elephant is like the elephant."

(7) If you talk of cutting off somebody's head in the presence of a child, he will always be staring at the man's neck.

Another type of parental responsibility which is an integral part of Yoruba child training has to do with the kind of conversation parents carry on in front of their child. On one occasion, the senior members of a Yoruba family were engaged in an evening conversation in the presence of their child. The young boy's father was talking about a neighbor in a very destructive manner. The boy was listening with unusually keen attention. The boy's mother noticed this and she became nervous and impatient as she listened to her husband. Soon, her patience ran out, and she suddenly sent her son on an errand. While the boy was away, she said to her husband, "If you talk of cutting off somebody's head in the presence of a child, he will always be staring at the man's neck." With this proverb from the wife, the destructive talk about the neighbor immediately ceased. This is an excellent example of the proverb as communication, and in fact as most effective communication. But what exactly is being communicated? If a parent expresses his bias about a person or refers to what he considers to be a fault in the person in the presence of his child, the child will always remember this bias or alleged fault whenever he sees the person in question. The proverb is urging that the parent take care not to transmit his personal bias to his child.

(8) We use a closed fist for tapping our chest.

With regard to the relationship between a child and his siblings, proverbs play an important role in showing how one child should behave towards another. Yoruba parents are very anxious to have unity among their children and they believe that a lack of such unity would have a serious disruptive effect upon the family's solidarity. They are, therefore, constantly on guard to insure that sibling unity is encouraged. A situation where there has been some evidence of intersibling rivalry or conflict will probably elicit a proverbial comment from a parent or older relative. For example, suppose one of two or three brothers is courting a girl. Ordinarily the other brothers visit the girl to show their interest in their brother's life and to display commendable family unity. If, however, the brothers fail to do this and either of the parents notices this, he might urge them to visit the girl by saying, "We use a closed fist for tapping our chest. " In this proverb, one finds reference to traditional gestures. Inasmuch as gestures are often functionally equivalent to proverbs (in that they summarize a situation, pass judgment, or recommend a course of action), this is not surprising. The "closed fist" is an expression of unity and strength, while tapping the chest with the fist is a characteristic gesture indicating boasting. The gestural message is that unity is a desideratum of which the family is proud and furthermore a family without it is in no position to boast.

(9) A child trying to act like an older person will find that his age gives him away.

The importance of the principle of seniority and relative age in Yoruba social structure and verbal behavior has been described in detail by Bascom (1942). These factors are definitely manifested in the relationship between a child and his younger or older sibling. A younger sibling is expected to be deferential to an older child. It should be realized that it is not just that age is crucial with respect to Yoruba interpersonal relationships, but that its influence upon a particular relationship is in some sense never-changing. A younger brother is at and by birth destined to be a younger brother. But it is not just relative age which is fixed. There is apparently a notion of absolute age, especially in regard to the cultural distinction between child and adult. The suggestion that age is an almost absolute regulator or indicator of behavior, impossible to escape, is made in a proverb: "A child trying to act like an older person will find that his age gives him away. " This might be cited in a situation in which a child was trying to act like an older person, but the child because of his age was unable to act properly. Let's say a boy gets married at a relatively early age (e.g. under 20) or a girl (under 15) does this and the marriage does not work out well. An older person, perhaps the parent, might comment either to the child or to someone else upon the unhappy marriage by quoting the proverb which would convey the opinion that the child should have waited to get married until he was old enough.

(10) A white fowl does not know it is old.
(11) When a child acts as a child, a man should act as a man.

If a younger child is criticized for trying to act older than his years, so also is an older child criticized for acting like someone younger than his years. In a situation where an older sibling has fallen short of his obligations towards one or more younger siblings, he may be chastised for his failure. When the parents are not at home, for example, the oldest child is expected to assume the responsibility for the other children's acting properly. He is also supposed to see that the children do not hurt themselves. If for any reason he is careless, and one child goes outside to a place where he is ordinarily not permitted to go, and if the child hurts himself, the oldest child will be censured by the parents upon their return. Had the senior sibling fulfilled his responsibilities, the

younger child would not have been hurt. The parents might say, "A white fowl
does not know it is old", or more probably "When a child acts as a child, a
man should acts as a man." Both these proverbs could also be used appropriately in contexts in which an adult does not act as an adult should. The significance of a white fowl depends upon the fact that white chickens are culturally
regarded as distinct from red, black, and other color chickens. White fowl are
used solely for sacrificial and ritual purposes, although the sacrificial chicken
is eaten by the participants after the ceremony which has been prescribed by a
diviner. The proverb suggests that the white fowl does not comprehend its higher status with respect to other chickens. Thus the proverb could be used in a
situation in which an elder (not necessarily with white hair) does not appear to
know, or act in accordance with, his privileged position relative to younger individuals. The second proverb is more hortatory in that it implies that a child
cannot help acting as a child, which places the burden of regulatory responsibility squarely upon the shoulders of oldest sibling present.

(12) The hand of a child cannot reach the high shelf, nor can that of an older
person enter a calabash.

In Yoruba culture, there is not only a principle of seniority (Bascom) but also
a principle of reciprocal responsibility. The young have a responsibility to the
old and the old have a responsibility to the young. More concretely, the child
has obligations to his parents; the parents have obligations to their child. The
younger sibling has obligations to older brothers and sisters; the older sibling
has obligations to his younger brothers and sisters. The interdependence between an individual and his elders is metaphorically rendered by the proverb:
"The hand of a child cannot reach the high shelf, nor can that of an older person enter a calabash." For a child to reach his goal, the aid of an elder is essential. Things which children cannot do for or by themselves must be done for
them by their elders. On the other hand, there are tasks which elders can perform only with difficulty, if at all. For such tasks, children are expected to
serve their elders. The proverb might be employed in a situation like the following. An uncle (paternal or maternal) asks a nephew, or any older individual
asks a younger one to go on several errands such as fetching water from a
pond. The youth does this many times. Then one day the younger person asks
the older for a favor. He sees that the older person has some pineapples and
he asks to be given one to eat. The older person refuses. The following day the
older person asks the younger to go on another errand, but the younger refuses
to go. Later the older one is talking to another person of the same age as himself, not necessarily a relative, and he complains of the younger person's behavior. The third party responds by quoting the proverb as a means of explaining the appropriateness of the youth's conduct.
    Notice how pale are the explanation of the proverb and the analytical phrase
about principle in comparison with the proverb itself. Folklore is both communication and art. It has been studied as art more than as communication. Yet if it
is studied as communication, its artistic qualities should not be overlooked.
Even in translation, this last proverb offers proof that there is art in the communication.

Discussion

Much more might be learned about the import of each of these proverbs and the conditions governing their use through field study in an indigenous setting. Some provisional observations, however, can be made here.

Apparently the most important Yoruba rules for the use of proverbs have to do with the identity of the participants in the speech situation. It is the identity of the addressor which seems crucial for the genre to be used at all, and the identity of the addressee, or audience, which seems crucial to the appropriate use of a particular proverb.

Regarding the genre as a whole, the main consideration seems to be the age of the person speaking relative to the age of the addressee. The speaker is normally older for some proverbs, equal in age for others. Some proverbs might be appropriate to either case. Younger persons are not wholly excluded, but Yoruba etiquette dictates that a younger person's use of a proverb in the presence of an older person must be marked by a prefatory apology. The standard politeness formula runs something as follows: "I don't claim to know any proverbs in the presence of you older people, but you elders have the saying...."

Of the present examples, it seems safe to say that an elder person would probably address numbers 8, 9, 10, and 11 to a younger person; e.g. a parent might say them to his child (but the elder need not be a parent). In contrast, numbers 3, 5, 6, 7, and 12 would be more likely to be addressed by an elder to another elder person, e.g. by a husband to his wife or by an adult to a friend or relative. Numbers 1, 2, and 4 could be used by either seniors to juniors or by age equals.

The topics or situations which might appropriately elicit a proverb are primarily concerned with a younger person's behavioral responsibilities toward his elders and an elder's behavioral responsibilities toward younger individuals. Numbers 1, 4, and 8 refer to a child's obligations to his family; numbers 2, 3, 5, 6 and 7 refer to a parent's obligations to his child; and numbers 9, 10, 11, and 12 refer to behavior proper to one or the other or both. It is clear that the identity of the addressee is crucial with regard to whether a particular proverb is appropriate or not. For example, a child would most probably be a suitable addressee for numbers 1 and 8, but a child would rarely, if ever, be the addressee of numbers 3 and 7. In fact it is doubtful whether number 7 would be used to any addressee if the child in question were even present. The point is that the presence or absence of individuals other than the principal addressee may be an important factor governing the use of particular proverbs in speech (but not in drumming).

The use of proverbs is not restricted by need for knowledge of any special code other than the Yoruba language itself, so far as we know. Neighboring or other foreign languages are not, for example, used, as they are among the Jabo (Herzog 1945) for purposes of concealment and mocking, so far as our data go. Nor is use of proverbs conditional upon skill in creative and adaptive change in message form. By the very nature of fixed-phrase genres of verbal art, the messages are culturally standardized in form and content. The creativity and adaptation lie rather in the successful application of these traditional materials to new situations. The relation between use of proverbs and channel, however, requires special consideration.

Proverbs and channel

Although most proverbs are transmitted by speech, some on occasion are communicated by drums. The type of drum (there are more than twenty different types of Yoruba drums) which is very often used to transmit proverbs is the "dundun" described by Bascom (1953b). Although drummed proverbs may be used to insult an individual (especially in struggles for political office or for coveted titles), generally drumming is a channel of communication utilized for ceremonial purposes, such as a funeral, a marriage, a naming ceremony, or the installation of a chief. Proverbs may be drummed on any of these occasions so long as the particular proverb is deemed appropriate by the drummer or by the person hiring the drummer, appropriate in terms of the particular situation and the particular addressee. It is, however, somewhat less likely that proverbs would be used as often in funeral ceremonies as in happier events such as marriages.

Certain families specialize in drumming and the skill is passed on within the family (Laoye 1954). Part of the training in drumming is the accumulation of both a large store of proverbs and the knowledge of the appropriate occasions for their use. Thus drumming is a channel not equally available to all members of Yoruba culture. However, a nondrummer could ask a drummer to drum an honorific or congratulatory proverb for a friend's marriage. The drummer receives payment for this. With regard to a drummed proverb honoring a marriage, the nominal addressee is considered to be the bridegroom, not the bride. (This is related to the bias inherent in Yoruba patrilineal social organization.)

The techniques of drumming generally and drumming proverbs specifically are too complex (Bascom 1953b) to be adequately treated here, but, essentially, suprasegmental patterns are extracted from the spoken versions of the proverb and the addressee is able to recognize the proverb whether he actually articulates the segmental phonemes or not. By moving the left arm by which the drum is held, the shape of the drum is varied, hence the tone is varied. The relative pitch differences and the rhythmic sequence of the drum tones are culturally perceived as being similar to the tone sequence found in particular proverbs (as is not the case among the Jabo according to the ethno-theory of Herzog's informants [Herzog 1945]).

(13) It will in no way hurt him if it falls upon him. A tree which fails to hold up a person when he leans against it will in no way hurt him if it falls upon him.

This proverb is one of several which are possibly more often drummed than spoken. The proverb would be most appropriate in a situation in which a person dismisses the possibility of another person's being able to do him harm. For example, suppose a boy asks an older relative for money to attend school. The elder promises to support the boy. Later the elder fails to provide this support. Then the boy may bitterly complain to a friend about this relative's action or lack of it. The friend tells him that he shouldn't talk that way about this relative, because he might find out and as a result he might try to make trouble for

the boy. The boy might then reply with the proverb to convey the idea that anyone who was too feeble to help another was surely too weak to be able to do that
person any harm. In this context, the proverb would be spoken, not drummed.
The situation, in part, determines the channel.

A situation in which the proverb would be drummed rather than spoken might
be one like the following. A man is seeking a title, such as chief. A friend who
has money and influence in the community promises to use them in his behalf.
However, when the time comes, the wealthy man fails to honor his promise.
The title-seeker is angry and he complains to many people about this breach of
faith. Some of these people warn him about speaking ill of such an important
person and some point out possible dangerous consequences, such as the rich
person's using his influence against him. The would-be chief decides to hire a
drummer, and he directs him to drum the proverb in order to tell the people of
the community that in his opinion, since the man had shown himself to be too
weak to live up to his pledge to support him, he was clearly in no position to
hurt him, even if he did use his influence to oppose the attempt to get the title.

One extremely interesting aspect of the relation between channel and proverb
concerns the effect of the former upon the form of the proverb. One might conjecture, for example, that it may be more than coincidence that the drummed
proverb mentioned above has in Yoruba a clear ABA form, a form also common
in Yoruba songs as well as in other traditional materials communicated by
drum. Moreover, the ABA form is not common in spoken Yoruba proverbs.

Another proverb which is drummed more than it is spoken has the same ABA
form.

(14) It is palm-oil that I carry. Person bearing rock, please don't spoil that
which is mine. It is palm-oil that I carry.

This proverb is used to refer to situations in which one person has something
of great value whose worth could be totally destroyed by the act of a thoughtless
person. The proverb might be drummed in a situation where an important person with a good reputation is threatened by an irresponsible young man with no
reputation. The latter envies the important man's position and prestige and he
seeks to spread malicious rumors such as that the man has taken bribes. Thus
a man who has a reputation worth little is in a position to destroy the fine reputation of an honorable man as pieces of rock can ruin palm-oil. The threatened
man might hire several drummers and tell them of the situation, but in this
case perhaps he might not indicate the specific proverb to use. One of the drummers decides to employ the particular proverb because he judges it to be appropriate.

If there is a definite correlation between channel and proverb form, this has
important theoretical implications. For one thing, it would suggest that stylistic
studies of folklore genres without taking channels into account might be misleading. What folklorists think is chance variation may in fact be a reflection
of channel alternatives. The correlation could also provide a way of gleaning
information from the scores of bare texts already reported. It might be possible, for example, to tell from the form alone that a particular Yoruba proverb

could have been transmitted by drums.

As mentioned in the preceding section, the presence or absence of particular individuals is not important if the channel selected is drumming rather than speech. Drumming is a public, speech a private, channel. In terms of addressees, drumming is nonexclusive, speech exclusive. Spoken proverbs would normally be addressed to an individual or to a relatively small number of individuals. Drummed proverbs, in contrast, would be addressed to a larger group of individuals or to one individual in that situation where it was important that the message be made public. This latter factor suggests that situational circumstances are more crucial than addressees with respect to the selection of drumming as a channel for proverbs. In any event, the investigation of differences in a single genre of folklore as it is communicated in diverse channels represents a potentially rich area of inquiry.

Conclusion

If folklore is communication, then the ways in which it is used as communication must be taken into account. The study of folklore should include both the study of lore and the study of folk. The study of lore alone without reference to the folk by whom it is used is incomplete and may even be misleading. To borrow from a recent American indictment of the commercialism of Christmas ("Let's put the Christ back in Christmas"), we might urge- "Let's put the folk back into folklore. "

Proverb texts*1

In the following texts, standard Yoruba orthography is employed. Two tones are indicated as: High Tone (/), and Low Tone (\). The phonetic equivalents of Yoruba orthography include: e is ∈ , s is š, p is kp, and o is ɔ. The reader is reminded that many collections of proverbs made by folklorists and linguists consist of just what is presented in this appendix. If the reader seriously doubts the necessity of collecting context, let him ask a non-Yoruba friend what some of these proverbs mean.

a   ki fí ìyá   eni dákú sere
we not use mother one faint play
(1) One should not say in jest that his mother is fainting.
abiikó   akoigbó   ode   ni o ti   kó   ogbón wá   ilé
untrained intractable outside is he have learned wisdom come home
(2) Untrained and intractable children would be corrected by outsiders.
bí a bá   fi owó òtún na   omo eni a fi òsì fà   á   móra
if we should use hand right beats child one we use left draw him to self
(3) If a man beats his child with his right hand, he should draw him to himself with his left.
agemo   bí   omo rè ná   ài mo jó   di   owó rè
chameleon produces child his already not know dance becomes hand his

(4) The chameleon has produced its child; the child is expected to know how to dance.

maṣe fi ìwà   jo   mí ọmọ olè ni olè jo
do not use behavior resembles me child thief is thief resembles

(5) Do not be like me: A thief's child takes after its parents.

ọmọ àjànàkú ki ya   ràrá ọmọ tí erin   bí erin   ni
child elephant not becomes dwarf child that elephant born elephant is

njọ
resembles

(6) The offspring of an elephant cannot become a dwarf; the offspring of an elephant is like the elephant.

a ki sọrọ orí bíbé   lójú   ọmọdé lórùnlórùn ní ima
we not talk head cutting before child   at the neck is will

wo   olúwarè
look the person

(7) If you talk of cutting off somebody's head in the presence of a child, he will always be staring at the man's neck.

àgbájo owọ́ ni a fi nsọ àyà
together fist is we use tap chest

(8) We use a closed fist for tapping our chest.

bí ọmọdé bá   fé se ìse àgbà ojọ́ orí rè kò jé
if child happens want do deed elder day head his not allow

(9) A child trying to act like an older person will find that his age gives him away.

adie funfun kò mọ   ara rè ní àgbà
fowl white not know self his as elder

(10) A white fowl does not know it is old.

bí ọmọdé bá   nse ọmọdé àgbà a ma se àgbà
if child happens doing child elder he will act elder

(11) When a child acts as a child, a man should act as a man.

ọwọ ọmọdé kò tó   pepe owọ́ àgbàlàgbà kò wo   àkèrègbè
hand child not reach shelf hand elder   not enter calabash

(12) The hand of a child cannot reach the high shelf, nor can that of an older person enter a calabash.

b´ó wó lu ni kò lè pa ni
if it falls hits one not can kill one

igi tí a f´ èhìn tì tí ko gba ni duro
tree that we put back lean that not hold one stand

b´ó wó lu ni kò lè pa ni
if it falls hits one not can kill one

(13) It will in no way hurt him if it falls upon him. A tree which fails to hold up a person when he leans against it will in no way hurt him if it falls upon him.

epo   ni mo rù
palm-oil is I   carry

onfyangí   ma   ba t´emi jẹ́
rock bearer do not — mine —   (ba + jẹ = spoil or ruin)

epo   ni mo rù
palm-oil is I   carry

(14) It is palm-oil that I carry. Person bearing rock, please don't spoil that which is mine. It is palm-oil that I carry.

NOTES

*1 All the Yoruba proverbs cited in this paper were contributed by Arewa, who learned them about 1945 in his native village of Oke-agbe in Western Nigeria. He also provided the translations and explanations of the proverbs. The authors are indebted to Dell Hymes for invaluable comments and suggestions.

5

METAFOLKLORE AND ORAL LITERARY CRITICISM

The theoretical assumption that folklore was limited to a survival and reflection of the past was a crippling one for the study of folklore in context. For if in fact folklore did reflect only the far distant past, then clearly there was no point in bothering to attempt to collect the <u>present</u> context of folklore. A past-oriented folklore collector would tend to regard his informants as relatively unimportant carriers of precious vestigial fragments, fragments which might prove useful in the central task of historically reconstructing the past. For the execution of historico-comparative studies, one needed only minimal information concerning the place and date of collection. It is clear that for the kinds of theoretical and methodological questions that nineteenth century folklorists were asking, e. g. "what was the original form of an item of folklore and what were the genetic relationships between various forms or subtypes of that item of folklore?", place and date of recording were sufficient.

In the twentieth century with the increasing amount of ethnographic fieldwork, it became glaringly apparent that folklore reflected the present as well as the past and that there was certainly a context in which folklore was used. Nevertheless, custom is strong even among scholars and the "butterfly" or "object-curio-collecting" philosophy has continued. Long lists of proverbs are published in folklore journals accompanied by no explanation of either use or meaning. Anthropologists append to their ethnographies a token section consisting of folktales and myths but with little or no comment on their relationship to other aspects of the culture. The "object-collecting" philosophy is itself a survival of the antiquarian days of folklore studies. Folklore texts without contexts are essentially analogous to the large numbers of exotic musical instruments which adorn the walls of anthropological or folk museums and grace the homes of private individuals. The instrument is authentic as is the folklore text, but the range of the instrument, the tuning of the instrument, the function of the instrument, and the intricacies of performing with the instrument are rarely known.

It was Malinowski who was most vociferous in calling for context. In his important 1926 essay "Myth in Primitive Psychology", he repeatedly pointed out the fallacy of collecting mere texts, calling them mutilated bits of reality. Here again is the notion of folklore as fragments, but not fragments of the past, fragments of the present. In one formulation, Malinowski observed, "The text, of course, is extremely important, but without the context it remains lifeless."

Reprinted from The Monist 50 (1966), 505-16.

(Malinowski 1954:104). More recently, Bascom (1954) has continued the call for context. Auguring well for future folklore field research is Goldstein's (1964) praiseworthy concern for context in his valuable Guide for Field Workers in Folklore. He specifically lists "folklore processes" as one of the principal kinds of folklore data to be obtained in the field (p.23). In another recent development in the study of folklore context, it has been suggested that the ways and means of using folklore are just as highly patterned as the materials of folklore themselves. The identification of the rules for the use of an item of folklore, or the "ethnography of speaking folklore" as it has been termed, suggests that to the "laws" of form (Olrik) and the "laws" of change (Aarne) may be added the "laws" of use.*1 The discovery of such laws or rules opens a new area of folklore research.

The current interest in the collection of context, however, has partially obscured the equally necessary and important task of collecting the meaning(s) of folklore. One must distinguish between use and meaning. The collection of context and preferably a number of different contexts for the same item of folklore is certainly helpful in ascertaining the meaning or meanings of an item of folklore. But it cannot be assumed that the collection of context per se automatically ensures the collection of meaning. Suppose a folklorist collected the following Yoruba proverb:

A proverb is like a horse- when the truth is missing, we use a proverb to find it.*2

Let us assume that he also collected the typical context of this proverb in which it is employed in an introductory capacity prior to uttering another proverb which was designed to settle a particular dispute. The introductory proverb announces to the audience that the arbitrator is planning to use a proverb and reminds them of the great power and prestige of proverbs in such situations. But from this text and context, does the collector know precisely what the proverb means? What exactly is meant by comparing a proverb to a horse? While the meaning(s) of a proverb are unquestionably involved in an individual's decision whether or not the quotation of that particular proverb is appropriate in a given context, the folklore collector may miss the meaning(s) even though he has faithfully recorded text and context. One cannot always guess the meaning from context. For this reason, folklorists must actively seek to elicit the meaning of folklore from the folk.

As a terminological aid for the collection of meaning, I have proposed "oral literary criticism" (Dundes 1964b; Arewa and Dundes 1964). The term is obviously derived from "literary criticism" which refers to a host of methods of analyzing and interpreting works of written literature. Even a beginner in literary criticism soon discovers that there are alternative and rival interpretations of one and the same work of art. The identical phenomenon occurs in the case of folklore which for the sake of the discussion we may call "oral literature" (although this unfortunately tends to exclude nonverbal folklore). For each item of oral literature, there is a variety of oral literary criticism. This is an important point inasmuch as folklorists, despite the fact that they are accustomed to thinking of variation in the texts of folklore, often wrongly assume that there is only one correct meaning or interpretation. There is no one right interpretation of an item of folklore any more than there is but one right version of a game or song. (We must overcome our penchant for monolithic perspectives as exemplified in monotheism, monogamy, and the like.) There are multiple meanings and interpretations and they all ought to be collected. One could ask ten different informants what each thought a given joke meant and one might obtain ten different answers. It is difficult to determine the gamut of interpretation because there has been comparatively little collection of oral literary criticism.

The interpretation which is made is inevitably from the collector's point of view. There is nothing wrong with analytic as opposed to native interpretations, but the one does not eliminate the need for the other. Unfortunately, in a few instances, the analyst-collector suggests that his interpretation is really the natives' own interpretation. Melville Jacobs, for example, tries to "see the literature as it appeared to Chinooks"(Jacobs 1959a:3), but one wonders if the Chinooks would have agreed with Jacobs' interpretations. Jacobs has reconstructed oral literary criticism but this may not be the same as the oral literary criticism he might have collected. The nature of his criticism is revealed in his discussion of Clackamas Chinook humor when he speaks of his methodology. "...I enumerated 130 instances in the Clackamas collection where I was certain that an audience at a folkloristic recital responded with smiles or laughter" or "...I took each of the 130 fun situations and attempted to pinpoint each fun-generating factor or stimulus to humor which I believe to have been present in them" make the analytic bias clear (Jacobs 1959a:178-79). Jacobs was not present at a Clackamas Chinook tale-telling session – he collected the tales from a highly acculturated informant in relative isolation – and he can give little more than educated guesses. Even in our own culture, it would be difficult to guess whether or not a "funny" story got a laugh and more particularly to know just at what points in the joke laughs were stimulated. One must not only record laughter (distinguishing types of laughter - a giggle, a bellylaugh), but one must try to find out what was funny and why the audience members laughed or did not laugh.

It is not easy to collect oral literary criticism. Much of it has probably never been consciously formulated. Yet the meanings and traditional interpretations of folkloristic materials are transmitted from individual to individual and from generation to generation just as is folklore itself. But some types of oral literary criticism are easier to collect than others and it might be well to mention them first.

One source of oral literary criticism comes from folklore itself rather than directly from the folk. There are a limited number of folkloristic commentaries on folklore. As there is a term "metalanguage" to refer to linguistic statements about language, so we may suggest "metafolklore" to refer to folkloristic statements about folklore. Examples of metafolklore or the "folklore of folklore" would be proverbs about proverbs, jokes about joke cycles, folksongs about folksongs and the like. Metafolklore is not necessarily intra-genre. There are proverbs about myths, for example. The previously cited Yoruba proverb would be an instance of metafolklore. It is a folkloristic commentary about a folklore genre, namely, the proverb. "A proverb is like a horse: when the

truth is missing, we use a proverb to find it. " This clearly indicates an attitude towards a key function of proverbs in Yoruba culture, the function being
the determination of truth in problem situations or disputes. Of course, since
metafolklore is still, after all, folklore, it is necessary to elicit oral literary
criticism of the metafolkloristic texts themselves. The meaning of the Yoruba
proverb, according to one informant, is that by mounting a horse, as opposed
to goats, sheep, dogs, and other animals found among the Yoruba, one can
quickly obtain a superior perspective. From the back of a horse, one can see
further than one can from the ground and the immediate local problem may be
seen in a new and better light. A proverb is like the horse inasmuch as it also
provides a speedy and efficacious means of getting above the immediate problem-
situation and of placing it in a perspective which is more likely to result in
finding a just and proper solution.

An example of a metafolkloristic joke is the following: It was a dark and
stormy night and this guy goes up to this old farm house. He's a salesman and
he says to the farmer, "I'm a salesman, my car broke down, and I need a place
to stay. " And the farmer says, "That's all right, but there's just one thing, we
have no extra rooms to spare so you'll have to sleep with my son. " And the
salesman says, "Oh my God, I must be in the wrong joke. " Here is a folk comment on the nature of the traveling salesman joke cycle. Invariably the jokes
involve the seduction of the farmer's daughter and/or wife. In most jokes in the
cycle, as you may know, the farmer explains to the salesman that he can stay
but that the only available space is in his daughter's room. This is thus a joke
about a joke cycle and it draws attention to one of the critical content features
of the cycle. Once again, one could elicit oral literary criticism of this bit of
metafolklore. One might find, for example, that the substitution of homosexuality for heterosexuality is particularly significant in the light of our culture's
taboo against homosexual activities. The mere suggestion of such activities to
a traveling salesman, the epitome of unrestrained heterosexual impulse, is so
shocking as to call a halt to the story. In other words, at the very mention of
homosexuality, the American male wants out because this activity is "wrong":
the salesman is in the wrong joke. (The breaking out of the joke is analogous
to the breaking of the "fourth wall" in theatrical parlance. Actors normally regard the proscenium as the fourth wall of a room. Occasionally, an actor will
break the convention and will speak directly to the audience. Some plays, like
this traveling salesman joke, specifically call for the breaking of the conventional vehicle.)

Sometimes the metafolklore may comment on the formal features rather than
on the content of folklore. For example, consider the following metafolkloristic
joke based upon the "knock, knock" cycle.

Knock!
Who's there?
Opportunity.

Here attention is drawn to the distinct characteristic reduplicative opening formula of jokes in this cycle: knock, knock. The use of just one "knock" is incorrect, but is rationalized by reference to a proverb: "opportunity only knocks

once". Such parodies of and plays on folkloristic forms can be useful sources of the folk's own attitudes towards their folklore.

Another source of overt literary criticism besides metafolkloristic texts consists of the asides or explanatory commentary made by raconteurs as they tell tales or sings songs. These asides are sometimes unwisely eliminated by the overscrupulous editor but they should not be. Two examples from a Potawatomi informant may illustrate the nature of these asides. At the beginning of one tale, my informant said, "Well there was once, there was a little boy. There was always a little boy, you know, and..."*3 The line "There was always a little boy" is a folk confirmation of one of the important characteristics of certain folktales, namely that the protagonist is a little boy. Such a comment might be particularly valuable if the folklorist-collector did not know in advance what kinds of tales were in his informant's repertoire. The comment indicates that there are a great many tales with little boys in them and it also serves to authenticate the particular tale he is recounting. It is as if to say that traditional tales must have little boys in them as protagonists and so in this traditional tale I am about to tell there is this required stereotyped character.

Another self-critical aside made by my informant came in a version of Big Turtle's War Party. In the mock plea (Motif K 581.1, drowning punishment for turtle) episode, the villagers are devising ways to kill the captured turtle. First they discuss throwing him into a kettle of boiling water, but the turtle threatens to splash the water and scald their children. Next, the villagers suggest tying him to a tree and shooting him with buckshot - at which point the narrator observed "I don't know whether they had any buckshot in those days or not" before concluding with the final throwing of the turtle into a river à la the tarbaby rabbit into the briarpatch. This commentary challenges the historical accuracy of the tale. Given the time setting of this American Indian tale - when animals were like people, the occurrence of such an obvious acculturated element of material culture as buckshot upset the sensibilities of my sensitive storyteller. However, he did not deny or alter the traditional tale as he knew it. He merely inserted a partial disclaimer, thereby expressing his own parenthetical doubts.

The problem with metafolklore and with the raconteur's asides is that they provide at best only an incomplete picture of the folk's evaluation of their folklore. For some folklore, no metafolklore has been recorded; for some genres few asides have been published. What is needed is the rigorous and systematic elicitation of oral literary criticism. A tale or song might be treated by the folklorist-collector much as a modern psychiatrist treats a dream. As the psychiatrist asks his dreamer-patient to "free associate" and to comment on the various elements in the dream, so the folklorist-collector should ask his informant to "free associate" in the same manner, attempting to explain or comment on each element in the tale. Too often the text-hungry folklorist immediately after the recitation of a tale or song will say, "That's fine, do you know any more like that..." and he will not patiently seek to have the informant provide a folk exegesis of the tale just told. Perhaps the collector should consider the item of folklore collected as a projective test or should we say "projective text" and in that event he should ask the informant to make up a story about the story.

Even more desirable would be to elicit the oral literary criticisms of both raconteur and audience. The meaning for the tale teller is not necessarily the same as the meaning for the audience or rather the different meanings for different members of the audience. It is incredible that folklorists speak of the meaning of a folktale. Moreover, the existence of multiple meanings suggests communications blocks. One might assume that if A and B, members of the same culture, both know a given folklore text that this text serves as a strong bond linking A and B. However, if A and B interpret the text differently, then A's addressing it to B might result in misunderstanding rather than understanding. The following may serve to illustrate multiple meanings.

There is a folk metaphor (proverbial phrase) "to have an axe to grind" and to me it means to have a bias as a lobbyist might have. If I said, "Watch out for so and so, he has an axe to grind", I would be warning against accepting what that individual said at face value inasmuch as his words or actions would be influenced by what I considered to be a vested interest. Archer Taylor told me that he thought the metaphor connoted the asking of a favor inasmuch as it takes two men to grind an axe, one to spin the whetstone and the other to hold the axe. Thus if one individual came to another and announced that he had an axe to grind, he would be asking the other person to stop what he was doing and help him grind the axe. The dictionary supports this interpretation by saying "to have an object of one's own to gain or promote".*4 However, there is another traditional meaning of this metaphor, the meaning of "grudge". According to informants, "to have an axe to grind" is similar to having a "bone to pick" with someone. One informant related that if he had neglected to do one of his assigned household chores, say taking out the garbage at the end of the day, the next morning his mother would say to him "I've got an axe to grind with you, you didn't take the garbage out last night". The informant explained that "I've got an axe to grind with you" meant "There's going to be friction, i.e. sparks were going to fly, just as sparks fly when an axe is ground". (I discovered that my wife also uses this meaning. Our neighbor's dog occasionally knocks over and rifles our garbage can. My wife indicated that she would think it appropriate to call up our neighbor and say, "I have an axe to grind with you", meaning there was something she was angry about.) Here then are two distinct interpretations of the same folk metaphor.

In some instances the meaning may be fairly constant, but the evaluation of the common meaning may vary. For example, the proverb "A rolling stone gathers no moss" means that a person who moves around from place to place, not staying in any one place for very long, will never belong to a place, or look as though he belongs to that place. The oral literary critical difference concerns whether this is good or bad. In the older tradition, it was bad and the proverb might be cited to keep someone from roaming too far and wide, to urge him to stay at one place. But in modern usage, at least in some quarters, the accumulation of moss is considered to be a negative characteristic and the "rolling stone" is conceived of as the ideal unencumbered life. Admittedly these differences could be gleaned from printed contextual instances of the proverb in novels and newspapers, but the point is that folklore collectors ought to obtain direct oral interpretations of the proverb at the time of collection.

As has been noted, it is not always easy to elicit oral literary criticism. The

folk know and use folklore without bothering to articulate their esthetic evalu-
ations. For some types of oral literary criticism, e. g. symbolism, an indirect
method of eliciting might be recommended. The problem in symbolism is that
the folk may not be completely conscious of the one or more symbolic meanings
of an element of folklore. This is understandable in view of the fact that it is
often the taboo activities and ideas which find expression outlets in symbolic
form. If the folk consciously recognized the symbolic significance of the joke
or folksong element, this element might not be able to continue to serve as a
safe, socially sanctioned outlet. (Cf. the popular belief that analysis of a work
of art interferes with or ruins one's enjoyment of it.) Fortunately, much of the
symbolism in folklore is baldly stated and may be obvious enough to some of
the members of the culture concerned. But the study of symbolism would surely be greatly advanced if symbolic interpretations of folklore were obtained
from the folk rather than from Freudian folklorists. No one likes to accept an
ex cathedra pronouncement that a shoe can symbolize female genitalia. Even
the folkloristic "evidence" such as is provided by nursery rhymes among other
genres leaves the issue in some doubt.

> There was an old woman who lived in a shoe
> She had so many children she didn't know what to do.

People don't live in shoes and the possible connection between a woman's living
in a shoe and having lots of children requires explanation. The sequel verse:
"There was another old woman who lived in a shoe, she didn't have any children, she knew what to do" suggests the sexual nature of the symbolism with
the implicit statement that a knowledge of contraceptive measures can allow a
woman to live in a shoe and not have children. One might also consider the
possible symbolism in:

> Cock a doodle doo!
> My dame has lost her shoe
> My master's lost his fiddling stick
> And doesn't know what to do. *5

Maybe there isn't a reference to a woman who has lost her vagina matched by
a man who has lost his phallus, but if not, the logical connection between a
shoeless dame and fiddle stick-less master remains to be seen. But the point
is that one should not guess at such interpretations, one should go to the primary sources and ask the folk. Let field data prove or disprove armchair
guesswork. What does the shoe suggest to the informant? Can the informant
draw a picture of the old woman and her shoe? Perhaps a modified Thematic
Apperception Test based upon the nursery rhyme (or other folklore) can be devised and administered. While it may be true that not all informants will be
equally facile in articulating oral literary criticism, some will be able to do
so. Even a passive bearer of tradition (as opposed to the active bearer who
tells the tale or sings the song) may be able to contribute an interpretation.
Folklorists should be just as anxious to collect variant interpretations of a folksong's meaning as they are to collect variants of the folksong's text!*6

As a final argument for the collection of oral literary criticism, I would note the interpretation of the world folklore itself, especially among the folk. The meaning of "folklore" in the phrase "That's just folklore" is similar to one of the meanings of myth, namely falsehood, error, and the like. I suspect that it is this pejorative connotation which has encouraged some folklorists to consciously avoid the term, substituting instead "verbal or spoken art", "oral or folk literature", and many others. More serious is the fact that this "folk" interpretation of the word "folklore" makes it difficult for the discipline of folklore and its practitioners to gain academic status. If folklore is error, than a Ph. D. in folklore is the height of folly, and the notion of a whole discipline devoted to error is unthinkable in the academic context of the search for truth. To use the term folklore without an awareness of the folk interpretation of the term is unwise.

One final point concerns the necessity for the continued and repeated attempts to elicit oral literary criticism. It is a commonplace that each generation reinterprets anew its folklore, but do we have records of these interpretations and reinterpretations? Sometimes the text is altered to fit new needs, but probably it is the interpretation of texts which changes more. The task of collecting oral literary criticism from a folk can never be completed any more than the task of collecting folklore from that folk can be. Even if both texts and interpretations remained almost exactly the same over a long period of time, this would still be well worth knowing. It might be an important index of the overall stability of that folk. Here also is an opportunity to use the scores of texts without commentary which line library shelves and archives. These texts may be taken <u>back into the field</u> and folk <u>explication de texte's</u> sought. Our goal for future folklore collection should be fewer texts and more contexts, with accompanying detailed oral literary criticisms.

NOTES

*1 See Arewa and Dundes (1964). For the laws of folklore form, see Axel Olrik's classic paper "Epic Laws of Folk Narrative". For the laws of folkloristic change, see Aarne (1913).

*2 In Yoruba, the proverb is:

Òwe   l'e̩s̩in   ò̩rò̩: bi ò̩rò̩ bá sonù
proverb is horse word if word got lost
òwe   l'a   fo   ńwá   a
proverb is we use finding it

For the proverb and its explanation, I am indebted to E. Ojo Arewa.

*3 This first example was published, see Dundes (1965a:139). The second example has not yet been published.

*4 <u>Webster's New World Dictionary of the American Language.</u> This is the meaning found in The Oxford Dictionary of English Proverbs, 17; Taylor and Whiting (1958).

*5 The rhyme of the old woman who lived in a shoe is number 546 in the canonical Oxford Dictionary of Nursery Rhymes, ed. Iona and Peter Opie. The Opies suggest (p. 435) that "the shoe has long been symbolic of what is personal to a woman until marriage". The Opies do not mention the sequel verse which dates from the 1890's in American Ozark tradition. See Hickerson and Dundes (1962). As for the "Cock a doodle-doo" rhyme, number 108 in the Opies' collection, one finds not even an oblique circumlocutory hint of any symbolic interpretation. Nursery rhymes should really be studied further. One wonders, for example, why the three blind mice (Opies' number 348) tried to run after the farmer's wife. If it were an Oedipal theme, then the cutting off of the presumptuous mice's tails would be appropriate symbolic castration.

*6 It should be mentioned that recently a number of folklorists have observed that the meaning of the folklore to the folk must be investigated. For typical statements see Legman (1964:285); Goldstein (1964:23, 106, 140). Linda Degh, in a description of the future tasks of folklore collectors (written in Hungarian) urges folklorists to leave the explanations to the storyteller and the members of his audience, see Ethnographia 74 (1963), 1-12.

SECTION TWO

STRUCTURAL ANALYSIS
OF FOLKLORE

6

FROM ETIC TO EMIC UNITS IN THE
STRUCTURAL STUDY OF FOLKTALES

Traditionally, the study of folklore in general and folktales in particular has
tended to be diachronic rather than synchronic. The emphasis has clearly been
upon the genesis and development of folkloristic materials rather than upon the
structure of these materials. Folklorists of the late nineteenth century were
much more concerned with how folklore came into being than with what folklore
was. Genetic explanations were considered sufficient to define the nature of
folklore. Thus the solar mythologists claimed that the bulk of folkloristic materials was primitive man's poetic translation of celestial phenomena such as
the rising and setting of the sun. After the "eclipse of solar mythology" as
Richard M. Dorson (1955) has so felicitously phrased it, there came the Anthropological School. The members of this group were convinced that folklore evolved from historical facts and primordial customs. In the course of the unilinear
evolution of all cultures, there were preserved vestigial remains of the archaic
origins. These remains were termed survivals in culture, and the study of
these survivals was called folklore. The modern version of this form of diachronic study is fostered by the advocates of the myth-ritual theory who claim
that all myth evolves from ritual. Since no attempt is made to explain the ultimate origin of the ritual, one can see that the question of genesis has been
dropped in favor of the question of evolutionary developments. Similarly, in the
most modern method of folklore study, the so-called Finnish historical-geographical method, questions of ultimate origin are eschewed. The aim of this
method is the delineation of the "complete life history of a particular tale"
(Thompson 1946:430). The users of the historical-geographical method attempt
to determine the paths of dissemination and the process of development of folkloristic materials. By assembling all the known versions, of a particular tale,
the folklorist seeks to reconstruct the hypothetical original form of the tale.
There is, however, no attempt to explain how this original form may have come
into being in the first place. Thus there has been a movement away from the
early interest in genesis and cause towards an interest in the process of transmission and evolutionary development. But in any case, the study of folklore
has remained diachronic.

All three approaches to folklore - the mythological, the anthropological, and
the historical-geographical - are alike not only in that they are diachronic, but
also in that they are comparative. All three utilize materials from many cultures. This was why it became apparent to folklorists, no matter which of these

Reprinted from the Journal of American Folklore 75 (1962), 95-105.

approaches they favored, that for comparative studies there had to be some convenient means of referring to individual parts or pieces of folkloristic items as well as to these items as wholes. In the second place, in order to have trustworthy comparison, one needed to operate with comparable units. This was particularly important to the members of the Finnish school inasmuch as it was precisely the differences of some of the smaller units of a given folktale upon which the conclusions of a historical-geographical study were often based. Unfortunately, the system of units which was developed was primarily intended to answer only the first need, that is, of supplying a means of referring to individual parts and pieces of folklore as well as to large chunks of folklore. The criterion of having genuine comparable units did not enter into the construction of either the motif-index or the Aarne-Thompson tale-type index. Thus however useful the motif-index and tale-type index may be as bibliographical aids or as means of symbol shorthand, their basic units, namely the motif and tale type, do not provide an adequate basis for comparative studies.

In order to see the inadequacy of the motif and tale type as units to be used in the comparative study of the folktale, one must have some idea of what any kind of a basic unit should consist of. Units are utilitarian logical constructs of measure which, though admittedly relativistic and arbitrary, permit greater facility in the examination and comparison of the materials studied in the natural and social sciences. It is important that units be standards of one kind of quantity (e. g. units of heat, length, and so forth). Units can be conceived as being abstractions of distinct entities which may be combined to form larger units or broken down into smaller units. There is an infinitude of units since they are man-made categorical attempts to describe the nature of objective reality. With a relativistic perspective, one can see that no matter what unit one considers, other smaller subunits may be postulated. Historically, this is what has happened in the development of the neutron from the atom which in turn developed from the molecule. A minimal unit may thus be defined as the smallest unit useful for a given analysis with the implicit understanding that although a minimal unit could be subdivided, it would serve no useful purpose to do so.

Folklorists are not alone with regard to encountering difficulties in defining appropriate units. As Kluckhohn (1953:517) points out: "Most anthropologists would agree that no constant elemental units like atoms, cells, or genes have as yet been satisfactorily established with culture in general." On the other hand, in one area of anthropology, namely linguistics, such units as the phoneme and the morpheme have been delimited. Roman Jakobson remarks in connection with the phoneme that "Linguistic analysis with its concept of ultimate phonemic entities signally converges with modern physics which revealed the granular structure of matter as composed of elementary particles." (Kluckhohn 1953:517, n. 24). However, most anthropologists and linguists seem to feel that the units of linguistics, although extremely useful in the study of language, are of little or no use outside the linquistic area (Voegelin and Harris 1952; Kluckhohn 1953). One notable exception is Kenneth Pike, who has even tried to employ linguistics-like units in an analysis of all human behavior. In his ambitious Language in Relation to a Unified Theory of the Structure of Human Behavior, Pike makes a number of stimulating theoretical statements which appear to be applicable to folklore. Although Pike makes no mention of folklore by name, he begins his study with an analysis of a party game which falls, of course, in the realm of folklore. If one examines Pike's theoretical presentation, one can see, that it may well be that folklorists can profit from the model provided by linguists. True, it is always dangerous to use ready-made patterns since there is the inevitable risk of forcing material into the prefabricated Procrustean pattern. However, this technique is justified if it aids in solving a problem, in this instance, namely the determination of units in folklore. It therefore remains to be demonstrates that first, the motif and tale type are nonstructural, or to use Pike's apt term, etic units, and second that there are empirically observable structural or emic units in folktales which may be discovered through the application of quasi-linguistic techniques.

One cannot criticize the motif on the basis of its not being monomial or indecomposable. As has already been stated, any unit can be subdivided into smaller units. However, the motif is open to criticism as a unit in that it is not a standard of one kind of quantity. Thompson's discussion of the motif makes this clear. According to Thompson, a motif is "the smallest element in a tale having a power to persist in tradition".[*1] It is noteworthy that in this definition, the crucial differentia is what the element does (i.e. persists in tradition) rather than what the element is. The definition is thus diachronic rather than synchronic. Thompson speaks of three classes of motifs. First there are actors; second, are "items in the background of the action - magic objects, unusual customs, strange beliefs and the like"; and third there are "single incidents" which, according to Thompson, "comprise the great majority of motifs". Exactly what an incident is is never stated. If motifs can be actors, items, and incidents, then they are hardly units. They are not measures of a single quantity. There are, after all, no classes of inch or ounce. In addition, the classes of motifs are not even mutually exclusive. Can one conceive of an incident which does not include either an actor or an item, if not both? It is reiterated that without rigorously defined units, true comparison is well-nigh impossible. Can an actor be compared with an item?

Perhaps the most important theoretical consequence of the use of the motif as a minimal unit has been the tendency to regard motifs as totally free entities which are independent of contextual environments. Moreover, the superorganic abstraction is often given a life of its own. When Thompson in speaking of motifs asks: "Do some combine freely everywhere?" the wording is no accident. The abstract units are the subject of the verb and the question is whether they do the combining. This is made clear by Thompson's (1946:426) following question: "Are some isolated, living an independent life as a single-motif tale-type?" (italics mine). But the most critical consequence of chopping up folklore into motifs is that mentioned above, namely that the motif is considered to be a completely isolable unit. Furthermore, such a unit is often assumed to be able to enter freely into limitless combinations. Lowie (1908), for example, speaks of a "perfectly free" element of folklore which could appear in various combinations.

Yet if motifs are truly free to combine, then the larger unit, the tale type, appears to be on somewhat shaky ground. A type, according to Thompson, is "a traditional tale that has an independent existence". Once again, it may be seen that the tale type is not defined in terms of morphological characteristics.

Instead, just as in the case of the motif, the criterion of existence through time is employed. Thompson notes that a complete tale or type is "made up of a number of motifs in a relatively fixed order and combination". If the motifs are in a relatively fixed order, then it appears to be unlikely that they "combine freely everywhere". However, if one presumed from the description of a tale type that a tale type was simply a unit made up of smaller units called motifs, one would have to take account of the fact that one class of motifs, namely incidents, may serve as "true tale-types", and, in fact, according to Thompson (1946:415-16), "By far the largest number of traditional types consist of these single motifs." If this is so, then the distinction between motif and tale type seems somewhat blurred.

The Hungarian folklorist Hans Honti (1939) has given probably the best description of the tale type as a unit. He observes that there are three possible ways of looking at the tale type as a unit. First, the tale type is a binding together of a number of motifs; second, the tale type stands as an individual entity in contrast with other tale types; and third, the tale type is, so to speak, a substance which is manifested in multiple appearances called variants. Honti then points out that in purely morphological terms, a tale type is only a formal unit when contrasted with other tale types. He rejects the other two types of unity after making a comparison with botanical classification. He notes that plants are composed of similar morphological elements: roots, stalks, leaves, and so on. However much these elements may differ in different types, they are uniform within individual types. Thus man can put plants into a structurally based classification system according to the constitution of their roots, stalks, leaves, and so on. But, in the case of folktales, the type is either made up of a variable combination of motifs or a great number of variants. In other words, the constituent elements of folktales, according to Honti, are not constant, but rather extremely variable. This makes strictly morphological classification difficult. It should be noted here that folklorists have somehow sensed that there is something of a fixed pattern in the arrangement of motifs in a folktale, but at the same time they have realized that the motifs may vary considerably. The very heart of the matter of folktale analysis is to ascertain what is constant and what is variable. This may well involve the distinction between form and content.*2 Form would be the constant while content would be the variable. In this light, one can see that the Aarne-Thompson tale typology is based upon the content, that is, the variable.

Aarne has three major divisions of folktales: Animal Tales, Ordinary Folktales, and Jokes and Anecdotes. The second division, which is the largest, has numerous subdivisions including: A. Tales of Magic, B. Religious Tales, C. Novelle or Romantic Tales, and D. Tales of the Stupid Ogre. Moreover, subdivision A., Tales of Magic, is further subdivided into: Supernatural Adversaries, Supernatural or Enchanted Husband (Wife) or Other Relatives, Superhuman Tasks, Supernatural Helpers, Magic Objects, Supernatural Power or Knowledge, and Other Tales of the Supernatural. Aarne then groups his tales, which by the way were restricted to collections from northern and western Europe, under these subjective headings. Only the Formula Tales category, which is listed under Jokes and Anecdotes, may be said to be based upon structural criteria.

One can see from even a cursory examination that this classification is not based upon the structure of the tales themselves so much as the subjective evaluation of the classifier. And yet this is all that folklorists have in the way of tale typology. If a tale involves a stupid ogre and a magic object, it is truly an arbitrary decision whether the tale is placed under II A, Tales of Magic (Magic Objects), or II D, Tales of the Stupid Ogre. With regard to the subdivisions of Tales of Magic, where would one classify a folktale in which a superhuman task is resolved by a supernatural helper who possesses supernatural power? Perhaps the best illustration of the fact that Aarne-Thompson typology is based upon the variable and not upon the constant may be found by examining tale types which differ only with respect to the dramatis personae. In the Animal Tale (Type 9), The Unjust Partner, there is a version listed in which in the division of the crop, the fox takes the corn while the benighted bear takes the more bulky chaff. Under the Tales of the Stupid Ogre, one finds Tale Type 1030, The Crop Division. It is the same story except that the dramatis personae are a man and an ogre. Under the Stupid Ogre listing, Aarne notes that the tale sometimes appears with a fox and a bear as the principals, and in fact he even comments in his preface to the type index upon this duplication of materials:"This narrative has been listed among the ogre tales, to which apparently it originally belonged; but it is also found with a note as to its proper place, among the animal tales as a transaction between fox and bear or man and bear. " This example is by no means unique. One may see the same kind of distinction with regard to differences in the dramatis personae by comparing such tale types as 4 and 72; 43 and 1097; 123 and 333; 153 and 1133; 250 and 275; and 38, 151, and 1159; to name just a few. *3

Another serious difficulty with the tale type as a unit is the fact that often one or more tale types are included in another tale type. This is analogous to the occurrence of actor and item motifs in incident motifs. Thus in some versions of Tale Type 1685, The Foolish Bridegroom, there appears the incident in which the fool, when told to cast "good eyes" at the bride, throws ox-eyes and sheep-eyes on the plate. This "incident" also appears as Tale Type 1006, Casting Eyes, listed under Tales of the Stupid Ogre. This blending and incorporation of tale types is indicated by the fact that in the case of a complex tale such as Type 300, Dragon Slayer, there are no less than eight other tale types which the classifiers recognized were sometimes commingled. One can see that even Honti's claim, that tale types were morphological units in that one tale type contrasted with other tale types, is not demonstrable. Actually, any professional folklorist engaged in folktale research knows very well that folktales, as collected from informants, very often are combinations of two or more Aarne-Thompson tale types. The point is that no matter how useful the Aarne-Thompson index may be in locating critical studies and variants, the Aarne-Thompson tale type as a structural unit of folklore leaves much to be desired. In fairness, it should be stated that neither Aarne nor Thompson ever intended the index to be more than a reference aid. "It is, of course, clear that the main purpose of the classification of traditional narrative, whether by type or motif, is to furnish an exact style of reference, whether it be for analytical study or for the making of accurate inventories of large bodies of material. If the two indexes can in this way promote accuracy of terminology and can act as keys to unlock large inaccessible stores of traditional fiction, they will have fulfilled their purpose." (Thompson 1946:427).

However, what has happened is that this laudable index terminology has begun to be thought of as a kind of typology. Some folklorists tend to regard Tale Type 1030, The Crop Division, as a generic kind of unit. What is more, because the Aarne-Thompson tale typology has achieved international currency and has done a great deal to facilitate international folktale research, folklorists are afraid to introduce an entirely new system. For example, Honti notes that if tales could be arranged according to a theoretically appropriate morphological system instead of a theoretically inadmissible logical system, it might be somewhat easier to work through folktale material. Nevertheless, he states his conviction that this does not constitute enough reason to replace the well-established Aarne-Thompson system. He comments on the inconvenience which would result from putting the catalogs of the various national folklore archives under a new system (Honti 1939:317). This kind of thinking is very dangerous and leads to intellectual stagnation, which the field of folklore can ill afford. In any field of learning, particularly in the natural or social sciences, if something is faulty or inadequate and recognized as such, it should be changed. Folklorists are supposed to study tradition, not be bound by it. Tradition and convenience are hardly sufficient reasons for scholars to perpetuate an acknowledged error. Comparative studies in folklore require carefully defined units, and if the motif and Aarne-Thompson tale type do not meet these needs, then new units must be devised.

New units have been suggested through the application of something like linguistic methodology to folkloristic materials. In particular, a Russian folklorist, Vladimir Propp, in 1928 published Morphology of the Folktale. In this work Propp pays tribute to Joseph Bédier for being the first to recognize that folktales contained invariable and variable elements. However, Bédier, whose key work, Les Fabliaux, was published in 1893, despite an attempt to express these related elements schematically, failed to determine the exact nature of the invariable units. Propp, borrowing the schematic technique, set himself the task of defining the invariable units of folktales.

Propp's aim was to delineate a morphology of fairy tales, and by fairy tales, he meant those tales classified by Aarne between 300 and 749, which Aarne termed "Tales of Magic". Propp's study was synchronic, which was in marked contrast to the rest of folklore scholarship. Propp hoped to describe the fairy tale according to its component parts and to indicate the relationship of these components to each other and to the whole. He begins by defining a new minimal unit, the function. He did this because he noticed that the names of the dramatis personae as well as their attributes changed but that the actions or functions of the dramatis personae did not change. In other words, to use an example mentioned previously, on a functional level, the tale of Tale Type 1030, Crop Division, is the same whether the dramatis personae are animals or humans. Hence Propp (1958:19) states that "The functions of a folktale's dramatis personae must be considered as its basic components; and we must first of all extract them as such." To illustrate how the minimal constituent unit of the function may be extracted from the dramatis personae, Propp, drawing material from four separate fairy tales, gives the following example:

1. A king gives an eagle to a hero. The eagle carries the hero (the recipient) away to another kingdom.
2. An old man gives Sučenko a horse. The horse carries Sučenko away to another kingdom.
3. A sorcerer gives Ivan a little boat. The boat takes him to another kingdom.
4. The princess gives Ivan a ring. Young men appearing from out of the ring carry him away into another kingdom and so forth.

Clearly, though the dramatis personae vary, the function is the same. Structurally speaking, it does not matter whether the object which carries the hero to another kingdom is an eagle, a horse, a boat, or men. Propp then proceeds to further define the function, and his further definition of the function is one of the most revolutionary and important contributions to folklore theory in decades.[4] Propp (1958:19) states that "an action cannot be defined apart from its place in the process of narration." This single statement reveals the unmistakable fallacy of thinking of folklore in terms of isolated motifs. The action or function can only be defined in its place in the process of narration. Honti, who was not familiar with Propp's work, had said that it was difficult to conceive of a motif other than as part of a type (1939:308), but Propp went much further. Not only is the minimal unit to be considered as part of a type, but it must also be considered with respect to where it occurs in that type.

Propp does succeed in distinguishing between the constant and the variable in folktales. He notes: "Functions serve as stable, constant elements in folktales, independent of who performs them, and how they are fulfilled by the dramatis personae." (p.20). After analyzing a randomly selected sample of 100 Russian fairy tales, Propp was able to draw the following startling conclusions. First, the number of functions known in the fairy tale is limited. In fact, Propp discovered that there are thirty-one possible functions. Furthermore, the sequence of functions is always identical. This does not mean that all thirty-one functions are in every fairy tale, but only that "the absence of several functions does not change the order of those remaining". As a result of his analysis, Propp is able to suggest a new unit to replace the Aarne-Thompson tale type. "Tales evidencing identical functions can be considered as belonging to one type. On this basis, an index of types can be created not relying upon plot features which are essentially vague and diffuse but, rather, upon exact structural features." Propp finds that every one of the 100 tales in his sample will fit into one formula and he concludes that "All fairy tales, by their structure, belong to one and the same type."(pp. 21, 95).

The distinction between the old minimal unit, the motif, and the new minimal unit, the function, may be seen very well in terms of Kenneth Pike's valuable distinction between the etic and the emic. The etic approach is nonstructural but classificatory in that the analyst devises logical categories of systems, classes and units without attempting to make them reflect actual structure in particular data. For Pike, etic units are created by the analyst as constructs for the handling of comparative cross-cultural data (1954:9-10, 20). In contrast, the emic approach is a mono-contextual, structural one. "An emic approach must deal with particular events as parts of larger wholes to which they are related and from which they obtain their ultimate significance, whereas an etic approach may abstract events, for particular purposes, from their context or local system of events, in order to group them on a world-wide scale without essential reference to the structure of any one language or culture." "... emic units within this theory are not absolutes in a vacuum, but rather are points in a system, and these points are defined RELATIVE to the system. A unit must be studied, not in isolation, but as a part of a total functioning componential system within a total culture. It is this problem which ultimately forms the basis for the necessity of handling emics as different from etics.... "(pp. 10, 93). Pike believes that the emic structure is a part of the pattern of objective reality and is not merely the construct of the analyst. Whether one follows Pike on this point or whether one considers that emic units are like beauty in being solely in the eyes of the beholder, one can see that the distinction between structural and nonstructural units is sound. For a complete discussion of the distinction between etic and emic (coined by using the last portions of the words phonetic and phonemic), one should consult Pike's work.

Pike's delineation of the simultaneous trimodal structuring of emic units is of considerable importance for folktale analysis. Pike's three modes are the feature mode, the manifestation mode and the distribution mode. At the risk of oversimplifying Pike's elaborate scheme, one might translate the modes into Propp's analysis by seeing the feature mode as exemplified by the function, the manifestation mode by the various elements which can fulfill a function, and the distribution mode by the positional characteristics of a particular function, that is, where among the thirty-one possible functions it occurs. One reason for bothering to put Propp's analysis in Pike's terminology is an extraordinary verbal coincidence. Pike's minimum unit of the feature mode is the EMIC MOTIF or MOTIFEME (p. 75). In other words, Propp's function in Pike's scheme of analysis would be called a MOTIFEME. Since the term function has not yet achieved any amount of currency among folklorists, it is here proposed that MOTIFEME be used instead.

With the establishment of the structural unit, MOTIFEME, one can see the usefulness of the term ALLOMOTIF for those motifs which occur in any given motifemic context. Allomotifs would bear the same relationship to motifeme as do allophones to phonemes and allomorphs to morphemes. The term MOTIF would continue to be used, but only as an etic unit like the phone or morph. The difference between etic and emic analysis of folktales, that is the difference between analysis by motif and analysis by motifeme, is considerable. For example, Propp's twelfth function or motifeme refers to the hero's being tested, interrogated, or attacked in preparation for his receiving either a magical agent or helper. For instance, a prospective donor may test the hero by assigning him difficult tasks. On the other hand, the twenty-fifth motifeme involves the assignment of a difficult task, usually by the villain. In other words, etically, or in terms of motifs, the same motif may be used in different motifemes. This means that the mere analyzing of folktales into motifs may be misleading. Folklorists are accustomed to treat all occurrences of a particular motif as being of equal or identical significance. This is, in Pike's theory, tantamount to treating homophonous or homomorphic forms as identical in meaning (p. 48). However, one might legitimately ask how one recognizes the appropriate motifeme for a particular motif. If one observes a specific motif, how can one ascertain which motifeme it subserves? Propp addresses himself to this very question. Again, it is the notion of a function or motifeme in the frame of sequential context, i. e. in situ. It is always possible to define a function or motifeme according to its consequences. Accordingly, if the receiving of a magical agent follows the solution of a task, then the motif belongs to the twelfth motifeme and it is clearly a case of the donor testing the hero. If, on the other hand, the receipt of a bride and a marriage follow, then the motif belongs to the twenty-fifth motifeme, the imposition of a difficult task.

It is not only important to realize that the same motif may be used in different motifemes, but it is equally important to realize that different motifs may be used in the same motifeme. Thus the helpful animal could be a cow, cat, bird, fish, and so on. Recalling that motifs are actors and items, it is obvious that for a given function or motifeme, there may be literally hundreds of motifs which would be appropriate. (Of course, not all "appropriate" motifs would necessarily be traditional, i. e. actually found in folktales.) An example of the alternation of motifs is provided by the different versions of the Potiphar's wife story. This is the story of a son-figure whom a mother-figure tries to seduce. When the son-figure refuses, the mother-figure accuses the son of attempting to violate her, whereupon a father-figure metes out punishment to the son-figure. In many versions the punishment is blindness. In other versions, the hero's feet are cut off. In probably the oldest known version of the tale, that of "The Story of the Two Brothers", dating from the fourteenth or thirteenth century B. C., the son-figure, Baîti, castrates himself.*5 One could say that the consequences of the seduction attempt include the cutting off of the hero's leg or phallus and blindness. Since these consequences are distributionally similar, they would appear to be part of the same motifeme, that is, they would appear to be allomotifs. Castration and blindness do not seem to be in complementary distribution but rather appear to be in free variation. In fact , it is probable that one element could be substituted for the other without changing the plot structure. In this light, a curious Greek version of the Potiphar's wife story becomes a little more intelligible. Phoenix, the son of Amyntor, was accused by Phthia, Amyntor's concubine, of having violated her. The father, on the strength of the concubine's false accusation of seduction, blinded his son and cursed him with childlessness.*6 If blindness and castration are allomotifs, then the connection between blindness and childlessness is not so remote.

An example of allomotifs in the folklore of a primitive culture may be found in the North American Indian test tales. In Boas's (1916) important study of the Tsimshian versions of the test theme, a jealous uncle or brother subjects the hero to tests. In order to obtain a wife, the hero must survive any one of the following elements: a snapping door, caves which open and close, a closing tree cleft or canoe, a clam with crushing shells, dangerous animals guarding a door, or a vagina dentata. All these elements appear to be allomotifs of the same motifeme, which, incidentally, looks very much like Propp's twenty-fifth motifeme, "A difficult task is proposed to the hero".

The notion of allomotifs has important theoretical implications for the Finnish historical-geographical method. In this method, considerable significance is placed upon the differences occurring in the variants of a given tale. By plotting the time (historic) and place (geographic) of a given story element. one attempts in this method to reconstruct the original form of the tale and its mode of development and dissemination. If, however, the arsenal of a storyteller included allomotifs, that is, if there are two or more traditional motifs any of which would fulfill a particular motifeme, then the analyst would have to be extremely cautious in evaluating such alternations. This would also explain why a given storyteller might tell the same tale differently upon different occasions. The choice of a specific allomotif (e.g. an obscene one) might be culturally conditioned by the type of audience. Furthermore, what folklorists have hitherto considered as two separate tale types or blends of tale types might be rather a case of the alternation of allomotifs or allomotif clusters. As Propp points out, although the storyteller apparently creates within a definite sequence of motifemes, he is "absolutely free in his choice of the nomenclature and attributes of the dramatis personae" (1958:102).

The phenomenon of the limiting nature of a sequential formula of motifemes merits study. It would be of interest, for example, to ascertain whether there is an absolute minimum number of motifemes necessary for the construction of a folktale. Propp speaks only of an upper limit. It would also be interesting to know if the sequence corresponded in any way with the structure of other cultural elements, such as ritual. In addition, a psychological study of the motifemic sequence might help to elucidate the etiology of the pattern. It should be noted that as yet no attempt has been made to see if there is motifemic patterning in folktales other than fairy tales, to say nothing of the other genres of folklore. Moreover, it has not yet been determined whether motifemic patterning varies from culture area to culture area. It is not even known whether or not there is such patterning in the folktales of primitive cultures. Motifemic analysis of all types of folktales in all types of cultures must be accomplished before any reliable comparative work may be attempted. Just as comparative linguistics is based upon emic analysis (Pike 1954:8, 18; Lado 1957:10), so ultimately must comparative folklore and mythology. In other words, solid synchronic analysis is needed to define adequately the formal structural characteristics of folkloristic genres before truly meaningful diachronic, i.e. historical, studies may be undertaken.

It seems safe to say that the emic unit of the motifeme (Propp's function) marks a tremendous theoretical advance over the etic unit of the motif. With regard to larger units, such as tale types, Propp was quite right when he said that "Types do exist, not on the level outlined by Aarne, but on the level of the structural properties of folktales...."(p. 10). However, the use of the emic unit should not be construed as in any way replacing the need for the etic units. The emic unit replaces the etic unit as a structural unit to be used as the basis for comparative studies; but with respect to the practical matters of classification and cataloging, there is certainly a definite place for etic units. As Propp himself observed, his basic task was "clearly the extraction of the 'genera'"(p. 24). Claude Lévi-Strauss (1960), in a lengthy commentary on Propp's work, notes that before such formalistic studies, folklorists tended to ignore what folktales had in common, but that after formalistic analysis, folklorists are deprived of the means of seeing how folktales differ. If Propp has found, so to speak, a "generative grammar" for Aarne-Thompson tale types 300 to 749, how can individual variants of the same structural tale type be distinguished? The point is that a structurally based tale typology does not in any way eliminate the need for a practical index such as Thompson's. As Honti suggested, synthetic and morphological typology should not be used instead of analytical indices and systems, but in addition to them. Assuming that there may be different formulaic sequences of motifemes for different kinds of folktales or for folktales in different culture areas, there could well be a tale-type index based upon morphological criteria. But this index would be in addition to the Aarne-Thompson type-index and would be cross-referenced so that a folktale scholar could tell at a glance what Aarne-Thompson tale types belonged to which morphological tale types. As Pike notes, etic analysis must precede emic analysis. It is therefore obvious that folklorists need both and further that they should not mistake the one for the other.

The structural study of folklore has really just begun. Except for a few scattered studies such as Sebeok's (1953) study of charms,*7 there has been very little work of this kind. With the aid of the rigorous definition of structural units, the future of structural studies in folklore looks promising indeed.

NOTES

*1 For Thompson's discussion of the motif, see The Folktale, 415-416.

*2 Form is not here considered as separate from meaning. There is wisdom in Pike's notion of a form-meaning composite in contrast to form without meaning or meaning without form. See Pike (1954:74, 99, 150).

*3 This discussion is based upon Stith Thompson's revision of Antti Aarne (1928). However, none of the duplication has been eliminated in Thompson's 1961 revision of the tale-type index.

*4 The importance of this particular theoretical point was not noted by either Taylor (1959) or Jacobs (1959c).

*5 The various versions of the Potiphar's wife story may be found in Bloomfield (1923) and Penzer (1923). The story of the Two Brothers may be found in Maspero (1915).

*6 Apollodorus The Library, trans. J. G. Frazer, The Loeb Classical Library (London, 1921), II, 75. It is interesting that psychoanalysts consider that blindness may, in certain situations, be a symbolic equivalent of castration. This suggests that an examination of the allomotifs or different culturally determined localizations in the motifemes of borrowed international tales may provide insight into the system of symbolic equivalents employed in a given culture.

*7 Unfortunately, most linguists err in treating linguistic units such as the morpheme as structural units of the folktale. This was pointed out by J. L. Fischer (1960) when he observed that if a folktale were translated from one language to another, the structure of the folktale might well remain the same though the linguistic structure would obviously change.

7

STRUCTURAL TYPOLOGY IN NORTH AMERICAN INDIAN
FOLKTALES

There can be no rigorous typology without prior morphology. In the case of
North American Indian folktales, the lack of morphological units and analyses
has precluded typological statements. The extent of the morphological void is
illustrated by the fact that the casualist theory of American Indian folktale composition is still widely held. According to this view, American Indian folktales
are composed of random unstable conglomerates of motifs. In 1894, the English
folklorist Joseph Jacobs, in discussing primitive folktales generally, remarked
(1894:137), "Those who have read these tales will agree with me, I think, that
they are formless and void, and bear the same relation to good European fairy
tales as the invertebrates do to the vertebrate kingdom in the animal world."
In 1916, Franz Boas made a similar statement (1916:878): "European folk-lore
creates the impression that the whole stories are units and that their cohesion
is strong, the whole complex very old. The analysis of American material, on
the other hand, demonstrates that complex stories are new, that there is little
cohesion between the component elements, and that the really old parts of tales
are the incidents and a few simple plots." Recently, Melville Jacobs (1959:127)
criticized Boas for not carrying over to the field of folklore a structural approach, which he used successfully in the study of language and plastic-graphic
art.

It is true that while the structural or pattern approach was sweeping through
linguistics, psychology, ethnomusicology, and anthropology proper in the 1920's
and 30's, folklore as a discipline remained oriented to a narrowly historical approach dedicated to atomistic studies. In 1934, there appeared Benedict's Patterns of Culture; in 1933, Helen Roberts published "The Pattern Phenomenon
in Primitive Music", as well as her study Form in Primitive Music. In linguistics, Sapir's Language (1921) and "Sound Patterns in Language", (1925) were
followed by Bloomfield's Language (1933) and Swadesh's "The Phonemic Principle", (1934). Köhler's Gestalt Psychology (1929) and Koffa's Principles of Gestalt Psychology (1935) reflected the same theoretical movement in psychology.
In the thirties, the search for patterns was itself a pattern of culture. However,
in the field of folklore, there was apparently no interest in a holistic synchronic
approach. The major piece of folklore scholarship of the middle thirties was
Stith Thompson's mammoth Motif-Index of Folk Literature, lexicon par excel-
lence, epitome of the atomistic emphasis in folklore. The culture lag in folklore
theory has unfortunately increased since the thirties, and this is one reason why

Reprinted from the Southwestern Journal of Anthropology 19 (1963), 121-30.

there have been so few notable theoretical advances in folklore.

One of the few exceptions is Vladimir Propp's Morphology of the Folktale published in 1928. By morphology Propp (1958:18) meant "the description of the folktale according to its component parts and the relationship of these components to each other and to the whole". Propp, after defining and isolating a morphological unit which he termed "function", proceeded to analyze morphologically one hundred consecutive märchen, a random corpus of tales, from the celebrated Afanasiev collections of Russian folktales. In analyzing the functions, that is, the units of plot narrative structure, of these hundred tales, Propp discovered that there was a limited number of functions, namely thirty-one, and that the sequence of these functions was fixed. This did not mean that all thirty-one possible functions necessarily occurred in any one given folktale, but rather that those which did occur did so in a predictable order. Having completed his morphology, Propp was able to proceed to typology, and he concluded (1958:21) that all Russian fairy tales, on morphological grounds, belonged to one and the same structural type.

In applying Propp's morphological framework to American Indian folktales, I have adopted some of the terminology and theory of Kenneth L. Pike, as expressed in the latter's Language in Relation to a Unified Theory of the Structure of Human Behavior (Dundes 1962a). Propp's function becomes thus a motifeme, instead, which permits the associated notions of motif and allomotif. Folktales may thus be defined as sequences of motifemes. The motifemic slots may be filled with various motifs and the specific alternative motifs for any given motifemic slot may be labelled allomotifs. With the aid of this combined Proppian/Pike structural model, I was able to discern a number of clear-cut structural patterns in North American Indian folktales.

A large number of American Indian folktales consist of a move from disequilibrium to equilibrium. Disequilibrium, a state to be feared and avoided if possible, may be seen as a state of surplus or of lack, depending upon the point of view. The disequilibrium may be indicated by a statement that there is too much of one thing or too little of another. In the hoarded object tales, in which such objects as game, fish, food-plants, water, tides, seasons, sun, light, fire, and so forth are not available to the majority of mankind or to most of the members of a tribe, there is very often an initial statement of the socially or universally felt lack. An initial state of flood may be interpreted as either too much water or too little land, but in any case, there is the undesirable state of disequilibrium, which I will call "lack". Folktales can consist simply of relating how abundance was lost or how a lack was liquidated. In other words, something in excess may be lost or something lost or stolen may be found. Both of these situations fall under the rubric of moving from disequilibrium to equilibrium.

One structural type of American Indian folktale then consists of just two motifemes: Lack (L) and Lack Liquidated (LL). In the Malecite version of "The Release of Impounded Water", a monster keeps back all the water in the world (L). A culture hero slays the monster, which act releases water (LL). A Wishram tale based upon the same motifeme pattern is as follows: "A people on the Columbia had no eyes or mouths (L). They ate by smelling the sturgeon. Coyote opened their eyes and mouths (LL). " In an unpublished Upper Chehalis tale: "Once upon a time the world started going to pieces. A mint with lots of runners decided to

sew it back together. It did so, and saved the world. " There are not a great
many tales which consist of only two motifemes, but there are some. The two
motifeme sequence may be said to constitute a minimum definition of an American
Indian folktale.

A much more common motifeme sequence is one with the following four motifemes: Interdiction, Violation, Consequence, and an Attempted Escape from the
Consequence (abbreviated Int, Viol, Conseq, and AE). The Attempted Escape
is an optional rather than obligatory structural slot. A tale may end with the
Consequence. Furthermore, if there is an attempted escape, the attempt may
be successful or it may be unsuccessful. The presence of the fourth motifeme,
Attempted Escape, may depend upon the particular culture or particular informant within that culture. Similarly the success or failure of the attempt may also
depend upon these factors.

A few examples may illustrate the nature of this folktale pattern. Notice the
diversity of content within the identical structural form. In a Swampy Cree tale,
a little boy is told by his sister not to shoot at a squirrel when it is near the
water (Int). The boy shoots at a squirrel near water (Viol) and when he seeks to
retrieve his arrow from the water, he is swallowed by a fish (Conseq). Eventually, the fish is directed to swim to the sister, who cuts it open, thereby re-
leasing her brother (AE). In a Lillooet tale, an old man warns some boys out
fishing not to mockingly call for a whale to come (Int). The boys laugh and continue calling (Viol) whereupon a whale comes and swallows them (Conseq). The
whale is directed to a certain beach where the people cut it open, permitting the
boys to escape (AE). In an Onondaga tale with parallels among Eskimo, Plains
and Woodlands peoples, a group of children is warned to stop dancing (Int). The
children refuse (Viol) and are translated to the heavens (Conseq) where they become the Pleiades. The ending of a tale with an explanatory motif is common in
American Indian folktales. The explanatory motif is not structurally obligatory;
it functions rather as a stylistic terminal marker or literary coda. Sometimes
the interdiction is implicit rather than explicit. In "The Rolling Rock", trickster
offends a rock by taking back a present (e.g. a robe) which he has previously
given it, or by defecating on the rock (Viol). The rock rolls after him in pursuit
(Conseq). The protagonist usually escapes through the helpful intervention of
friendly animals who destroy the rock (AE). In a Tlingit tale, some boys pull a
piece of drifting seaweed out of the water on one side of their canoe and put it
in again on the other (Viol). Permanent winter results (Conseq). In a Kathlamet
cognate, the interdiction is explicit. The people of a town are forbidden to play
with their excrements (Int). A bad boy does play with his (Viol) and the next
night snow begins to fall. Winter comes permanently and people start to die of
hunger (Conseq). The people escape these consequences by leaving the bad boy
to die on the ice (AE). There is great variety of content in these tales; that is,
there are a great number of allomotifs. This is what has led some anthropologists to believe that American Indian folktales lacked cohesion. However, the
sequence of motifemes is exactly the same in these tales. Motifemically speaking, there is great cohesion between the component elements, contrary to what
Boas thought.

Longer American Indian folktales may be composed of combinations of shorter
motifeme patterns. A common six motifeme combination consists of Lack,

Liquidation of Lack, Interdiction, Violation, Consequence, and Attempted Escape. In Orpheus, a man loses his wife (L), but regains her or can regain her (LL) if he does not violate a taboo (Int). Inevitably the man breaks the taboo (Viol) and loses his wife once again (Conseq). As an illustration of how diverse content can occur within a common structural frame, the Orpheus tale may be compared with the Zuni tale of "The Little Girl and the Cricket". A girl discovers a singing cricket and wants to take it home (L). The cricket goes home with her (LL), but warns her that she must not touch or tickle him (Int). The girl in playing with the cricket tickles him (Viol) and the cricket bursts his stomach and dies (Conseq). In tabular form, the two tales are as follows:

Motifemes	Orpheus	Girl and Cricket
Lack	Man wants to bring wife home from the dead	Girl wants to bring cricket home from fields
Lack Liquidated	Man does so	Girl does so
Interdiction	Man is warned not to look back at wife	Girl is warned not to touch cricket
Violation	Man looks back	Girl touches cricket
Consequence	Man's wife dies	Cricket dies
Attempted Escape	— — — — — — — — — —	— — — — — — — — — —

It should be noted that the consequence may be a form of lack, as it is in the Orpheus tale, for example. This suggests that in folktales where there is no initial lack given, there may occur a sequence of motifemes causing a state of lack. Usually the lack is the result of some unwise action or more specifically the result of a violation of an interdiction. Thus in some versions of earthdiver, the lack is stated initially: "Once there was no earth. Water was where the earth is now." On the other hand, the flood may be caused, as in the Upper Chehalis account, by foolishly flaunting a taboo. In the latter account Thrush is not allowed to wash his dirty face (Int), but he is induced to do so (Viol). After Thrush washes his face, it begins to rain heavily until the water rises and covers everything (Conseq). Then Muskrat dives four times for the necessary dirt in the usual earthdiver sequence (AE).

It is important to realize that these structural motifemic alternatives are not limited to any one historical tale; these alternatives may be found in many tales. In the widespread tale of Eye-Juggler, the trickster may simply lose his eyes (L) and regain them (LL). However, in many Plains versions, the two motifeme sequence is expanded. Trickster wishes to be able to imitate a man who is able to throw his eyes into the air and replace them (L). Trickster is given the power (LL), but he is warned that his eyes may only be thrown four times or that they may not be thrown too high or near trees (Int). Trickster disobeys (Viol) and loses his eyes (Conseq). On the basis of structural analysis, one might say that in _any_ tale which begins with an initial lack, it is theoretically possible for _that_ tale to begin with an interdiction whose violation causes the lack. If this is so, then a knowledge of the alternative structural patterns might be of considerable use in constructing and evaluating historical-geographical hypotheses concerning individual folktales. What folklorists have previously considered to be sub-types of a particular tale may be manifestations of much more general structural pattern alternation.

While it is clear that American Indian folktales are definitely structured inasmuch as they are composed of specific statable sequences of motifemes, it must be understood that all the existing motifeme patterns are not discussed above. Another common pattern, for example, consists of Lack, Deceit, Deception, and Lack Liquidated (Dundes 1964). Yet these few illustrative patterns should be sufficient to support the thesis that American Indian folktales are structured. But structural analysis is not an end in itself and the question might be raised: what is the significance and use of the structural analyses of folktales?

First, typological statements can be made. As Roman Jakobson observed in commenting upon the Boasian approach to the study of American Indian languages, structural similarities should be pointed out. He noted, "Certain grammatical phonemic types have a wide continuous distribution without corresponding lexical similarities." (Jakobson 1939:192-193). Voegelin and Harris (1947:596) have made similar statements. They have said, for example, that "Structural comparability of languages may be stated independently of their genetic relationships." Just as Van Gennep noted that a common structural pattern characterized a variety of rites of vastly different content, that is, that the sequential pattern of separation, transition, and incorporation could be found in rites dealing with birth, puberty, marriage, death, and so forth, so common structural patterns in folktales of quite diverse content may be clearly delineated.

A second significant benefit accruing from structural analysis is a new technique of gaining insight into the cultural determination of content within transcultural forms. If a folklorist aligns all the tales with the same structure reported in a given culture, that is, aligns them motifeme by motifeme, he may then easily note whether or not a specific motifeme is manifested by a particular motif. For example, after aligning a number of Cheyenne tales based upon the Interdiction/Violation pattern, I discovered that invariably the interdiction forbade the use of a special power more than four times. In some cases, the content of the tale was considerably altered by Cheyenne informants to make it possible for this particular motif to occur. In a Cheyenne version of "Rolling Rock", one does not find the usual offense to the rock. Instead, trickster sees a man who can command stones to turn over without touching them and he desires this power (L). He is given the power (LL) on condition that he use it no more than four times (Int). He loses count, uses the power for a fifth time (Viol) and the stone pursues him (Conseq). A nighthawk saves trickster by breaking the stone into pieces (AE). Similarly, in an unusual version of "Bungling Host", trickster is given the power of scraping flesh from his back for food provided that he does not repeat the process more than four times. The cultural predilection for the "not more than four times" motif might have been noticed from the reading of one tale, but then again it might not have been. It is no longer necessary to employ so subjective an empirical approach. One need only align, or superimpose, all the tales in a culture based upon a particular motifeme pattern and then sight down the various motifs filling a particular motifemic slot.

Another benefit of structural analysis lies in the area of prediction in an acculturation situation. If one knows the structure of European folktales and the structure of American Indian folktales, one can predict with reasonable certainty what changes will occur when a European tale is borrowed by an American Indian group. For example, the Zuni version of Aarne-Thompson tale type 121, "Wolves Climb on Top of One Another to Tree", is instructive. In the European tale, some wolves resort to climbing on top of one another to capture someone in a tree. When the lowest wolf runs away, the others all fall. In the Zuni version of this tale, Coyote wants to climb up a cliff to get some corn (L). Coyote gathers together his fellow coyotes and the group decides to ascend the cliff by holding on to one another's tail or by holding on to corn cobs inserted in their anuses (LL). The coyotes are all warned not to break wind (Int). However, the last coyote does so (Viol), causing the whole chain to tumble down. All the coyotes are killed (Conseq).

Whereas formerly folklorists were content merely to identify European tales among the North American Indians, it is now possible to show exactly how European tales have been cast in the mold of traditional American Indian folktale patterns, in this case, that of the Interdiction/Violation motifeme sequence. It is interesting to note that one of the most striking structural differences between European and American Indian folktales concerns the number of motifemes intervening between a pair of related motifemes, such as Lack and Lack Liquidated. The number of intervening motifemes may be considered as an indication of what may be termed the "motifemic depth" of folktales. American Indian tales have far less motifemic depth than European folktales. In the latter, Lack (Propp function 8a) and Lack Liquidated (Propp function 19) are widely separated whereas in American Indian tales a lack is liquidated soon after it is stated. It is possible that the lesser motifemic depth of American Indian tales may account in part for the absence of either native or borrowed cumulative folktales among the American Indians, inasmuch as cumulative tales often consist of an extensive interconnected series of lacks to be liquidated within the frame of an initial lack and final liquidation of that lack. Such hypotheses might be tested by planting tales of a given structural pattern in a culture and re-eliciting them after a given period of time.

Perhaps the most exciting contribution of structural analysis lies in the uncharted area of cross-genre comparison. Rarely have folklorists attempted to compare the different genres of folklore. In fact, on the contrary, with respect to the genres of folktale and superstition, there has been within recent years an attempt to divide the field of folklore study into the two divisions of folk literature and folk custom. Herskovits, for instance, accepts this "dual mandate" as he terms it (1946:93) and Bascom in an unequivocal statement (1953a:285) maintains that folklore to the anthropologist includes myths and tales but does not include folk custom or folk belief.

Yet, morphological analysis of the two genres reveals that a common structural pattern may underlie both. In a recently published structural study (Dundes 1961:28), I proposed the following tentative generic definition of superstition: "Superstitions are traditional expressions of one or more conditions and one or more results with some of the conditions signs and others causes. " The formula for superstitions may be stated simply as "If A, then B", with an optional "unless C". In a category of superstitions which I have termed "Magic", fulfillment of one or more conditions <u>causes</u> one or more results. The Chippewa believe, for example, that throwing dogs or cats into a lake will cause a storm. However, in "Conversion" superstitions, an undesirable result may be neutralized or even reversed so that a desirable result ensues. Thus in magic superstitions, there is a conditional action, which if fulfilled leads to a result. But there may be an accompanying conversion superstition which, employed as a counteractant, permits an individual to avoid or nullify the undesirable result of the magic superstition. Perhaps now the parallel between the structure of the Interdiction/Violation motifeme sequence in folktales and the structure of superstition may be seen. Consider the following Zuni folktale and superstition:

Folktale		Superstition	
Int:	A girl is warned not to hunt rabbits	Condition:	If a woman eats the wafer bread from the deer hunt
Viol:	She does		------------
Conseq:	A cannibalistic monster appears	Result:	she will have twins
		Counteractant:	unless the bread is
AE:	The twin Ahaiyute save the girl		passed around the rung of her house ladder four times

One must not be deceived by the apparent lack of an analogue to the Violation motifeme. In superstitions, it is always assumed that the condition will be fulfilled, or in other words, that the interdiction will be violated. It thus appears that it is possible to compare folktales and superstitions. Moreover, it would be interesting to know whether there is any significant correlation between the forms of folktales and superstitions of the same culture, especially with respect to the more or less optional Attempted Escape motifeme and the counteractant portion of superstitions. One would think that in cultures where there is a great preponderance of attempted escapes from the consequences of violating interdictions in folktales, there would be an analogous high incidence of counteractants or conversion superstitions. It should also be noted that this structural pattern may be found in other folkloristic genres. For example, in games, there are inevitably rules. If the rules are broken (and breaking the rules may be part of the game), there may be a penalty. Then depending upon the particular game or the particular version of the game, there may or may not be a means of nullifying or escaping the penalty.

The importance of structural analysis should be obvious. Morphological analysis of American Indian folktales makes it possible for typological descriptive statements to be made. Such statements, in turn, make it possible for folklorists to examine the cultural determination of content, to predict culture change, and to attempt cross-genre comparison. It is to be hoped that structural analyses of the folklore of other geographical areas, e.g. Africa, will reveal whether or not certain structural patterns are universal.

8

ON GAME MORPHOLOGY: A STUDY OF THE STRUCTURE
OF NON-VERBAL FOLKLORE

Are children's games a form of non-verbal folklore and folktales, a form of verbal folklore, structurally similar? I am suggesting they are and also that there are many other non-verbal analogues to verbal folklore forms. Consequently, the definition of folklore should not be limited to verbal materials.

Although structural analysis, as an effective means of descriptive ethnography, has been applied to a number of types of folklore expression, it has not been employed in the study of children's games. Yet games, in general, and competitive games, in particular, are obviously patterned. In competitive games, the participants are aware that play is governed by definite limiting rules. The application and the interrelationship of these rules result in an ordered sequence of actions by the players, and these action sequences constitute the essential structure of any particular game.

In order to delineate the structure of a game, or any other form of folklore, one must have a minimum structural unit. Only with such a unit can there be any precise segmentation of the continuum of game action. As a trial unit, I propose to use the motifeme, a unit of action which has been used in structural studies of folktales (Dundes 1962a, 1963b). One obvious advantage of employing the motifeme is that if game action can, in fact, be broken down into motifemes, then it would be relatively easy to compare the structure of games with the structure of folktales.[*1]

Before examining the pronounced similarities in game and folktale structure, it is necessary to emphasize one important difference between the two forms. The difference is dimensionality. The folktale is concerned with conflict between protagonist and antagonist, but the sequence of plot actions is unidimensional. Either the hero's actions or the villain's actions are discussed at any one moment in time at any one point in the tale. Vladimir Propp, a Russian folklorist, published in 1928, a thought-provoking examination of fairy tales and devised a distribution of functions (motifemes) among the dramatis personae of the tales (Propp 1958). He noted, for example, that functions VIII (villainy), XVI (struggle), and XXI (pursuit) belong to the villain's sphere of action. Certainly, functions IV (reconnaissance) and V (delivery) in Propp's analysis are villain and not hero actions. In games, however, one finds a contrast: there are at least two sequences of actions going on simultaneously. When A is playing against B, both A and B are operating at the same time, all the time. This is theoretically true in folktales, but only one side's activities (usually the hero's) are described

Reprinted from New York Folklore Quarterly 20 (1964), 276-88.

at a given point in the tale. A folktale is, therefore, a two-dimensional series of actions displayed on a one-dimensional track, or, conversely, a game is, structurally speaking, a two-dimensional folktale.

In his notable discussion of folktale morphology, Propp drew particular attention to function VIII, villainy. In this function, a villain causes harm or injury to one member of a family by abducting a person or stealing an object, etc., thus creating the actual movement of the folktale (p. 29). At the same time, he astutely observed that a folktale could begin with the desire to have something or a deficiency or lack as a given ground-rule. In the analysis, Propp considered lack (function VIIIa) as morphologically equivalent to villainy (function VIII). If a folktale did not begin with a state of lack, then a state of lack could be created by an act of villainy. This same distinction can also be applied to the structure of many games. A game can begin with an object which is missing, or the object may be hidden before play begins. In some games nothing is missing, but the initial portion of game action (corresponding to Propp's "initial" or "preparatory" section of the folktale, functions I-VII) brings about the requisite state of lack or insufficiency. In games of the first type, an individual may hide from the group (as in "Hare and Hounds") or the group may hide from an individual ("Hide and Seek"). In games of the second type, an individual or object may be abducted or captured, which also results in a lack. This happens, for example, in the child-stealing game of "The Witch". Other chracteristics shared by both folktales and games will become apparent in the following discussion of several specific games.

In "Hare and Hounds" (Gomme 1964:I, 191), the boy chosen as the Hare (the choosing by counting out rhymes or other means may be construed as pre-game activity) runs away to hide. Usually a fixed time span, a specific number of minutes, or counting to some arbitrary number, marks the formal beginning of the chase, much as the iteration of an opening formula marks the passage from reality to fantasy in the beginning of a folktale. In fact, some games actually have opening formulas such as "Ready or not, here I come". The game, then, begins with a lack, the missing Hare. The quest, so popular in folktales, is equally popular in games. The Hounds attempt to find and catch the Hare, just as the hero in folktale seeks to liquidate the initial lack (function XIX).

Note, however, that two sets of actions, or motifeme sequences, are involved in the game. One action is from the point of view of the Hounds, the other from the perspective of the Hare. The sequences include the following motifemes: lack, interdiction, violation, and consequence.*2 In one motifemic sequence, the Hounds want to catch the Hare (lack). They are required to catch him before he returns "home", a place agreed upon previously, (interdiction). If the Hounds fail to do so (violation), they lose the game (consequence). In the second motifemic sequence taking place simultaneously with the first, the Hare wants to go "home" (lack), but he is required to arrive there without being caught by the Hounds (interdiction). If he fails to do so (violation), he loses the game (consequence). It is possible to win the game, by liquidating the lack, by either of two actions: catching the Hare or returning "home" safely. But it is impossible for both Hare and Hounds to win and also impossible for both Hare and Hounds to lose. Here is another point of contrast with folktales. In folktales, the hero always wins and the villain always loses. In games, however the outcome is not so regular or predictable: sometimes the Hare wins, and sometimes the Hounds win. As Caillois has pointed out, one characteristic of competitive games is that the opponents are equal and, in theory, each opponent stands the same chance of winning. *3

The game of "Hare and Hounds" might be structured as follows:

	Lack	Interdiction	Violation	Consequence
Hare	wants to go home	without being caught by Hounds	is caught (isn't caught)	loses game (wins game)
Hounds	want to catch Hare	before he arrives back home	do not catch Hare (do catch Hare)	lose game (win game)

The double structure is also illuminated by comparison with analogous folktale structure. From the Hare's point of view, one could say there was a hero pursued (function XXI) and that the hero is rescued from pursuit (function XXII), assuming the Hare wins. The game-folktale analogy is even closer in those versions in which the Hare is required to leave signs, such as strips of paper, to mark his trail. In folktales, when the hero runs from his pursuer, he often places obstacles in the latter's path. These objects mark the trail, but also serve to delay the pursuer. From the point of view of the Hounds, i.e. with the Hounds as heroes, the Hare appears to serve as a donor figure, inasmuch as the dropped slips of paper are "magical agents" (identified as function XIV) which aid the hero-Hounds in liquidating the initial lack. *4 The donor sequence, then, is another point of similarity between games and folktales.

In a popular American children's game which Brewster (1953:164) calls "Steps", the leader, or "it", aids the others in reaching him (to tag him) by permitting various steps, such as baby steps, giant steps or umbrella steps. In this game, the donor figure grants the privilege of using certain "magical" steps. The fact that the magical aid is not granted until the hero is tested by the donor is also a striking parallel to folktale morphology. After the donor, ("it") permits the number and type of steps, (e.g. four baby steps), the recipient ("hero") is required to say "May I?" If the latter passes the politeness test, he is permitted to take the steps which bring him closer to his goal. However, should he neglect to express the etiquette formula, the donor will penalize him by ordering him to step backwards, thus moving him away from the goal. More often than not in folktales, civility or politeness to the donor will provide the needed magical agents while discourtesy deprives the would-be hero of these same agents.

In some games, the presence of a donor sequence appears to be optional rather than obligatory, as is also true in folktales. In "Thimble in Sight" (Newell 1963:152; Brewster 1953:46) an object, such as a thimble, is hidden. Actually, the object is supposed to be visible but not obvious. The children seek to discover or notice the object (lack). As each child does so (lack liquidated), he indicates his success by exclaiming a verbal formula such as "rorum torum corum", much as the successful player in "Hide and Seek" announces his return "home" with the phrase "Home free". (These verbal formulas would appear to be analogous to closing formulas in folktales.) In this form of "Thimble in Sight" there is no donor sequence but in some versions, the hider aids the thimble-seekers by giving helpful clues such as "You're freezing" or "You're cold", when the seeker is far away from the quest-object, and "You're warm" or "You're burning", when the seeker is close to the object. In such versions, the seeker could presumably request assistance from the donor by asking, "Am I getting warm?" Nevertheless, since the game can be played without the donor sequence, it is clear that the sequence is structurally not obligatory.

The frequency of the donor sequence in games and folktales also demands attention. One would suspect, for example, that since the donor sequence is comparatively rare in American Indian folktales, as compared with Indo-European folktales, the donor sequence would be infrequent in American Indian games. The presence or absence of such a sequence might even be correlated with magic and religion. If a person can make magic or seek a religious vision as an individual, then the need for a donor might be less than in those cultures in which experts or intermediaries supply magic or religion.

So far, mention has been made of a number of games in which the initial lack is part of the given. The game's action does not begin until an object or person is removed or secreted. "It" may absent himself in order to produce the initial lack situation. However, in "The Witch" the lack is the result of "it's" abducting someone.*5 In this game, the parallel to folktale structure is also apparent. A mother leaves her seven children, named after the days of the week (Propp's function I, "One of the members of a family is absent from home" - still bearing in mind that Propp's morphological analysis was made of folktales and not games). Before leaving, the mother tells her children, "Take care the Old Witch does not catch you" (function II, "An interdiction is addressed to the hero"). The witch enters and the children do not take heed (function III, "The interdiction is violated"). The witch pretends that the children's mother has sent her to fetch a bonnet (function VI, "The villain attempts to deceive his victim in order to take possession of him or of his belongings"). The child goes to get the bonnet (function VII, "The victim submits to deception and thereby unwittingly helps his enemy"). The witch abducts one of the children (function VIII, "The villain causes harm or injury to one member of a family"). The mother returns, names her seven children, and thus discovers that one of her children is missing. The remaining children cry, "The Old Witch has got her" (function IX, "Misfortune or shortage is made known"). The sequence of motifemes is repeated until the witch has abducted all the children. This action is analogous to the repetition of entire moves in folktales, e.g. elder brothers setting out successively on identical quests.

The mother then goes out to find the children (function X, "The seeker agrees to or decides upon counteraction", and function XI, "The hero leaves home"). The mother encounters the witch and asks her for information about the whereabouts of her children. In the standard ritual dialogue, one finds possible traces of the standard donor sequence, as identified by functions XII-XIV. In this game, the witch functions as donor. The mother finally arrives at the place where her children are being held captive (function XV, "The hero is transferred, reaches, or is led to the whereabouts of an object of search"). This function or motifeme is of great significance to the structural analysis of both games and folktales. Propp remarks "Generally the object of search is located in another or different kingdom." Anyone familiar with children's games will recall that many make mandatory the penetration of the opponent's territory. In "Capture the Flag", the object of the search is the opponent's flag, clearly located in the "enemy's kingdom".

Now the mother discovers her lost children (function XIX, "The initial misfortune or lack is liquidated"), and mother and children pursue the witch. The one who catches the witch becomes the witch in the next playing of the game. In folktales, a pursuit often follows the liquidation of the initial lack, but more commonly the villain pursues the hero (function XXI, "The hero is pursued"). The hero inevitably escapes (function XXII, "The hero is rescued from pursuit"). Propp remarks that "a great many folktales end on the note of rescue from pursuit." The same might be said of games. In many games, "it", or the villain, is the one who pursues the "hero"-seekers after the latter have obtained the quest-object, such as the flag in "Capture the Flag". Of course, one reason why the game of "The Witch" is similar to folktales is the fixed nature of the outcome! The witch never wins, just as the villain in folktales never wins.

Critics have been sceptical of Propp's morphological analysis on the grounds that he limited his material to Russian fairy tales. Competent students of the folktale, however, are aware that most, if not all, of the tales Propp analyzed can, in fact, be classified according to the Aarne-Thompson system as tale types. Others complain that Propp was too general and that his functions apply to literary as well as to folk materials. It is true that Propp's concept can be correlated to the plot structure of Beowulf and to most of the Odyssey (Cf. his functions XXI to XXXI with the end of the Odyssey). Clearly, the game of "Old Witch" contains a number of Propp's functions and, in one sense, the game appears to be a dramatized folktale. Moreover the "Old Witch game bears a superficial resemblance to the Aarne-Thompson tale type 123, "The Wolf and the Kids". But what is important here is that the morphological analysis of folktales appears to apply equally well to another genre of folklore - traditional games, thereby providing further confirmation of the validity of Propp's analysis.

When one perceives the similarity between the structure of games and folktales it is also possible to see parallels among special forms of the two genres. For example, one type of folktale is the cumulative tale. In these tales (Aarne-Thompson types 2000-2199), one finds chains of actions or objects. Usually, there is repetition with continual additions. In ballads this stylistic feature is termed "incremental repetition." Stith Thompson, in his discussion of tales of this type, noted, but without further comment, that they had "something of the nature of a game"(1946:230,234). This game-tale analogy is obvious in "Link Tag" in which "it" tags someone. The tagged person must take hold of the tagger's hand and help him tag others; the next one tagged joins the first two and so on (Brewster 1953:67). (The same structure is obviously found in those folk dances in which couples or individuals form ever-lenthening chains.)

Another sub-genre analogy might be trickster tales (or jokes) and pranks. In trickster tales and in most pranks or practical jokes, the primary motifemes are fraud and deception (Propp functions VI and VII) so there can even be an exact identity of content as well as form in folktales and games (Brewster 1953: 120-26). For example, in some versions of tale type 1530, "Holding up the

Rock", a dupe is gulled into believing that he is holding up a wall. But "Hold up
the wall" is a hazing stunt at Texas Agricultural and Mechanical College, in
which, according to one report, a student is required to squat with his back
against a wall as if supporting it (Eikel 1946). A more surprising example is
the prank analogue of tale type 1528, "Holding Down the Hat", in which victims
were fooled into grabbing feces concealed under a hat (Caldwell 1945:50). Perhaps the greatest similarity in trickster tale and prank morphology is their
common parodying of standard folktale and game structure. Instead of liquidating
an actual lack, a false lack is feigned. Thus the unsuspecting initiate is sent
snipe-hunting, armed with a sack and a flashlight, or an apprentice is persuaded
to seek some quest-object which, according to the occupation group, may be
striped paint, a board-shortener or a left-handed monkey wrench.

The morphological similarity between game and folktale suggests an important principle which may be applied to other forms of folklore. Basically, these
different forms derive from the distinction between words and acts. Thus, there
is verbal folklore and non-verbal folklore. The distinction is made most frequently with respect to myth and ritual. Myth is verbal folklore or, in Bascom's
(1955) terms, verbal "art". Ritual, in contrast, is non-verbal folklore or non-
verbal art. Myth and ritual are both sacred; folktale and game are both secular.
(Whether all games evolved from ritual is no more or less likely than the evolution, or rather devolution, of folktales from myths.) Whereas folklorists have,
for some time, known of the similarities between myth and ritual, they have
not recognized the equally common characteristics of folktale and game. Moreover, they have failed to see that the verbal/non-verbal dichotomy applies to
most, if not all, of the standard genres of folklore. The proverb, clearly an
example of verbal folklore, has for its non-verbal counterpart the gesture.
They are functionally equivalent as both forms may sum up a situation or pass
judgment on a situation. Riddles are structurally similar to proverbs in that
both are based upon topic/comment constructions, but they are distinct from
proverbs in that there is always a referent to be guessed (Georges and Dundes
1963:113,117). Non-verbal equivalents include a variety of difficult tasks and
puzzles. The distinction between proverbs and riddles applies equally to gestures and non-oral riddles. The referent of the gesture is known to both the em-
ployer of the gesture and his audience before the gesture is made; the referent
of the non-oral riddles is presumably known initially only by the poser. *6

Superstitions are also illuminated by this verbal/non-verbal distinction. Folklorists have long used terms such as "belief" and "custom" or "practice" in
discussions of superstitions. In this analysis, practices or customs would be
examples of non-verbal folklore since actual physical activity is involved. The
distinction may even apply to folk music. If folk narrative, for example, is set
to music, it would then be termed folksong; if a game were set to music, it
would then be termed folk dance. (Note that the etymology of the term "ballad"
supports this distinction.) I am not implying that folksong derives from folk
narrative or that folk dance derives from game but only suggesting that these
supposedly disparate genres have much in common. For example, the basic
sequence of lack and lack-liquidated found in folktales and games is also found
in folk dance. In many dances, a couple is separated, or from the man's point
of view, he has lost his partner (lack). The remainder of the dance consists of

reuniting the separated partners (liquidating the lack). *7 Moreover, the leaving of home and returning home occurs in folktales, games, folk dances and folk music. Structurally speaking, it does not matter whether "home" is a house, a tree, a position on a dance floor or a note.

The techniques of structural analysis should be applied to genres of folklore other than games and folktales. These forms, from the design of quilt patterns to tongue-twisters, can be defined structurally. One would guess that such analyses will reveal a relatively small number of similar structural patterns underlying these apparently diverse forms.

Specifically, I have tried to demonstrate that at least one non-verbal form of folklore, children's games, is structurally similar to a verbal form, the folktale. If, then, there are non-verbal analogues (e. g. games) for verbal folklore forms (e. g. folktales), then folklore as a discipline cannot possibly be limited to the study of just verbal art, oral literature, or folk literature, or whatever similar term is employed. Kenneth Pike (1954:2) has observed that "Verbal and non-verbal activity is a unified whole, and theory and methodology should be organized or created to treat it as such. "*8 It is time for folklorists to devote some of the energies given over to the study of verbal folklore to the study of folklore in its non-verbal forms. Compared to folk narrative and folksong, such forms as folk dance, games, and gestures have been grossly neglected. *9 Admittedly there are complex problems of transcription but surely they are not insuperable.

NOTES

*1 A recent interesting study (Roberts, Sutton-Smith, and Kendon 1963) demonstrates that folktales and games are strikingly similar models of competitive situations and that folktales with strategic outcomes are positively correlated with the occurrence of games of strategy in given cultural settings. However, the comparison of game and folktale content was limited to a generalized consideration of "outcomes". The delineation of game structure should facilitate this type of cross-cultural study.

*2 One should remember that an interdiction is a negative injunction. Compare, for example, "Don't open your eyes" with "Keep your eyes closed". It should also be kept in mind that one form of consequence can be lack, while another form can be liquidation of lack (Propp's functions VIIIa and XIX). Brian Sutton-Smith (1959) lumps game action into a cover-all term, "The Game Challenge". While he does discuss the structure of game time and space, he does not really conceive of games as linear structural sequences of actions nor does he appear to be aware that there are two distinct sets of action sequences in the game he analyzes, "Bar the Door", one set for the person who is "it", the central player, and one set for the children who attempt to run past "it" as they go from one base to the other.

*3 Caillois (1961:14). The double set of rules existing in games makes their analysis somewhat different from the analysis of folktales. Sometimes the two patterns are distinct in that there is no rapid change from one set of rules to the other for an individual player. In baseball, for example, the rules of "offense" apply for the team at bat until three men have been put out. Similarly, the rules of "defense" for the team in the field apply for the same period. At the end of the period, the teams exchange places (and rules). However, in other games, such as basketball or football, the rules can change at any time. In football, an intercepted pass or a recovered fumble by the team on defense immediately transforms the defense team into an offense team, and the same action immediately transforms the team previously on offense to a defense team. In "How many miles to Babylon?" described in Brewster (1953), players who attempt to run from one end of a rectangular space to another may be caught by the player in the middle; they now belong to that player and aid him in catching others trying to cross the field.

*4 It is quite likely that magical gestures such as touching a certain tree, crossing one's fingers, or assuming a certain "safe" position (such as squatting in "Squat Tag") are analogous to the host of magical agents which protect protagonists in folktales.

*5 Gomme (1964:II, 391-96). For a New York State version called "Old Witch", see Sneller (1964).

*6 For examples of non-oral riddles, see Jan Brunvand (1960). Note that this form of folklore is defined negatively, in terms of the presumably primary verbal form: riddles. In the same way, the term "practical joke" represents a qualifying of the primary term "joke", which is also verbal. Even the term used here of "non-verbal folklore" continues the same bias in favor of the primacy of verbal forms. At least gestures are not called non-oral or non-verbal proverbs.

*7 In the structure of folk dance, the same distinction is found of beginning either with a state of lack or causing a state of lack by an act of villainy. Some dances have an "it" who is without a partner (lack) and who seeks to obtain one (lack liquidated). Other dances begin with couples, but during the dance one or more couples become separated (lack) and reunite only at the end of the dance (lack liquidated). For an interesting study of dance morphology, see Szentpal (1958); also Martin and Pesovár (1961).

*8 These categories of "verbal" and "non-verbal" folklore are arbitrary distinctions which do not necessarily reflect objective reality. Obviously jump rope rhymes, counting out rhymes, and finger rhymes involve both words and actions.

*9 Krappe (1930) gives these forms short shrift. The unfortunate trend continues. One looks in vain for extended mention of these forms in annual folklore bibliographies, works in progress lists, and surveys of folklore research.

9

THE STRUCTURE OF SUPERSTITION

Of the twenty-one definitions of folklore contained in the Standard Dictionary of
Folklore, Mythology and Legend, nine make reference to superstitions. Of these
nine, two use folk belief and superstition as interchangeable terms for the same
genre of folklore, while six other definitions, including Stith Thompson's, specifically mention both beliefs and superstitions and by so doing, imply separate dis-
tinguishable items. Unfortunately, the Dictionary does not include a definition of
what professional folklorists mean by the term superstition. Nor, incidentally,
are terms like "beliefs", "custom", or "practice" defined. In the absence of standard definitions of materials which are unquestionably in the province of the folklorist, each collector is, of course, completely free to call whatever he likes
superstition. Most collectors, as a matter of fact, do not even bother to try to
define superstition. This raises obvious problems with regard to the classification of superstitions, and not surprisingly there are approximately as many
schemes for the classification of superstition as there are collections of superstitions.

In 1900, Samuel Adams Drake remarked that "Superstition is not easily defined."(Drake 1900:7). In the 1959 edition of the Encyclopaedia Britannica, H.
J. Rose, writing on superstition, noted that superstition is "not easy to define".
Fifty-nine years of folklore scholarship has apparently not made the task of definition any easier. Even a cursory glance at a few of the attempts to define superstition reveals some of the difficulties. Frazer (1927:166) and Tylor (1958:72)
considered superstitions as survivals, that is, as beliefs and practices of savagery and barbarism which had survived among the more civilized peoples.
Such a definition would appear to preclude the possibility of new superstitions
arising, such as those collected about baseball, for example (Hyatt 1935:432-34).
A definition by Alexander H. Krappe contrasts superstition with religion. "Superstition", he says, "in common parlance, designates the sum of beliefs and practices shared by other people in so far as they differ from our own. What we believe and practice ourselves is, of course, Religion."(Krappe 1930:203). A
consequence of Krappe's definition is that if superstitions are practiced only
among other people, then by definition we can have no superstitions. Actually
Krappe compromises slightly when he concludes: "It will be best, then, to define as 'superstition' any belief or practice that is not recommended or enjoined
by any of the great religions such as Christianity, Judaism, Islam and Buddhism."
(p. 204).

In criticizing Krappe's definition, one may note the fundamental fallacy of almost all definitions of superstition. The definitions never deal with the material

Reprinted from Midwest Folklore 11 (1961); 25-33.

itself but rather with opinions about the material. The arbitrariness and relativity of opinion or belief make it of dubious value for purposes of defining. If
one Christian sect endorses the practice of making the sign of the cross to ward
off bad luck, is the practice no longer a superstition? The same difficulties
arise in the definition of mythology. Mythology believed in or endorsed by authority is called religion while religion without belief is mythology. One must remember that the Greeks did not call their religion mythology. It may well be,
ethnologically speaking, very important to note that religious narratives not
believed are myths while religious beliefs not believed are superstitions, but
this observation does not constitute an adequate definition of either myth or
superstition. Thus while the collector should as a matter of course record
whether or not a superstition is believed, belief is not a reliable criterion for
defining superstition. Certainly, in practice, folklorists do not refuse to collect
an item simply because the informant does not believe it.

The majority of definitions of superstition not only depend upon the notion of
belief, but in addition postulate elements of fear and irrationality. Bidney (1953:
294), for example, says that a superstition is "a mode of fear based on some
irrational or mythological belief and usually involves some taboo". According
to Bidney, beliefs in which there is no element of irrational fear should be distinguished from genuine superstitions. Thus if the informant has an irrational
fear of a black cat's crossing his path, the collector has found a superstition.
If the informant merely remembers a statement about a black cat that his grandfather used to make, the collector has something else. Defining superstition in
terms of irrational fear is an example of a definition in terms of genesis. The
definition postulates the origin of superstition. But even assuming the genesis
through irrational fear is correct, one cannot assume that the genetic cause of
a cultural item is identical with the cause for the continuity or persistence of
that item. *1 Moreover the explanation of the original cause of an object does
not necessarily explain what that object is.

Perhaps the most common definition of superstition is that which employs the
criterion of validity in the sense of objective scientific truth. Thus H. J. Rose
defines superstition as "the acceptance of beliefs or practices groundless in
themselves and inconsistent with the degree of enlightenment reached by the
community to which one belongs". Puckett (1926:571) defines superstition in
much the same way: "Superstition at any time would seem to be those beliefs
not receiving the sanction of the more advanced mores of that generation. " Both
of these definitions are relativistic inasmuch as there is no way of determining
exactly what the degree of enlightenment of a given community is or what constitutes the advanced mores of that community. The groundlessness of the practices is irrelevant. As a matter of fact, some superstitions have been scientifi-
cally verified, especially weather signs (Puckett 1929:513-14). The homeopathic
magic of many cures in folk medicine has, of course, been found to be the
scientific basis of immunization through inoculation. Truth should not be a criterion in defining superstition. There are true as well as false superstitions.
In the case of cures, for example, even "false" cures can be effective with many
of the psychosomatic illnesses (Richmond and Van Winkle 1958:115). Another
factor to be considered is that scientific truth is itself relative. In fact, much
of the scientific truth of the past such as astrology lives on in the form of super-

stitions. Who knows which of the present-day scientific truths will withstand the test of time?

If genetic and the other definitions mentioned cannot be relied upon, how then may superstitions be defined to such an extent that one would know a superstition when he came across one? Such a definition might be achieved by considering what superstitions are, rather than emphasizing how they came about or whether or not they are true or believed. In other words, the definition should be descriptive, utilizing criteria of form rather than criteria of genesis or belief. One striking attempt to define superstitions in this way was made by Puckett in his Folk Beliefs of the Southern Negro of 1926. Puckett distinguishes between "control-signs" and prophetic signs. Control signs, which can be either positive or negative, are those signs "which allow of human control" (p. 312). Puckett derives a formula for control signs which is: "If you (or some one else) behave in such and such a manner, so and so will happen." (p. 312). Prophetic signs, according to Puckett, are "those undomesticated causal relationships in which the human individual has no play". Under prophetic signs Puckett includes omens of good and bad luck, weather signs, and dream signs. With prophetic signs "man has no control and submits helplessly to the decrees of nature" (p. 312). Puckett's formula for prophetic signs is: "If something (outside of your control) behaves in such and such a manner, so and so will result." (pp. 312, 439). Puckett is to be commended for trying to define superstitions in terms of form. However, his definition and classification are not wholly acceptable.

Following Puckett in part, the following tentative definition of superstition is offered. Superstitions are traditional expressions of one or more conditions and or more results with some of the conditions signs and others causes. This is meant as a generic definition of superstition. There are superstitions with but one condition and one result. For example, "If a dog howls, it's a sign of death". On the other hand, superstitions involving divination often have multiple conditions. For example, "In the spring the first mourning dove you hear cooing, take off one of your stockings or socks, turn it wrongside out and in the heel will be a hair, the color of the hair of the person you're going to marry". By and large, results are usually singular but occasionally they may be plural: "In dog days, dogs are liable to go mad and snakes are blind" or "If mourning doves nest close to your house, it's good luck and you're a nice person". With regard to formalistic features, Puckett was correct in noting that the majority of superstitions have a condition marker, namely "if". However, it is important to realize that the absence of a condition marker such as "if" or "when" does not mean that a condition is absent. For example, specific conditions are implicit in the following superstitions: "Friday begun will never be done"; "A red sunrise is a sign of bad weather". Often the condition is stated in terms of an imperative injunction such as: "Don't ever return borrowed salt, it's bad luck", "Never cut your fingernails on Sunday", and "Never move your broom". Of course, if the results are indicated, such superstitions could be restated in terms of Puckett's formula (e. g. If you return borrowed salt, you'll have bad luck).

With regard to classification, one can see that, generally speaking, superstitions can be grouped either by condition or by result. Neither is entirely satisfactory and a combination of both unavoidably duplicates material. For ex-

ample, if all superstitions were classified according to conditions, then a folklorist interested especially in signs of death would have to read through all the
superstitions dealing wi th dogs and hoes in order to cull the appropriate items.
On the other hand, if superstitions are classified by results, as is most common,
under such categories as birth, marriage, luck, etc., the folklorist interested
in superstitions concerning dogs or hoes would have to read through all the
superstitions. Indexes, naturally, are of some assistance but one does not know
which of fifty entries on dogs deal with superstitions in which the dog is in the
condition. Ideally, superstitions should be presented twice, first according to
condition and second according to result. However, this is clearly not practical.
A possible solution is to classify by condition and in addition to provide an index
of results. The reason for condition classification is that frequently only the
condition is collected. In the example mentioned previously of "Never cut your
fingernails on Sunday", only the condition is present. The informant was asked
about the consequences of disobeying the injunction, but she did not know. Puckett
suggests that indefinite consequences, i.e. good or bad luck, are a later weak-
ening of superstitions which originally had specific consequences such as marriage or death (p.577). If there is any kind of an evolution of superstition, it
well may be from specific results to the omission of any stated result. If this
is the case, then clearly the condition is of prime importance and accordingly
it should be made the basis of classification. One difficulty with condition classification, however, is the determination of the most significant condition. For
example, what is the significant condition in the following superstition? "You
go out on May the first and get a snail and place that snail on a shoebox lid and
place it under your bed and the next morning, the name of the person you're
going to marry will be spelled out". Is it the date, the snail, the shoebox, or
the placing of the shoebox and snail under the bed?

Having formulated a tentative definition of superstition in terms of grammatical conditions and results, there remains the task of distinguishing categories
of superstitions. If one analyzes the relationship between the conditions and the
results, one finds three basic categories of superstitions. One category corresponds to Puckett's prophetic signs. This category, which for the sake of convenience will be termed simply "Signs", consists of portents and omens which
man may read. Signs are usually made up of single conditions and results and
they often serve as the basis of prediction. Thus if one notes a ring around the
moon, one can predict rain. Many of the signs come from human activity but it
is extremely important to note that all "Sign" human activity is purely accidental or coincidental. Such activity includes dropping knives and forks, experiencing an itching nose, hand, or foot, dreaming, and so on. Actually the greater
number of signs are non-human in nature consisting chiefly of celestial, animal,
and plant indicators. One characteristic of signs is that the signs themselves
are unavoidable, although in some instances the consequent effects may be
avoided. One cannot avoid a ring around the moon. Similarly, one cannot avoid
the howling of a dog or the sight of a black cat, since these are accidentally occurring phenomena not subject to human volition. In the same way, one cannot
avoid the accidental dropping of knives and forks. There is, however, an even
more important characteristic of sign superstitions.

Puckett speaks of prophetic signs as causal relationships and, in fact, others

have made much the same comment. Lévy-Bruhl (1936:47), in discussing such
matters among primitives, notes that omens not only announce the desired success but are a necessary condition of it and they guarantee and effect it. Having
assumed causality, Lévy-Bruhl is puzzled by signs and results which occur simultaneously. An example of a modern superstition illustrating this would be: "If
you see a falling star, someone in the family is passing beyond". Lévy-Bruhl
is forced to concede that "in such circumstances sign does not really seem to
imply cause" (p. 61). An empirical examination of sign superstitions reveals
that the relationship between condition and result is non-causal. The ring around
the moon does not cause the rain; it indicates only that rain will come. The ultimate cause of the rain (as well as that of the ring around the moon) is simply
not stated. Here it is necessary to distinguish antecedence from causality. As
W.R. Halliday (1913:375) noted: "Mere priority is not causality." A sign is not
a necessary efficient cause. Since there are a number of sign superstitions for
the same result, for example, rain, no one sign is necessary in the sense of
being a sine qua non. It can rain if there is not a ring around the moon. As a
matter of fact, in daytime when the moon is not ordinarily visible, there are
other signs. "When the hoot owls holler in daytime, it's a sign of rain". However, the sign is usually a fixed indicator. If there is a ring around the moon,
it will rain.

The second category of superstitions, which will be termed "Magic", corresponds to Puckett's "Positive and Negative Control Signs". Magic superstitions
often consist of multiple conditions and they serve as a means of production or
prescription rather than prediction. In contrast to sign superstitions, human
activity in magic superstitions is intentional rather than accidental. In fact, in
this category, intentional human activity occurs in most of the superstitions,
although not in all. Since the human activity is intentional, it is also avoidable.
One can avoid bad luck by not walking under a ladder. Whereas sign superstitions
are non-causal, magic superstitions are causal. A given effect or result will
not occur unless the conditional activity does. The fulfillment of the condition
is efficient cause. (There is still, of course, the formal cause which makes
possible the efficient cause.) Again the variety of means to the same end
suggests that no condition or conditions of a magic superstition can be considered a sine qua non either. What is most significant in comparing sign and magic
superstitions is the distinction between predicting the future and making the
future (Halliday 1913:42). Instead of foretelling rain, death, and bad luck, one
can, using magic superstitions, produce rain, death, and bad luck. Thus instead
of predicting rain from seeing a ring around the moon, one can produce rain by
turning a dead snake's belly up. Implicit also is the contrast between human
passivity and activity. Man is passive with regard to signs, but definitely active
with regard to magic. In cases where agents other than man occur in magic
superstitions, there is usually still some noticeable activity. Moreover, one
could differentiate sign from magic in terms of belief and practice. A sign
superstition entails belief only; whereas a magic superstition in its entirety
involves belief and practice. Of course, as has already been noted, many magic
superstitions are no longer practiced and in many cases no longer believed.
Nevertheless, in theory at least, one can see that no practice was ever involved
in experiencing the result of a sign superstition.

Magic superstitions frequently make use of ritual, and this may be seen by examining such magic superstitions as cures and divinations.*2 The reason that divination is placed in this category is that it is man's actions which cause the results. In a sense, man is producing signs similar to those which occur naturally. However, whereas celestial or accidental plant, animal, or human signs cannot be avoided, divination procedures can. Furthermore, they can be repeated as often as necessary or desired, that is, as many times as it takes for the divination to "come out right". Not only can one pull petals off hundreds of daisies but according to an informant, one can beat the system by starting with "He loves me not". This is unquestionably human control. Water-witching is a form of divination which involves a magically produced rather than an accidentally produced sign. Accordingly, divination is considered magic superstition and not sign superstition.

Perhaps the most interesting category of the three, might be termed "Conversion". This is a hybrid category in which, for the most part, sign superstitions are converted into magic superstitions. Still other conversion superstitions are simply magic superstitions in which one or more of the preliminary conditions is a sign. A few conversion superstitions arise from the neutralizing or reversal of magic superstitions. This third category includes planting signs, wishes, and counteractants (i. e. form of counter-magic). One cannot plant corn with the best chances of success until the whippoorwill calls. One cannot wish unless one sees a shooting star or similar sign. One cannot avoid the bad luck caused by a black cat's crossing his path unless or until a black cat does cross his path. It is important to notice that the preliminary sign alone has either no effect or a different meaning. The call of a whippoorwill by itself cannot cause a good corn crop nor can the sight of a shooting star by itself bring about wish-fulfillment. In conversion superstitions, man's activity is required. This is not so in the case of sign superstitions. No activity is required in interpreting either the shooting star or whippoorwill's call as a sign of death.

A great number of conversion superstitions appear to represent man's struggle against undesirable sign or magic superstitions. Puckett wrongly assumes that the Negro as opposed to the European is unique in opposing the inevitable (p.484). As a matter of record, wherever undesirable results are feared, that is, either unwanted results of sign or magic superstitions, conversion superstitions have been collected. For example, for the sign superstition in which bad luck results from spilling salt, there are numerous counteractants including, of course, the common practice of throwing some over one's left shoulder. For the magic superstition in which bad luck results from bringing a hoe in the house, the counteractant consists of backing out the same door by which one entered. These two counteractants are both neutralizing conversion superstitions in that the proper action cancels the undesirable result. However, there are also counteractants which do more than neutralize. Such counteractants convert evil to good. This change is often brought about through the act of wishing. For example, it is bad luck to retrace one's steps for a forgotten article. This bad luck may be averted by many means, one of which is the simple act of sitting down. But the following counteractant does more than neutralize: "If you start anywhere and have to turn back, you sit down and make a wish and they say it'll come true". Another example of wishing as a conversion factor occurs in connection with the sign superstition: "If you drop a comb, you'll be disappointed". Stepping on the comb neutralizes this superstition but wishing changes a potentially maleficent situation into a beneficial one. "If you drop a comb, step on it, make a wish and don't say a word until someone asks you a question". While it is usually unwise to generalize from a few examples, one is tempted to see a kind of evolution from a superstition with an undesirable result to a neutralizing conversion superstition to a final conversion superstition in which the individual stands to gain rather than lose. If this assumption is correct, it would explain the occurrence of the neutralizing element, (e. g. sitting down, stepping on the comb) in the final version of the superstition as the result of a process of accretion.

Although the above discussion is based upon a comparatively small number of superstitions, and for that reason may well not apply to all superstitions, it is hoped that other folklorists may be stimulated to work out a more precise definition and a better classification scheme for superstitions. To recapitulate, superstition was tentatively defined as traditional expressions of one or more conditions and one or more results with some of the conditions signs and others causes. Moreover, three categories of superstitions were distinguished: Category I, Signs; Category II, Magic; and Category III, Conversion.

NOTES

*1 Bidney is, of course, well aware of this distinction. In fact it is to his enlightening discussion of Malinowski's identification of social function with historical origin (1953:226-30) that I owe my awareness of the theoretical problem involved.

*2 Violetta Halpert, in her illuminating article "Folk Cures from Indiana", commented upon the magical nature of cures. In her tripartite classification of cures, she noted (p. 12) that "in the physical cures, the power of the cure lies in the substance itself; in the physio-magical group, in the procedure for the curative use of the object; in the magical group, in the healer." Halpert errs in not seeing all portions of her classification as magical because actually her classification scheme represents an isolation of three important elements of magic ritual: a magic object, a procedure, and the personal power of the magician. (The three element analysis of magic ritual was suggested by Professor David Bidney.)

10

TOWARD A STRUCTURAL DEFINITION OF THE RIDDLE

(with Robert A. Georges)

An immediate aim of structural analysis in folklore is to define the genres of folklore. Once these genres have been defined in terms of internal morphological characteristics, one will then be better able to proceed to the interesting problems of the function of folkloristic forms in particular cultures. Furthermore, morphological analysis may reveal that a given structural pattern may be found in a variety of folklore genres.*1 At the present time, however, cross-genre comparison is greatly impeded by the lack of adequate morphological definitions of the individual genres. One example of such an inadequately defined genre is the riddle.

Folklorists are in unanimous agreement that the riddle is a proper object for study by them. Yet thus far no folklorist has been able to give a definition of the riddle employing concrete and specific terms. The early definitions identify the riddle with metaphor. Aristotle was probably the first to define the riddle in this way.*2 In this classical tradition fall definitions similar to the one proposed by Gaston Paris. He defined the riddle as "a metaphor or a group of metaphors, the employment of which has not passed into common use, and the explanation of which is not self-evident".*3

Another observation concerning the formal characteristics of riddles drew attention to the frequent presence of an apparently irreconcilable contradiction or incongruity. Once again, Aristotle was one of the first to comment on this: "The very nature indeed of a riddle is this, to describe a fact in an impossible combination of words (which cannot be done with the real names for things, but can be with their metaphorical substitutes)...."*4 The most comprehensive discussion of this characteristic of riddles is contained in a doctoral dissertation by Robert Petsch (1899). In his analysis of what he terms die wirklichen Volksrätsel 'the true riddle', Petsch distinguishes five elements: (1) introductory frame element, (2) denominative kernel element, (3) descriptive kernel element, (4) block element, and (5) concluding frame element.*5 Petsch admits that riddles containing all five elements are extremely rare. Certainly they are not common in English oral tradition. Petsch himself remarks that one or both of the frame elements are frequently lacking. He also realizes that the block element is absent even more often. This may be the reason why Petsch's five-element analysis has not been utilized to any great extent.

A definition of the riddle which takes into account both metaphor and block is that of Archer Taylor, who among modern folklorists has contributed most to

Reprinted from the Journal of American Folklore, 76 (1963), 111-18.

riddle scholarship. In 1938, Taylor recognized that the forms of the riddle had never been adequately described (Taylor 1938:3). Taylor proposed the following definition in 1943: "The true riddle or the riddle in the strict sense compares an object to another entirely different object."(Taylor 1943:129)*6 A further refinement by Taylor is the analysis of riddles into two descriptive elements, one positive and one negative. These elements, he claims, constitute "the essential structure of the riddle". Taylor's negative element corresponds to Petsch's block. According to Taylor, the positive element is metaphorical, in terms of the answer, though the listener is led to understand it in a literal sense. In contrast, the negative descriptive element is correctly interpreted literally. Thus in the riddle "Something has eyes and cannot see" (Irish potato, 277a),*7 the positive descriptive element "eyes" is metaphorical in terms of the answer "potato", while the negative descriptive element "cannot see" is unequivocally literal. In this definition, the answer is implied by the details of the positive descriptive element, which mislead the listener because he wrongly assumes that a figurative description is a literal one. "The negative descriptive element", says Taylor, "can be recognized immediately because it seems to be impossible". Taylor (1943:130) summarizes his definition: "In other words, a true riddle consists of two descriptions of an object, one figurative and one literal, and confuses the hearer who endeavors to identify an object described in conflicting ways. " In a later reformulation of his definition, Taylor (1952:I, 286) states that a true riddle "consists of a vague general description and a specific detail that seems to conflict with what had gone before. "

One indication of the limitation of Taylor's definition is the fact that it does not apply to many of the texts in his English Riddles from Oral Tradition, one of the most comprehensive riddle collections in any language. Taylor says that his collection includes "only true riddles", but a large number of examples do not appear to be true riddles in terms of his own definition. Positive and negative descriptive elements, for example, are not found in the following representative riddles from Taylor's corpus: "Hump back, smoove [smooth] belly" (self-heater, 45a); "My fader have a horse, /Go everywhere he like" (pumpkin vine, 419); "What goes all down street and comes back home, and sits in the corner and waits for a bone?" (shoe, 453c); "A bird flyin' an' one sittin'" (a woman married an' one single, 473); "A gully with two notch in it" (purse, 1107).

Not only are there metaphorical riddles without blocks, but there are also riddles without either blocks or metaphors. The following riddles consist of no more than a literal description: "Wha' live in de river?" (fish, 98); "Wha' flies in de sky an' come down low an' ketch people chicken?" (hawk, 360); "Red outside, / White inside" (apple, 1512); "Me riddle, me riddle, / Something bear on a tree, when it is ripe it is red" (pomegranate, 1084a); "Runs and jumps, stops and humps" (rabbit, 220). Taylor is undoubtedly right in considering these texts riddles, but they do not possess the major formal features of the true riddle as he defines it.

Some folklorists have recognized that there can be riddles without metaphors and blocks. For example, Sokolov (1950:282), after defining the riddle as "an ingenious question, expressed usually in the form of a metaphor", notes that the metaphorical character of the riddle does not appear to be obligatory and that riddles may be encountered "in the form of a direct question, without any figurative meaning of the words which enter into it".*8 Similarly, Taylor (1951a:697-98, n. 72) does admit in a footnote that riddles may consist of non-contradictory descriptions, and that some riddles are no more than literal descriptions.

The narrowness of Taylor's definition of the true riddle is further revealed when one observes that even in riddles which do have both positive and negative descriptive elements, the positive element is not necessarily metaphorical, nor the negative one literal. The following two riddles contain positive and negative elements, but the positive element is not metaphorical: "What goes to the branch and drinks and don't drink?" (cow and bell, 247b); "When it come, it does not come; when it does not come, it come" (rat and corn, 945). By the same token, it is the negative as well as the positive element in the following riddle which should be interpreted metaphorically by the listener: "I know something got hand an' don't wash its face" (clock, 301). It is clear, then, that there is a need for a definition for the riddle which will be broad enough to include traditional texts such as the ones cited above which apparently fall outside Taylor's definition of the true riddle. At the same time, the definition should be narrow enough to exclude other materials whose morphological characteristics indicate that they are specimens of another genre.

The best way to arrive at a definition of the riddle is through structural analysis, since definitions based on content and style have proved to be inadequate. While it is possible to discuss the style of riddles, it should not be confused with the structure of riddles. Only two of Petsch's five elements are structural ones - the descriptive kernel element and the block element. The opening and closing formulas in riddles, as in folktales, are stylistic devices whose presence is optional and whose absence does not affect the overall structure of the genre. Although anthroplogists have been interested in studying many aspects of culture structurally - e.g. language and kinship - those studying riddles have eschewed the structural approach. Melville and Frances Herskovits (1958:55), for example, assert that they are concerned with the riddle's "cultural role in the complex of the spoken arts, rather than with its structural form". Thus William R. Bascom (1949) in his analysis of Yoruba riddles limits his comments on structure to the statement that "the basic form of the Yoruba riddle is an enigma presented by two statements which appear to be mutually contradictory, incongruous or impossible". He then proceeds to make a stylistic analysis which consists primarily of analyzing linguistic patterns rather than the patterns of folkloristic structure. Because of this, he is forced to employ as many as twenty-nine formulas for the fifty-five riddles in his corpus.*9

In order to define the riddle structurally, it is first necessary to delineate a minimum unit of analysis. It is here proposed that the unit be termed descrip-tive element, following Petsch and Taylor. A descriptive element consists of both a topic and a comment. The topic is the apparent referent; that is, it is the object or item which is allegedly described. The comment is an assertion about the topic, usually concerning the form, function, or action of the topic.*10 In the riddle "Twenty-fo' horses set upon a bridge" (teet' in yer gum, 507), the topic is "Twenty-fo' horses", and the comment is "set upon a bridge". This riddle, then, consists of one descriptive element. The riddle "It has a head, but can't think" (a match, 272) consists of two descriptive elements; the first,

"It has a head", and the second "but can't think". In some riddles there is no specific linguistic unit such as a pronoun for the topic. Consider "Many eyes,/ Never cries" (potato, 276). This riddle consists of two descriptive elements, and it could, of course, be rewritten with no change in meaning or structure as "It has many eyes, but it never cries".

A minimum unit of analysis having been defined, it is now possible to present a tentative structural definition of the riddle: A riddle is a traditional verbal expression which contains one or more descriptive elements, a pair of which may be in opposition; the referent of the elements is to be guessed.*11 There are two general categories of true riddles. The two categories are differentiated by the presence or absence of descriptive elements in opposition. Riddles which lack descriptive elements in opposition may be termed nonoppositional riddles. Those with descriptive elements in opposition are oppositional riddles.

Nonoppositional riddles may be literal or metaphorical. In literal nonoppositional riddles, the riddle referent and the topic(s) of the descriptive element(s) are identical. In "Wha' live in de river?" (fish, 98), the referent and the topic are both "fish". Likewise, the topic and the referent are identical in the following examples: "Wha' set up on fo' block?" (house, 733); "My fader had a tree, it bear fruit, outside green and inside white" (coconut, 1085); "Wha' makes de nes' on de ma'sh?" (ma'sh-hen, 355); "I know something that sleeps all day and walks at night" (spider, 255); "Got somet'in' yeller inside an' green outside" (pumpkin, 1503a).

In metaphorical nonoppositional riddles, the riddle referent and the topic(s) of the descriptive element(s) are different. In the riddle "Two rows of white horses on a red hill" (teeth, 505a), the topic is horses, but the answer is teeth. Additional examples of nonoppositional metaphorical riddles are the following: "A lady in a boat/With a yellow petticoat" (egg, moon, 647, 648); "Two brothers side by side all day and at night they go to rest" (pair of boots, 992); "Mary Mack all dressed in black,/Silver buttons down her back" (coffin, 656); "A crowd of little men livin' in a flat-top house" (matches in a box, 907); "My father have ten trees in his yard an' two taller than the rest" (fingers, 1041). It should be emphasized that in nonoppositional riddles, both literal and metaphorical, the constituent descriptive elements are not in opposition. There is sometimes a change in a descriptive detail, as in the riddle "Goes up white and comes down yellow" (egg, 1550a), but there is no contradiction involved.*12

Oppositional riddles are characterized by the occurrence of an opposition between at least one pair of descriptive elements. The presence of opposition is implicit in Petsch's block element and in Taylor's notion of two conflicting descriptions of an object. However, no one has ever attempted to give a more detailed morphological analysis of the nature of oppositional riddles. A theoretical basis for such an analysis was outlined by Aristotle, who was interested in the structure of riddles. As was mentioned above, he commented upon the relation of metaphor and riddle and upon the frequent presence of apparently impossible combinations.*13 There are at least three distinct kinds of oppositions in oppositional riddles in English oral tradition: (1) antithetical contradictive, (2) privational contradictive, and (3) causal contradictive.

In the antithetical contradictive opposition, apparently only one of the two descriptive elements in opposition can be true. Often the second of the contradictory descriptive elements is a categorical negation of the first element. The riddle "What goes to the branch and drinks and don't drink?"(cow and bell, 247b) is composed of three descriptive elements, the second and third of which are in antithetical contradictive opposition. Other examples of riddles containing this type of opposition are: "This corner, this corner is no corner at all" (ring, 1411); "When it come, it does not come; when it does not come, it come" (rat and corn, 945); "A man who was not a man, /Killed a bird that was not a bird/ On a tree that was not a tree, /With a gun that was not a gun" (it means that a little boy killed a butterfly with a power gun on a cane tree, 824); "As I was goin' up London Bridge, /I met three living people. /They were neither men, women or children" (was a man, a woman, and a child, 837a); "I went to London but because I didn't go I came back" (watch, 130b). It is also possible to have antithetical contradictive opposition implied rather than stated directly. In these cases, the second descriptive element does not categorically deny the first, but rather another assertion is made which contradicts the first. Antithetical contradictive opposition is implied in the following riddles: "I am rough, I am smooth;/I am wet, I am dry;/My station is low, my title high;/My king my lawful master is, /I am used by all, though only his" (highway, 578); "Large as a house, /Small as a mouse, /Bitter as gall, /And sweet after all" (pecan tree and nut, 1272); "Somet'ing live in water/Still water kill it" (salt, 1008); "What turns and never moves?" (a road, 131); "Light as a feather, /Nothing in it. /A stout man can't hold it/More than a minute" (breath, 1660b). In riddles of this type, the answer may consist of more than one object.

The privational contradictive opposition results when the second of a pair of descriptive elements is a denial of a logical or natural attribute of the first. Very often it is the principal function of an object which is denied. This is the case in the following riddles: "Something has an ear and cannot hear" (ear of corn, 285); "Got two eyes and can't see" (potato, 277b); "Something has a nose and can't smell" (teapot, 286); "What has legs, /But cannot walk?" (chair, 306a); "What has teeth and can't bite?" (comb, 299b). It is also possible to have a whole object deprived of one or more of its parts as in these examples: "What has hands/ and no fingers?" (clock, 22); "My father have a house without window or door" (egg, 1132); "What has a head, / But no hair?" (pin, 3); "A tub came without a bottom" (ring, 1172a); "What has four legs and only one foot?" (bed, 75d). Finally, there are privational contradictive oppositions in which an associative part or function is denied. Thus in the riddle "Something has fingers but no toes" (glove, 23), fingers and toes are usually associated with each other, since they are both parts of the same object, namely the human body. However, toes, the second of the two parts, is denied. Other riddles which illustrate this opposition are: "Something have a head, but no body" (pin, 1); "Something has a tongue and no mouth"(shoes, 17); "Something has legs but no body" (chair, 26); "One hun'ed windows an' no do'" (fish-net, 1130i); "Somet'in have hoof, no head, no tail" (table, 28). An associated function of the same object may also be denied, as in these examples: "What chew all the time and don't swallow?" (it is a cane-mill, 241); "What smokes, but cannot chew?" (smoke, 244); "Under de water, / Over de water, / Yet not touch de water" (a lady passin' ower de water wid a pail o' water on her head, 165a); "Can holler, but can't talk" (a train, 230). Most of the privational contradictive oppositions in English riddles involve comparisons with the human body.

The third type of opposition is termed causal contradictive. In this type of opposition, the first descriptive element consists of an action performed by an object or upon an object. In some causal contradictive oppositional riddles the second of the pair of descriptive elements explicitly denies the expected or natural consequence of the action contained in the first descriptive element. Examples of this type of riddle include: "What goes to the mill every morning and don't make no tracks?" (the road, 181); "What eats and eats and never gets full?" (a sausage-grinder, 237); "What jumps into the water and out again and don't get wet?" (egg in a duck's belly, 170b); "Four bottles of milk, uncarked, turn down, and not a drap can come out" (cow breasts, 1199c); "Ofttimes it has been divided,/And yet it can't be seen where it has been divided" (vessel going through the water, 1666). In other causal contradictive oppositional riddles, the second descriptive element contains an assertion which is contrary to the expected or natural consequence. The second assertion in the riddle "Stick a hog at its head and it bleed at its tail" (pipe, 383) is contrary to the expected result, namely that the hog will bleed at its head. Further examples of this causal contradictive opposition are found in the following riddles: "What is it even though it's locked in can get out?" (fire, 112); "My father make a door an'it was too short; he cut it and it become longer" (grave, 1111d); "What's full and holds more?" (pot full of potatoes when you pour water in, 1457); "What grows larger the more you contract it?" (debt, 1698). The causal contradictive opposition is unlike the antithetical contradictive opposition in that there is no complete negation of one descriptive element by another. Nor is there a part or function of an object lacking as there is in the privational contradictive opposition. One of the distinguishing characteristics of the causal contradictive opposition is its time dimension. The two descriptive elements in opposition are separated by time. Specifically, one is necessarily prior to the other. In contrast, antithetical and privational contradictive oppositions are synchronic; that is, the descriptive elements in opposition are not separated by time.

In summary, the riddle has been defined as a traditional verbal expression which contains one or more descriptive elements, a pair of which may be in opposition; the referent of the elements is to be guessed. Two general categories of riddles are (1) nonoppositional, in which there is no contradiction to be found in one or more descriptive elements, and (2) oppositional, in which at least one pair of descriptive elements is in contradiction. The nonoppositional riddles may be literal or metaphorical, but in either case there is no apparent contradiction involved. Oppositional riddles are almost always metaphorical or a combination of metaphorical and literal descriptions. There are three kinds of oppositions: (1) antithetical contradictive, (2) privational contradictive, or (3) causal contradictive.

Former definitions of the riddle, as discussed above, have tended to ignore the large body of nonoppositional riddles. Furthermore, those scholars who have recognized the frequent presence of an opposition in oppositional riddles have failed to distinguish the various types of oppositions. All these oppositions must be included in a comprehensive definition of the riddle. Definitions based upon a single one of the oppositions do not account for either those riddles with the other oppositions or for the nonoppositional riddles. As was pointed out above, Taylor wrongly concluded that the true riddle consists of both a figurative and a literal description of an object, or a vague general description and a conflicting specific detail. While Taylor's definition applies to riddles containing the privational contradictive opposition, it certainly does not apply to the antithetical and causal contradictive riddles. Since Taylor's definition does not include the nonoppositional riddles either, it cannot be said to apply to the majority of riddles in his English Riddles from Oral Tradition. The riddle of riddle structure may not be entirely solved, but at least a frame of referents has been proposed.

NOTES

*1 An analysis showing the existence of an identical structural pattern in certain North American Indian folktales and superstitions has recently demonstrated the possibility of cross-genre comparisons. The analysis is contained in Dundes (1964). For an analysis showing a common pattern in legends and folktales, see Dundes (1962d:171).

*2 In The Rhetoric, Bk. III, Ch. 2, Aristotle says: "Good riddles do, in general, provide us with satisfactory metaphors: for metaphors imply riddles, and therefore a good riddle can furnish a good metaphor."

*3 Paris' definition and many other earlier definitions are summarized by Tupper (1910:xii–xiii). For a more recent discussion of the riddle as metaphor, see Christiansen (1958).

*4 The Poetics, Ch. XXII.

*5 For Petsch's list of the five constituent elements of the true riddle and his discussion of their frequency of occurrence, see (1899:49–50).

*6 The same definition is found in Taylor (1951a:1).

*7 All examples given in this paper are taken from Taylor (1951a). The numbers following the answers are the numbers Taylor uses.

*8 Sokolov, however, does not appear to realize that riddles may consist of blocked as well as unblocked metaphors.

*9 It is interesting that there has been another attempt to analyze Yoruba riddles. In referring to his unpublished analysis, Robert Plant Armstrong says that he "used the formal nature of the riddle to achieve a pair of 'immediate constituents' representing the riddle itself, which was viewed as the compounding metaphor, and the answer, viewed as a resolution of that metaphor" (Armstrong 1959:161).
The independence of folkloristic structure from linguistic structure may be illustrated by comparing two versions of the same riddle: "What has eyes and

can't see?" and "It has eyes and can't see". Disregarding intonational patterns, which are not indicated in most collections of printed texts, there appears to be, from a linguistic perspective, a syntactic difference between the two texts, namely one is an interrogative sentence and the other is declarative. Folkloristically speaking, the two belong to the same structural pattern which is outlined in the present paper.

*10 For a discussion of topic and comment constructions, see Yuen Ren Chao (1959). Charles F. Hockett (1958:201) applies the topic-comment analysis to English sentences.
Proverbs also consist of a topic-comment structure. However, the proverb merely makes an assertion which requires no answer. The referent of a proverb is usually a person or situation known to both narrator and audience before the proverb is uttered. In the riddle, the referent is presumably initially known only to the riddler. For a preliminary statement of proverb structure, see Dundes (1962e:37).

*11 By traditional we mean that the expression is or was transmitted orally and that it has or had multiple existence. Multiple existence means that an expression is found at more than one period of time or in more than one place at any one given time. This multiple existence in time and/or space usually, though not necessarily, results in the occurrence of variation in the expression.

*12 It is important to distinguish between a change in state and a genuine opposition. There is a change of state in "It goes upstairs red and comes downstairs black" (a warming pan, 1556), but there is no contradiction. In contrast, in the riddle "It's white's milk / An' as black's coal, / An' it jumps on the dyke / Like a new shod foal" (magpie, 1379), there is an apparent contradiction, because it is impossible for an object to be completely black and completely white at the same time.
It is essential to distinguish between linguistic and folkloristic structure. The presence of a linguistic negative construction in a riddle does not mean that the riddle contains an opposition. There are riddles found in Asia, for example, which contain a linguistic negative construction but which are clearly nonoppositional riddles. The negative construction in these riddles merely eliminates one possible answer to the riddle. It does not in any way contradict the preceding descriptive element. A typical example is the following Russian riddle: "She is red [pretty], but she is not a maid; she is green, but she is not a grove of trees" (carrot) (Sokolov 1950:284). A Bihar example is: "It has a red crest, yet is not a cock; it has a green back, yet is not a peacock; it has a long tail, yet is not a monkey; and it has four feet, yet is not a horse" (garden lizard) (Mitra 1901:36).

*13 See notes 1 and 3 above. We are indebted to Pierre Maranda for drawing our attention to Aristotle's discussion of oppositions in The Categories, X. However, the application of a modified form of the Aristotelian theory of oppositions to English riddles is our own.
It should be noted that a given riddle may consist of a combination of nonoppositional and oppositional descriptive elements. This is the case in the riddle "What's round as an egg, has eyes and can't see?" (potato, 277d).

11

ON THE STRUCTURE OF THE PROVERB

The study of the proverb has fascinated a great many scholars from a variety of disciplines and this may account for the vast bibliography of works devoted to the proverb.*1 Most of the scholarship - as opposed to mere reportorial collection - has tended to be historical in emphasis. Commonly the goal is to discover proverb cognates among peoples with related languages or to propose possible places and times of origin for individual proverbs.

In the twentieth century, thanks in part to the influence of the social sciences, there has been a shift away from purely literary and historical studies of proverbs.*2 There have been detailed field investigations of the concrete contexts in which specific proverbs are uttered.*3 It has been suggested that there may be laws or rather principles of usage governing the decision-making process which results in the citation of one proverb rather than another, or rather than no proverb.*4 With regard to content analysis, there have been attempts to correlate proverb content with national character and to extrapolate worldview from proverbs.*5 In the area of "applied folklore" there have been a number of interesting practical uses of proverbs. Proverb reasoning tests have been devised as a means of attempting to measure various mental skills. (In these tests, individuals are presented with a given proverb and then asked to select the one proverb of a list of five which most nearly resembles the initial proverb.) Other proverb tests allegedly serve as diagnostic tools in the identification of possible schizophrenics. The assumption underlying the tests is that schizophrenics are unable to read metaphorical proverbs as metaphors but only as literal statements.*6

In view of the considerable attention which the proverb has continued to receive, it comes as something of a surprise to learn that the proverb has never been adequately defined. Archer Taylor begins his important book on the proverb with the following defeatist statement: "The definition of a proverb is too difficult to repay the undertaking .... An incommunicable quality tells us this sentence is proverbial and that one is not. Hence no definition will enable us to identify positively a sentence as proverbial." When asked about this pessimistic statement, Professor Taylor remarked that in a way his whole book constituted a definition of the proverb.*7 B.J. Whiting, another leading literary scholar, takes more or less the same stance: "To offer a brief yet workable definition of a proverb, especially with the proverbial phrase included, is well nigh imposs-

This paper was originally presented at a Symposium in Palermo "Strutture E Generi Della Letteratura Etnica" in April, 1970.

ible. " Moreover, he goes on to claim that definitions are not really needed anyway. "Happily, no definition is really necessary, since all of us know what a
proverb is. "*8 Now it may well be that all of us do know what a proverb is, but
it seems incredible that if this is so, someone could not articulate this supposedly common knowledge. I submit that a definition of the proverb genre, even a
most tentative definition, should be useful to any form of proverb research, be
it a historical investigation of a single proverb or be it a search for national
character traits in an extensive proverb corpus from a single culture.

The proverb may best be defined in structural terms. Purely functional definitions are inadequate inasmuch as other genres of folklore may share the same
function(s) as proverbs. For instance, most functional definitions of proverbs
make mention of "summing up a situation" or "recommending a course of action". Clearly gestures and narrative exampla among other genres of folklore
may involve the same functional criteria. This is not to demean the genuine utility of functional considerations, but only to affirm the necessity for internal
rather than external formal definitional criteria. The critical question is thus
not what a proverb does, but what a proverb is.

Another reason for attempting a structural analysis of the proverb is that it
would represent a valuable test case for the structural analysis of folklore generally. If it is truly possible to analyze the structure of the genres of oral literature, then it ought to be possible to analyze the structure of proverbs in particular. All of the general theoretical problems associated with structural analysis
are relevant to the proverb. These problems include: the nature of the basic or
minimum structural units, the persistent question of if and where the continuum
is or can be meaningfully segmented, and the inevitable controversy as to
whether the units of analysis are really in the data (God's truth) or are only a
heuristic device found exclusively in the mind of the analyst (Hocus-Pocus).*9
The great advantage of using proverbs rather than folktales, myths, or ballads
is obviously the relative simplicity of the genre. It makes sense therefore to
attack the crucial theoretical questions of structural analysis by focusing upon
a simple proverb rather than a complex myth.

In the past we find there have been several discussions which have been concerned with proverb structure. In 1947, Kimmerle attempted to devise a classification of folk sayings which included proverbs. However, her schema was
closely tied to linguistic and syntactic formulas. Not all of her seventeen categories were relevant to proverbs and the use of such grammatical distinctions
as the presence of a predicate noun or predicate adjective or direct object
suggests that her analysis was more of surface structure than deep structure,
to employ the Chomsky metaphor.*10 While it is true that it is possible to
"parse" proverbs, so to speak, it is highly questionable whether parts of speech
per se can significantly illuminate the structure of proverbs. It is not that there
isn't linguistic structure. To the extent that proverbs are composed of words,
there would have to be linguistic structure involved. The question is rather
whether there are underlying patterns of "folkloristic structure" as opposed to
"linguistic structure" which may be isolated.*11

One problem which arises with respect to isolating possible folkloristic structures which may underlie proverbs has to do with whether one is analyzing proverb image, proverb message, or proverb architectural formula.*12 For exam-

ple, there appear to be a finite number of proverb compositional or architectural formulas. There is "Better _____ than _____"(e. g. Better late
than never, Better safe than sorry, Better bend than break). Other common
proverb formulas include: "A _____ is a _____" (e. g. A bargain is a
bargain); "_____ _____(s) never _____"(e. g. Barking dogs never
bite); "_____ or _____"(e. g. do or die); and the Wellerism "_____,
said the _____(as he _____)"(e. g. I see said the blind man as he
picked up his hammer and saw.)*13

Proverb formulas appear to be relatively independent of image and to a lesser
extent message. "Better late than never" does not mean the same as the Italian
proverb "Better a mouse in the mouth of a cat than a man in the hands of a lawyer". There is, to be sure, a commonality of semantic message to the extent
that in both cases, the first item, let us call it "A", is deemed better than the
second item "B". But the messages are quite different. In one, an individual
may be urged not to go to a lawyer, in the other, an individual is urged to go
(somewhere) -- even though it is late. Since "not going" is not the same as
"going", the message would appear to be distinct from the overall formula
"Better _____ than _____."

Finnish proverb scholar Kuusi (1966:98) also observes that the message or
referential aspect of proverbs is not tied to the image employed. That is to say
that the same or similar message may be communicated by different images.
The proverb "He who is bitten by a snake fears even a rope" is in terms of semantic import quite similar to the French proverb "A scalded cat fears even cold
water" and both proverbs are similar in message to the Greek proverb "Whoever is burned on hot squash blows on the cold yogurt". The images differ; the
messages do not. The question then with respect to structural analysis is: precisely what is it that is being analyzed? The Turkish proverb "You cannot make
a stallion out of a donkey by cropping its ears" has a similar message to "You
can't make a silk purse out of a sow's ear", yet the images are different. What
exactly should be subjected to structural analysis? the image, or the underlying
formula: "you can't make a _____ out of a _____" which is seemingly independent
of any one specific image? I believe it should be the underlying frame or formula
rather than the image. Different proverb images are rather like different Aarne-
Thompson tale types. The point is that differences in content do not necessarily
mean that there are correlative differences in underlying structure. As Propp's
syntagmatic model may underlie many different Aarne-Thompson tale types and
as Lévi-Strauss's paradigmatic model may underlie many different South American Indian myths, so the would-be analyst of proverbs should seek a syntagmatic
or paradigmatic model for proverbs.*14

A recent ambitious attempt to bare the nature of proverbs tends to concentrate
upon content rather than form. Initially stimulated by working with a collection
of Samoan proverbs, G. B. Milner (1969a) has suggested that proverbs might be
defined as traditional sayings consisting of quadripartite structure.*15 According to Milner's theory, the four quarters (minor segments) of a proverb are
grouped into two "halves" (major segments) which "match and balance each
other". The opening half Milner terms the "head" while the second half is labelled the "tail".

Milner then examines the word or words in each quarter and determines whether it or they have a plus or minus value. Thus in the proverb "Soon ripe, soon rotten" the values are assigned by Milner as follows:

+	+	
soon	ripe	(which means that the head is +)
+	-	
soon	rotten	(which means that the tail is -)

Within each half of a saying, Milner argues, the two quarters may both be plus (as in "soon ripe") or both be minus or they may be opposites (as in "soon rotten"). If both quarters are plus or both quarters are minus, the meaning of the whole half is considered to be positive. If the quarters are opposites, the whole half is considered to be negative. By this reasoning, any proverb consists of a positive or negative "head" followed by a positive or negative "tail". Having established this general scheme, Milner can assign any individual proverb to one of sixteen possible classes. These sixteen are reduced to four main classes (each consisting of four subclasses). Class A has a positive head and a positive tail; Class B has a negative head and positive tail; Class C has a positive head and negative tail; and Class D has a negative head and a negative tail. Within each main class, there are four different means of achieving the end. For example, in Class A, the four quarters may be of any of the following schemes: + + + +; - - - -; + + - -; - - + +. The other main classes are similarly broken down into subclasses (Milner 1969a:200-01).

Unfortunately, there are several difficulties with Milner's scheme, though these difficulties in no way minimize the novelty of Milner's analysis. For one thing, Milner's analysis seems to have no other end than that of classification. It is not clear what the advantage is of being able to assign a given proverb to one of Milner's sixteen classes. Another problem arises from Milner's assumption of the logical priority of his basic quadripartite proverb structure. From this assumption, Milner is led to speculate that any proverbs not possessing four "quarters" must be mere survivals from an earlier fuller form. In his words, ". . . it is likely that a very large number of tripartite, bipartite and unipartite idioms current today, were once quadripartite, and have been eroded by the familiarity of usage" (1969a:202). This is not only a form of throwing away empirical data that doesn't fit a theory, but is itself a "survival" of English survival theory in which it is invariably assumed that the full, original form in the past has evolved or rather devolved through time suffering such ravages of attrition that only a fragment remains.*16 Milner's hint that the fundamental quadripartite structure of proverbs may ultimately be related to the "fourness" of the Jungian mandala is also extremely speculative. But there are other theoretical difficulties.

One issue recognized by Milner himself is the subjective nature of the assignment of plus and minus values to the four quarters. And he does give two contrasting analysis of the same proverb, "Rolling stones gather no moss". The Scottish and English interpretations of the meaning of the proverb necessitate different value assignments. In England, the stones refer to the stones in a brook and those stones rarely move. Moss is considered to be wealth, prosperity, etc. Hence the Milner formulation for the English meaning of the proverb is:

```
        -           +
    Rolling      stones          (the head is -)
                       .
    gather       no moss         (the tail is -)
       +         (-      +)
                     -
```

In Scotland, however, the stones are thought to be the cylindrical stones of an old fashioned roller. Such stones must not be idle or else moss (lichen) will grow on them. In the Scottish context, then, rolling is plus, stones are plus, gather is plus and no-moss is plus.

```
        +           +
    Rolling      stones          (the head is +)

    gather       no moss         (the tail is +)
       +         (-      -)
                     +
```

Thus though the proverb continues to manifest a four part structure, the English and Scottish meanings involve different plus-minus patterns. (One wonders also if given this variability whether one could make such plus or minus assignments without close consultation with informants. If this is so, then one could not by definition make such assignments just by looking at the text alone.)

But Milner doesn't see the subjectivity of some of his other examples. For instance, he makes the following analysis of the proverb "England has mild winters but hard summers".

```
                    +         +
    (England has)  mild     winters      (the head is +)

            but    hard     summers      (the tail is -)
                    -         +
```

Milner places the proverb in his Class C (Positive head; Negative tail). However, it seems to me that one could very well argue that the value to be assigned to "winters" should be "minus", not "plus". And the point here is not simply that Milner mislabelled one of his quarters, but rather that he is the victim of a much too atomistic analysis. For whatever the structural units of a proverb may be, they cannot be defined apart from their relationship to the rest of the proverb. Milner's error lies in trying to assign plus or minus values to each of the quarters as though the other three quarters were not present. Just so there is no mistake, let me quote Milner's own views in his own words: "Within each half, the two quarters have <u>independent</u> values which modify and affect each other (<u>but do not modify the quarters of the other half</u>)." (Milner 1969a: 200; emphasis mine). My point is that one cannot understand the structural significance of "winters" in the proverb "England has mild winters but hard summers" without taking "summers" into account. Clearly, "winters" and "summers" are in opposition (just as "mild" and "hard" are in opposition). This is, in my view, a fundamental weakness in Milner's scheme of analysis. Whether one favors syntagmatic or paradigmatic structural analysis, one cannot define any structural element in total isolation from the whole syntagmatic sequence or the whole paradigm.

My own approach to proverb structure assumes that there is a close relationship between proverb structure and riddle structure. While there is no doubt that there are important functional differences between these two genres, e.g. riddles confuse while proverbs clarify, I believe that structurally speaking there are major similarities. First of all, both proverb and riddle depend upon "topic-comment" constructions.*17 A minimum proverb or riddle consists of one descriptive element, that is to say, one unit composed of one topic and one comment. It is true that in riddles the referent of the descriptive element is to be guessed whereas in proverbs the referent is presumably known to both the speaker and the addressee(s). And that is one of the principal differences between proverbs and riddles.

Several scholars have drawn attention to the similarity of my previous structural definitions of proverb and riddle, arguing that if the only difference is that in the riddle "the referent of the descriptive element(s) is to be guessed", this is not a structural difference.*18 I think that it is a structural difference, especially in the case of oppositional riddles inasmuch as the answer (referent) provides the means of resolving the apparent opposition. In proverbs which are oppositional, the opposition normally remains unresolved. The initial situation which stimulated the utterance of the proverb in the first place may or may not resolve the opposition delineated in the proverb. In oppositional riddles, the answer always resolves the opposition. One reason for this is that frequently the oppositions in riddles are only pseudo or pretended oppositions. In oppositional proverbs, the oppositions are genuine ones and are not to be easily resolved at all.

Other folklorists have previously observed the similarities in the construction of proverbs and riddles. The Russian folklorist Sokolov (1950:285) cites an example: "Nothing hurts it, but it groans all the time." If the text is used as a proverb, it refers to a hypocrite and a beggar. If used as a riddle, it refers to a swine. Sokolov is incorrect, however, when he contends it is only by means of a single change of intonation that a proverb is transformed into a riddle. It is obviously not intonation per se which is the critical causal factor. Instead, it is the context in which the text is cited. If the text is being used to refer to a hypocrite known to both the speaker and the audience, the text functions as a proverb. If the speaker wishes to test an addressee, then he may state the text as a question using an appropriate interrogatory intonation pattern. The context or rhetorical intention of the speaker determines the intonation pattern and the genre distinction. The intonation is a concomitant feature, a signal or indicator of the genre, but hardly a "cause" of the genre.

The double life of a text as both proverb and riddle is apparently not that uncommon. In a Burmese example, we find the same phenomenon (Dundes 1964b). The text: "The one who does not know about it may walk over it; the one who knows about it will dig it up and eat it." As a riddle, the referent (answer) is a potato or any crop that grows underground. As a proverb, the statement is applied in many different situations where someone is ignorant of something valuable that is not readily apparent but which is close at hand. If such texts can be employed as both proverbs and riddles, then it should not be surprising to discover that the structures of proverbs and riddles are similar. It is also interesting in this connection to remark that in cultural areas where proverbs seem to be absent or scanty, riddles appear to be likewise. Among North and South American Indians, there are relatively few proverbs and riddles. One wonders if any culture has the one genre without the other. Structurally speaking, one is tempted to argue that the existence of one makes the presence of the other logically possible.

As there are non-oppositional riddles, so there are non-oppositional proverbs. Those proverbs which consist of a single descriptive element, such as, "money talks", would be examples of non-oppositional proverbs. Note that with the minimum structural definition of a proverb as one descriptive element (consisting of one topic and one comment), it is theoretically impossible to have a one word proverb. According to this definition, one would have to have at least two words to have a proverb. There are traditional one word items of folk speech, but these would not be proverbs. *19

Before discussing the nature of oppositional proverbs, it might be well to consider for a moment the proverb with respect to what linguist Kenneth Pike (1954: 83) has termed "identificational-contrastive" features. In such linguistic units as the phoneme and the morpheme, the sub-units or allo-units demonstrate a combination of both identificational and contrastive features. Thus, for example, two allophones of the English phoneme /p/ as manifested in "pit" and "tip" share common articulatory characteristics (identificational) but differ with regard to aspiration (contrastive). Initial "p" in English is aspirate whereas final "p" in English is inaspirate. (This is in contrast to the French phoneme /p/ where, for example, initial "p" is normally inaspirate.) I am not concerned with the validity of the identificational-contrastive distinction in linguistics so much as with using it as a means to analyze proverb structure. I believe that multi-descriptive element proverbs are composed of analogous identificational-contrastive features. Some proverbs are primarily identificational; some are primarily contrastive; and some are combinations or composites of identificational and contrastive features.

The reason I refer to multi-descriptive element proverbs is that proverbs which consist of just one descriptive element cannot be oppositional. English examples of one descriptive element proverbs include: "Money talks", "Opposites attract", and "Time flies". One descriptive element proverbs cannot be said to be as common as multi-descriptive element proverbs. Nevertheless, they do exist and consequently any definition of the proverb must take them into account.

I should also like to raise briefly the question of metaphor and its relationship to proverb structure. In a previous analysis of riddle structure, it was pointed out that nonoppositional riddles could be either literal or metaphorical (Georges and Dundes 1963). In other words, the structure of riddles did not depend upon whether the riddle was a literal or a metaphorical description. The same seems to be true of proverbs. Just as nonoppositional riddles may be either literal or metaphorical so nonoppositional proverbs may be either literal or metaphorical. Representative literal nonoppositional English proverbs include: "Honesty is the best policy"; "The customer is always right"; "Haste makes waste"; "Virtue is its own reward"; "Experience is the best teacher"; "Discretion is the better part of valor". Some scholars may prefer to call literal proverbs by some other term, e. g. aphorism, but structurally speaking, literal proverbs appear to be similar to metaphorical proverbs.

If we imagine an axis, one end of which represents identificational features and the other end of which represents contrastive features, then what I have previously termed the "equational proverb" falls close to the identificational end.*20 Moreover, if the equation consists explicitly of an identity as in "A bargain is a bargain", "Business is business", "Let bygones be bygones", "Boys will be boys" or "Enough is enough", then there are virtually no contrastive or oppositional features. Generally equational proverbs of the form A = B are identificational rather than contrastive. Examples of equational proverbs include: "Time is money"; "Seeing is believing", and many of the literal non-oppositional proverbs mentioned above. Proverbs of the form "He who $\underline{A}$ is $\underline{B}$" seem to be transformations of the basic A = B formula. "He who laughs last laughs best" suggests that "laughing last" = "laughing best". Similarly, "He who hesitates is lost" implies that "hesitating" = "losing". In much the same fashion, proverbs with the formula "Where there's an $\underline{A}$, there's a $\underline{B}$", would appear to be another transformation of the basic equational formula. "Where there's life, there's hope" tends to argue that "life" = "hope". "Where there's smoke, there's fire" would be reduced to "smoke" = "fire". "Where there's a will, there's a way" might be rendered as "will" = "way". (In the last two examples, there is a postulated equivalence of cause and effect. In the first, an effect, smoke, is presumed to mean its cause, fire. In the second, will is assumed to causally lead to a way. But whether cause = effect or effect = cause, the equational structure is maintained.)

Another transformation of the equational structure consists of a series of two or more descriptive elements. These descriptive elements are often linked by a repetition of either the topic or comment: "Many men, many minds"; "First come, first served". I believe that either of these series could be written in normal equational form with no loss of meaning: many men = many minds; first come = first served. Interestingly enough, it is usually the first term of two in a nonoppositional series or equation which is identical, e. g. "Monkey see, monkey do"; "coffee boiled is coffee spoiled"; "a friend in need is a friend in deed (indeed)"; "handsome is as handsome does"; "a penny saved is a penny earned"; "nothing ventured, nothing gained"; "out of sight, out of mind". Occasionally, there are series which are more coordinate or conjunctional than equational. Examples are "Live and learn", "Live and let live", "Laugh and grow fat" and "Love 'em and leave 'em".

Let us now turn to oppositional proverbs. There seem to be a number of different forms of opposition which are found in proverbs. One of the simplest is negation.*21 Negation in this sense denies an identificational equation. "Two wrongs don't make a right". Here we have the basic formula A ≠ B. The opposition is strengthened by "two" ≠ "one" and by "wrong" ≠ "right". Similarly, "One Swallow does not make a summer". "Swallow" ≠ "summer". Presumably, many swallows do indicate that summer has arrived, thus the "one" is implicitly contrasted with "many". I suggest that all the proverbs based on formula that "A is less than B" or "A is greater than B" (which would include all the proverbs with the familiar formula Better ____ than ____) are contrastive rather than identificational proverbs. "Hindsight is better than foresight. " Hindsight certainly does not equal foresight. Rather the two entities are contrasted. And this is the point really: All proverbs are potentially propositions which compare and/or contrast. Comparing originally referred to finding similarities or identificational features in common; contrasting referred to delineating differences. Other examples of A is greater than B include "His eyes are bigger than his belly" and "Fingers were made before forks".

In investigating the nature of the oppositions found in proverbs, one is tempted to see a certain parallel to the types of oppositions found in oppositional riddles. In a previous study, three types of opposition in English riddles were distinguished: antithetical contradictive, privational contradictive, and causal contradictive (Georges and Dundes 1963). Each of the three types can be produced by either affirmation or negation. Accordingly, antithetical contradiction in riddles can come from statements that A = B; A ≠ B (which incidentally is a beautiful illustration of the combination of identificational and contrastive features) or via affirmation: A = B; A = C (where B ≠ C) (Georges and Dundes 1963).

Antithetical contradiction might be said to be analogous to complementary distribution in linguistic theory. If you have A, then you can't have B; if you have B, you can't have A; (When /p/ occurs initially in English, you will automatically have the aspirate p allophone and never the allophone. If /p/ occurs at the end of an English word, you will automatically have inaspirate p, never aspirate p - unless you wish to signal great stress or emphasis as in asking a thief to "stop"!) There seem to be proverbs which demonstrate such complementary distribution. "You can't have your cake and eat it too. "If you have your cake, you obviously can't have eaten it. If you eat it, then you no longer have it. "Having your cake" is thus mutually exclusive with "eating it". This form of oppositional proverb is evidently of considerable antiquity, judging from its occurrence in Sumer. Consider the following Sumerian text (Kramer 1959:121):

The poor man is better dead than alive
If he has bread, he has no salt,
If he has salt, he has no bread,
If he has meat, he has no lamb,
If he has a lamb, he has no meat.

Having both meat (dead) and the lamb (alive) is just as impossible as having one's cake and eating it too. Another Sumerian illustration:

Who builds like a lord, lives like a slave;
Who builds like a slave, lives like a lord. *22

Evidently, building like a lord and living like a lord are in complementary distribution; they cannot co-occur.

Complementary distribution, it should be noted, can occur even if there is no explicit signal of negation. In the well known international proverb "When the cat's away, the mice will play" there is an opposition between presence and absence in addition to the obvious contrast between cat and mice (which also entails "one" versus "many"). If cats are present, then mice are absent; if cats are absent, then mice are present. Cats and mice, according to the proverb are thus in complementary distribution and cannot co-occur.

Although one can have opposition without explicit negation, it is more common to have opposition produced through overt negation. It is important to realize that the negation need not be limited to the verb as in A ≠ B. Either A or B can be negative (as non-A or non-B). In this respect, Milner was on the right track in attempting to assign plus and minus values to constituent elements of proverbs. However, I would argue that the negation is, more often than not, explicit and therefore one does not need to employ subjective value judgments to determine whether or not negation is a factor. Consider the proverb "No news is good news". Here the negation occurs in the first descriptive element. There is opposition insofar as there is a question as to how no news can be "news" at all, much less good news. But clearly the absence of news may be good news. Thus as in the cat and mice proverb "Absence" = "presence".

It would appear that negation occurs more often in the second or final descriptive element of multi-descriptive element proverbs. For example, consider "Rolling stones gather no moss". The negative is the "no" in "no moss". Yet the negation is presumably caused by the comment in the first descriptive element, namely "rolling". If we consider the proverb as "stones which roll are stones which gather no moss", then it is the act of rolling which rules out the accumulation of moss. If a stone rolls, it can't have moss; if a stone has moss, it can't have rolled. Notice that this analysis holds regardless of whether moss is deemed a good thing or a bad thing. Structure is more or less independent of meaning although to be sure there will always be conscious or unconscious meanings attached to any given structure. In the same way, it is the "barking" in "Barking dogs never bite" which precludes biting. The negative equation might be written "barking dogs are not biting dogs". Although the proverb is normally understood metaphorically, it is perfectly true, physically speaking, that it is impossible for a dog to bark and bite at the same time. Thus "barking" and "biting" may be said to be in complementary distribution insofar as they are mutually exclusive activities. One is tempted to generalize that there seems to be a formulaic pattern _____ _____s never _____, in which the presence of the initial factor means the absence of the last. It is "watching" which prevents boiling (in "A watched pot never boils"); it is "too many" which negates the broth (in "Too many cooks spoil the broth") and it is the "dead" which precludes taletelling (in "Dead men tell no tales"). *23

There are other examples of oppositional proverbs which contain oppositions remarkably similar to the antithetical contradictions of riddles. "A straight stick is crooked in the water" ("straight" = "crooked"). A most interesting German proverb in this connection is "He who rules, must hear and be deaf, see and be blind". "Seeing and being blind" is surely reminiscent of riddle oppositional structure. (Cf. What has eyes and cannot see? A potato.) There are also proverb analogues for privational contradiction where a logical part or attribute of an object is denied. "The mob has many heads but no brains" would be a proverb of this type. (This is quite similar to the riddle for a match: "It has a head, but can't think.)

There are even proverb parallels for causal contradictives where normal effects or consequences are denied. There are, of course, numerous non-oppositional causal proverbs in which A simply causes B, e.g. "Practice makes perfect"; "Haste makes waste"; "Familiarity breeds contempt". Ideally, the effect should be parallel to the cause: "As you sow, so shall you reap." However, in oppositional causal proverbs, the cause is denied or deemed impossible. "You can lead a horse to water but you can't make him drink." If one leads a horse to water, one might expect the horse to drink or possibly that one could force him to drink. The opposition results from the contrast of what "can" be done and what "can't" be done. One "can" lead a horse to water but one "can't" make him drink. Again, there is an obvious riddle parallel, "What goes to the branch [stream] and drinks and doesn't drink?" (Cow and bell). Other causal contradictive proverbs include: "you can't make a silk purse out of a sow's ear"; "one can't be in two places at the same time"; "you can't get blood from a turnip". In these and other proverbs, A cannot produce or yield B.

Still another form of causal opposition occurring in proverbs plays upon the possibility of having the normal effect being illogically placed before the cause. The proverb seemingly reverses the usual chronological priority of actions A and B in "Don't lock the barn door after the horse has been stolen", "Don't set the cart before the horse", "Don't count your chickens before they are hatched", "Catch the bear before you sell its skin".

In attempting to distinguish between identificational versus contrastive features in proverbs or between nonoppositional and oppositional proverbs, one needs to bear in mind that not all proverbs fall neatly into just one category. As has already been suggested, some proverbs contain both identificational and contrastive features. Westermarck noted some years ago in his brilliant introductory essay on the nature of the proverbs he had collected in Morocco that in some proverbs there is a tendency to have two or more parallel assertions while in others there is a predilection for antithesis and contrast. With respect to the latter, he even went so far as to indicate that subjects could be contrasted, predicates could be contrasted, or both subjects and predicates could be contrasted (1930:5-6). I agree with Westermarck's observations except that I would employ the terminology of "topic" and "comment" in place of his subject and predicate, and I would underline his suggestion that parallel and contrastive features may occur in one and the same proverb. I would also speculate that the phenomenon of simultaneous identification/contrastive features might be a characteristic of proverbs in all cultures where the genre is found.

Perhaps the most common means of building opposition in proverbs is to utilize one or more of a number of traditional semantic contrastive pairs. In English these include:

one	versus	two
few		many
young		old
old		new
little		great
near		far
weak		strong
worst		best
easy		hard

always	versus	never
good		bad
black		white
before		after
today		tomorrow

It should be made clear that this is only a partial list. It should also be noted that no one member of any of these pairs is always superior. In the "one" versus "two" sometimes "one" is preferred, sometimes "two". For example, in many of the "A is greater than B" proverbs, one can find "One A is better than two B's" (e. g. "One hour's sleep before midnight is better than two after ") but one can also find "Two A's are better than one" as in "Two heads are better than one". (Then again, sometimes "one" = "two" as in "A bird in the hand is worth two in the bush" though of course it is the contrast between "in the hand" and "in the bush" which balances the numerical inequity.)

In causal proverbs, the obvious contrast between cause and effect is heightened by the use of such pairs. For example, "A little spark kindles a great fire" has not only the contrast between spark and fire but also "little" and "great". The same opposition is found in "Great oaks from little acorns grow". A different pair is employed in "A black hen will lay a white egg", but the oppositional principle is the same.

Some proverbs contain both oppositional and nonoppositional features. For example, there is an equational proverb: "The longest way round is the shortest way found". There is an equation which implies an identificational feature, but the equation involves "longest" = "shortest" which is clearly oppositional. Consider "One man's meat is another man's poison" in which "meat" (life) = "poison" (death). Or "An ounce of prevention is worth a pound of cure" in which "ounce" = "pound". The equational structure provides a frame suggesting identification, but the content within this frame contains contrastive features. Another example is "Easy come, easy go". "Coming" and "going" are in opposition, but the two instances of "easy" constitute an identity. The same sort of combination occurs in "Win a few; lose a few". One could say that in such proverbs there is not only the opposition between members of a contrasting semantic pair (e. g. coming-going, winning-losing) but also the opposition caused by having both an identity and a contrast in the same proverb!

Less ambiguous are the multi-descriptive element proverbs in which both topics and comments are members of contrastive pairs. Here are some examples: "The spirit is willing but the flesh is weak" (spirit/flesh; willing/weak); "United we stand, divided we fall" (united/divided; stand/fall); "Man proposes but God disposes" (man/God; proposes/disposes); "Last hired, first fired" (last/first; hired/fired); "Here today, gone tomorrow" (present/absent; today/ tomorrow); "Jack of all trades and master of none" (Jack/master; all/none); "Penny wise and pound foolish" (penny/pound; wise/foolish). In a proverb like "Many are called but few are chosen", it is clear that "many" are opposed to "few" and that "being called" ≠ "being chosen".

From this we can see that there does seem to be a continuum from non-opposition to opposition. One can have a set of topic-comment constructions which are parallel or in series and are not in opposition: "Many men, many minds";

"First come, first served". One can have a set in which either the topic or the comment is parallel or identical with the remaining element in opposition "Easy come, easy go". Finally, one can have a set in which both topics and comments are in opposition: "Last hired, first fired".

One of the most striking contrasts between terms in series and terms in opposition is provided by the difference between proverbs of the form "Live and learn" on the one hand and proverbs of the form "Do or die" on the other. There is no opposition or contradiction between living and learning. On the contrary, to live is to learn. Living = learning. But "doing" and "dying" are in opposition. If one does not do, one dies. If one dies, one cannot do. The same is true for "sink or swim", "put up or shut up", "fish or cut bait", "shape up or ship out", "publish or perish", etc. In alternative structure proverbs, the terms are normally in complementary distribution, that is, they are mutually exclusive. And as has already been noted, complementary distribution in proverbs represents one of the strongest forms of opposition.

In summary then, the proverb appears to be a traditional propositional statement consisting of at least one descriptive element, a descriptive element consisting of a topic and a comment. This means that proverbs must have at least two words. Proverbs which contain a single descriptive element are nonoppositional. Proverbs with two or more descriptive elements may be either oppositional or non-oppositional. "Like father, like son" would be an example of a multi-descriptive element proverb which was nonoppositional; "Man works from sun to sun but woman's work is never done" would be an example of a multi-descriptive element proverb which is oppositional (man/woman; finite work/infinite or endless work). Non-oppositional multi-descriptive element proverbs emphasize identificational features, often in the form of an equation or a series of equal terms; oppositional proverbs emphasize contrastive features often in the form of negation or a series of terms in complementary distribution. Some proverbs contain both identificational and contrastive features. The means of producing opposition in proverbs is strikingly similar to the means of producing opposition in riddles. However, whereas the oppositions in riddles are resolved by the answer, the oppositional proverb is itself an answer to a proverb-evoking situation, and the opposition is posed, not resolved. In this sense, proverbs only state problems in contrast to riddles which solve them.

The above analysis is most tentative and needs to be empirically tested with proverb materials from a variety of cultures. To the extent that the proverb is a cross-cultural genre of folklore, there should be a cross-culturally valid definition of the proverb. One research possibility resulting from the above analysis concerns the discernment of oicotypes.*24 Do all cultures which have proverbs have the same proverb structural types? For example, which cultures have equational proverbs consisting of perfect identities as "Enough is enough"? There are also possible oicotypes of content. Do all cultures which have proverbs have contrastive pairs emphasizing time and quantity, for example?

It may well be that the foregoing discussion is based upon too limited a sample and that close analysis of proverbs from Asian and African cultures will require considerable revision of the distinctions outlined above. It is also likely that insofar as proverbs are traditional propositions, they should properly be studied by scholars with expertise in symbolic logic and related disciplines. However, for the time being, I am encouraged to find some confirmation of the importance of oppositional structure in proverbs as found in two famous "definitions" of proverbs. One is Cervantes' suggestion that proverbs are "short sentences drawn from long experience". And equally supportive as "short" versus "long" is the beautiful definition attributed to Lord Russell which suggests that proverbs are: "The wisdom of many, the wit of one."*25

NOTES

*1 For an entry into proverb scholarship, see Bonser and Stephens (1930) and Moll (1958).

*2 For an excellent survey of recent proverb studies, see Kuusi (1957).

*3 An exemplary field investigation of the proverb is Hain (1951).

*4 For a discussion of the proverb with respect to communication rules, see Arewa and Dundes (1964).

*5 For a discussion of proverbs and national character, see Raymond (1954); for proverbs and worldview, see Shimkin and Sanjuan (1953).

*6 See Gorham (1956) and Elmore and Gorham (1957). The difficulty in interpreting metaphor as metaphor may also be related to certain forms of aphasia, see Jakobson and Halle (1956). For another practical use of proverbs, see Baumgarten (1952).

*7 Taylor (1962). Professor Taylor's remark was a personal communication to the author.

*8 Whiting (1952:331). Whiting has even made a survey of previous definitions of the proverb but his own definition leaves much to be desired, e.g. "It is usually short but need not be; it is usually true, but need not be." See Whiting (1932). Whiting does suggest that true proverbs be distinguished from proverbial phrases or what I would term "folk metaphors". This is a thorny question. However, I would agree that true proverbs can be distinguished from proverbial comparisons or folk similes. Structurally, they do not appear to be transformationally equivalent. The proverb "Love is blind" does not occur as a folk simile "as blind as love". By the same token, the folk simile "as blind as a bat" does not occur as "A bat is blind".

*9 For a discussion of the God's truth versus the Hocus-Pocus positions with respect to the reality of structure in folklore, see Dundes (1964:57).

*10 Kimmerle (1947). I believe that Noam Chomsky's search for "deep structure" as opposed to "surface structure" is intellectually similar to Freud's interest in the latent content as opposed to the manifest content and to Jung's interest in archetypes. In the same way, Lévi-Strauss tries to isolate the paradigmatic structure which underlies syntagmatic structures. See Dundes (1968a: xii) for a discussion of this point. Chomsky, Jung, and Lévi-Strauss are all looking for universals in the form of "deep structure", "archetype" and a binary oppositional paradigm.

*11 For a discussion of the distinction between "folkloristic structure" and "linguistic structure", see Georges and Dundes (1963:117, nn. 15, 18).

*12 These three aspects of proverbs have been well differentiated by Kuusi (1966).

*13 In the tripartite structure of the Wellerism, the third portion appears to be structurally optional rather than obligatory. Thus one can have Wellerisms of the form: _____ said the _____. See Taylor (1962). On the other hand, the third portion is usually present as it is this section which puts the first portion - the quotation or proverb - in a new and often humorous light.

*14 For a discussion of the distinction between syntagmatic and paradigmatic structures, see Dundes (1968a:xi-xiii).

*15 A shorter statement of Milner's scheme is Milner (1969b). A fuller account is Milner (1969c).

*16 For a discussion of this theoretical position, see Dundes (1969).

*17 For a discussion of topic-comment constructions, see Dundes (1962e), or Georges and Dundes (1963).

*18 One such scholar is Charles T. Scott (1969); see esp. p. 124. The criticism is also contained in Scott (1965). The same criticism was made independently by Nathhorst (1968).

*19 This brings up two points with respect to Milner's analysis. First of all, if "money talks" is a bona fide proverb, then must we assume that it was once part of a larger quadripartite proverb? I would say that although there are proverbs with what Milner terms quadripartite structure, it would be wrong to claim that all proverbs have or had this one structure. The basic unit of proverbs seems to me to be a topic-comment construction and Milner's quadripartite structure is essentially a doubling of the basic structure. The second point concerns Milner's reference to "unipartite idioms". I doubt that there is a one word proverb. Milner's one example is really an allusion to a proverb rather than a proverb per se. If there are truly unipartite proverbs, I should like to see some examples.

*20 Dundes (1962e:37-38). In this initial discussion of the equational proverb, I failed to make any mention of oppositional proverbs.

118

*21 The relationship of negation to equation is not altogether clear. In folktales, for example, Propp (1958:27) noted that "A command often plays the role of an interdiction". "Keep your eyes closed" would be a command; "Don't open your eyes" would be an interdiction. I found the same difficulty in defining disequilibrium in American Indian narratives. A flood could be construed as too much water or too little land! See Dundes (1964c:61-64). Similarly, riddle oppositions can be produced by affirmation or by negation. The role of negation in folkloristic structure should be the subject of a separate investigation.

*22 Kramer (1959:125). Milner (1969b:382), gives a number of examples in which the order of words in the first half is inverted in the second half, e. g. "Those who speak don't know; those who know don't speak". He claims this type of formula A B
        B A
is quite widespread, occurring, for instance, in Chinese and African proverbs.

*23 The initial factor seems to be equally crucial in equational proverbs. In "The early bird catches the worm" it is the "earliness" which = the worm. In "A new broom sweeps clean", it is the "newness" which = cleanliness.

*24 For a discussion of the concept of oicotype, see Dundes (ed.) (1965:219-20) and Bødker (1965:220).

*25 I wish to thank the members of an informal seminar on structural analysis who met weekly during the Winter Quarter of 1970. I am especially indebted to Angie Berry, Rob Hanford, Bess Hawes, Dr. William Hendricks, Bill Herzog, Sharon Heuga, Toni Ihara, Ed Kahn, Mellie Lopez, Gail Schow, Barbara Vogl, Fred Walden, and Marcia Walerstein for their stimulating suggestions.

SECTION THREE

THE PSYCHOANALYTIC APPROACH

12

ON THE PSYCHOLOGY OF COLLECTING FOLKLORE

Within recent decades, professional folklorists have placed more and more emphasis upon obtaining biographical and other background information about informants. A collector of folklore is expected to do more than merely indicate his sources. He is encouraged to provide just as much pertinent data describing his informants as possible. The purpose is presumably to aid in relating folklore to individual bearers of tradition and more especially to cultural context. In contrast to the previous practice of studying folklore materials in the abstract, the sociological and psychological study of folklore is facilitated by this new interest in particular informants. Nevertheless, one aspect of the collecting situation remains singularly untouched. While folklorists may be coming closer to an answer to the perennial question of why individuals tell tales, sing folksongs, etc., the motivation of folklorists in collecting folklore in the first place is rarely considered. Richard Dorson, however, does ask, in an important article on collecting folktales, "Why does the collector gather and publish tales?" (Dorson 1957:54).

In order to answer this question satisfactorily, it will probably be necessary to study background information on the collectors of folklore. Unfortunately, most of the famous collectors, although they do occasionally give numerous details about their various informants, fail to give relevant biographical material about themselves. In the absence of such material, the psychology of collecting folklore must of necessity remain largely a matter of conjecture. The following consideration of this question is admittedly speculative, but it is sincerely hoped that the hypothetical framework suggested will be supported or refuted by forthcoming data provided by honest self-critical collectors of the future. No attempt is made here to discuss the scientific value of folkloristic materials collected nor are the various uses to which folklore may be put considered. Only the underlying psychological motivation for the collecting of folklore is the subject of the present inquiry.

It has long been recognized that collecting folklore is akin to collecting other objects. W. W. Newell in the very first issue of the Journal of American Folklore quotes Charles G. Leland on the popular opinion of the collection of folklore, "that it amounts to gathering mere literary bric-abrac and collecting traditionary postage-stamps and buttons" (Newell 1888d). More recently, Louise Pound expressed a similar view, but with the additional remark that folklore was a more worthwhile object for collection than many other materials diligently collected.

Reprinted from the Tennessee Folklore Society Bulletin 28 (1962), 65-74.

Teachers, clergymen, attorneys, writers, and others often feel prompted
to hunt out the traditions, legends, songs, and tales of their own region.
Why not? Such persons are of much the same type as those who search for
antique furniture, old glassware, and the like. Some may call them dilettantes,
but surely their hobbies are acceptable enough; and often, too, their activities
are helpful to specialists. Indeed, popular traditions seem to me more laudable for collection than do many of the objects now often gathered ardently,
such as match covers, pictures of ball players and cinema stars, and among
children, of backs of playing cards and even of colored milk bottle tops.
(Pound 1952).*1

Dorson (1957:55), however, suggests that the aimless collection of folklore is
really not so different from collecting less laudable materials when he states,
"A collector guided by no larger purpose than the desire to accumulate new
species of texts might as well collect buttons or butterflies. " If collecting folklore is one aspect of the collecting tradition in general, then perhaps the motivation for collecting folklore is related to the motivation for collecting objects
in general.

At the beginning of this century, it was assumed that there was a collecting
instinct and that this instinct was manifested in the diverse collecting activities
of children.*2 Later studies of children's collecting sought to avoid raising the
question of the instinctive character of collecting, although by and large the
feeling was that the assumption of a collecting instinct was premature and that
collecting was attributable not to a hereditary predisposition so much as to en-
vironmental conditioning.*3 The collecting instinct, therefore, became the collecting tendency. However, the environmentalists had difficulty in explaining
why frequently the object collected was of little apparent value (e.g. bottle tops,
match covers, etc.).

Probably the most comprehensive attempt to elucidate the rationale underlying collecting activities is that formulated by psychoanalysts. According to
psychoanalytic theory, the etiological basis of collecting was anal erotism.
Briefly, Freud suggested that individuals from infancy onward find genuine
physical pleasure in the act of defecation. However, at least in Western society,
the child is soon made aware of adult demands that this activity should be strictly regulated. Toilet training consists largely of conditioning an infant to control
his excretory activity. Psychoanalysts further claim that this controlling or
holding back becomes in itself a source of pleasure. According to Ferenczi
(1956a:271), "The excrementa thus held back are really the first 'savings' of
the growing being, and as such remain in a constant, unconscious inter-relation-
ship with every bodily activity or mental striving that has anything to do with
collecting, hoarding, and saving. " Moreover, from the Freudian point of view,
the infant has a natural curiosity concerning the fecal material he produces. But
the infant's attempts to explore and play with this material are almost inevitably
discouraged by adults and the child is gradually introduced to a succession of
less undesirable substances ranging from mud pies to sand piles to modeling
clay and finger paints (Ferenczi 1956a:272-74). From this perspective, "Collecting is a sublimation of anal-retentive desires, and the collector's pleasure
in it is a continuation of his infantile-narcissistic pleasure in his own feces. "
(Fenichel 1954:148). Actually, there appear to be two separate contributing

factors to the genesis of collecting activity and Karl Abraham (1948b:373) makes an important distinction between, on the one hand, the act of excretion which provides pleasure, and on the other hand, the products of the excretory process in which an individual may find pleasure.

Although Freud in his paper, "Character and Anal Erotism", did speak of three characteristics of anal character: orderliness, parsimony, and obstinacy, he did not mention collecting specifically (1949c:45). Rather it was Ernest Jones who referred to collecting when he developed Freud's insights in greater detail in his paper "Anal-Erotic Character Traits". Jones noted that there were basically two opposing tendencies resulting from anal conditioning: "the tendencies to keep and postpone production and to produce feverishly". He suggested that the two tendencies might be termed the "retaining" and the "ejecting" tendencies (Jones 1950:428, n. 6). Combining these two contrasting tendencies with the possibilities of sublimation and reaction formation, Jones delineated a fourfold typology of anal characterology. He was, of course, careful to say that these four classifications are by no means mutually exclusive.

The first classification is retaining-sublimation and its two aspects are "the refusal to give and the desire to gather". In discussing this classification, Jones makes the categorical statement that all collectors are anal-erotics. The second classification is retaining-reaction formation. Reaction formation, in contrast to sublimation which consists of selecting a socially acceptable substitute for a tabooed object or activity, is basically a total rejection of the original pleasure-seeking tendency. Thus pleasure is found, not in dirtiness, but in cleanliness. Cleanliness is often extended into orderliness. Individuals of this disposition are prone to systematize and organize so that objects may be neatly placed in their proper place. The third classification is ejection-sublimation. Individuals in this category are generous and apt to "give out" material. Sublimation may be evidenced by the desire to manipulate the material and to mould it or create out of it. The fourth classification, namely ejection-reaction formation is somewhat similar to the second classification in that it is characterized by a denial of an interest in dirt. Individuals of this type take little interest in their material or mental productions and often seek to discard or get rid of them.

Although the Freudian notion of anal character is by no means universally accepted, even critics admit that it is "the most clearly-drawn picture in Freud's album of characterology".*4 The relevance of the Freudian hypothesis to the psychology of collecting folklore is somewhat dependent upon the idea of occupational determinism. Among psychoanalysts, there are those who insist that people choose vocations (usually unconsciously) on the basis of particular individual infantile conditioning. In fact, it has even been suggested that anal erotics would do well in occupations involving collecting and systematic indexing, as in positions as museum curators or archivists.*5 An example of an anally conditioned occupation choice might be found in the life of Benvenuto Cellini who, in addition to collecting pebbles, shells, and eventually gems, decided at the age of fifteen to become a goldsmith. Gold is a common symbolic equivalent of feces as numerous folklore motifs testify, and the aesthetic pleasure obtained from beating and moulding gold is derived from an early activity, namely the infantile real or fantasied play with excrement.

Though most folklorists are skeptical of psychoanalysis, to say the least, perhaps some may see the application of Freudian theory to the psychology of the collecting of folklore as well as to the specific methods employed in the treatment and study of folklore. In addition, considerable light may be shed upon the personalities of various well-known folklorists.

First of all, folklore as an object of collection is often regarded as a useless product of human activity. Just as cancelled stamps, empty beer bottles, etc., in one sense represent waste products, folklore has historically also been regarded in much the same way. For example, when the indefatigable Danish collector, E. Tang Kristensen, obtained a new teaching position he had sought, a member of the parish council concerned said to him, "We won't have you, you take up so much of your time with rubbish. . . ."(Craigie 1898:200). In fact, folklorists are still trying to convince both the public and the Foundations that folkloristic materials are valuable and worth collecting.

Another curious fact is the professional folklore collector's insistence that the material be entirely oral. It must come from the mouths of informants, and preferably not from printed sources. In other words, the collector stands ready to gather the precious material as it falls from a body aperture, namely the oral cavity. In Freudian parlance, this might be construed as displacement from below upward. Strangely enough, there is often the feeling that as soon as the material is put on paper, it is somehow less authentic. It is also of interest that if folklore is considered as survivals or if it is remembered that folkloristic material is often first encountered in early childhood, then collecting folklore is, in part, collecting materials of the past and possibly in particular the materials of childhood. (No doubt many non-folklorists consider the study of folklore as something of a regression to childhood.)

It is somewhat of a surprise to discover that part of the accepted methodology of folklore scholarship may be related to the psychology of collecting folklore. Collecting usually implies some order, namely that the objects collected are subject to some kind of classification. Bearing in mind Jones' second classification of anal character (retaining-reaction formation) with its emphasis upon orderly, systematic arrangement, one can appreciate the following statement, written not with reference to folklore, but about collecting in general: "The striving for form also manifests itself in the tendency of modern collectors to follow a specific sequence in forming and arranging collections, as well as in the desire to complete definite 'sets' or series of exhibits. The nature of these sequences will vary according to the subject of the collection itself. They may be historical or geographical. . ." (Rigby and Rigby 1944:75-76). The historical-geographical method is, of course, a highly organized and systematic form of collecting! This may be seen by noting the representational or relational aspects of collections in general. W. N. Durost, in giving a basic definition of a collection stresses this very point. He suggests that the use or the value of the object collected is of secondary importance for purposes of definition. A collection may or may not be of practical use or of culturally recognized value. What is important, according to Durost, are the representational or relational criteria. He points out that if an object or idea is valued chiefly for the relation it bears to some other object or idea, or objects, or ideas, such as being one of a series, part of a whole, a specimen of a class, then it is the subject of a collection (Durost 1932:10). One can see that the historical-geographical method entails collecting specimens of a class: for example, versions of a single tale type. The more specimens or versions one can amass, presumably the better the study. The idea of considering an object in terms of its being one of a series calls to mind the ballad collector who specializes in collecting numbers in Child's closed canon. A ballad collector obtaining a Child ballad is like a stamp collector obtaining an important stamp in a certain series. D. K. Wilgus (1959: 247-48) mentions the penchant of American ballad collectors for collecting Child numbers and refers, for example, to Reed Smith's score sheets showing which collectors in which states had collected the most Child ballads.*6

Another aspect of folklore scholarship relating to the classificatory aspect of collecting may be seen by recalling the elaborate book classification scheme of Samuel Pepys. Pepys collected books (and also ballads) but later shifted his interest to arranging his collection. In a letter of August 10, 1663, he remarked that his chief delight was in the neatness of everything and that he could not be pleased with anything unless it was very neat, which he admitted was a strange folly. He had all his books bound alike and he arranged them symmetrically according to size. In order still to be able to use his library Pepys devised a complex cataloging system which provided for the numbering and lettering of shelves and books. According to one account of Pepys' system, a key catalogue was prepared and "by consulting this for the title desired one could locate the volume's position on the shelves by number: i. e. , the first book on the front row on the shelf fourth from the top in Press One would be marked '1. 4a. 1' " (Rigby and Rigby 1944:240). Had Pepys lived several centuries later, he might have compiled a motif index.

One can now see how Jones' classifications may be used to distinguish different emphases among folklorists. Some folklorists are primarily interested in collecting (retaining-sublimation) while others are specialists in a classificatory kind of collection (retaining-reaction formation). It might be noted that the latter's reaction formation is clearly revealed by their opposition to discussing so-called "dirty" folklore, or even acknowledging its existence. For example, classification schemes might very well simply omit portions which have to do with obscene materials. The anal retentive nature of some collectors is manifested by their putting their manuscripts or tapes in a secret or locked place, often denying others access to their materials. Frequently, they refuse to publish. By a curious verbal coincidence (which is probably no accident), one often hears such collectors described as "sitting on" their material. ("Sitting tight" has somewhat the same connotation. "Tight" commonly means stingy in the sense of being reluctant to part with something (Jones 1949:429, n. 1). Here is the significance of Abraham's distinction between the pleasure of the act of excretion and the pleasure in possessing the products of excretion. To illustrate this type of folklorist, i.e. one who loves to collect but who hates to publish, is not difficult. (Cf. the two aspects of Jones' first classification: the desire to gather and refusal to give.) One example should suffice. It should not be necessary to state that no disrespect is intended nor is there any attempt to minimize the efforts of one of the most important collectors of American folklore in the following consideration of Frank C. Brown.*7

Frank C. Brown was an enthusiastic and tireless collector, but he simply could not bring himself to publish. Though a volume of folklore was scheduled to appear by Christmas of 1914, the first volume of Brown's material did not appear until 1952, years after his death. Members of the North Carolina Folklore Society, not understanding Brown's personality pattern, began dropping their memberships in protest over Brown's failure to publish his wealth of materials. (Incidentally, one of the purposes of this study is to make folklorists more tolerant of the foibles of some collectors and at the same time to urge those who have material to make it available to others.) The anal retentive nature of Brown's behavior is apparent in a statement opposing the suggestions made by members of the Society. He said, "I am quite sure that I am not going to give up my own materials to anybody." Brown obviously felt that the materials, though taken from others, were his personal possessions. He is a prime example of the collector described in the following passage written by a non-Freudian:

> All the desires and interests which contribute toward making any sort of individual into a collector are given focus by the fact of personal possession. From the small boy to the great connoisseur, the joy of standing before one's accumulated pile and being able to say, "This belongs to me!" is the culmination of that feeling which begins with the ownership of the first item. (Rigby and Rigby 1944:35).

Newman I. White observes that Brown was "tenacious of his manuscripts" and that "he allowed nothing to stop him", a personality trait in accord with the third of Freud's characteristics of anal character, obstinacy. Brown was especially interested in ballads and he took great pride in building up the number of Child ballads discovered in North Carolina. He was very pleased that he had been able to gather more than fifty numbers of the canonical series. Howover, his pleasure was confined to collecting. His own statement of his attempts to publish confirm his personality pattern. "When I try to write an article, I almost invariably lose interest in it before I get my notes copied. My interest is at fever heat in making an outline and in making a rough draft, but as soon as this has been made, somehow my interest lags and I almost become sick when I feel that is is necessary to tear the thing to pieces and rewrite it." Apparently Brown could not bear to touch anything that he produced. Here also is clearly indicated his inability to part with or destroy anything he amassed or created. This is in marked contrast to Jone's fourth classification in which individuals take little interest in their materials and, in fact, seek to get rid of them. Brown gave only two papers at the North Carolina Folklore Society meetings and in view of his unmistakable anal character traits, it is noteworthy that one of them was entitled: "Treasure Hunting in North Carolina".[*8] Treasure is a common coprophilic symbol, particularly when it is removed from the "bowels" of the earth in buried form.

While the anal retentive folklore collector is loath to publish, the anal ejective collector is, on the contrary, often feels compelled to publish. Frequently the publication is extremely "regular". Ferenczi (1956a:277, n. 1) refers to the latter type of anal personality as "tolerant on the matter of dirt, extravagant, and easy-doing".[*9] However, sometimes the anal ejective seeks to mould or manipulate his material. Here may be found one possible reason for the production of fakelore.[*10] The material is reshaped according to the aesthetic standards of the anal ejective. Consequently, coarse or dirty elements are fastidiously "eliminated". If this kind of reaction formation and sublimation is combined with the general anal ejective tendency, then such individuals would be quite likely to publish regularly "treasuries" of doctored or re-worked texts. This is in contrast to the anal ejective who is tolerant of, if not attracted by "dirty" materials (e.g. jokes). The latter would also publish regularly, but the materials would be left pretty much as collected, that is, with the crude elements remaining. *11 This practice would undoubtedly annoy the fakelorist who goes to great lengths to eliminate such details in his attempt to deny any anal basis to the collection and study of oral tradition. One fakelorist, several years ago, wrote a letter to the officers of the American Folklore Society protesting the work of a collector who insisted upon presenting texts as they were related by the folk. The true nature of the anal-oral quarrel was unwittingly suggested when the author of the letter asked indignantly if the officers of the Society wanted a toilet in their dining room. Of course, to anyone who felt impelled to reshape or mould material, nothing could be more shocking than to be confronted with the anal reality so scrupulously avoided.

Although, as has been mentioned previously, biographical data on collectors is rarely available, one might, nevertheless, suggest certain possible personality characteristics of collectors of folklore. For one thing, it is very likely that they collect other items, such as books (some of which may be in languages they cannot really read), musical instruments (some of which they may be unable to play), records, bibliography, stamps, etc. Walter Anderson, for example, is a bibliographer and numismatist (Kiefer 1947:30). Some folklore collectors may have the habit of reading in the bathroom. (According to psychoanalysts, such reading is an act of incorporation intended to balance the material which is lost through defecation Fenichel 1953:374; Abraham 1948b:385, n. 1 .) If they are anal ejective and enjoy seeing their material in print, they may very well have the habit of looking at their feces after producing it. (The relationship between publishing and bowel habits was supported by the case of one collector who, soon after he started publishing scattered articles in various journals, began to suffer from repeated diarrhea. It would be interesting to know whether those folklorists who have difficulty in publishing ever suffer from constipation. Unfortunately, there is no data available on this point and it is doubtful if those in a position to provide data would be self-sacrificing enough to furnish it!) If they are anal retentive, they may have the habit of never being able to throw anything out. It has been noted that "An unwillingness ever to throw anything away, while in itself not enough to make a collector, is certainly a characteristic directly related to collecting." (Rigby and Rigby 1944:97). Thus it is no suprise to learn that the celebrated Norwegian collector Asbjörnsen is described as being "virtually incapable of destroying a scrap of paper if anything was written on it" (Christiansen 1953:14).

While this by no means exhausts the possible anal personality characteristics of collectors of folklore, it is at least an indication of some possible ones. It is to be hoped that someday there will be enough data to explain more fully the psychology of collecting folklore as well as numerous other forms of collecting activity. It may well turn out that the reasons why folklorists collect folklore are related to the reasons why certain members of the folk collect folklore, the latter in some cases becoming prize informants for the professional folklorist. *12

NOTES

*1 Harold Laurence Leisure's autobiographical account of his change from an "incorrigible collector of such bulky objects as books, old glass antiques", to an enthusiastic collector of folklore, also attests to the affinity of various collecting activities. See Leisure (1940).

*2 G. Stanley Hall (1891) referred to the collecting instinct as an "almost universal force in human nature". He suggested that this instinct be studied inasmuch as it was the basis of much of scientific research, pointing out that even the gathering of data about collecting depended upon this very instinct. The first important study of children's collections was Burk (1900). This study as well as subsequent ones are surveyed by Durost (1932).

*3 Witty and Lehman (1930:113,124). For an enlightening discussion of the interrelationship between instinctual drives and cultural environment with regard to collecting activity, see Fenichel (1938).

*4 Orlansky (1949:17). A survey of the Freudian position may be found in Karpman (1948). For a lucid account of the limitations involved in the application of even a modified form of Freudian theory to a non-Western society, see S. H. Posinsky (1957).

*5 Geza Roheim has repeatedly maintained that occupation choice is determined by infantile conditioning. See Roheim (1934) or (1943). The specific suggestion of vocations ideally suited for anal erotics is made by White (1923).

*6 Somewhat analogous to the collecting of Child numbers by ballad scholars is the collecting of Aarne-Thompson tale types by folktale specialists. Taylor (1951) mentions Anders Allardt who printed in full one example of each Aarne-Thompson tale type.

*7 I am indebted to Jan Brunvand for suggesting Frank C. Brown as a possible example of a folklore collector with some of the personality traits described in this study. All of the data on Brown cited comes from White (1952).

*8 The identification of folklore and treasure is not uncommon. For example, the first paragraph of Pearce (1954-55:20), makes extensive use of the equation: "A folklore hunt is like a search for buried treasure: all the clues are present in both, but the secret is illusive no matter how earnest the pursuit. Perhaps with folk treasure the yield is more often productive. My experience in searching for the author of the Las Palomas-Pastores play had all the elements of a treasure hunt. Unlike many a chase after hidden gold, this mystery was solved, and the solution may open the way to solving other mysteries and uncovering more folklore treasure."

*9 In view of the hypothetical partial anal erotic basis of the prejudice against Negroes - Negroes are commonly considered as being black, smelly, and dirty - it is noteworthy that the few eminent American folklorists who have recently collected Negro material are "tolerant on the matter of dirt" and have even collected and published obscene, i.e. "dirty" folklore. For the suggestion that there may be an anal erotic reason for Negro prejudice, see Kubie (1937).

*10 See Dorson p. 170 (1950) for a discussion of his term "fakelore".

*11 It should, of course, be obvious that for the scientific study of folklore, it is imperative that texts should not be altered or changed in any way by the professional folklorist for purposes of publication. Even the most careful minimal editing risks destroying potential data.

*12 The striking similarity between informants with large repertoires and professional folklore collectors has recently been noted by Seeger (1962).

13

EARTH-DIVER: CREATION OF THE MYTHOPOEIC MALE

Few anthropologists are satisfied with the present state of scholarship with re-spect to primitive mythology. While not everyone shares Lévi-Strauss's extreme pessimistic opinion that from a theoretical point of view the study of myth is "very much the same as it was fifty years ago, namely a picture of chaos" (1958:50), still there is general agreement that much remains to be done in elucidating the processes of the formation, transmission, and functioning of myth in culture.

One possible explanation for the failure of anthropologists to make any no-table advances in myth studies is the rigid adherence to two fundamental prin-ciples: a literal reading of myth and a study of myth in monocultural context. The insistence of most anthropologists upon the literal as opposed to the sym-bolic interpretation, in terms of cultural relativism as opposed to transcultural universalism, is in part a continuation of the reaction against 19th century thought in which universal symbolism in myth was often argued and in part a direct result of the influence of two dominant figures in the history of anthro-pology, Boas and Malinowski. Both these pioneers favored studying one culture at a time in depth and both contended that myth was essentially nonsymbolic. Boas often spoke of mythology reflecting culture, implying something of a one-to-one relationship. With this view, purely descriptive ethnographic data could be easily culled from the mythological material of a particular culture. Mali-nowsky argued along similar lines: "Studied alive, myth, as we shall see, is not symbolic, but a direct expression of its subject matter" (1954:101). Certain-ly, there is much validity in the notion of mythology as a cultural reflector, as the well documented researches of Boas and Malinowsky demonstrate. However, as in the case of most all-or-nothing approaches, it does not account for all the data. Later students in the Boas tradition, for example, noted that a comparison between the usual descriptive ethnography and the ethnographical picture ob-tained from mythology revealed numerous discrepancies. Ruth Benedict (1935) in her important Introduction to Zuni Mythology spoke of the tendency to idealize and compensate in folklore. More recently, Katherine Spencer has contrasted the correspondences and discrepancies between the ethnographical and mytho-logical accounts. She also suggests that the occurrence of folkloristic material which contradicts the ethnographic data "may be better explained in psycho-logical than in historical terms" (1947:130). However, anthropologists have tended to mistrust psychological terms, and consequently the pendulum has not

Reprinted from American Anthropologist 64 (1962), 1032-51.

yet begun to swing away from the literal to the symbolic reading of myth. Yet it is precisely the insights afforded by advances in human psychology which open up vast vistas for the student of myth. When anthropologists learn that to study the products of the human mind (e. g. myths) one must know something of the mechanics of the human mind, they may well push the pendulum towards not only the symbolic interpretation of myth but also towards the discovery of universals in myth.

Freud himself was very excited at the possibility of applying psychology to mythology. In a letter to D. E. Oppenheim in 1909, he said, "I have long been haunted by the idea that our studies on the content of the neuroses might be destined to solve the riddle of the formation of myths...." (Freud and Oppenheim 1958:13). However, though Freud was pleased at the work of his disciples, Karl Abraham and Otto Rank, in this area, he realized that he and his students were amateurs in mythology. 'In the same letter to Oppenheim he commented. "We are lacking in academic training and familiarity with the material." Unfortunately, those not lacking in these respects had little interest in psychoanalytic theory. To give just one example out of many, Lewis Spence in his preface to An Introduction to Mythology stated: "The theories of Freud and his followers as to religion and the origin of myth have not been considered, since, in the writer's opinion, they are scarcely to be taken seriously." What was this theory which was not to be taken seriously? Freud wrote the following: "As a matter of fact, I believe that a large portion of the mythological conception of the world which reaches far into the most modern religions, is nothing but psychology projected to the outer world. The dim perception (the endopsychic perception, as it were) of psychic factors and relations of the unconscious was taken as a model in the construction of a transcendental reality, which is destined to be changed again by science into psychology of the unconscious" (1938:164). It is this insight perhaps more than any other that is of value to the anthropologist interested in primitive myth.

There is, however, an important theoretical difficulty with respect to the psychoanalytic interpretation of myth. This difficulty stems from the fact that there are basically two ways in which psychoanalytic theory may be applied. A myth may be analyzed with a knowledge of a particular mythmaker, or a myth may be analyzed without such knowledge. There is some doubt as to whether the two methods are equally valid and, more specifically, whether the second is as valid as the first. The question is, to employ an analogy, can a dream be analyzed without a knowledge of the specific dreamer who dreamed it? In an anthropological context, the question is: can a myth be interpreted without a knowledge of the culture which produced it? Of course, it is obvious that any psychoanalyst would prefer to analyze the dreamer or myth-maker in order to interpret more accurately a dream or myth. Similarly, those anthropologists who are inclined to employ psychoanalysis in interpreting myths prefer to relate the manifest and latent content of myths to specific cultural contexts. However, this raises another important question. Do myths reflect the present, the past, or both? There are some anthropologists who conceive of myths almost exclusively in terms of the present. While tacitly recognizing that traditional myths are of considerable antiquity, such anthropologists, nevertheless, proceed to analyze a present-day culture in terms of its myths. Kardiner's theory of folklore, for instance, reveals this bias. Speaking of the myths of women in Marquesan folklore, Kardiner observes, "These myths are the products of the fantasy of some individual, communicated and probably changed many times before we get them. The uniformity of the stories points to some common experience of all individuals in this culture, not remembered from the remote past, but currently experienced." According to Kardiner, then, myths are responses to current realities. (1939: 417,214). Roheim summarizes Kardiner's position before taking issue with it. "According to Kardiner, myths and folklore always reflect the unconscious conflicts of the present generation as they are formed by the pressure brought to bear on them by existing social conditions. In sharp contrast to Freud, Reik, and myself, a myth represents not the dim past but the present." (1940:540).

The evidence available from folklore scholarship suggests that there is remarkable stability in oral narratives. Myths and tales re-collected from the same culture show considerable similarity in structural pattern and detail despite the fact that the myths and tales are from different informants who are perhaps separated by many generations. Excluding consideration of modern myths (for the myth-making process is an ongoing one), one can see that cosmogonic myths, to take one example, have not changed materially for hundreds of years. In view of this, it is clearly not necessarily valid to analyze a present-day culture in terms of that culture's traditional cosmogonic myths, which in all likelihood date from the prehistoric past. An example of the disregard of the time element occurs in an interesting HRAF-inspired cross-cultural attempt to relate child-training practices to folk tale content. Although the tales were gathered at various times between 1890 and 1940, it was assumed that "a folk tale represents a kind of summation of the common thought patterns of a number of individuals ..." (McClelland and Friedman 1952:245). Apparently common thought patterns are supposed to be quite stable and not subject to cultural change during a fifty year period. Thus just one version of a widely diffused North American Indian tale type like the Eye Juggler is deemed sufficient to "diagnose the modal motivations" of the members of a culture.

Nevertheless, Kardiner's theoretical perspective is not entirely without merit. Changes in myth do occur and a careful examination of a number of variants of a particular myth may show that these changes tend to cluster around certain points in time or space. Even if such changes are comparatively minor in contrast to the over-all structural stability of a myth, they may well serve as meaningful signals of definite cultural changes. Thus, Martha Wolfenstein's comparison of English and American versions of Jack and the Beanstalk (1955) showed a number of interesting differences in detail, although the basic plot remained the same. She suggested that the more phallic details in the American versions were in accord with other cultural differences between England and America. Whether or not one agrees with Wolfenstein's conclusions, one can appreciate the soundness of her method. The same myth or folk tale can be profitably compared using versions from two or more separate cultures, and the differences in detail may well illustrate significant differences in culture. One thinks of Nadel's (1937) adaptation of Bartlett's experiment in giving an artificial folk tale to two neighboring tribes in Africa and his discovery that the variations fell along clear-cut cultural lines, rather than along individualistic lines.

However, the basic theoretical problem remains unresolved. Can the myth as a whole be analyzed meaningfully? Margaret Mead in commenting briefly on

Wolfenstein's study begs the entire question. She states: "What is important here is that Jack and the Beanstalk, when it was first made up, might have had a precise and beautiful correspondence to the theme of a given culture at a given time. It then traveled and took on all sorts of forms, which you study and correlate with the contemporary cultural usage" (Tax 1953:282). The unfortunate truth is that rarely is the anthropologist in a position to know when and where a myth is "first made up". Consequently, the precise and beautiful correspondence is virtually unattainable or rather unreconstructible. The situation is further complicated by the fact that many, indeed, the majority of myths are found widely distributed throughout the world. The historical record, alas, only goes back so far. In other words, it is, practically speaking, impossible to ascertain the place and date of the first appearance(s) of a given myth. For this reason, anthropologists like Mead despair of finding any correspondence between overall myth structure and culture. Unfortunately, some naive scholars manifest a profound ignorance of the nature of folklore by their insistent attempts to analyze a specific culture by analyzing myths found in a great many cultures. For example, the subject of a recent doctoral dissertation was an analysis of 19th century German culture on the basis of an analysis of the content of various Grimm tales (Mann 1958). Although the analyses of the tales were ingenious and psychologically sound, the fact that the Grimm tales are by no means limited to the confines of Germany, and furthermore are undoubtedly much older than the 19th century, completely vitiates the theoretical premise underlying the thesis. Assuming the validity of the analyses of the tales, these would presumably be equally valid wherever the tales appeared in the same form. Barnouw (1955) commits exactly the same error when he analyzes Chippewa personality on the basis of a Chippewa "origin legend" which, in fact, contains many standard North American Indian tale types (Wycoco). It is clearly a fallacy to analyze an international tale or widely diffused myth as if it belonged to only one culture. Only if a myth is known to be unique, that is, peculiar to a given culture, is this kind of analysis warranted. It is, however, perfectly good procedure to analyze the differences which occur as a myth enters another culture. Certainly, one can gain considerable insight into the mechanics of acculturation by studying a Zuni version of a European cumulative tale or a native's retelling of the story of Beowulf. Kardiner is at his best when he shows how a cultural element is adapted to fit the basic personality structure of the borrowing culture. His account of the Comanche's alteration of the Sun Dance from a masochistic and self-destructive ritual to a demonstration of feats of strength is very convincing. (1945:93).

If it is theoretically only permissible to analyze the differentiae of widely diffused myths or the entire structure of myths peculiar to a particular culture, does this mean that the entire structure of widely diffused myths (which are often the most interesting) cannot be meaningfully analyzed? This is, in essence, the question of whether a dream can be analyzed without knowledge of the dreamer. One answer may be that to the extent that there are human universals, such myths may be analyzed. From this vantage point, while it may be a fallacy to analyze a world-wide myth as if it belonged to only one culture, it is not a fallacy to analyze the myth as if it belonged to all cultures in which it appears. This does not preclude the possibility that one myth found in many cultures may

have as many meanings as there are cultural contexts (Boas 1910b:383). Nevertheless, the hypothesis of a limited number of organic human universals suggests
some sort of similar, if not identical, meaning. It should not be necessary to
observe that, to the extent that anthropologists are scientists, they need not
fear anathematic reductionism and the discovery of empirically observable universals. The formula $e = mc^2$ is nonetheless valid for its being reductionistic.

A prime example of an anthropologist interested in universals is Kluckhohn.
In his paper, "Universal Categories of Culture", Kluckhohn contends that "The
inescapable fact of cultural relativism does not justify the conclusion that cultures are in all respects utterly disparate monads and hence strictly noncom-
parable entities" and "Valid cross-cultural comparison could best proceed from
the invariant points of reference supplied by the biological, psychological, and
socio-situational 'givens' of human life" (1953:520,521). Of even more interest
is Kluckhohn's conviction that these "givens" are manifested in myth. In "Recurrent Themes in Myths and Mythmaking", he discusses "certain features of
mythology that are apparently universal or that have such wide distribution in
space and time that their generality may be presumed to result from recurrent
reactions of the human psyche to situations and stimuli of the same general order" (1959:268). Kluckhohn's recurrent themes appear somewhat similar to
Freud's typical dreams. Although Freud specifically warned against codifying
symbolic translations of dream content and, although he did clearly state his belief that the same dream content could conceal a different meaning in the case
of different persons or contexts, he did consider that there are such things as
typical dreams, "dreams which almost every one has dreamed in the same
manner, and of which we are accustomed to assume that they have the same
significance in the case of every dreamer" (1938:292,39). While there are not
many anthropologists who would support the view that recurrent myths have
similar meaning irrespective of specific cultural context, that does not mean
that the view is false. For those who deny universal meanings, it might be mentioned that the reasons why a particular myth has widespread distribution have
yet to be given. The most ardent diffusionist, as opposed to an advocate of poly-
genesis or convergence, can do little more than show how a myth spreads. The
"how" rarely includes the "why". In order to show the plausibility of a symbolic
and universal approach to myth, a concrete example will be analyzed in some
detail.

One of the most fascinating myths in North American Indian mythology is that
of the earth-diver. Anna Birgitta Rooth in her study of approximately 300 North
American Indian creation myths found that, of her eight different types, earth-
diver had the widest distribution. Earl W. Count who has studied the myth for a
number of years considers the notion of a diver fetching material for making
dry land "easily among the most widespread single concepts held by man" (1952:
55). Earth-diver has recently been studied quite extensively by the folklorist
Elli Kaija Köngäs (1960) who has skillfully surveyed the mass of previous pertinent scholarship. The myth as summarized by Erminie Wheeler-Voegelin is:

> In North American Indian myths of the origin of the world, the culture hero
> has a succession of animals dive into the primeval waters, or flood of waters,
> to secure bits of mud or sand from which the earth is to be formed. Various

animals, birds, and aquatic creatures are sent down into the waters that cover the earth. One after another animal fails; the last one succeeds, however, and floats to the surface half dead, with a little sand or dirt in his claws. Sometimes it is Muskrat, sometimes Beaver, Hell-diver, Crawfish, Mink who succeeds, after various other animals have failed, in bringing up the tiny bit of mud which is then put on the surface of the water and magically expands to become the world of the present time. (1949:334).

Among the interesting features of this myth is the creation from mud or dirt. It is especially curious in view of the widespread myth of the creation of man from a similar substance (Frazer 1935:4-15). Another striking characteristic is the magical expansion of the bit of mud. Moreover, how did the idea of creating the earth from a particle of dirt small enough to be contained beneath a claw or fingernail develop, and what is there in this cosmogonic myth that has caused it to thrive so in a variety of cultures, not only in aboriginal North America but in the rest of the world as well?

Freud's suggestion that mythology is psychology projected upon the external world does not at a first glance seem applicable in the case of the earth-diver myth. The Freudian hypothesis is more obvious in other American Indian cosmogonic conceptions, such as the culture hero's Oedipal separation of Father Sky and Mother Earth (Roheim 1921:163) or the emergence myth, which appears to be man's projection of the phenomenon of human birth. This notion of the origin of the emergence myth was clearly stated as early as 1902 by Washington Matthews with apparently no help from psychoanalysis. At that time Matthews proposed the idea that the emergence myth was basically a "myth of gestation and of birth". A more recent study of the emergence myth by Wheeler-Voegelin and Moore makes a similar suggestion en passant, but no supporting details are given (1957:73-74). Roheim, however, had previously extended Matthews' thesis by suggesting that primitive man's conception of the world originated in the prenatal perception of space in the womb (1921:163). In any event, no matter how close the emergence of man from a hole in Mother Earth might appear to be to actual human birth, it does not appear to help in determining the psychological prototype for the earth-diver myth. Is there really any "endo-psychic" perception which could have served as the model for the construction of a cosmogonic creation from mud?

The hypothesis here proposed depends upon two key assumptions. The two assumptions (and they are admittedly only assumptions) are: (1) the existence of a cloacal theory of birth; and (2) the existence of pregnancy envy on the part of males. With regard to the first assumption, it was Freud himself who included the cloacal theory as one of the common sexual theories of children. The theory, in essence, states that since the child is ignorant of the vagina and is rarely permitted to watch childbirth, he assumes that the lump in the pregnant woman's abdomen leaves her body in the only way he can imagine material leaving the body, namely via the anus. In Freud's words: "Children are all united from the outset in the belief that the birth of a child takes place by the bowel; that is to say, that the baby is produced like a piece of faeces" (1953: 328). The second assumption concerns man's envy of woman's child-bearing role. Whether it is called "parturition envy" (Boehm) or "pregnancy envy"

(Fromm), the basic idea is that men would like to be able to produce or create valuable material from within their bodies as women do. Incidentally, it is this second assumption which is the basis of Bruno Bettelheim's explanation of puberty initiation rites and the custom of couvade. His thesis is that puberty rites consist of a rebirth ritual of a special kind to the effect that the initiate is born anew from males. The denial of women's part in giving birth is evidenced by the banning of women from the ceremonies. Couvade is similarly explained as the male's desire to imitate female behavior in childbirth. A number of psychoanalysts have suggested that man's desire for mental and artistic creativity stems in part from the wish to conceive or produce on a par with women (Jones 1957: 40; Fromm 1951:233; Huckel 1953:44). What is even more significant from the point of view of mythology is the large number of clinical cases in which men seek to have babies in the form of feces, or in which men imagine themselves excreting the world. Felix Boehm makes a rather sweeping generalization when he says: "In all analyses of men we meet with phantasies of anal birth, and we know how common it is for men to treat their faeces as a child." (1930:455; see also Silberer 1925:393). However, there is a good deal of clinical evidence supporting the existence of this phantasy. Stekel (1959:45), for example, mentions a child who called the feces "Baby". The possible relevance of this notion to the myth of the origin of man occurred to Abraham (1948a:320), Jung (1916:214), and Rank (1922:54). Jung's comment is: "The first people were made from excrement, potter's earth and clay." (Cf. Schwarzbaum 1960:48). In fact, Jung rather ingeniously suggests that the idea of anal birth is the basis of the motif of creating by "throwing behind oneself" as in the case of Deucalion and Pyrrha. Nevertheless, neither Abraham, Jung, nor Rank emphasized the fact that anal birth is especially employed by men. It is true that little girls also have this phantasy, but presumably the need for the phantasy disappears upon the giving of birth to a child. (There may well be some connection between this phantasy and the widespread occurrence of geophagy among pregnant women Elwin[1949: 292, n. 1].)

Both of the assumptions underlying the hypothesis attempting to explain the earth-diver myth are found in Genesis. As Fromm points out (1951:234), the woman's creative role is denied. It is man who creates and, in fact, it is man who gives birth to woman. Eve is created from substance taken from the body of Adam. Moreover, if one were inclined to see the Noah story as a gestation myth, it would be noteworthy that it is the man who builds the womb-ark. It would also be interesting that the flood waters abate only after a period roughly corresponding to the length of human pregnancy. Incidentally, it is quite likely that the Noah story is a modified earth-diver myth. The male figure sends a raven once and a dove twice to brave the primordial waters seeking traces of earth. (Cf. Schwarzbaum 1960:52, n.15a.) In one apocryphal account, the raven disobeys instructions by stopping to feast on a dead man, and in another he is punished by having his feathers change color from white to black (Ginzberg 1925:39, 164). Both of these incidents are found in American Indian earth-diver myths (Rooth 1957:498). In any case, one can see that there are male myths of creation in Genesis, although Fromm does not describe them all. Just as Abraham, Jung, and Rank had anal birth without pregnancy envy, Fromm has pregnancy envy without anal birth. He neglects to mention that man was created

from dust. One is tempted to speculate as to whether male creation myths might
be in any way correlated with highly patriarchal social organization.

Of especial pertinence to the present thesis is the clinical data on phantasies
of excreting the universe. Lombroso, for example, describes two artists, each
of whom had the delusion that they were lords of the world which they had excreted from their bodies. One of them painted a full-length picture of himself,
naked, among women, ejecting worlds (1895:201). In this phantasy world, the
artist flaunting his anal creativity depicts himself as superior to the women who
surround him. Both Freud and Stekel have reported cases in which men fancied
defecating upon the world, and Abraham cites a dream of a patient in which he
expelled the universe out of his anus (Freud 1949b:407; Stekel 1959:44; Abraham
1948a:320). Of course, the important question for the present study is whether
or not such phantasies ever occur in mythical form. Undoubtedly, the majority
of anthropologists would be somewhat loath to interpret the earth-diver myth as
an anal birth fantasy on the basis of a few clinical examples drawn exclusively
from Western civilization. However, the dearth of mythological data results
partly from the traditional prudery of some ethnographers and many folklorists.
Few myths dealing with excretory processes find their way into print. Nevertheless, there are several examples, primarily of the creation of man from excrement. John G. Bourke (1891:266) cites an Australian myth of such a creation
of man. In India, the elephant-headed god Ganesh is derived from the excrement
of his mother (Berkeley-Hill 1921:330). In modern India, the indefatigable Elwin has collected quite a few myths in which the earth is excreted. For instance,
a Lanjhia Saora version describes how Bhimo defecates on Rama's head. The
feces is thrown into the water which immediately dries up and the earth is
formed (1949:44). In a Gadaba myth, Larang the great Dano devoured the world,
but Mahaprabhu "caught hold of him and squeezed him so hard that he excreted
the earth he had devoured.... From the earth that Larang excreted, the world
was formed again" (1949:37). In other versions, a worm excretes the earth, or
the world is formed from the excreta of ants (1949:47; 1954:9). An example
closer to continental North America is reported by Bogoras. In this Chukchee
creation myth, Raven's wife tells Raven to go and try to create the earth, but
Raven protests that he cannot. Raven's wife then announces that she will try to
create a "spleen-companion" and goes to sleep. Raven "looks at his wife. Her
abdomen has enlarged. In her sleep she creates without effort. He is frightened,
and turns his face away." After Raven's wife gives birth to twins, Raven says,
"There, you have created men! Now I shall go and try to create the earth."
Then "Raven flies and defecates. Every piece of excrement falls upon water,
grows quickly, and becomes land." In this fashion, Raven succeeds in creating
the whole earth (Bogoras 1913:152). Here there can be no doubt of the connection between pregnancy envy and anal creation. Unfortunately, there are few
examples which are as clear as the Chukchee account. One of the only excremental creation myths reported in North America proper was collected by Boas.
He relates (1895:159) a Kwakiutl tale of Mink making a youth from his excrement. However, the paucity of American Indian versions does not necessarily
reflect the nonexistence of the myth in North America. The combination of puri-
tanical publishing standards in the United States with similar collecting standards may well explain in part the lack of data. In this connection it is note-

worthy that whereas the earlier German translation of Boas' Kwakiutl version refers specifically to excrement, the later English translation speaks of a musk-bag (1910a:159). Most probably ethnographers and editors alike share Andrew Lang's sentiments when he alludes to a myth of the Encounter Bay people, "which might have been attributed by Dean Swift to the Yahoos, so foul an origin does it allot to mankind" (1899:166). Despite the lack of a great number of actual excremental myths, the existence of any at all would appear to lend support to the hypothesis that men do think of creativity in anal terms, and further that this conception is projected into mythical cosmogonic terms.

There is, of course, another possible reason for the lack of overtly excremental creation myths and this is the process of sublimation. Ferenczi in his essay, "The Ontogenesis of the Interest in Money"(1956), has given the most explicit account of this process as he traces the weaning of the child's interest from its feces through a whole graduated series of socially sanctioned substitutes ranging from moist mud, sand, clay, and stones to gold or money. Anthropologists will object that Ferenczi's ontogenetic pattern is at best only applicable to Viennese type culture. But, to the extent that any culture has toilet training (and this includes any culture in which the child is not permitted to play indiscriminately with his feces), there is some degree of sublimation. As a matter of fact, so-called anal personality characteristics have been noted among the Yurok (Posinsky), Mohave (Devereux), and Chippewa (Barnouw, Hallowell). Devereux (1951:412) specifically comments upon the use of mud as a fecal substitute among the Mohave. Moreover, it may well be that the widespread practices of smearing the body with paint or daubing it with clay in preparation for aggressive activities have some anal basis. As for the gold-feces equation, anthropologists have yet to explain the curious linguistic fact that in Nahuatl the word for gold is teocuitlatl, which is a compound of teotl 'god', and cuitlatl 'excrement'. Gold is thus "excrement of the gods" or "divine excrement" (Saville 1920:118). This extraordinary confirmation of Freudian symbolism, pointed out by Reik as early as 1915, has had apparently little impact upon anthropologists blindly committed to cultural relativism. (See also Roheim 1923:387. However, for an example of money/feces symbolism in the dream of a Salteaux Indian, see Hallowell 1938.) While the gold-feces symbolism is hardly likely in cultures where gold was unknown, there is reason for assuming that some sort of sublimation does occur in most cultures. (For American Indian instances of "jewels from excrements" see Thompson 1929:329, n.190a. In this connection, it might be pointed out that in Oceanic versions of the creation of earth from an object thrown on the primeval waters, as found in Lessa's recent comprehensive study [1961], the items thrown include, in addition to sand, such materials as rice chaff, betel nut husks, and ashes, which would appear to be waste products.) If this is so, then it may be seen that a portion of Ferenczi's account of the evolutionary course of anal sublimation is of no mean importance to the analysis of the earth-diver myth. Ferenczi states: "Even the interest for the specific odour of excrement does not cease at once, but is only displaced on to other odours that in any way resemble this. The children continue to show a liking for the smell of sticky materials with a characteristic odour, especially the strongly smelling degenerated produce of cast off epidermis cells which collects between the toes, nasal secretion, ear-wax, and the

dirt of the nails, while many children do not content themselves with the moulding and sniffing of these substances, but also take them into the mouth" (1956b:
273). Anyone who is familiar with American Indian creation myths will immediately think of examples of the creation of man from the rubbings of skin (Thompson 1955:Motif A 1263. 3), birth from mucus from the nose (Motif T 541. 8. 3),
etc. The empirical fact is that these myths do exist! With respect to the earth-
diver myth, the common detail of the successful diver's returning with a little
dirt under his fingernail is entirely in accord with Ferenzci's analysis. The
fecal nature of the particle is also suggested by its magical expansion. One
could imagine that as one defecates one is thereby creating an ever-increasing
amount of earth. (Incidentally, the notion of creating land masses through defecation has the corollary idea of creating bodies of water such as oceans through
micturition [Motif A 923. 1]. For example, in the previously mentioned Chukchee
myth, Raven, after producing the earth, began to pass water. A drop became a
lake, while a jet formed a river.)

The present hypothesis may also serve to elucidate the reasons why Christian
dualism is so frequently found in Eurasian earth-diver versions. Earl Count
considers the question of the dualistic nature of earth-diver as one of the main
problems connected with the study of the myth (1952:56). Count is not willing to
commit himself as to whether the earth-diver is older than a possible dualistic
overlay, but Köngas agrees with earlier scholars that the dualism is a later
development (Count 1952:61; Köngas 1960:168). The dualism usually takes the
form of a contest between God and the devil. As might be expected from the
tradition of philosophical dualism, the devil is associated with the body, while
God is concerned with the spiritual element. Thus it is the devil who dives for
the literally lowly dirt and returns with some under his nails. An interesting
incident in view of Ferenczi's account of anal sublimation is the devil's attempt
to save a bit of earth by putting it in his mouth. However, when God expands
the earth, the stolen bit also expands, forcing the devil to spit it out, whereupon mountains or rocks are formed (Köngas 1960:160-61). In this connection,
another dualistic creation myth is quite informative. God is unable to stop the
earth from growing and sends the bee to spy on the devil to find a way to ac-
complish this. When the bee buzzes as it leaves the devil to report back to God,
the devil exclaims, "Let him eat your excrement, whoever sent you!" God does
this and the earth stops growing (Dragomanov 1961:3). Since the eating of excrement prevented the further growth of the earth, one can see the fecal nature
of the substance forming the earth. In still another dualistic creation myth,
there is even an attempt made to explain why feces exists at all in man. In this
narrative, God creates a pure body for man but has to leave it briefly in order
to obtain a soul. In God's absence, the devil defiles the body. God, upon returning, has no alternative but to turn his creation inside out, which is why man has
impurities in his intestines (Campbell 1956:294). These few examples should
be sufficient to show that the dualism is primarily a matter of separating the
dross of matter from the essence of spirit. The devil is clearly identified with
matter and in particular with defecation. In a phrase, it is the devil who does
the dirty work. Thus Köngas is quite right in seeing a psycho-physical dualism, that is, the concept of the soul as being separable from the body, as the
basis for the Christian traditional dualism. However, she errs in assuming

that both the creator and his "doppelgänger" are spiritual or concerned with the spiritual (1960:169). Dualism includes one material entity and, specifically in earth-diver dualism, one element deals with dirt while the other creates beauty and valuable substance from the dirt.

Earth-diver has been previously studied from a psychoanalytic perspective. Géza Róheim, the first psychoanalytic anthropologist, made a great number of studies of the folklore and mythology of primitive peoples. In his earlier writings, Róheim tended to follow along the lines suggested by Freud, Abraham, and Rank in seeing folk tales as analogous to dreams (1922:182), but later, after he discovered, for example, that the Aranda word altjira meant both dream and folk tale (1941:267), he began to speculate a more genetic relationship between dream and folk tale or myth. In a posthumously published paper, "Fairy Tale and Dream" (1953a), this new theory of mythology and the folk tale is explained. "To put this theory briefly: It seems that dreams and myths are not merely similar but that a large part of mythology is actually derived from dreams. In other words, we can not only apply the standard technique of dream interpretation in analyzing a fairy tale but can actually think of tales and myths as having arisen from a dream, which a person dreamed and then told to others, who retold it again, perhaps elaborated in accord with their own dreams"(1953a:394; for a sample of Róheim's exegesis of what he terms as dream-derived folk tale, see 1953b). The obvious criticism of this theory has been made by E. K. Schwartz in noting that "one can accept the same psychoanalytic approach and techniques for the understanding of the fairy tale and the dream, without having to accept the hypothesis that the fairy tale is nothing else but an elaboration of a dream" (1956:747-48). Thus Schwartz, although he lists 12 characteristics of fairy tales which he also finds in dreams, including such features as condensation, displacement, symbolism, etc., does conclude that it is not necessary to assume that fairy tales are dreams. Róheim, in The Gates of the Dream, a brilliant if somewhat erratic full-length treatment of primitive myth and dream, had already addressed himself to this very criticism. He phrases the criticism rhetorically: "Then why assume the dream stage, since the unconscious would contain the same elements, even without dreams?" His answer is that the dream theory would explain not only the identity in content but also the striking similarity in structure and plot sequence (1951:348). Actually, the fundamental criticism is not completely explained away. There is no reason why both dream and myth cannot be derived from the human mind without making the myth only indirectly derived via the dream.

Róheim's theory comes to the fore in his analysis of earth-diver. In fact, he even states that the earth-diver myth is "a striking illustration of the dream origin of mythology" (1951:423). Róheim has assumed the existence of what he calls a basic dream in which the dreamer falls into something, such as a lake or a hole. According to Róheim, this dream is characterized by a "double vector" movement consisting both of a regression to the womb and the idea of the body as penis entering the vagina. In interpreting the earth-diver as an example of this basic dream, Róheim considers the diving into the primeval waters of the womb as an erection. Of considerable theoretical interest is Róheim's apparent postulation of a monogenetic origin of earth-diver: "The core of the myth is a dream actually dreamed once upon a time by one person. Told and retold it became a myth. . . . " (1951:428). Actually, Róheim's over-all theory of the dream origin of myth is not at all necessarily a matter of monogenesis. In fact, he states that it is hardly likely as a general rule that an original dream was dreamed by one person in a definite locality, from which the story spread by migration. Rather, "many have dreamed such dreams, they shaped the narrative form in many centers, became traditional, then merged and influenced each other in the course of history" (1951:348).

The validity of Róheim's interpretation of earth-diver depends a great deal on, first of all, his theory of the dream origin of myth and, secondly, the specific nature of his so-called basic dream. Once could say, without going so far as to deny categorically Róheim's theoretical contentions, that neither the dream origin of myth nor the existence of the "basic dream" is necessary for an understanding of the latent content of the earth-diver myth. Curiously enough, Róheim himself anticipates in part the present hypothesis in the course of making some additional comments on earth-diver. In discussing the characteristic trait of the gradual growth of the earth, Róheim cites an Onondaga version in which he points out the parallelism between a pregnant woman and the growing earth. From the point of view of the present hypothesis, the parallelism is quite logically attributable to the male creator's desire to achieve something like female procreativity. Thus the substance produced from his body, his baby so to speak, must gradually increase in size, just as the process of female creativity entails a gradually increasing expansion. (Here again, the observation of the apparently magically expanding belly of a pregnant woman is clearly a human universal.) Róheim goes on to mention what he considers to be a parallel myth, namely that of "the egg-born earth or cloacal creation". As will be shown later, Róheim is quite correct in drawing attention to the egg myth. Then following his discussion of the Eurasian dualistic version in which the devil tries to keep a piece of swelling earth in his mouth, Róheim makes the following analysis: "If we substitute the rectum for the mouth the myth makes sense as an awakening dream conditioned by excremental pressure" (1951:429). In other words, Róheim does recognize the excremental aspects of earth-diver and in accordance with his theory of the dream origin of myth, he considers the myth as initially a dream caused by the purely organic stimulus of the need to defecate. Róheim also follows Rank (1912, 1922:89) in interpreting deluge myths as transformations of vesical dreams (1951:439-65). Certainly, one could make a good case for the idea that some folk tales and myths are based upon excremental pressures, perhaps originally occurring during sleep. In European folklore, there are numerous examples, as Freud and Oppenheim have amply demonstrated, of folk tales which relate how individuals attempt to mark buried treasure only to awake to find they have defecated on themselves or on their sleeping partners. It is quite possible that there is a similar basis for the Winnebago story reported by Radin (1956:26-27) in which Trickster, after eating a laxative bulb, begins to defecate endlessly. In order to escape the rising level of excrement, Trickster climbs a tree, but he is forced to go higher and higher until he finally falls down right into the rising tide. Another version of this Trickster adventure is found in Barnouw's account of a Chippewa cycle (1955:82). The idea of the movement being impossible to stop once it has started is also suggested in the previously cited Eurasian account of God's inability to stop the earth's growth. That God must eat excrement to stop the movement is thematically similar to another Trickster version in which Trickster's own excrement, rising with flood waters, comes perilously close to his mouth and nose. However, the fact there may be "excremental pressure myths" with or without a dream origin does not mean that excremental pressure is the sole underlying motivation of such a myth as earth-diver. To call earth-diver simply a dream-like myth resulting from a call of nature without reference to the notions of male pregnancy envy and anal birth theory is vastly to oversimplify the psychological etiology of the myth. Róheim, by the way, never does reconcile the rather phallic interpretation of his basic dream with the excremental awakening dream interpretation of earth-diver. A multi-causal hypothesis is, of course, perfectly possible, but Róheim's two interpretations seem rather to conflict. In any event, Róheim sees creation myths as prime examples of his dream-myth thesis. He says, "It seems very probable that creation myths, wherever they exist, are ultimately based on dreams" (1951:430).

The idea of anal creation myths spurred by male pregnancy envy is not tied to the dream origin of myth theory. That is not to say that the dream theory is not entirely possible but only to affirm the independence of the two hypotheses. In order to document further the psychological explanation of earth-diver, several other creation myths will be very briefly discussed. As already mentioned, Róheim drew attention to the cosmic egg myths. There is clinical evidence suggesting that men who have pregnancy phantasies often evince a special interest in the activities of hens, particularly with regard to their laying of eggs (Eisler 1921:260,285). The hens appear to defecate the eggs. Freud's famous "Little Hans" in addition to formulating a "lumf" baby theory also imagined that he laid an egg (1949b:227-28). Lombroso (1895:182) mentions a demented pseudo-artist who painted himself as excreting eggs which symbolized worlds. Ferenczi, moreover, specifically comments upon what he calls the "symbolic identity of the egg with faeces and child". He suggests that excessive fondness for eggs "approximates much more closely to primitive coprophilia than does the more abstract love of money" (1950:328). Certainly, the egg-creation myth is common enough throughout the world (Lukas 1894), despite its absence in North America. It is noteworthy that there are creations of men from eggs (Motifs T 542 or A 1222) and creation of the world from a cosmic egg (Motif A 641). As in the case of feces (or mud, clay, or dirt), the cloacal creation is capable of producing either men or worlds or both.

Another anal creation myth which does occur in aboriginal North America has the spider as creator. The Spider myth, which is one of Rooth's eight creation myth types found in North America, is reported primarily in California and the Southwest. The spider as creator is also found in Asia and Africa. Empirical observation of spiders would quite easily give rise to the notion of the spider as a self-sufficient creator who appeared to excrete his own world, and a beautiful and artistic world at that. Although psychoanalysts have generally tended to interpret the spider as a mother symbol (Abraham 1948a:326-32; cf. Spider Woman in the Southwest), Freud noted at least one instance in folklore where the thread spun by a spider was a symbol for evacuated feces. In a Prussian-Silesian tale, a peasant wishing to return to earth from heaven is turned into a spider by Peter. As a spider, the peasant spins a long thread by which he descends, but he is horrified to discover as he arrives just over his home that he could spin no more. He squeezes and squeezes to make the thread longer and then suddenly wakes up from his dream to discover that "something very human had happened to him while he slept" (Freud and Oppenheim 1958: 45). The spider as the perfect symbol of male artistic creativity is described in a poem by Whitman entitled "The Spider". In the poem, the spider is compared to the soul of the poet as it stands detached and alone in "measureless oceans of space" launching forth filament out of itself (Wilbur and Muensterberger 1951:405). Without going into primitive Spider creation myths in great detail, it should suffice to note that, as in other types of male myths of creation, the creator is able to create without any reference to women. Whether a male creator spins material, molds clay, lays an egg, fabricates from mucus or epidermal tissue, or dives for fecal mud, the psychological motivation is much the same.

Other cosmogonic depictions of anal birth have been barely touched upon. As Ernest Jones has shown in some detail (1951a:266-357), some of the other aspects of defecation such as the sound (creation by thunder or the spoken word), or the passage of air (creation by wind or breath), are also of considerable importance in the study of mythology. With respect to the latter characteristic, there is the obvious Vedic example of Pragapati who created mankind by means of "downward breathings" from the "back part" cited by Jones (1951a:279). One account of Pragapati's creation of the earth relates the passing of air with the earth-diver story. "Prajapati first becomes a wind and stirs up the primeval ocean; he sees the earth in the depthts of the ocean; he turns himself into a boar and draws the earth up" (Dragomanov 1961:28). Another ancient male anal wind myth is found in the Babylonian account of Marduk. Marduk conquers Tiamat by the following means: "The evil wind which followed him, he loosed it in her face.... He drove in the evil wind so that she could not close her lips. The terrible winds filled her belly" (Guirand 1959:51). Marduk then pierces Tiamat's belly and kills her. The passage of wind by the male Marduk leads to the destruction of the female Tiamat. Marduk rips open the rival creator, the belly of woman, which had given birth to the world. There is also the Biblical instance of the divine (af)flatus moving on the face of the waters. Köngas (1960:169) made a very astute intuitive observation when she suggested that there was a basic similarity between the spirit of God moving upon the primeval water and the earth-diver myth. The common denominator is the male myth of creation whereby the male creator uses various aspects of the only means available, namely the creative power of the anus.

Undoubtedly anthropologists will be sceptical of any presentation in which evidence is marshalled á la Frazer and where the only criteria for the evidence appears to be the gristworthyness for the mill. Nevertheless, what is important is the possibility of a theory of universal symbolism which can be verified by empirical observation in the field in decades to come. Kluckhohn, despite a deepseated mistrust of pan-human symbolism, confesses that his own field work as well as that of his collaborators has forced him to the conclusion that "Freud and other psychoanalysts have depicted with astonishing correctness many central themes in motivational life which are universal. The styles of expression of these themes and much of the manifest content are culturally determined but the underlying psychological drama transcends cultural difference" (Wilbur and Muensterberger 1951:120). Kluckhohn bases his assumptions on the notion of a limited number of human "givens", such as human anatomy and physiology. While it is true that thoughts about the "givens" are not "given" in the same sense, it may be that their arising is inevitable. In other words, man is not born with the idea of pregnancy envy. It is acquired through experience, that is, through the mediation of culture. But if certain experiences are universal, such as the observation of female pregnancy, then there may be said to be secondary or derived "givens", using the term in an admittedly idiosyncratic sense. This is very important for the study of myth. It has already been pointed out that from a cultural relativistic perspective, the only portion of mythology which can be profitably studied is limited to those myths which are peculiar to a particular culture or those differences in the details of a widely diffused myth. Similarly, the literal approach can glean only so much ethnographic data from reflector myths. Without the assumption of symbolism and universals in myth, a vast amount of mythology remains of little use to the anthropologist. It should also be noted that there is, in theory, no conflict between accepting the idea of universals and advocating cultural relativism. It is not an "either/or" proposition. Some myths may be universal and others not. It is the all-or-nothing approach which appears to be erroneous. The same is true for the polygenesis-diffusion controversy; they also are by no means mutually exclusive. In the same way, there is no inconsistency in the statement that myths can either reflect or refract culture. (The phrase was suggested by A. K. Ramanujan.) Lévi-Strauss (1958:51) criticizes psychoanalytic interpretations of myth because, as he puts it, if there's an evil grandmother in the myths, "it will be claimed that in such a society grandmothers are actually evil and that mythology reflects the social structure and the social relations; but should the actual data be conflicting, it would be readily claimed that the purpose of mythology is to provide an outlet for repressed feelings. Whatever the situation may be, a clever dialetic will always find a way to pretend that a meaning has been unravelled." Although Lévi-Strauss may be justified insofar as he is attacking the "Have you stopped beating your wife?" antics of some psychoanalysts, there is not necessarily any inconsistency stemming from data showing that in culture A evil grandmothers in fact are also found in myth, while in culture B conscious norms of pleasant grandmothers disguise unconscious hatred for "evil" grandmothers, a situation which may be expressed in myth. In other words, myths can and usually do contain both conscious and unconscious cultural materials. To the extent that conscious and unconscious motivation may vary or be contradictory, so likewise can myth differ from or contradict ethnographic data. There is no safe monolithic theory of myth except that of judicious eclecticism as championed by E. B. Tylor. Mythology must be studied in cultural context in order to determine which individual mythological elements reflect and which refract the culture. But, more than this, the cultural relative approach must not preclude the recognition and identification of transcultural similarities and potential universals. As Kluckhohn said, "... the anthropologist for two generations has been obsessed with the differences between peoples, neglecting the equally real similarities -upon which the 'universal culture pattern' as well as the psychological uniformities are clearly built" (Wilbur and Muensterberger 1951:121). The theoretical implications for practical field work of seeking psychological uniformities are implicit. Ethnographers must remove the traditional blinders and must be willing to collect <u>all</u> pertinent material even if it borders on what is obscene by the ethnographer's ethnocentric standards. The ideal ethnographer must not be afraid of diving deep and coming up with a little dirt; for, as the myth relates, such a particle may prove immensely valuable and may expand so as to form an entirely new world for the students of man.

14

SUMMONING DEITY THROUGH RITUAL FASTING

Fasting, in the sense of total abstinence from all food, is found in religious
ritual among a great many peoples. Although fasting has often been confused
with specific individual food taboos, it should not be, as Hocart (1948) has pointed out. While fasting may be employed at various life-cycle rites of passage,
e. g. as a formalized expression of mourning, or as a prescribed prelude to
marriage, it is perhaps most commonly found as a means of placing the faster
in a relationship with the supernatural. More particularly, fasting often serves
as a ritual means of summoning deity.

In his extensive survey of fasting among the North American Indians, Blumensohn suggests that in the case of the Central Algonkian, the use of the fast as a
means of putting the faster into a personal relation with the supernatural is especially prominent. In fact, Blumensohn (1933) goes so far as to contend that
this use of fasting to promote a personal relation with the supernatural is peculiar to the Central Algonkian. In contrast, Radin (1914) in his general discussion
of North American Indian religion lists fasting as the first item under "The
Methods of Bringing Spirits into Relation with Man", not restricting it to any
particular culture area or tribe. It is not pertinent to the present study to ascertain just how widespread the practice of using fasting to enter into a relationship with the supernatural is. It is sufficient to note that clearly fasting is so
used. The present study is an attempt to explain the psychological origin of the
practice.

There have been a number of explanations offered as to the origin of ritual
fasting in general. None of them, however, satisfactorily explain why it is the
specific act of an individual's abstention from eating which apparently can magically induce or force a deity to approach. Spencer suggested that the practice
of offering all the available food to the dead caused temporary famine, which
was later stimulated by voluntary fasting. Mallery (1888:202) rightly called this
hypothesis more ingenious than satisfactory. Westermarck (1907:403), who made
an extended study of fasting, proposed the idea that fasting connected with mourning was the result of the fear of swallowing food polluted with the contagion of
death. It should be observed that even if Westermarck's hypothesis were valid
for death fasts, it would not illuminate the practice of fasting to summon a deity
inasmuch as no food polluted by death is involved. MacCulloch, in the tradition
of the British anthropological school of folklorists, sought a historical fact as
the basis of the custom. He argued that it derived from man's frequent periods

Reprinted from American Imago 20 (1963), 213-20.

of enforced fasting resulting from a "scarcity of or difficulty in obtaining food" (1951:759).

The question arises as to just how natural periods of famine could account for a ritual action designed to put an individual into contact with a supernatural being. A modern explanation is that fasting causes physiological weakness such that dreams and visions are more easily induced. Radin, for example, states that among American Indians, fasting was undergone "to superinduce religious feeling" (1914:367). However, this type of explanation is probably post hoc in the same way that the fear of trichinosis is as the rationale underlying the Jewish taboo against eating pork. Certainly, it is doubtful whether any American Indian would offer this rationalization for the practice. More likely the explanation would be closer to one offered by a Yale educated Winnebago born circa 1884: "Fasting is a universal practice among Indians. Sometimes they go without food from four to ten days at a time. The purpose of these fasts, in which I often took part, is to gain the compassion and blessing of some spirit, <u>in order that he may come and reveal himself.</u> "(Cloud 1916:401; italics mine).

A simple but plausible explanation of ritual fasting as a means of summoning a deity is implicit in Kardiner's extension of Freud's seminal concept of the infantile origin of religion. Freud, in speaking of man's relationship to deity, noted that "it has an infantile prototype, and is really only the continuation of this. For once before one has been in such a state of helplessness: as a little child in one's relationship to one's parents. " (Freud 1957; see also Jones 1951b: 195). Freud also explained animism in these terms: "When he personifies the forces of nature man is once again following an infantile prototype. He has learnt from the persons of his earliest environment that the way to influence them is to establish a relationship with them, and so, later on, with the same end in view, he deals with everything that happens to him as he dealt with those persons. "(Freud 1957:36). Kardiner's contribution consists of adding the dimension of cultural relativism to Freud's insight. He suggested that since parental care varies in different cultures, the infantile concept of the parents will likewise vary and thus the resultant concepts of deity will necessarily vary. He further observed that not only are the concepts of deity bound to vary from culture to culture in accordance with varying infantile concepts of the parent, but the means of communicating with and soliciting aid from the deity will be similarly determined. According to Kardiner (1945:234), how divine help is solicited or forfeited differs in different cultures as determined by the specific experiences of the child. Kardiner's view is as follows:

> ...the character of the demands made on the deity and the conditions under which such help can be solicited, are derived from the disciplines to which the child is subjected. He is thus taught the primary techniques by which aid can be secured from a more powerful individual. If the disciplines established by the parent are severe, the means of placating the god must likewise be associated with privations and punishments to establish the conditions for reinstatement of the conditions for being loved (1939:473).

Armed with these concepts, one is able to suggest why fasting is a perfectly natural technique for soliciting aid from a deity.

In many cultures, and particularly in those in which poor (i. e. sporadic, in-frequent) maternal care prevailed, it is probable that most infants would have in common the experience of feeling and enduring hunger for a considerable time before the supreme being looking after the helpless infants arrived. If this association of hunger with the arrival of the succoring parent became firmly rooted, then it would not be impossible for the idea to develop that the chances of the parent's coming were better, the more hungry the child was. Thus, trans-posing the infantile situation, the hungrier the suppliant, the faster he feels the god should come. Since the parent did come when the child was hungry (and in primitive societies this may have been the only time when parents or parent-surrogates heeded the cries of infants), it is natural to fast (i. e. to make one-self hungry) to cause the deified parent to come. The physiological fact that fasting did weaken the body and mind in such a way that visions were more fre-quent was undoubtedly a factor confirming the infantile logic.

If this hypothesis is valid, then one can see why fasting should be so common a means of attempting to "bring spirits into relation with man" to borrow Radin's phrase. The inherent correctness of the statement made by the educated Winne-bago, Henry Roe Cloud, that the purpose of fasting is to "gain the compassion and blessing of some spirit, in order that he may come and reveal himself", is also strikingly demonstrated. The present hypothesis also puts some of the older explanations in a new light. Inasmuch as the normal means of a mother's fulfilling her food-providing role entails breast feeding, Robertson Smith's (1957:434) thesis that "fasting is primarily nothing more than a preparation for the sacramental eating of holy flesh", may well be figuratively true. The same may be said of Bell's (1931:134) statement that "The Polynesian feels that in partaking of food he is linking himself with the gods. "

The hypothesis may also be useful in elucidating some of the other functions of ritual fasting, such as funeral fasts. If death is conceived of in terms of pro-longed absence, and if prolonged absence may, from the infantile point of view, be translated into the deprivation of a food supply, then the immediate conse-quence of the departure (death) of a parent would be hunger. The fact that feast-ing very often occurs soon after a funeral fast is probably a reflection of an ambivalent attitude towards the dead. Freud (1938:855) has suggested that the taboo of the dead originates from the opposition "between the conscious grief and the unconscious satisfaction at death. " The curious combination of ex-pressions of sorrow and joy at funeral rituals has long been noted by folklorists (see, for example, Sokolov 1950:166, 224). The fast could be an expression of an individual's sorrow and loss, while the feast could be an expression of joy and gain. Incidentally, the ambivalence of the attitude towards the dead may well be the reason why riddles are often used in mourning ritual. Riddles, structurally speaking, usually consist of a juxtaposition of two apparently ir-reconcilable elements, e. g. what has eyes, but cannot see. The answer (po-tato) resolves the apparent contradiction and permits the two elements to co-exist. Presumably, by means of the principle of imitative magic, answering a riddle would aid in resolving the contradiction between fast and feast, that is, the contradiction resulting from the simultaneous feelings of sorrow and joy. In the same way, the riddle may function as a structural model intended to rec-oncile symbolically the mutually exclusive polarities of life and death. *1

The use of fasting as a prerequisite to marriage ritual may also be clarified by the infantile origin hypothesis. *2 Marriage ritual often consists simply of a woman's offering food to a man. If the man accepts the food, the marriage is considered solemnized. The offering of food by a woman to a man may well be a derivation from the infantile feeding situation and thus the bestowing of food may be understood as a primary act of love. If this is so, then the function of fasting is clear. If to be hungry is to want love, then the hungrier one is, the more love he needs and wants. If one fasts, then one produces a state of hunger which is construed as a state of desire for love.

Another type of ritual fasting is that employed by a creditor to recover goods withheld by a debtor. According to Clift (1909:163), the creditor camps on the debtor's doorstep and fasts. This ritual act legally forced the debtor to yield his goods. The idea that fasting could cause someone to give up an item withheld is in accord with the infantile origin hypothesis.

The present hypothesis may apply to ritual fasting as it occurs in funeral, marriage, and legal customs, but it was proposed principally to explain why fasting is used so frequently as a means of summoning a deity. It may not be amiss to point out that fasting before Communion is found in some forms of Christianity. In this connection, it is interesting that Charlemagne's attempt to enjoin fasting after Communion did not succeed. Hocart (1940:145) attributed this failure to "the introductory character of fasting", but in terms of the present scheme, the placing of the fast after the Communion would be contrary to the sequence of a lack and the lack liquidated as found in the infantile feeding situation.

If Kardiner is correct in his notion that cultural differences in the means of soliciting aid from a deity are attributable to differences in child care, then it would be interesting to ascertain whether or not there was any correlation between longer periods of religious fasting with poorer (by our standards) infant care. Presumably, the longer the infant had to wait for the parent, the longer the prescribed period of religious fasting would be. One would expect to find a positive correlation between deities who did not respond to prayer and who appeared only after long periods of fasting or severe self-mortification and poor infant care. By the same token, belief in the efficacy of prayer and little or no serious fasting would be likely to be found in cultures where infant care was good. In general, this is the case in contemporary American culture. Indeed, in this culture, parental care is often so profuse as to be administered even if not requested (schedule rather than demand feedings), and consequently there is less need for prayer, since the deity provides automatically. In such a culture, one would not expect to find much enthusiasm for the notion of summoning a deity by means of fasting. On the other hand, in primitive cultures such ritual abstinence is likely to continue so long as minimum maternal care of the young prevails.

NOTES

*1 Claude Lévi-Strauss suggested that the purpose of myth is to provide a logical model capable of overcoming a contradiction. He did not, however, refer to riddles in this connection. Recently, he compared the solved riddle with incest. "Like the solved riddle, incest brings together terms destined to remain separated: the son unites with the mother, the brother with the sister, as does the answer in successfully joining the question, contrary to every expectation." See Lévi-Strauss (1958:65) and (1960a:22). In the present analysis of riddle structure, it is the riddle answer which reconciles the two or more unrelated elements contained in the riddle question. This analysis illuminates another important function of riddles, namely their use in courtship ritual. Seeking a riddle answer is seeking a means of relating two unrelated terms. Furthermore, the answer (relationship) is concealed and secret. Once the answer has been given (or figuratively, the marriage-solemnizing act performed), the two un-related terms are related and the relationship is no longer secret. In this sense, riddles could serve as miniature models of marriage.

*2 For examples of courtship ritual fasting, see Westermarck (1922:544-45).

15

THE FATHER, THE SON, AND THE HOLY GRAIL

There are two basic subdivisions to the psychoanalytic approach to literature, divisions that fall along the traditional lines between historical-biographical criticism and "new criticism". In the former category, the critic seeks to analyze the author through his works and by so doing illuminate those works. The "new criticism" category, by analyzing in a vacuum, so to speak, is more obviously open to attacks of arbitrary symbol-mongering. The theoretical problem involved in psychoanalytic "new criticism" may be stated analogically as: can a dream by analyzed without a knowledge of the dreamer? This is an especially crucial question with regard to folkloristic material inasmuch as the authors are simply not known. The primary clue to the answer to this question comes from an examination of the extraordinary structural uniformity of folkloristic material and the literary works based thereupon.

Nowhere has this similarity in structure been more noticeable than in hero cycles, such as that of Arthur, for example. One of the most significant studies of this structure was made by Raglan in The Hero, first published in 1936. Raglan was not primarily concerned with describing the structure and patterning of hero cycles per se. His avowed aim in The Hero was to demonstrate folklore's lack of historicity and to trace the evolution of such cycles from myths which, he suggested, had in turn evolved from ritual (1956:41,141). He hoped that by showing the identity of incident and incident-sequence in the lives of a considerable number of heroes, it would become obvious that none of the heroes' adventures could be relied upon as bonafide history. His method resulted from his accidental discovery that many of the incidents contained in the Oedipus story also occurred in the accounts of Theseus and Romulus (p. 173). He then tabulated a sequential list of twenty-two incidents in the hero-pattern:

(1) The hero's mother is a royal virgin;

(2) His father is a king, and

(3) Often a near relative of his mother, but

(4) The circumstances of his conception are unusual, and

(5) He is also reputed to be the son of a god.

(6) At birth an attempt is made, usually by his father or his maternal grandfather, to kill him, but

(7) He is spirited away, and

(8).Reared by foster-parents in a far country.

Reprinted from Literature and Psychology 12 (1962), 101-12.

(9) We are told nothing of his childhood, but

(10) On reaching manhood he returns or goes to his future kingdom.

(11) After a victory over the king and/or a giant, dragon, or wild beast,

(12) He marries a princess, often the daughter of his predecessor, and

(13) Becomes king.

(14) For a time he reigns uneventfully, and

(15) Prescribes laws, but

(16) Later he loses favour with the gods and/or his subjects, and

(17) Is driven from the throne and city, after which

(18) He meets with a mysterious death,

(19) Often at the top of a hill.

(20) His children, if any, do not succeed him.

(21) His body is not buried, but nevertheless

(22) He has one or more holy sepulchres. (p. 174-75).

Raglan attempted to "fit the pattern" on twenty-one heroes of tradition. Each of these twenty-one test case heroes was given a score equal to the number of the twenty-two pattern incidents which occurred in his traditional life history. Some of these scores were: Oedipus, 22; Theseus, 20; Romulus, 18; Dionysos, 19; and Arthur, 19. From these and the other scores, Raglan concluded that the accounts of the heroes were not historical, although he did admit the possibility that

> ...the heroes were real persons whose stories were altered to make them conform to a ritual pattern.... The fact that the life of a hero of tradition can be divided up into a series of well-marked features and incidents - I have taken twenty-two, but it would be easy to take more - strongly suggests a ritual pattern. I doubt whether even the most fervent euhemerist would maintain that all these resemblances are mere coincidences... (p. 186).

Raglan maintained that the hero formula stemmed from a particular ritual; namely, ritual regicide. "The original ritual, so far as can be judged from the general pattern, was based on the existence of a king who was killed and replaced annually. " (p. 148; see also p. 150, 161). But the ultimate origin of the pattern is not explained by Raglan. Myth and ritual, he feels, are probably derived from "a common source", but what that common source might be, there is no hint (p. 148; see also Thompson 1958:105).

Curiously enough, Raglan was totally unaware that twenty-five years earlier, in 1909, a twenty-five-year-old student of Freud named Otto Rank had published a monograph, The Myth of the Birth of the Hero, covering much of the same material.*1 In this monograph, Rank examined fifteen hero cycles, including those of Oedipus, Moses, Jesus, and Tristram, and discovered "a series of uniformly common features... from which a standard saga, as it were, may be constructed. " (Rank 1959:65). Though Rank's outline is not identical with Raglan's, it is quite similar, particular if one remembers that Rank was primarily interested in the first part of the cycle, that is, the birth of the hero. Rank's pattern is:

The hero is the child of most distinguished parents, usually the son of a king.

His origin is preceded by difficulties, such as continence, or prolonged
barrenness, or secret intercourse of the parents due to external prohibition
or obstacles. During or before pregnancy, there is a prophecy, in the form
of a dream or oracle, cautioning against his birth, and usually threatening
danger to the father (or his representative). As a rule, he is surrendered to
the water, in a box. He is then saved by animals, or by lowly people (shep-
herds), and is suckled by a female animal or by a humble woman. After he
has grown up, he finds his distinguished parents, in a highly versatile fashion.
He takes his revenge on his father, on the one hand, and is acknowledged, on
the other. Finally he achieves rank and honors. (p. 65).

Rank, unlike Raglan, does not find the origin of the pattern in ritual. Instead
he explains it on the basis of infantile thought. More particularly, he sees the
myth as essentially a projection of the so-called family romance. The king and
queen represent the father and the mother, but whereas in actuality the youth
wishes to remove the father, in the myth the father tries to get rid of the child.
The mechanism is, of course, projection. Other elements of the pattern are explained in terms of the traditional Oedipus Complex. Thus, the virgin birth represents a complete repudiation of the father (Rank 1959:81; see also Jones 1951c
and d). The unusual circumstances of conception are similarly motivated. The
idea that the mother does not really welcome the father's sexual advances is
suggested by the fact that the father gains access to the mother by deceit or, in
the case of Arthur, by magic. The hero's conquest of a king, giant, or wild
beast is in this light the triumph over the father, while the marriage with the
queen or princess is, of course, the epitome of Oedipal wish-fulfillment. What
is important here is that the pattern of the hero in folklore and literature is
interpreted in terms of human activity. Because of the historical importance of
folklore theory in literary criticism, which anyone familiar with Jessie L.
Weston's work will doubtless acknowledge, it might be well to develop this last
point before proceeding to the Arthurian material.
    In general, past interpretions of hero patterns fall into two categories: cel-
estial and ritual. In the first category, human activity is seen as representing
the interaction of solar and lunar phenomena, and accordingly heroes are considered sun gods. In this celestial light, Oedipus becomes "the solar hero who
murders his procreator the darkness; he shares his couch with his mother, the
gloaming, from whose lap, the dawn. He has been born; he dies, blinded, as
the setting sun."*2 This theory is actually an excellent example of projection.
Advocates of this method of interpretation are

... in a position similar to that of the creators of the myths in that they strive
to disguise certain shocking motives by relation to nature, by projection of
the offensiveness upon the external world and thus to deny the mental reality
underlying the myth formation by the construction of an objective reality.
This defence tendency has probably been one of the chief motives for the mythical projection of shocking thoughts upon cosmic processes, and its possibility for reaction formation in the service of explanation of myths is naively
considered by the founders of the nature-mythological method of interpretation as an especial advantage of their method. Thus Max Müller avows that

"by this method, not merely do meaningless saga attain a real significance but that one may thereby eliminate some of the revolting traits of classical mythology and ascertain their true meaning. " (Rank and Sachs 1916:34; see also Rank 1959:11).

The second category, ritual, which has had a marked effect upon Arthurian criticism, brings interpretation down to earth but persists in projection. Solar heroes become ritual participants in seasonal rites. The son-father combat is interpreted as a ritual version of spring's eternal conquest over winter. Thus, for example, with regard to the Grail materials, Weston (1957:163) makes the following statement:

After upwards of thirty years spent in careful study of the Grail legend and romances I am firmly and entirely convinced that the root origin of the whole bewildering complex is to be found in the Vegetation Ritual, treated from the esoteric point of view as a Life-Cult, and in that alone. (Emphasis is Weston's).

Although a sexual element in the Grail legend is noted both by Weston (1957: 75) and by Roger Sherman Loomis (1927:262), they tend to follow Frazer (1951: 156-58) in regarding it, not as an end in itself, but merely as an effective bit of sympathetic magic to produce a good crop yield (Weston 1957:52-64, 75). Ritual-oriented critics take the primary phenomena to be aspects of vegetative rebirth just as celestial-oriented critics consider solar phenomena to be primary. These presumed primary phenomena or events are only acted out or symbolized by human actors. With the insights afforded by psychoanalysis, one might argue that it is, after all, the human activities and motives which are primary and that these activities and motives, especially in taboo areas, are projected upon external non-human events. This is not to deny that man has always had a very vital interest in celestial matters and in vegetative fertility. The matter is primarily one of emphasis.

Since Arthurian criticism has tended to be influenced by the succession of folklore theories (e. g. Arthur is seen as a sun god or vegetation spirit), it is somewhat surprising that little has been done in the way of psychodynamic analysis. Certainly the rigid unilinear evolutionary theory of Frazer has become passé, at least in anthropological circles. It is especially surprising in view of the fact that much of Malory's material, not to mention other Arthurian romance materials, contains numerous elements which would appear to have considerable psychological significance. This may perhaps be seen in connection with Arthur himself.

A number of critics have noted that there are two Arthurs. This may have come from an awareness of the fact that Malory's Arthur plays more than one role. However, the dual nature of Arthur has not been adequately defined. Among the attempts to delineate this dualism is the frequently stated vague notion that there is a mythical Arthur and a historical Arthur (Raglan 1957:78). This notion, however, does not materially aid in defining Arthur's dualism. Another statement concerning two Arthurs is made by Roger Sherman Loomis (1927:353), who says, "Arthur, we may conclude, was both man and god. " This, of course, amounts to a restatement of the mythic-historic dichotomy. It is not

a conflict between supernatural and natural elements which gives a reader the
impression that there are two Arthurs. The dualism is psychological. There is
Arthur the son and Arthur the father. In terms of the hero pattern, initially
Arthur is a young hero, and he remains a young hero until he achieves the throne.
Upon becoming king, Arthur becomes a father figure and accordingly tends to
assume the role of "villain" in the hero pattern, which can be seen, for example, in his position as foil to Lancelot. Since the narrative is not in strict
chronological order (and since unconscious material is, at best, never noted
for its adherence to either logic or chronology), Arthur often appears to change
rapidly from one role to the other. In folklore, as in dreams, dimensions of
time and space are irrelevant, and consequently such matters as the passage
of time or the age of anyone are inevitably vague. It is often not clear in a particular episode whether Arthur is young (i.e. a hero) or old (i.e. a paternal
king figure).

To make a solar pun: it is the rise of the son which constitutes the bulk of the
heroic pattern. Arthur is conceived through Uther Pendragon's tricking, with
Merlin's aid, the Duchess Igraine (I, 7).*3 In accordance with the pattern,
Arthur is raised by a couple who he thinks are his real parents (I, 8). Incidentally, Raglan (1957:183) points out that Arthur is apparently in no danger at
birth; nevertheless he is removed from his royal surroundings. (Actually, the
best example of the foster-parent incident to appear in Malory occurs in the
story of Sir Tor. Aries, the poor cowherd, brings up Sir Tor as his son just as,
in the Bible, Joseph, the poor carpenter, brings up a noble son. When questioned the wife of Aries confesses that before her marriage she was taken by force
by a knight whom Merlin reveals as King Pellinore (I, 74). In the apocryphal
Christian version, Mary is similarly pregnant before her marriage to Joseph.)*4

To return to Arthur, it is significant that he becomes king by pulling the
sword from the rock (I, 11). This is a traditional test for the hero-son (D 1654.
4. 1)*5 and Galahad, for example, also passes this test successfully. The phallic
symbolism of the sword suggests the importance of this ritual act. The fact that
other males are unable to move the sword suggests their impotence as contrasted with the virility of the hero. From an Oedipal viewpoint, the son wishes to
interrupt and, in fact, to end sexual intimacy between his parents. Thus the act
of withdrawing the royal sword which is wedged in the stone is reserved for the
royal son. In some versions of this incident, it is specifically stated that the
sword originally belonged to the hero's father (cf. E 373.2 and T 645.1). Once
the son possesses the royal sword, he becomes king and thereby gains possession of the queen. This symbolism is perhaps more obvious in the story of
Balin. In this story, a damsel comes to court wearing a sword, and she asks
that a pure hero draw it (H 1313). At this point, Arthur, who is now a king and
thus a paternal figure, is unable to draw the sword (I, 47) while Balin draws it
easily (I, 48). It is also of interest that Arthur obtains Excalibur from the Lady
of the Lake, who would appear to be a maternal water figure (I, 49).

The youthful Arthur's Oedipal characteristics may also be seen in his adventures with giants. Perhaps the most ferocious of these adversaries was the one
who, like King Rience, had a coat made of kings' beards and who had raped the
Duchess of Brittany. In Malory's words: "...he hath murdered her in forcing
her, and hath slit her unto the navel." The hero Arthur fights the giant with

appropriate viciousness: "And the king hit him again that he carve his belly and cut off his genytours, that his guts and his entrails fell down to the ground" (I, 137). In psychodynamic terms, Arthur is initially threatened with the cutting off of his beard. The cutting of hair is a common castration equivalent, as may be seen in the story of Samson's loss of strength or the custom of tonsuring priests pledged to celibacy (Róheim 1952:370, Jones 1951c:206, and Freud 1913). The infantile conception of parental intercourse as a combat in which the father cruelly overpowers the mother has been frequently noted (Freud 1900:496, 1917: 327-28; see also Stekel 1959:49-50). In such a conception, it is not infrequent that the phallus is thought to physically harm the victimized mother (Freud 1917: 328, Klein 1960:332). Moreover, from the infant's relativistic perspective, adults are seen as powerful giants. In this light, it is entirely in keeping with the hero pattern (Raglan's eleventh incident) that Arthur vanquish and castrate the giant.

If there were really any doubt that the young Arthur has Oedipal characteristics, one could point out the fact that Arthur, like Oedipus, does not originally know who his father is and that through this ignorance he commits incest with his sister, the Queen of Orkney (I, 35). It is only after Arthur commits this crime that he learns the true identity of his parents. As in the Oedipus myth, the circumstances of the raising of the hero by foster parents permits the hero to encounter his kin as if he were not related to them. As a foreigner, the hero is not denied access to his mother or sister. Only after the incest taboo is broken is the disguise stripped off.

In order to show just how important the son-hero is in Malory's work, and in addition to consider Arthur as father, it may be profitable to examine briefly the stories of Lancelot, Tristram, and Galahad. With regard to the first two, one can see that the love of a knight for his sovereign queen may well contain an Oedipal motif. This possibility is strengthened if the knight and the king are said to be related as nephew to uncle, for example. The relationship of nephew to uncle in medieval literature is too complex to be treated here. However, Farnsworth in his Uncle and Nephew in the Old French Chansons de Geste considers the relationship a survival from primitive matriarchy. Ernest Jones (1951e), in discussing the Tristram and Lancelot stories in particular, concludes that the displacement from father to uncle is analogous to the displacement of the mother attachment to the sister. If one assumes that Lancelot was not the original lover of Guinevere but rather that he replaced Gawaine who was, in fact, Arthur's nephew, then it is clear how the disguised Oedipal theme became attached to Lancelot.[*6]

The similarities between the stories of Lancelot and Tristram have been noticed by Arthurian scholars (Weston 1901:114, n. 1), and Weston suggests that the Lancelot story was greatly influenced by the earlier Tristram story (pp. 1, 207). Certainly the parallels in Malory are striking. While hunting, Tristram is accidentally shot in the thigh by an archer before an important duel (II, 122). Lancelot, while sleeping in the woods before the jousts, is accidentally shot in the buttocks by a lady archer (II, 308). Tristram sleeps with a lady who, though not Isoud, is equally desired by King Mark, "for they loved both one lady"(I, 257). (In the Bédier 1945:75 retelling of the Tristram story, the lady in question is Isoud.) Tristram leaves a tell-tale blood stain (I, 258). Lancelot in sleeping with

Guinevere also leaves a blood stain (II, 324-325). It is of interest to note just
how the bleeding came about in Lancelot's case. According to Malory and also
Chrétien, Lancelot injures himself in breaking down the bars in the process of
entering the window of Guinevere's chamber. This is reminiscent of the way in
which the heroine's action in the folktale of the Forbidden Chamber (Tale Type
311)*7 is discovered. When she opens the forbidden door or enters the forbidden chamber, often the key becomes bloody (C 913). If one assumes that the
chamber is a female sexual symbol (Freud 1917:169-71), then the incident becomes transparent. The fact that blood may reveal defloration by appearing
upon the key or hand (male symbol) is, of course, physiologically normal. It is,
however, true that whereas the girl in the Forbidden Chamber tale is actually
a virgin, the same cannot be said for Guinevere or Isoud. Here one must remember that in the Oedipal ideal the hero's mother is a virgin (Jones 1951c:
210, 1951d:361). The same window symbolism occurs again when the queen re-
buffs her lover. In the story of Tristram, it is Kehydius, a would-be lover of
Isoud, who jumps out of a bay-window, to King Mark's astonishment (I, 324).
However, it is Tristram who goes mad and runs around naked (I, 326). Lancelot,
after being rebuffed by the queen, jumps out of the bay-window of her chamber
and like Tristram goes mad and runs about with scanty clothing (II, 135, 145).
Aside from the implications of the rebirth symbolism of leaping from the window
and the nakedness, it is important to notice that there are such parallels in the
adventures of Tristram and Lancelot. With regard to Arthur, it is obvious that
in Lancelot's story, Arthur is no longer the youthful hero but rather the cuck-
olded husband adversary. However, curiously enough, Lancelot also plays the
latter role in the celebrated Grail legend.

With such a plethora of critical works on the Grail*8 it is truly presumptuous
to theorize at all about the Grail without reading deeply in the literature. Moreover, to attempt to treat the subject of the Grail en passant in several paragraphs
when whole books have proved inadequate is equally foolhardy. Having apologized
for my temerity, I shall simply add one more interpretation to the long list of
interpretations of the Grail. Weston (1957:75, 99, 205) commented upon the sexual symbolism of the Grail vessel and spear, and Roger Sherman Loomis (1927:
262) remarked that the way the spear bleeds into the vessel is "distinctly suggestive of a sexual symbolism". However, critics have had difficulty in reconciling
the phallic nature of the Grail with its role as a provider of food. In connection
with the latter, Loomis (1927:232) notes that one property of the Grail is "its
denial of food to the unworthy". The fact that the Grail furnished an apparently
inexhaustible supply of food has led a number of critics to identify the Grail
with the cauldron of Dagda, the Celtic cauldron of plenty (Weston 1957:73).
Weston objects to this identification and points out that the food-supplying vessel
in Arthurian materials is such that "whatever its form, Cup or Dish, it can
easily be borne (in uplifted hands, entre ses mains hautement porté) by a maiden,
which certainly could not be postulated of a cauldron!"(1957:73) The most important clue Weston provides to the nature of the Grail is her distinguishing between the provision of food and the Grail as closely related but not identical
phenomena.

Nor is there any proof that the Vessel itself contained the food with which the

folk of the Grail castle were regaled; the texts rather point to the conclusion
that the appearance of the Grail synchronized with a mysterious supply of
food of a choice and varied character. There is never any hint that the folk
feed from the Grail... (1957:73).

The foregoing brief discussion of the Grail symbols when combined with one of
Weston's observations concerning the quest for the Grail show that this portion
of the Arthurian romance is not unlike those portions already discussed.

Weston noted that although several knights are mentioned as participating in
the Grail quest, only two, a father and a son, play the principal roles. According to Weston, Lancelot and his son were preceded by Perceval and his son who
were in turn preceded by Gawaine and his son.[*9] If the Grail is a female symbol (Róheim 1952:260, Jones 1951f:132), and if the quest for the Grail involves
a father and a son, then clearly it is the Oedipal theme once again. If the interpretation seems repetitious, one might argue that to a certain extent so is the
material being interpreted. Galahad is born of essentially a virgin mother. Before his conception, the prophecy was circulated that he, Lancelot's son, would
be better than his father (II, 130, 169, 194). This is a milder version of the Del-
phic Oracle's warning to Laius that his son would kill him. Galahad, like Arthur,
pulls the sword from the stone (II, 169). The female-stone symbolism is also
the basis of the Siege Perilous motif (cf. H 31.4 and P 11.5). The seat and the
Grail are both reserved for Galahad. The identity of these elements is hinted
at by a curious supernatural sign. Just before Galahad appears to take his place
in the Siege Perilous, "all the doors and windows of the palace shut by them-
self" (II, 167). Similarly, right before Galahad achieves the Grail, "all the doors
and windows of the palace were shut without man's hand" (II, 269). The appropriateness of the door and window symbolism, which has already been discussed,
to Galahad's situation is indicated by the fact that soon after the sign, Galahad
enters the palace. It is implied that the royal rooms are closed to everyone except the hero. The same sexual symbolism is employed in Lancelot's unsuccessful attempt to achieve the Grail. Lancelot comes to the door of the chamber in
which the Holy Grail lies. "And at last he found a chamber whereof the door was
shut, and he set his hand thereto to have opened it, but he might not"(II, 256).
Finally, Lancelot is permitted to look inside the chamber, but when he tries to
enter it he is knocked unconscious for twenty-four days (II, 257-258). Only
Galahad, the son, succeeds in entering the sacred chamber, which his father is
unable to enter.

The other elements of the Grail ritual do not contradict the Oedipal interpretation. The Maimed King, who, according to Weston (1927:119), is never a youthful character, is a castrated father figure. If Weston's analogy between the Grail
hero and the Son-Lovers Adonis and Attis is sound, then the features of the
wounded old Fisher King may be explained. The Maimed or Fisher King in some
versions suffers castration (euphemistically, a wounding in the thighs) because
of some unwise sexual adventure (Weston 1927:22, Loomis 1927:262) and, in
one version mentioned by Weston (1927:123), the wounding is self-inflicted. It
is noteworthy that Attis suffers castration after sexual intimacy with the Great
Mother Goddess (Jones 1951d:370, Freud 1913:924) and that, in another myth,
Oedipus inflicts a wound upon himself; namely, blinding, which is generally

considered to be symbolic castration (Freud 1913:907, n. 4). The question is, how does the Maimed King, who is a father figure, become castrated? The answer may lie in the idea that in an Oedipal fantasy in which the son succeeds in his desire without being punished, part of the success consists in the castration of the rival figure. It has already been pointed out that Arthur castrated the hostile giant who had threatened castration. In the Grail cycle, the father figure has been castrated as a punishment for sexual aggression, and he is compelled to wait for the mercy of the son figure to be cured. In the course of the curing, the son reasserts his priapic preeminence. Galahad takes the pieces of the broken sword which was supposed to have pierced Joseph of Arimathea's thigh and makes the sword whole again (II, 263; cf. H 1023. 8). As soon as he has repaired the sword, the Grail appears. In other versions the Grail is achieved by the asking of a question (C 651). This may well be analogous to the riddle asked by the Sphinx and answered by Oedipus. Just as Oedipus had to answer the riddle in order to become king and marry his mother, so the Grail hero had to ask the vital question in order to achieve the Grail. *10

If the quest for the Grail is the quest for the mother, then the combination of sexual and nutrimental characteristics of the Grail becomes quite reasonable. The mother, in addition to being a sexual object, is also regarded as a source of food. As the primordial dispenser of nourishment, the mother is in a position to withhold food as a means of punishment. This would explain Loomis's observation that one property of the Grail is its denial of food to the unworthy. The mother-Grail equation would also explain Weston's feeling that the appearance of the Grail was synchronized with a mysterious supply of food rather than complete identity of the Grail with the food-supplying vessel. Possibly the reason for the confusion of the two elements is a curious reworking of symbolism. Cups, goblets, and cauldrons are often female symbols. However, if an originally symbolic object is interpreted as a non-symbolic object, the symbolism becomes confused. Thus the symbolic hollow vessel became simply a food container. But even here the original symbolism is not completely concealed. The vessel is considered to provide an inexhaustible supply of food (D 1652. 1). The question is raised as to the origin of this motif. Is there anything in nature which will provide an inexhaustible supply of food, with the only condition being possession of or at least access to the magic object? The mother's breast would, from the infant's point of view, seem to be such an inexhaustible supply of food. The fact that the food-Grail is often borne by a maiden would tend to support this suggestion (II, 130). If this interpretation is valid, then it becomes clear how the Grail quest can have both a phallic and a food motivation. In this connection, it is important to note that almost all of the knights of the Round Table go on the Grail quest (II, 172). The quest is not just an individual's quest but a search for a thing desired by all men.

Perhaps one of the strongest bits of evidence for the Oedipal underpinnings of the Grail quest is a detail which has puzzled critics for some time. Despite the fact that a great majority of the knights of the Round Table, including Galahad, are engaged in seeking the Grail, the simple truth is that the Grail is to be found at the castle of Corbin, the home of Galahad! It is Galahad's grandfather, King Pelles, who is the Maimed King (II, 242). Weston (1901:168, n. 1) contends that this situation emphasizes the "absolute unreality" of the Galahad quest. "The hero knows all about the Grail, its keeper, where it is to be found, his own relation to it. He has grown up under its shadow as it were." In the present interpretation, it is, of course, perfectly natural for the Grail to be found at the home of the hero. In fact, one could argue that this emphasizes the "absolute reality" of the Galahad quest. It is noteworthy that neither the Celtic talisman theory nor the Christian relic theory nor the vegetation renewal theory of the Grail can adequately explain this curious detail. *11

The considerations of the Grail quest and the stories of Lancelot and Tristram suggest that the son-hero pattern lies at the heart of Malory's work. However, since the son-hero pattern requires a father as a foil, it is necessary for some characters to assume both father and son roles. Lancelot is a son figure in his relation to Arthur but a father figure in his relation to Galahad. Arthur as a son-hero has already been described; Arthur as a father-hero is perhaps best seen, not in his relation to Lancelot but in his relation to Mordred. When Merlin tells Arthur that he has committed incest with his sister, the Queen of Orkney, he also prophesies that the forthcoming product of this union will ultimately destroy Arthur (I, 37). Thereupon, Arthur, similar to the Pharaoh in the story of Moses and to Herod in the story of Jesus, orders a massacre of the innocents. Since Merlin had said that Arthur's destroyer was born on May Day, Arthur ordered that all children who were born on May Day be placed on a ship left to drift at sea. However, by chance, Mordred was saved and was brought up by a foster-father (I, 45). As a matter of fact, an analysis of Mordred's biography reveals that his life contains nineteen of Raglan's twenty-two incidents. Loomis compares Mordred's biography with that of Pope Gregory and notes the basic similarities. However, Loomis (1927:341) feels that the legend of Mordred is "saturated with Celtic lore". The story of Gregory (Tale type 933) is quite similar to the story of Oedipus (Tale type 931) - as Thomas Mann clearly recognized. The fact that the incidents of Mordred's life correspond to those of the Oedipal son-hero pattern would suggest that the legend of Mordred is not necessarily of exclusively Celtic provenience.

If one were given the unbiased facts of Mordred's life together with either Rank's or Raglan's statement of the hero pattern, one would be forced to conclude that Mordred was a hero. However, in Malory's work, Mordred is clearly no hero. Essentially Mordred is depicted as an unsuccessful hero, an "anti-hero". Whereas the true Oedipal hero gains possession of the father's wife upon replacing the father, Mordred meets with resistance from Guinevere when he seeks to marry her. It is interesting that in accounts other than Malory's, such as the versions of Layamon and Wace, Guinevere is portrayed as a willing sinner (Weston 1901:105-06). However, even in Malory's work, the Oedipal content is revealed when, for example, the Bishop of Canterbury warns Mordred that he must not wed his father's wife (II, 380). Mordred in disobeying the bishop's injunction does commit near-incest and does kill his father Arthur. Perhaps Weston is correct when she suggests that Mordred and Gawaine "really represent two sides of one original personality" (1901:109). One notes that Gawaine in Hamlet's situation sought to kill the main who has slept with his mother but that it was actually Mordred who struck the man, Lamorak, from behind (II, 69). At any rate, it is clear that Mordred's character must be taken into account apart from the incidents of the hero-pattern. After all, Lancelot as a lover of Guinevere also engages in a war against Arthur, but Lancelot remains true to his chivalric ethics. He tends to be the son who loves both father and mother and who is genuinely distressed at having to fight the father in order to possess the mother. Mordred, in contrast, hates both Lancelot (II, 339) and Arthur. Since Arthur did initially attempt to kill Mordred, Mordred is, of course, not without some justification for his actions. Generally speaking, however, Arthur as a father figure is honorable and lovable, and this is more than enough to compensate for Mordred's heroic pattern. It is true that in some father-and-son combats, such as, for example, Sohrab and Rustum, both father and son are heroes. But with Mordred as a villain, Arthur remains something of a heroic figure even in defeat. It is interesting that, although details are lacking, Malory's version of the Tristram story apparently has King Mark and Tristram killing each other (II, 335). In this case, as in Tennyson's "The Last Tournament", it is the father figure who is the treacherous villain, not the son.

As a result of this examination of Malory's Le Morte D'Arthur, it seems safe to say that father-son conflict in terms of the conventional hero pattern makes up much of the material. One must give credit to the perspicacious Jessie Weston for partly realizing this when she commented that she believed the deadly combat between father and son "to be of greater importance in heroic-mythic tradition than has yet been realised. " She suggested that "the father and son combat in heroic tradition really represents the 'slayer who shall himself be slain', the prehistoric combat of the Golden Bough. . ." (1901:109). She considers the story of Yvain as an example of this and comments: "What is it but the variant of a motif coeval with the earliest stages of human thought and religious practice... and how old this tale may be, Mr. Frazer has taught us. "(1901:72). The Frazer hypothesis is quite similar to Raglan's postulated ritual regicide. If one adds Freud to Raglan and Frazer, one finds that the custom of the slayer's taking the place of the slain, even to the extent of taking the wife of the slain, as in Yvain, is indeed an old tale; namely, the tale of Oedipus. Thus one finds Weston's intuitive insights supported.

NOTES

*1 Raglan (1957) specifically denies knowledge of Rank's work, stating: "I had not heard of Otto Rank before, and am sorry not to have read his book. "

*2 Rank (1959), citing Goldhizer (1876:125). For a similar interpretation see Cox (1881:120-26).

*3 All references to Malory's Le Morte D'Arthur are to the two-volume Everyman edition (London, 1956).

*4 The Lost Books of the Bible and The Forgotten Books of Eden (Cleveland, 1926), 30-31.

*5 Motif references are to Stith Thompson's six-volume Motif-Index of Folk-Literature.

*6 Weston (1901:108) thinks that "most probably" the original lover of Guinevere was Gawaine.

*7 Tale type references are to Thompson (1961).

*8 An annotated list of the older critical works on the Grail is found in A.E. Waite (1933:604-18). Recent studies include Holmes and Klenke (1959) and Locke (1960). Other Grail studies may be found by consulting Bulletin bibliographique de la société internationale Arthurienne.

*9 Weston's views are summarized by Anderson (1953:40).

*10 There has been considerable discussion of the sexual significance of the riddle of the Sphinx. See Freud (1917:327,1938b:595). For a psychoanalytic commentary on Aarne's folkloristic study of the riddle, see Róheim (1952:530). A similar interpretation is found in Wolfenstein (1954:97).

*11 The three principal Grail theories are summarized by Loomis (1927).

16

ON THE PSYCHOLOGY OF LEGEND

It is difficult to think of any area of folklore research which has continued to be as sterile and unrewarding as the study of legend. One reason for this is that the relatively few folklorists who specialize in legend have never been able to escape from the dreary concerns of endless collecting and hairsplitting classification debates. But the more important reason is that folklorists have utterly failed to convince anyone, including themselves, of the significance and relevance of legend with respect to the ultimate goal of understanding the nature of man. Collection per se does no more than provide necessary raw materials for interpretation. But without interpretation, the raw materials remain just that: raw materials. Classification attempts in which culturally relative a priori arbitrary schemes are proposed or imposed as possible universal categories have thus far proved little more than exercises in futility. Unless and until folklorists enter the area of interpretation, for example, what did and do specific legends mean? there is precious little hope of interesting folklore students and members of other disciplines in the masses of legend material in print and in archives.

Recent valuable surveys of legend research by Wayland Hand (1965) and Lutz Röhrich (1966) clearly indicate the major bias in contemporary legend scholarship. Collecting and indexing are presented as the principal research emphases. Chapter headings in Röhrich (1966) are essentially subgenre distinctions (based mostly on content features), such as "Totensagen", "Christliche Sagen", and "Historische Sagen". In these and other surveys, there is little or no evidence that legends have ever been - or could ever be - studied profitably from a psychological point of view. Nor is there much extended discussion of any kind of meaningful interpretation of legend materials, for it must be noted that the psychological approach to legend content is only one of several possible avenues to analysis. The glaring lack of mention of psychological studies raises the question as to whether legends can or cannot be usefully studied in terms of psychology. Is there perhaps something in the legend that makes it impossible to use for psychological studies? Or is it simply a matter of the professional folklorist's unwillingness to consider legends from this perspective, a possibility that if true might itself be the subject of an interesting psychological study? I suggest that folklorists once having admitted intellectually that legends contain fantasy proceed to dismiss this fact, blithely ignoring the total range of academic scholarship specifically concerned with the study of human fantasy.

Reprinted from American Folk Legend: A Symposium, ed. Wayland D. Hand (Berkeley, Los Angeles, London: University of California Press, 1971), 21-36.

No doubt if Hand or Röhrich had considered some of the classic psychological studies, their evaluation would have been negative. In the present context, how-ever, I believe it to be beside the point to lift an accusing finger at folklorists who ignore psychologists. It is equally pointless to rail at psychiatrists who make analyses of legends without the benefit of any knowledge of the tools of the trade of folklore. For why should the important task of analysing the traditional forms of fantasy we label legend be left to nonfolklorists anyway? Either folk-lorists must begin to try to interpret legend materials as traditional products of human fantasy, or they must forfeit any claim to be anything other than anti-quarian butterfly collectors and classifiers.

There are some characteristics of legend which make it a genre particularly valuable to the psychologically oriented folklorist. One of these is the temporal dimension of legends, a dimension that to my knowledge has not previously been spelled out in sufficient detail. William Bascom (1965) in his excellent survey article has delineated the standard European trichotomic division of folk or prose narrative into myth, folktale, and legend. The criteria include formal features (e.g. the presence or absence of opening and closing formulas), the element of belief, and the dimension of time. Generally, Bascom's discussion accurately reflects the categories used by European folklorists if not the folk. In fact, one could devise field experiments to test some of the criteria. An introductory folk-tale formula such as "Once upon a time" could be prefixed to a story from the Old Testament, for example, in Genesis. Presumably, if members of the audi-ence had strong religious convictions depending upon belief in the literal truth of the Old Testament, there would be some expression of outrage and indignation. "Once upon a time" means roughly that "everything that follows this fixed phrase utterance is fiction rather than truth". This is appropriate enough in the case of a fairy tale that breaks with reality in favor of a world of unreality, but it would presumably constitute an intolerable insult to members of an audience who be-lieve the story to be true.

In Bascom's discussion of the temporal dimensions of folk narrative, he notes that myths are set in the remote past while legends are set in the recent past. This, however may be too static a description and I believe it might be more useful to describe myth and legend in terms of segments of a time continuum bounded by either definite or indefinite end points. As a heuristic device, I would suggest the metaphor or image of an hourglass open at both ends. The hourglass would represent a true time axis and thus folktale would not be included in it. Folktales are outside true time. In European tradition at least, they occur at no particular time or at any time. In a way "Once upon a time" means literally that the story is perched above or outside of time. In contrast, myth and legend are in true time. In terms of the hourglass image, myth would be the bottom. Here one can see the value of the open-endedness of the hourglass metaphor. There is no time before myth. Myth-time is the earliest imaginable time, and it runs roughly up until the world and man were created in their present form. The time of the creation of world and man would be the middle of the hourglass. Legend, as both a European folk and analytic category, is set in postcreation time, that is, after the creation of man. Once Adam and Eve are created (as told in a myth), their historical or pseudohistorical adventures may be in legend form. Legend is thus the upper portion of the hourglass. Just as the beginning of myth-time is open-ended, however, so the end of legend-time is open-ended. The open-endedness is again relevant because in many cases, the action or plot of a legend is not completed in the narrative itself, and in fact the action continues into the present or even into the future. The house down the road continues to be haunted; the Flying Dutchman (motif E 511) continues to roam the seas; the Wandering Jew (motif Q 502. 1)*1 continues his woeful peregrination. Thus whereas the action of myth is normally completed in the narrative (although its consequences and implications may and indeed usually do persevere), the action of a legend may never be completed. What this means in part is that individuals may well feel closer to the action of legend than to the action of myth that happened long, long ago, and closer to the action of legend than to the action of folktale that never really happened. As a matter of fact, in many of those legends whose actions are not yet completed, the sense of immediacy may produce genuine fear or other emotion. This suggests that legend might be much more appropriate than myth and folktale for psychological studies.

The greater immediacy of legend in time is paralleled by immediacy of place. First we may see the contrast between myth and legend, on the one hand, and folktale, on the other. Whereas myth and legend are set in this world, folktale is set in another, a fictional world, a never-never land of make-believe. One leaves his own time and place to enter the fantasy and dream world of the folktale. In myth and legend, however, the fantasy is introduced into the time and place of the real world. Here we may distinguish legend from myth in terms of distantiation. Since myth occurred before the world was as it is now, it tends to be somewhat removed from the contemporary scene. Although myth does refer to the real world, the events were of such scope and took place so long ago (although the time period will vary with different peoples), that they may be much less immediate than local legends. Again this immediacy of space would seem to make legend primary source material for the study of fantasy. One does not escape the real world into legend; rather legend represents fantasy in the real world, an important point psychologically speaking. It is "true" fantasy, not to be confused with the "false" or fictional fantasy of folktale.

There is yet another characteristic of legends which makes them attractive to folklorists willing to consider a psychological approach, and interestingly enough it is a characteristic that is the despair of the more conservative collector-classifier folklorist. The characteristic concerns quantity and generative power. There are literally countless legends. As Wayland Hand (1965:439) has phrased it, "For the systematizer, folk legends seem endless." There are probably more legends than myths or folktales in most cultures. There is a finite number of basic myth types, for example, the creation of the world, origin of death, and so forth, but an infinite number of legends, especially local legends as opposed to migratory legends. Moreover, there are continual additions to the world's supply of legends. Each era contributes either new legends or at least new versions of old legends to the general corpus of texts. This does not seem to be the case for myths. If one uses the concept of myth in a folkloristic sense, that is, as a sacred narrative explaining how the world and man came to be in their present form, it is doubtful whether one will find many, if any, new myths created. Similarly, the majority of the folktales found in oral tradition at any one point in time are probably genetically related to older versions.

Legends, in contrast, can spring anew whenever an appropriate personage, place, or event is deemed legendworthy by a folk group. This does not mean, of course, that there are not traditional patterns of legend and that apparently "new" legends do not resemble earlier legends. The point is simply that if one is interested in the origin and development of folk narrative - an area of research clearly related to the province of psychology - then legend presents a much likelier subject than myth or folktale. New problems in society create new legends, and folklorists should capitalize on the opportunity to observe the legend formation process in progress. Thus the constant flow of new legends which bedevils the obsessive perfectionist collector-classifier who wants to obtain and/or index all known versions of all known legends represents a potentially enormous asset to the psychologically oriented folklorist.

Before attempting to illustrate the possibilities of a psychological approach to legend using specific American folk legends as examples, I should like to indicate that there is a considerable body of relevant scholarship, the bulk of which has not been written by folklorists. A random sampling might include Bonaparte (1946) on the legend of unfathomable waters, Isaac-Edersheim (1941) on the Wandering Jew, Róheim (1926) on the wild hunt, De Groot's (1965) extended study of the Saint Nicholas legend, and Spiro's (1967) insightful analysis of Burmese religious legends. Those seriously interested in exploring the scholarship should consult Grinstein's multivolume bibliographical aid, The Index of Psychoanalytic Writings, and perhaps also Psychological Abstracts for further references. Since it is, however, doubtful whether many folklorists will take the trouble of giving such psychological studies even a trial reading, I propose to present brief psychological interpretations of several representative American folk legends. But even if none of the particular interpretative suggestions are adjudged convincing - the question of "proving" any one interpretation beyond a shadow of a doubt is always unlikely when working with symbolic materials - I would hope that at least the exposure to such interpretations will demonstrate the advantages and indeed the necessity for a psychological approach to legend.

First, we might consider the story of George Washington and the cherry tree. Brunvand (1968:94) tends to demean this classic bit of apocrypha on the grounds that there is so little variation, and certainly it is true that the account does inevitably end with George confessing to his father, "I cannot tell a lie; I did it with my little hatchet." I suspect that this story comes as near to being known by virtually everyone in the United States as any other American legend we might name. Now what does the legend mean? Can it be usefully explicated in psychological terms? It is probably not historical and even if it were, its historicity could not possibly account for its continuing widespread popularity. Clearly, it functions as an exemplum to teach a moral lesson, to wit, a child should always tell the truth even when there is risk of anger or punishment. It is invariably implicit if not explicit that George's father did not punish George for the heinous crime of chopping down a favorite cherry tree. Rather one assumes that the lack of corporal punishment constituted a reward for telling the truth. But is the legend's role as a traditional argument-charter for telling the truth sufficient to explain its lasting appeal? I would suggest instead that there are other reasons, compelling psychological reasons, which may account for the appeal.

For one thing, the legend, brief as it is, involves a conflict between father and son. The son apparently has cut down a prize possession of his father, namely, his father's cherry tree. Does the act of chopping down a tree have any possible symbolic import? Well, if one can judge from "Jack and the Beanstalk", one might think so.*2 A son cutting down his father's tree might be indulging in a symbolic castration attempt. It is terribly tempting to make something of the fact that the tree in question is a cherry tree. Cherry in modern slang means virgin, one who has not yet experienced sexual intercourse. Thus George in cutting down his father's "cherry" tree makes the son's crime all the more impressive. Whether the cherry tree symbolizes George's mother, which he cut down and thereby prevented his father from enjoying, or whether the cherry tree represents George's father's phallus, which George effectively rendered impotent, the basic nature of the crime is clear. Note that whether it is George's mother who is cherry or George's father's phallus that is cherry, the upshot is the same inasmuch as in either case, George has succeeded in preventing his father from engaging in sexual activity. If George's mother were a virgin, like the mother of Jesus and the various heroes described by Raglan in his account of the hero pattern, then this would effectively deny that George's father and mother had ever had intercourse. If George's father's phallus were cherry, then similarly, its lack of sexual experience is implied. It is true that it is difficult to determine whether "cherry" had a sense of sexual innocence a century or so ago. On the basis of such evidence as the well-known riddle in Captain Wedderburn's Courtship (Child 46) in which a successful courting depends upon a man's explaining how there can be a chicken without a bone and cherry without a stone, one might think so . (Such privational contradictive riddles in which critical parts of wholes are denied can have sexual significance.)*3 In European tradition, moreover, one finds such motifs as D 1375. 1. 1. 4, Magic cherry causes horns to grow on a person, and D 1376. 1. 1. 2, Magic cherry makes nose long. In both cases, a magic cherry causes a body extremity to appear or lengthen ! Such motifs would support the notion that cherry and cherries have a sexual connotation in folk tradition. In any case, the fundamental psychological import of a son's cutting down his father's tree does not really depend upon the species of the tree. It might be safer simply to say that the indisputable sexual significance of "cherry" in our own day surely could be a factor in the continued popularity of the legend.

There are several other comments of a psychological nature which might be made. First of all, is the legend son or father oriented? I would argue that it seems to be slightly father oriented - at least to the extent that the son does not get away with cutting down his father's tree. In this respect, the George Washington cherry tree legend differs from the Jack and the beanstalk plot. In the latter, Jack cuts down the giant's stalk (with the help of a hatchet often thoughtfully provided by Jack's mother), and this kills the giant. In George's case, he has to confess his sins. In this respect, George's situation parallels that of Jesus Christ. Jesus is supposed to be a sacrifice by, for, or to God the father. The son yields to the greater power of the father and in that sense it may not be particularly important whether one is nailed to a phallic cross or to a cherry tree. What I should like to suggest here en passant is: (1) that Raglan's (1956) hero pattern actually applies more to legend than to myth - most of the heroes' lives he analyzes were either historical or pseudo-historical; (2) that the pattern's particulars have psychological significance, for example, the virgin birth is the ultimate repudiation of one's father having had intercourse with one's mother, as Otto Rank (1959:81; see also Dundes 1962f) noted; and (3) that to a limited extent the pattern is relevant to this legendary fragment of George Washington's life.*4

Finally, one might remark that there is additional evidence attesting to the fact that George Washington has assumed sexual symbolic significance as an American folk image. One thinks, for instance, of the allegations or even actual signs stating that "George Washington Slept Here". Why should it matter that George Washington <u>slept</u> in a particular house? Why not George Washinton ate here or visited here? That fact is that it is his presence in a <u>bed</u> of the house which the folk have singled out for emphasis. Perhaps by itself, this sleeping mania would not make much sense, but then we recall that George Washington is called the "father" of his country. Moreover, even the most adamant anti-Freudian would have to admit the possible phallic implications of the particular monument "erected" to honor the "father" of our country! All these bits and pieces of the George Washington image tend to support the thesis that there may be a psychological level to the familiar legend of George chopping down his father's cherry tree.

While still in a phallic frame of reference, let us turn to the modern American legend of "The Hook". This legend has been well reported by Linda Dégh (1968a), and the fact that she found forty-four versions indicates the legend's genuine popularity, at least among college age girls. The essence of the plot involves a couple in a car parked in a local lover's lane. (In Los Angeles, the scene is invariably Mulholland Drive; in Berkeley it is Tilden Park; in Oakland it is Skyline Drive.) The boy hoping to make out (sexually) turns on the car radio to find some soft music to set the stage. After several minutes of "necking", the couple is startled by a news flash that interrupts the music to say that a sex maniac has just escaped from the state insane asylum. The announcement also mentions that the one distinguishing feature of this man is that he has a hook in place of one arm. The girl is upset "cause she's just sure this guy is going to come and try and get in their car" (Dégh 1968a:92). Finally, after much argument, she convinces the boy to leave the area whereupon he suddenly starts the car and roars away. At the girl's home, she gets out of the car and sees "a hook hanging on the door".

What is this legend about? To say as Linda Dégh does that its function is to provide the chill of a good scare is not to say much in specific terms about its content. Dégh makes no real attempt to <u>interpret</u> the content of the legend, but rather limits herself to <u>surveying</u> the content. She remarks that some of the extended details found in the forty-four versions "emphasize the horrible looks of the hook-man, elaborating on the natural dread of the handicapped". I shall return later to the question of whether "handicapped" is really an appropriate epithet in view of the probable psychological meaning of the plot. Dégh also notes that some versions "concentrate on the fearful insistence of the girl or the disappointment of the boy, or the argument between the couple". I found most revealing her comment that "the most persistent motif is the one that renders credibility to the tearing off of the hook-arm". She also observes that "the boy's disappointment and suddenly recognized fear is an adequate expla-

nation for the jump start of the car: the boy gunned the motor as a typical teen-
ager while the girl rolled up the window with the hook arm caught in between."
Here we have a fine example of how a professional folklorist, one of the very
best, reports a legend. And yet the presentation is totally devoid of any real
discussion of the psychological significance of the content.

One clue to the meaning of the legend is provided by the information that the
narrative is normally told by girls to other girls. The majority of the informants cited by Dégh are girls. It thus appears to be a narrative from a girl's
point of view, a narrative that seems to summarize teen-age girls' fears about
parking with their boyfriends. In the legend, we find an expression of the so-
called double standard: the boy is expected to try to make out, the girl is expected to resist. According to the plot, the boy tries to set an appropriate mood for
a seduction or at least necking attempt. Part of the strategy involves turning on
the radio. But the ploy backfires when the real danger of parking in lover's lane
is announced by the radio, the conscience-like voice from society. "A sex maniac has escaped from the state insane asylum." From a girl's point of view,
previously nice boys sometimes act like sex maniacs when parked in a car on
a country road. And it is probably true that a boy feels that he has temporarily
escaped from some of the "institutional" pressures that normally inhibit him
once he is out parked in a romantic lonely lane. The radio announcement also
mentions that the sex maniac's distinguishing identifying characteristic is a
hook. The girl is frightened by the report of the hook that may have sexual over-
tones. Girls fear that boys out on dates will be "all hands", that is, that the
boy's hands will be constantly engaged in exploring various parts of the girl's
body. A "hook" could be a hand as in the expression "getting one's hooks into
somebody", but a hook could also be a phallic symbol. The typical fear of the
girl might then be that a boy's hand, signifying relatively elementary necking,
might suddenly become a hook (an erect, aggressive phallus).

At any rate, in the legend, the girl insists that the boy take her home. The
boy is unhappy because "you know he really had his plans for this girl" with the
plans clearly being of a sexual nature. If the hook were a phallic substitute,
then it would make perfect sense for the hook to be severed as a result of the
girl's instigating the sudden move to return home. One informant told me the
girl forced the boy to "pull out fast" referring ostensibly to driving the car away
hurriedly. One way of keeping a sexually aggressive boy at bay is to castrate
him! In terms of such symbolism, please note that it is entirely appropriate
that the hook be ripped off just as it had made contact with the girl's "door".
There is similar poetic justice in the version in which the girl winds up/closes
her "window" thereby catching the penetrating hook. The attempt to enter the
"body" of the car is seemingly a symbolic expression of the boy's attempt to
enter the body of the girl. (The general association of cars and sexuality among
teen-agers is also signaled by boys calling their cars hot rods and such auto-
mobile games as "padiddle" in which the first to observe a car at night with one
light - the other presumably being extinguished - can claim a kiss.)

If I am correct in this psychological reading of the legend, then it is not the
fear of an escapee from a mental instition but the fear of the sexual attack by
the girl's date which provides the emotional raison d'être of the story. If this
is so, then it is at least misleading and at worst wrong to claim that the story

is based upon the "natural dread of the handicapped". The girl in the story (and for that matter the girls who are telling and listening to the story) are not afraid of what a man lacks, but of what he has. The fact that frequently actual dates end with a parking visit to a local lover's lane might account for the great popularity of this legend. It reflects a very real dating practice, one which produces anxiety for both boys and girls, but particularly for girls.

A less popular but equally interesting legend is commonly found in medical schools. A group of medical students take a cadaver's hand or arm and put a coin in its fingers. They then head for a toll bridge, for example, the Golden Gate. The toll booth attendant reaches out to take the extended coin and is startled when the entire hand or arm is left behind by the driver as he speeds off. In Dorson's (1959a:259) version, the attendant drops dead of shock. This legend has not been studied, but it seems to be popular on both the East and West coasts. What is the meaning of the legend?

First of all, it is one of many legends told among medical students having to do with cadavers. Clearly, one of the first hurdles that new medical students encounter is learning to face and handle human bodies, both alive and dead. As we shall see later in the "Runaway Grandmother", Americans abhor touching a dead body, and they take great pains to keep children from even observing a cadaver. I am told that after an initial period of squeamishness, medical students soon get to the point of eating their bag lunches in the dissection room surrounded by various cadavers. The legend thus provides an outlet for the anxiety initially felt about treating a dead human body as a mere "nonhuman" object.

In the legend, the contrast between the medical students' cavalier and joking treatment of the body and the reaction of the toll booth attendant who represents the outside world is intentional. It is as if to say that the outside world finds the medical students' handling of a dead body shocking, and perhaps that a typical man on the street would be "scared to death" to cut up a corpse. This critical attitude towards medical students' handling of the human body is a long standing one, going back hundreds of years. The very fact that doctors were concerned with the body rather than with the mind was originally held against them. In essence, the idea of anyone's making his living by investigating a human body was felt to be repugnant, especially if the body was a dead one. (This attitude may still be true with respect to morticians.) This may be reflected in the legend by the toll bridge setting. The fact that future doctors use a cadaver arm to pay the toll suggests that they are using the limbs of others, perhaps of victims, to help pay their way in life. The connection between money (the coin) and the body part (the arm or hand) is clear. Doctors get their money in life from the sick, dying, or dead. Obviously, there are humanitarian goals at work too, but from one perspective the doctor obtains considerable wealth from the hands of his patients, even the ones who die. The doctor, after all, must charge a fee even if the operation fails and patient dies. No doubt new medical students may feel certain qualms about this. To make money from the pains of fellow human beings has its guilt-causing aspect. Thus the medical students, by offering the cadaverous arm with the coin attached to the toll-booth attendant, are reversing the normal roles. In the legend, it is not the doctor but the outside world who has to take the money from the dead man (and it is such a frightening experience that the attendant dies). It is interesting that the arm is left behind.

Perhaps this shows that the doctor is willing to put such things behind him once the necessary impersonal (as the relationship between toll collector and toll payer) pecuniary activity is completed. Doctors cannot afford the luxury of becoming too involved with or attached to their patients' ailments. They must learn to be able to work with living beings and treat the bodies of these beings with the same objectivity that they learned to use with cadavers. The legend then does more than make medical students more comfortable around cadavers, since it may well provide an expression for the basic anxiety connected with taking money from sick or dying human beings.

My final example is "The Runaway Grandmother", a legend that has been carefully reported by Linda Dégh (1968b) who indicates that the story is popular in many parts of Europe. Her summary of the basic plot includes a pleasure trip or family vacation in which an old grandmother is taken along. Shortly after arrival at the vacation spot, the grandmother dies. The vacation ends and the pleasure trip becomes a nightmare. Various obstacles hinder the disposal of the body, obstacles such as the remoteness of the area, the unavailability of mortuary facilities, crossing a national border, and so forth. Usually, the body is strapped on the top of the car for the return home. En route, the family stops to eat at a restaurant. Upon emerging from the restaurant, the family discovers that the car parked outside has been stripped of its contents including the body. In many versions, the whole car disappears. The legend may end at this point, although often there is a brief explanation of the difficulty in probating the will or collecting the insurance of the deceased in view of the absence of the body.

Here is an excellent example of a modern bit of fantasy, and it provides another appropriate test case for the feasibility of a psychological approach to legend. First, let us see what Linda Dégh has to say about the story. After commenting on its distribution and observing its appearance in newspapers in Hungary and Denmark, she notes that the European versions make more of the problem of smuggling the grandmother across a national border. Her suggestion that the fear and danger of going through customs is much more relevant to the European experience than to the American is surely a sound one (pp. 74-75). Less plausible is her suggestion that the story expresses "the fear of the return of the dead". This I suspect is a European folklorist familiar with revenant traditions misreading American versions of what may well be a cognate form of a European plot. Dégh is at least explicit: "The meaning of this legend is that the corpse has to receive a decent burial; it cannot just be left behind." She also claims "The real concern is: how to dispose of the body (at a decent place where it will rest and not haunt the survivors). The disappearance of the corpse results in the prolongation of the fear: she might return some day. "I find this unconvincing and frankly I fail to see the slightest bit of evidence in any of the texts cited by Dégh (or in the versions I know from California) that there is any chance of the grandmother coming back to haunt the family. If I am correct and the story is not about "the fear of the return of the dead", what then is the legend about?

One of the principal characteristics of folklore, according to psychoanalytic theory, is wishful thinking and wish fulfillment. Yet the majority of folklorists choose to ignore this insight. Such deliberate ignorance is part of the general reluctance to treat fantasy as fantasy. Folklorists seem to prefer studying lore as if there were no folk. If we look at "The Runaway Grandmother" as an expression of wishful thinking, we can, I think, see the content of the legend in a new light.

The problem is basically one of a geriatric nature: What does one do with grandmother? In a youth oriented society, a society that worships the future and rejects the past (Dundes 1969), there is no place for the older generation. Nuclear family units resent in-laws moving in even for a temporary visit. (Remember please that a grandmother is a mother-in-law.) Rather grandfathers and grandmothers are encouraged to settle elsewhere and more and more "old-age" retirement communities are being built to accommodate such exiles. In the legend, a family cannot even go on its once-a-year annual vacation without being plagued by grandmother. Grandmother cannot or will not be left home alone and so she must be taken along on the vacation trip. The fact that a pleasure becomes a nightmare, as Dégh phrases it, suggests that this is the central theme: grandmothers are de trop and their unwelcome presence transforms family pleasure into nightmare. If this is an accurate depiction of general American family attitudes toward grandmothers (though not on the part of grandchildren), then the nature of the wish is obvious: grandmother should die! Or to put it more metaphorically, grandmother should take a trip from which she doesn't return.*5 This is precisely what happens in the legend. The psychological purpose of the legend is thus to get rid of grandmother.

The wishful thinking aspect of the legend does not end with the death of the grandmother, for there is one striking unpleasant consequence of grandmother's death: what to do with the body? Americans dislike discussing death in front of children. In various versions of the legend, it is stated specifically that the parents did not want to alarm the children - this is one reason for strapping the body on top of the car. The children must be kept from direct contact with death at all cost, a philosophy that surely has consequences in adult attitudes towards the reality of violence and death. In any case, a secondary wish in the legend is manifest in the restaurant episode. While the family is at lunch, the body disappears. Someone else has removed the unpleasant consequence of grandmother's death from the scene. Here is a perfect reflection of American attitudes towards burials. Whereas in many societies in the world, it is the family that takes care of preparing the body for burial, in the United States, the family calls in a specialist who comes immediately to remove the body and take care of the funeral details. Normally, there may be some guilt felt by family members in calling in a perfect stranger to take care of their "beloved" grandmother. There is, I think we would agree, something unpleasant about calling in a paid professional to come take care of a corpse. Here in this legend not only is the body neatly removed but since it was stolen by strangers, the family need not accept responsibility for giving the body to strangers (that is, morticians). It was not the family's fault that the body was stolen. Thus the legend kills off grandmother and eliminates the body with a minimum of guilt. (There is a little guilt to the extent that someone might have stayed with the car to guard the body!)

The final element of the legend also has psychological significance. It is usually added casually as though it were not really part of the plot. It concerns the insurance and/or will probate. One of the primary reasons why Americans want grandmothers dead is related to capitalism. One way of "getting rich quick" is to inherit wealth from deceased relatives. Thus the whole wish in the legend might be expressed: (1) grandmother should die; (2) someone should steal the body so we do not have the bother, expense, and sadness of burying it; and (3) we shall get all of grandmother's money. Unfortunately, wish part 2 tends to rule out or at least delay wish part 3. If there is no body, then there is no proof of death, and the family must wait until the individual in question is declared legally dead. That such a crass mercenary motive does underlie the legend is made abundantly clear in many versions. For example, in Dégh's first text, right after the body is stolen, the narrator says "Well, it wasn't very funny even though it sounds like it because they have to wait seven years now to prove that Grandma is dead before they can collect any insurance." So while I would certainly agree with Dégh that the story is a genuine folk legend, I am not sure I accept her view that it is one "with hidden supernatural meaning stressing the unusual, the strange experience". It is perfectly possible that the American versions do derive from a European form in which supernaturalism and revenants play a central part. But I would maintain that the fear in the American versions is not that grandmother will return, but rather that she will not. The family would like the body to turn up so that they might enjoy their inheritance right away. In a few versions, it is stated that the family needed the body so as to prove that murder had not been committed (Dégh 1968b:69). The very suggestion that a family would murder its grandmother is fantastic, but it does support the general interpretation of wishful thinking offered here. Grandmother is a burden whether she is alive or dead. Even after she dies, she has to be carried by the family. The wish then is not just that she would die, but that she would die at a convenient time (definitely not during the annual two-week vacation), that somebody else will come to remove the body, and that there will not be too much trouble or delay in inheriting grandmother's wealth. In the legend, all the wishes are not fulfilled. Perhaps the guilt of taking grandmother "for a ride", to use the gangster phrase for liquidation of an enemy, requires that the family have to wait to collect their blood money. Still the primary wish of getting rid of grandmother is fulfilled.

In these brief speculative investigations of several popular American folk legends, I hope I have shown the rich potential that legends have for folklorists willing to consider a psychological approach. Even if one were to reject all the interpretations offered as being too subjective, farfetched, and unverifiable, one could still see the kinds of questions folklorists need to try to answer. Why is the legend of George Washington's cutting down his father's cherry tree as popular as it is? Are there many girls attacked by one-armed men wearing hooks, and whether there are or not, why should such a story appeal to hundreds of teen-age girls all over the United States? Why should medical students tell a story in which a coin held in a cadaver's hand is held out to a bridge toll booth attendant? Why should a legend involving a grandmother dying unexpectedly on a family vacation trip capture the imagination of a large segment of the American public? I do not believe that the mere recording of more texts or the protracted debates about genre definition and indexing can answer these questions, and I honestly think that if folklorists continue to be bogged down in the tedium of taxonomy then questions like these will not even be asked - much less answered.

174

NOTES

*1 One indication of the difficulty in defining genres of folk narrative is pro-
vided by the fact that Stith Thompson has listed the Wandering Jew as a tale
type (AT 777) which would imply that it is a folktale rather than a legend. For
a recent study of this plot, see Anderson (1965).

*2 For considerations of the symbolism of "Jack and the Beanstalk", see Alan
Dundes (ed.) (1965:103-113).

*3 For a discussion of the possible sexual symbolism of oppositional riddles
involving privational contradictions, see Dundes (1964b).

*4 There is good evidence that the folk reworkings of the biographies of his-
torical American heroes conform to a Raglanesque pattern. See Utley (1965).

*5 Another folk metaphor may be implied by placing the body in a sleeping bag
on top of the car (sleeping=death).

SECTION FOUR

THE ANALYSIS OF AMERICAN FOLKLORE

17

HERE I SIT - A STUDY OF AMERICAN LATRINALIA

Any American male who has ever had an occasion to enter a public bathroom such as one found in a railroad or bus terminal has surely observed at one time or another one of the many traditional inscriptions found on the walls of the facilities. In some quarters, e. g. in the rest rooms of some bars and café's, one finds the custom has been institutionalized in that a small slate and an accompanying piece of chalk are hanging on the wall. This allows individuals to write freely and at the same time it saves the establishment the expense of continually repainting walls.

Despite the widespread distribution of these inscriptions and despite the fact that many of them are demonstrably traditional, one looks in vain for extended collections of published texts and for any rational discussion of them or the practice of writing them. Most histories of the water closet (e. g. Pudney, Reynolds, Wright) do little more than recognize that such traditions exist. Typical is the remark made by poet John Pudney, author of The Smallest Room, who bothers to say (1954:130), "I must here resist the temptation urged on me by several men of letters to quote more freely from this poetry of the smallest room." Certainly there can be no doubt as to the antiquity of the genre. In the chapter devoted to latrines of John G. Bourke's classic Scatalogic Rites of All Nations, one finds references to the obscene poetry written in Roman latrines (1891:136). What little evidence is available in print does attest to the age and international spread of this popular form of written folklore. Gershon Legman, an authority on erotic folklore bibliography, mentions (1964:254,451) The Merry-Thought or The Glass-Window and Bog-House Miscellany of 1731, with the only known complete copy at Oxford. In the important journal of obscene folklore, Anthropophyteia, one finds a handful of brief collectanea, e. g. one entitled "Skatologische Inschriften", or ones by Fisher and von Waldheim, which indicates the

Reprinted from The Kroeber Anthropological Society Papers 34 (1966), 91-105. This paper was presented at the 1966 meeting of the California Folklore Society at Davis, California. I am indebted to many of my students and colleagues for contributing examples of latrinalia. Unless otherwise indicated, all materials were collected from men's rooms in Berkely and the surrounding Bay Area in 1964. I am especially grateful to psychologist Nathan Hurvitz who provided all of the items from Paris, Texas. My thanks also to Sam Hinton for his suggestion that the paper be entitled "Ars(e) Poetica". Explanations of the meaning of most of the slang terms appearing in the latrinalia may be found in the works by Read and Sagarin cited in the list of references for this paper.

presence of the form in modern Europe. A fair sampling of Mexican examples
appeared in a chapter "Grafitos en Los Comunes" in Jiménez' best-selling
Picardía Mexicana. The classic study of the form in America was made by
Allen Walker Read who privately published it in 1935 under the euphemistic
title, Lexical Evidence from Folk Epigraphy in Western North America: a
Glossarial Study of the Low Element in the English Vocabulary. The title page
of this eighty-three page monograph announced that the circulation was restricted to students of linguistics, folklore, abnormal psychology, and allied branches
of the social sciences.

Professor Read's term "folk epigraphy" raises the question of what to call
bathroom wall writings. The term graffiti is too broad in that it includes all
kinds of inscriptions and marks placed on walls. Moreover, the walls may be
any walls, not just bathroom walls. Professor Read included in his compilation
everything he saw on walls during an extensive sight-seeing trip made in the
western United States and Canada in the summer of 1928. Much of his material
is traditional in form only, but not content. The various homosexual rendez-
vous requests with listing of dimensions and telephone numbers are clearly traditional in form and are surely worth studying as indicators of one of the obvious functions of men's rooms in a culture which forbids homosexual activities.
However, the specific content of these assignation attempts is often idiosyncratic. The folklorist is primarily interested in those mural inscriptions which
are traditional in both form and content. Thus while he may record the hapax
logomena or one-time occurrences, he is more concerned with those which have
multiple existence, that is, those which are found with almost exactly the same
form and wording in many different places. Obviously, a one-time occurrence
may become traditional in time, but the vast majority of the nontraditional
graffiti are much too localized to diffuse easily. For the traditional inscriptions,
I propose the term latrinalia. This is preferable, I think, to the closest thing
to a folk term, "shithouse poetry" inasmuch as not all latrinalia is in verse or
poetic form.

Before examining the nature of latrinalia in America and discussing its significance, I should like to comment briefly on the failure of American social
scientists to study this kind of material. It is curious that it is perfectly permissible to investigate the graffiti of the past, say the graffiti of classical cultures, but it is not equally acceptable, academically speaking, to study the
graffiti of our own culture. The rationale is apparently that it is safe to study
the "once removed" whether once removed in space or time, but not so safe to
study what is all too readily available in one's immediate environment. Perhaps
one of the reasons why individuals are attracted to the discipline of anthropology
is that the "once removed" framework is provided. Archaeologists, practicing
"dirt archaeology", are free to dig into the bowels of the earth searching for
buried treasures among the remains of what men of the past produced. In this
connection, archaeologists have even begun to indulge in the analysis of cop-
rolites. Physical anthropologists are free to examine every part of the human
body in great detail. Ethnographers can perfectly properly go into the "field"
and voyeuristically observe exotic customs, the analogues of which they might
be embarrassed to watch at home in their own culture. (One is reminded of the
folk definition of anthropology: the study of man...embracing woman!) Even the

unusually great concern with the finer points of kinship may reflect an abiding and fundamental curiosity about basic family relationships. That ethnographies reflect the culture of the ethnographers as much as the people described cannot be doubted. Germane to the present study is the lack of data in standard ethnographies on defecation and urination. When, where, and how are these acts performed? When and how precisely is toilet training for infants introduced? One can read an entire ethnography without ever coming upon any reference to these daily necessities. The study of man must include all aspects of human activity.

Since ethnography, like charity, should begin at home (how can we possibly perceive the bias of our accounts without fully understanding our own culture?), the study of latrinalia is clearly a legitimate area of inquiry. One must not forget that it it humans who write on bathroom walls and humans who read these writings. As one writer has put it (Reynolds 1943:171-72), "Stereotyped and crude, our lavatory inscriptions are the measure of our social fixations; and that enterprising anthropologist who is said to be collecting photographs of them in all parts of the world should reveal more of the truth than all of the bombastic historians who will so soon be clothing our grotesque society with dignified phrases and political stercorations, representing its present antics as studied movements, to be explained in terms of high principles and rational conduct." So then let us proceed with our essay in hard core ethnography!

In American culture, anything which leaves the body from one of its various apertures is by definition dirty. The transition is immediate. Saliva is not defiling until it leaves the mouth. Similarly, nasal, ear, or eye secretions (with the possible exception of tears) are not offensive until they are removed from the body. The emitted materials are frequently as disgusting to the emitter as to others. Few Americans would be able to drink a glass of water into which they or someone else had just expectorated or even drooled. It is true that French or soul kissing allows for swapping spits, but in this case, the saliva is is encountered while still inside the mouth and it is presumably not deemed dirty. A more mundane example would be the removal of partly masticated food from the mouth. Since by definition anything which emerges from the body is dirty and disgusting, an unchewed morsel may present a social problem. Does one grasp it with the fingers or with an eating utensil? Is there any sense of embarrassment at removing the morsel in front of others and realizing the removal is being observed? How does one dispose of the chewed bit of gristle? Is it placed surreptitiously on one's plate and perhaps concealed with a convenient lettuce leaf? Of course, there is nothing inherently dirty. Man, not nature, makes dirt and one can say that dirt, like beauty, lies in the eyes of the beholder. The concept of dirt is part of culture and as such it falls into the province of the cultural anthropologist.

One of the few places where dirt may be displayed and discussed in American culture is the bathroom, private and public. Bathrooms, generally speaking, are status symbols and not infrequently houses are measured in part by the number of bathrooms they possess. It is in the home bathroom that the child is taught to deposit his feces and urine. Here is one place where he is allowed to manipulate his genitals and expose them to view, either his own view or the view of others. Not only are the genitals and buttocks exposed, but the products of micturition and defecation may also be observed. Later, in public rest rooms, the child soon learns that he must make public what has hitherto been private. He must urinate alongside strangers and in the course of so doing, he may observe the organs of others in the act just as these other individuals may observe him.

Despite the overt behavior, the culturally prescribed pretense that such activities do not exist, as manifested in the taboo against referring directly to them, continues. The large number of euphemisms attest to that. The private family idioms of the home, e.g. to go potty, to do number one (urination) or number two (defecation), to wee wee, to make a poo, etc., cannot be used in the public context. Children in school are taught to "excuse" themselves. (Note that to "excuse oneself" may carry the sense of apologizing!) The ironic part is that the child must go through the public confessional act of raising his hand to tell the teacher and all of his peers that he wishes to answer a "call of nature". The child soon learns the gamut of farfetched euphemisms ranging from "washing" or "freshening up" to "seeing a man about a dog", going to "shake hands with the head of the family", or trying to do something about the fact that one's "back teeth are floating". (For an extended discussion of such euphemisms, see Pudney 1954:20-37 and Sagarin 1962:69-74.) Note that the term lavatory literally refers to cleaning and thus to sinks, not toilets. Yet the word lavatory has become almost taboo and is now substituted for by newer euphemisms (Reynolds 1943:179). Once in the school bathroom, however, the behavior cannot be anything other than to the point. It is in the public school bathroom (termed boys' and girls' "basement" at my secondary school in Pawling, New York, though the rooms were not located in the basement) that important social interactions take place. Boys meet there to discuss the problems of the day while girls similarly go there to gossip. It is in many ways a place of comparative freedom from the normal restraints imposed by the adult world. The necessity of some sexual exposure no doubt contributes to the bathroom's role as a place of sanctioned license. It is in public bathrooms, particularly men's rooms, that one finds latrinalia.

The variety of latrinalia forms includes: (1) advertisements or solicitations, normally of a sexual nature; (2) requests or commands, often concerning the mechanics of defecating or urinating; (3) directions, which consist of false or facetious instructions; (4) commentaries, either by the establishment or by clients; and (5) personal laments or introspective musings. These categories are not hard and fast and they are not necessarily mutually exclusive. A sampling of each of the categories should serve to illustrate the nature of American latrinalia.

The majority of advertisements are probably not traditional in that individuals simply write their own names and telephone numbers. Furthermore, in view of the paucity of published materials, it is difficult to ascertain whether or not a number of items have appeared elsewhere. Typical "want ads", which may or may not be traditional, include:

1. For a good blow job, call 777 2024
   Bill, don't call, it's me, Bob.

2. I'm big. 9" long, 3" round, and ready to go.
   (In another hand) How big is your prick?

In view of the nontraditional content of most latrinalia advertisements, I will proceed to the more common traditional category of requests or commands. The following are usually placed near men's urinals:

3. Don't throw cigarette butts in the urinal –
   it makes them soggy and hard to light.

4. Please do not throw butts in the urinal.
   Do we piss in your ash trays?

This is strikingly similar in style to the private swimming pool sign which reads:

We don't swim in your toilet
Please don't piss in our pool.

The pool sign reflects, of course, the fact that Americans do in fact urinate in swimming pools (just as American infants urinate in their baths)!
A large number of urinal latrinalia specifically ask for care in aiming the stream of urine. Typical examples of this "toilet training" tradition include:

5. We aim to please.
   You aim too please.

6. It is our aim to keep this place clean.
   Your aim will help.

These are often written by the management. A common request urges men to stand close to the urinal to reduce the chances of spillage.

7. Stand up close. The next man might have holes in his shoes.

8. Stand close, the next person may be barefooted.

9. Stand up close
   The next fellow may be a Southerner
   And be barefooted. (Camp Maxey, Paris, Texas, 1945)

10. If your hose is short
    And your pump is weak
    You better stand close
    Or you'll pee on your feet.

11. Old rams with short horns
    please stand up close. (Fort Lewis, Tacoma, Washington, circa 1945;
    cf. Read 1935:20)

An appropriately localized version from New England is as follows:

182

12. Puritans with short muskets step up to the firing line. (Damiscotta, Maine, circa 1950)

Another example of latrinalia which is posted by the management rather than the customers is one found in diners' restrooms:

13. If you shit here, eat here
We don't want just the tail end of your business.

Occasionally, there are blason populaire latrinalia:

14. Shake well. Texas needs the water.

For the special case when a man urinates into a toilet rather than into a urinal, special instructions may be found:

15. Be like brother
Not like Sis
Lift the seat
When you take a piss. (New York City, 1924)

16. Be like Dad and not like Sis
Pull your lid before you piss. (Camp Maxey, Paris, Texas, 1945)

Some commands are concerned with toilet flushing.

17. Flush your toilets for Wichita's sake. (Hutchinson, Kansas, circa 1958; cf. Read 1935:20)

18. Flush twice: L. A. needs water.

19. Flush hard. It's a long way to the kitchen.

This insult to the chef is a reversal of the conception that man is a dirt-making machine which transforms food into feces. This conception is illustrated by a latrinalia verse in French which was found in Oxford, England, in 1947: "Ici tombent en ruines les merveilles de la cuisine." In the above text and the following, the "natural" procedure is reversed as feces becomes food.

20. Don't flush the toilet. The next man might be hungry. (Chicago, 1960)

21. Please flush the toilet.
We want the niggers to starve to death. (A Missouri café, 1965)

There is also some instruction designed to keep the toilet seat clean.

22. Here is the place we all must come
To do the work that must be done
Do it quick and do it neat
But please don't do it on the seat.

23. Boys we all must use this throne
    Please keep it clean and neat
    Shit down the hole God damn your soul
    And not upon the seat. (Camp Maxey, Paris, Texas, 1945)

The reference to "throne" recalls the euphemisms in other cultures which speak of going to the place where the king goes on foot or alone (Pudney 1954:97). A common American fantasy technique designed to minimize one's awe of a great personage is to imagine that individual at stool.

24. For those in a hurry
    With no time to sit
    Please lift the lid
    For a more direct hit. (Women's restroom, Berkeley, 1963)

This may refer also to the practice of many women of not actually sitting on a toilet seat but of squatting over it.
    One commentary complains about the nature of men's clothing as opposed to women's clothing with special reference to defecation.

25. Women women what a blessing
    You can shit without undressing
    But we poor men we sons of bitches
    We must strip or shit in our britches. (Camp Maxey, Paris, Texas, 1945)

The influence of television programs and such contemporary events as demonstrations by civil rights groups (e.g. the Congress of Racial Equality) is evident in some commands.

26. Smile, You're on Candid Camera.

This is usually written on the inside of the door of the toilet stall.

27. Stay seated. This is a Core shit-in. (University library, Berkeley campus,
                                          April, 1964)

Some commands or requests are bitter parodies:

28. Support mental health or I'll kill you.

In the "directions" category, one finds mostly parodies. In the following text, the accuracy of the first line and of the order of the remaining lines was questioned by the informant. It is, however, an excellent example of a latrinalia verse of the "how-to-do-it-yourself" variety.

29. If you want to shit at ease
    Place your elbows on your knees
    Place your hands upon your chin
    Work your asshole out and in. (cf. Read 1935:51, 73)

30. Directions to get to Texas: Go west until you smell shit - that's Oklahoma.
Then, go south until you step in it - that's Texas. (Manchester, New Hampshire, circa 1953)

31. In case of atomic attack...
    1. Put your hands over your ears
    2. Put your head between your legs
    3. Kiss your ass goodbye. You've had it.

32. In case of attack, hide under this urinal.
Nobody ever hits it. (Great Lakes, Illinois, 1951)

There are also false directions which are really a form of what folklorists sometimes call a catch. Repeated many times, each time in smaller writing is the line: "If you can read this come closer." Then at the bottom right below a minuscule version appears the line: "You are now shitting at a 45° angle." In similar vein is the sign on the ceiling over the urinal which says, "While you're reading this, you're peeing on your shoes."

The content of the latrinalia commentaries varies. Some are unexpectedly intellectual.

33. "God is dead." Nietzsche
"Nietzsche is dead." God

However, not many commentaries have this kind of sophistication. Few American latrinalia verses are as philosophical, for example, as the following latrinalia verse popular in Spain:

En este lugar cerrado
donde viene tanta gente
hace fuerza el más cobarde
y se caga el más valiente. (cf. Jiménez 1960:124)

The majority of American commentaries stay close to home. An "x" marked high over the wall of a men's urinal is accompanied by the explanatory line:

34. Anyone who can piss this high ought to be a fireman.

One wonders if there is any insight here into the psychological rationale underlying the motivation to become a fireman. (Note the slang term "hose" for penis and see text 10 in this paper.) One recalls the desire of many small boys to grow up to be firemen and the custom of adolescent boys of urinating on campfires to extinguish them (cf. Bettelheim 1955:166-167).

35. You are holding the future of America in your hands.

Here is a reminder during the act of urination that the same organ is one used for reproduction. Note the pseudo-patriotic responsibility to procreate.

One common commentary deals with the very real problem of those last drops of urine which all too often drip down into one's pants or down one's leg.

36. You can wiggle, jiggle, jump or dance
    But the last three drops go down your pants.

37. No matter how you dance and prance
    The last two drops go down your pants.

38. You can shake and shake as much as you please
    But there'll still be a drop for your B.V.D.'s.

An English version has a different rhyme for the same message:

39. However hard you shake your peg
    At least one drop runs down your leg.

The "shaking" is also found in other latrinalia.

40. You are now shaking your best friend
    And he stood up for you on your wedding night. (Camp Maxey, Paris,
    Texas, 1945)

However, the shaking act can be suspicious if carried on too long. Excessive manipulation of the genitals could be construed as masturbatory activity:

41. If you shake it more than three times, you're cheating. (cf. Read 1935:68)

There are other anti-masturbation verses.

42. Be a man, not a fool
    Pull the chain, not your tool.

43. This is a teepee
    For you to peepee
    Not a wigwam
    To beat your tomtom.

Another topic of commentaries is the cleanliness of toilets.

44. No need to stand on the toilet seat
    For the crabs in this place jump forty feet. (cf. Read 1935:40,44)

45. It does no good to line the seat
    The crabs here jump fifteen feet.

The last verse reveals the practice of putting sheets of toilet paper on the top of toilet seats as a means of avoiding contact with the seat. This folk custom has recently become formalized by the presence of paper seat cover dispensers.

There are occasional political latrinalia. Here are several demeaning presidential candidate Barry Goldwater:

46. When I look down, I see Goldwater.

47. Urine is goldwater; the only benefit is derived from the comfort of its removal.

Mathematics, the language of science, has exerted some influence:

48. The heat of the meat is inversely proportional to angle of the dangle.

The heat of the meat, that is, the state of sexual excitement, is directly proportional to the degree of erection. The greater the erection, the less the "angle of dangle". The internal rhyme in this last verse shows the poetic quality of latrinalia. (Poetic features are found in other obscenity. One thinks of the alliterative folk alternatives for saying "I've been screwed", to wit: to be "fucked by the fickle finger of fate" or to be "diddled by the dangling digit of doom".)
Another latrinalia comment on sexuality occurs in the folkloristic form of a toast:

49. Here's to the hole that never heals
    The more you rub it the better it feels
    All the water this side of hell
    Can't wash away the codfish smell. (Camp Maxey, Paris, Texas, 1945)

The language of advertising can be found too. A borrowing from a Ban deodorant advertisement was found in November, 1965, on a prophylactic dispenser in a Shafter, Nevada, restroom:

50. It takes the worry out of being close.

By far the best poetry is to be found in the personal laments or introspective musings category. One of the most popular of these is:

51. Here I sit broken hearted
    Tried (Came) to shit and only farted. (cf. Read 1935:50)

The sadness is actually economic inasmuch as one ordinarily pays to use most public toilets. One must make a small deposit <u>before</u> entering the toilet stall. The "failure to get one's money's worth", an important theme in American culture, is explicit in some versions.

52. Here I sit broken-hearted
    Paid a nickel and only farted.

This last verse has a traditional response:

53. Don't cry brother
    You had your chance
    I didn't have a nickel
    And shit (in) my pants.

There is also a combination of both verses:

54. Here I sit broken hearted
    Tried to shit and only farted.
    But think of the man who took the chance
    Tried to fart and shit his pants.

There are other examples of American latrinalia with the introductory <u>opening</u> formula "Here I sit".

55. Here I sit in stinking vapor
    Some sonuvabitch stole the toilet paper.

56. Here I sit in silent bliss
    Listening to the trickling piss
    Now and then a fart is heard
    Calling to the coming turd. (Los Angeles, 1918; cf. Read 1935:51, 81)

57. Here I sit in solemn bliss
    Listening to the dribble of piss
    And now and then a fart is heard
    Then followed by a thundering turd. (Camp Maxey, Paris, Texas, 1945)

These last two verses are obviously cognates and are related to the versions from Lake Tahoe and Visalia, California, reported by Read (1935:51).
    Noteworthy is the sound aspect of the process of elimination. Most people are ashamed of anyone's hearing the sound of their urinating or defecating. Even the sound of a toilet flush is embarrassing to some. The whole philosophy of pretending that the activity doesn't exist is of course threatened by the possibility of someone's hearing the unavoidable telltale sound. The listener, as opposed to the voyeur, is depicted in the following verse:

58. Sam, Sam, the janitor man
    Chief superintendent of the crapping can.
    He washes out the bowls and picks up the towels
    And listens to the roar of other men's bowels. (cf. Read 1935:39)

The sound is also involved in some of the onomatopoeic euphemisms, e.g. "tinkle" meaning to urinate.
    Some latrinalia explore the motivations for visiting bathrooms.

59. Some come here to sit and think
    But I come here to shit and stink. (Camp Maxey, Paris, Texas, 1945; cf.
                                        Read 1935:21, 49, 74)

60. Some come here to sit and think
    And some come here to wonder
    But I come here to shit and stink
    And fart away like thunder.

A comparison of the last two reveals how a two-line verse may be expanded into a four-line verse. In the following verse, the expansion utilizes a different rhyme scheme:

61. Some people come to sit and think
    Others come to shit and stink.
    But I just come to scratch my balls
    And read the bullshit on the walls.

All these latrinalia texts are representative and they should serve to illustrate the nature of this on-going mural tradition. However, these materials raise a number of questions. Probably the most intriguing questions about latrinalia are psychological. Why are they written at all and why in bathrooms? Why are they so much more common in men's rest rooms than in women's rest rooms?

There has been little theorizing about the psychological functions of latrinalia. Reynolds (1943:170) has stated that generations of lavatory wall writers simply write for the pleasure of breaking a taboo, presumably the taboo of referring to body elimination activities. Allen Walker Read suggests that latrinalia probably results from many different motivations. Nevertheless, he notes (1935:17) that, "A principal reason is the well-known human yearning to leave a record of one's presence or one's existence." If this is correct, the question remains, what is the psychological significance of a yearning to leave a record of one's presence?

Allen Walker Read has also observed (1935:17) that writing latrinalia is the same order of activity as the carving of initials or names on trees. Interestingly enough, psychoanalyst Ernest Jones tried to explain the latter custom in his famous paper on "Anal-Erotic Character Traits". Jones hypothesizes (1961: 432) that it may possibly be a derived and sublimated form of what he terms a "primitive smearing impulse", the desire that infants allegedly have to handle and manipulate their feces, a desire whose fulfillment is invariably forbidden by toilet-training conscious parents. People who carve or write their names are leaving a memento of themselves which may injure and spoil something beautiful. Although Jones makes no mention of latrinalia, I suggest that it may well stem from the same impulse to smear feces or dirt on walls. Dirty words are dirt by themselves, independent of the dirtiness of their referents. Certainly this theory would explain why the writing was placed on bathroom walls in particular. The fact that much of the content of latrinalia does refer to defecation and urination would tend to support the assertion that there is some relationship between the acts of writing on walls and playing with feces. Farfetched as this may sound to some, it is precisely the explanation given by the folk! In one of the best known latrinalia verses, the rationale for writing latrinalia is as follows:

62. Those who write on shithouse walls
    Roll their shit in little balls
    Those who read these words of wit
    Eat the little balls of shit.

Here is an explicit equation of the act of writing on walls with the manipulation of one's own feces. It could not be said any more plainly than "Those who write on shithouse walls roll their shit in little balls!"

From earliest childhood, the American is taught to deny his anus and its activities. The smearing impulse is redirected to suitable substitute activities: working with modeling clay, finger paints, or throwing mud pies (cf. Ferenczi 1956a). Using words, dirty words, some individuals finally do give vent to the impulse to sully walls. Since "dirt" is supposed to be deposited in the clean white receptacles found in bathrooms, what more flagrant act of rebellion than to place symbolic dirt on the very walls surrounding the receptacles!

While Freudian explanations are not popular in anthropological and folkloristic circles, the fact that the folk confirm the Freudian explanation must be taken into account and explained by anti-Freudians. The independent congruence of analytic and folk or native theories does, it seems to me, present a reasonably convincing argument. Noteworthy also in this connection is the fact that the second couplet of the above mentioned metafolkloristic text corroborates another psychoanalytic insight into toilet ritual. It has been suggested (Abraham 1948b: 385; Fenichel 1953:374) that the popular practice of reading while at stool is essentially an act of incorporation designed to balance the material which is lost through defecation. (The common rationale for such reading is the desire not to waste time. By reading in the bathroom, one can save time and make it more productive. Additionally the reading also permits and encourages the prolongation of the defecation act.) Thus "eating" the dirty words compensates for the evacuated fecal dirt. Once again, the folk apparently agree with the explanation: "Those who read these words of wit eat the little balls of shit."

A more recent localized bit of latrinalia appearing in Berkeley supports the writing-feces equation:

63. Don't write on our walls
   We don't shit in your notebooks.
                    The Regents

   What's found in our notebooks is shit anyway
                    The Students
                    (Main Library, U.C. Berkeley, 1965)

The equation of defecation and writing is not limited to American culture. Apparently in parts of Bulgaria, one who has gone to the "thinking place" is described as "thinking" or "writing" (Pudney 1954:25). The writing-defecation equation suggests that the academic motto "publish or perish", an oicotypal example of what might be termed the alternative structure proverb (cf. "do or die", "put up or shut up", "fish or cut bait", etc.), may be "shit or get off the pot" in symbolic disguise. One might remember that scholars are first supposed to amass great quantities of data from which they are expected to "get stuff out regularly" (Dundes 1962b). (Cf. the notion of weighing the output on the scales at the end of the year.)

The suggested anal erotic basis of writing may also explain why men rather than women write latrinalia. According to current theory, men the world over suffer from pregnancy envy (Bettelheim 1955, Dundes 1962g:1038). In essence, men are envious of women's ability to bear children and they seek to find various substitute gratifications, e. g. couvade behavior, having an intellectual "brainchild", calling their pet project their "baby", etc. Bettelheim has assembled a good deal of convincing anthropological evidence to document the pregnancy envy hypothesis. However, although Bettelheim does cite (1962:128) the instance of the Chaga men's practice of stopping up their rectums as a form of symbolic pregnancy, he does not see that males commonly use their anuses to provide substitutes for parturition. Feces, like babies, are produced by the body. When a man defecates, he is a creator, a prime mover. Women produce feces too, but since they can produce babies from within, there is less need for women to emphasize this type of body product. That women have less need of fecal substitute activities is suggested by the fact that few women indulge in sculpture, painting, blowing wind instruments, etc. (cf. Jones 1961:435, n. 4). Certainly in American culture, it is men who are more concerned than women with creative feces metaphors. It is usually men, not women, who are "full of it", who are "BS artists", who tell "cock and bull stories".

In American culture, the emphasis is on productivity and the male must make much more than feces. He must make something of himself and he must make a living. The word make is itself indicative of the productive component of defecation. An infant may be told to make water, make weewee, make B.M. , or just plain make (Sagarin 1962:47, 52). As an adult in a "man's world", he tries to make money or make time. Once he is successful, he may be told that he's got it made. "Time is money", the proverb says, but both time and money are symbolic fecal substitutes (Brown 1959:277; Carvalho Neto 1956b:125-148; Ferenczi 1956a; Dundes 1962g, 1962h; Jones 1961:425-427) as folk speech and other folklore so abundantly attests (cf. to be filthy rich, to be rolling in it, to have money up the ass, to make one's pile, to have time on one's hands, to pass time or piddle the time away, etc.). Time and money can be saved or hoarded; time and money can be spent or wasted. In American ideal culture, saving is valued. Think of all the money and time saving devices enjoyed by Americans. Yet in American real culture, prestige accrues to those who spend or waste time and money. If a man wants to make it big or make a splash, he has to produce, to put out. He can't sit tight; he can't sit on his material. Even God, a masculine figure, is termed a maker, which is entirely appropriate in view of the anal nature of man's creation, that is, man's being molded from dust or dirt (Dundes 1962g:1046). (Note also that the "fart-thunder" linkage so patent in the latrinalia hints at an infantile origin of thunder gods as Róheim (1952:515) almost says.)

The make metaphor also applies to genital matters. A man is expected to make out, to make a woman and to make love. The couching of genital affairs in anal terms is paralleled by the whole concept of dirty words in American culture. Dirty jokes, for example, are largely genital, not anal in content. Yet jokes about sex are called "dirty jokes". The word on the sign at Berkeley was an obscene word which no false acrostic, "Freedom Under Clark Kerr", could disguise, but it was thought of as a dirty word (cf. the filthy speech movement - no pun on movement intended!). One reason why genitality is considered to be "dirty" may be guilt by association. The organs concerned are recognized and identified first as producers of urine, that is, as producers of dirt. Later it is discovered that the sexual act is performed by the same dirt-producing instrument. This situation has been summed up by Yeats in his poem "Crazy Jane Talks With the Bishop" when he wrote: "But Love has pitched his mansion in the place of excrement." Here is dirt by association.

The desire to make one's mark or to leave something behind for posterity is also very likely involved in the writing of latrinalia. Defecation as a technique to mark a place for identification is found not only in folk tales (Freud and Oppenheim 1958:38) but among other forms of primate life who apparently demarcate territorial boundaries through urination and defecation (Harrisson 1963). The goal is also perhaps to achieve notice and immortality by producing dirt. A final example of latrinalia bears on this:

64. To the shithouse poet
In honor of his wit
May they build far and wide
Great monuments of shit.

One wonders about the significance of leaving great stone memorials. Many great men have taken an active part in designing and building that which was to remain after they had departed. There is the obvious phallic significance of some monuments. The Washington monument is certainly appropriate for the father of our country. But the majority are massive pieces of stone, often in the shape of little rooms or houses. (Writing on these walls involves epitaphs rather than latrinalia.) The psychology of making one's mark, of leaving some memorial behind, may be related to American males' desire to successfully compete with females who can "make" children as their form of immortality.

For those who may be skeptical of the theory that the psychological motivation for writing latrinalia is related to an infantile desire to play with feces and to artistically smear it around, I would ask only that they offer an alternative theory. For those who doubt that the greater interest on the part of males in latrinalia is related to anal creativity stemming from pregnancy envy, I would ask the same. It is all too easy to offer destructive criticism. We know that latrinalia exists. What we want to know is why it exists and what function it serves. One day when we have more information about the writers of latrinalia (and perhaps psychological projective tests administered to such writers) and when we have better cross-cultural data, we may be better able to confirm or revise the present attempt to answer the questions.

18

ON ELEPHANTASY AND ELEPHANTICIDE

(with Roger D. Abrahams)

The literature on the theory of humor and with and related subjects is vast and includes works by some of the greatest minds in Western history: Aristotle, Bergson, Freud, Meredith, and others more recent. These writers have tended to concentrate on two aspects of the humor problem: the structure of devices which make people laugh and what laughter does to individuals. [1] These philosophical or psychological commentators have attempted to analyze the reasons why people are amused. Nevertheless, there have been few attempts to discern the effect of time and place on the creation and dissemination of jokes and other witticisms. Though it is widely known that the "sense of humor" of one era or region differs from others, little of substance has been written to explain these differences. The effect of time and place on humorous devices becomes especially important in analyzing joke cycles, for here the jokes often achieve a spontaneous popularity and a widespread diffusion in a relatively short time. Yet the question remains unanswered as to why and how this phenomenon occurs. In hopes of taking one step toward this answer, we will investigate the latent content of one recent joke cycle, the elephant riddles, and discuss it in relation to certain important psychological and social factors in the lives of those who have transmitted these bits of jokelore. [2]

This investigation seems especially appropriate, for the elephant series is a recent one and has achieved a notoriety that may have surpassed even that of the "knock-knock", "little moron", or "sick joke" cycles. The elephant riddle, as with all of these cycles, utilizes a childish type of humor. It involves the simple, highly repetitive form of the conundrum, deriving a great deal of its humor from the restricted form and subject matter. Furthermore, the world presented in these jokes is whimsically topsy-turvy, based on the premise that elephants can climb trees and do all sorts of other wonderful acrobatic tricks (such as jump down from trees, climb into refrigerators and Volkswagens, fly, etc.).

The elephant jokes, then, are patently childish and nonsensical. In their insistence on childish forms and techniques, they emphasize the basically regressive nature of wit as suggested by Freud and his followers. [3] Wit is but one form of the comic, and the comic is a regressive means of achieving a temporary sense of freedom from superego or societal restraint. "Under the influence of the comic, we return to the happiness of childhood. We can throw off the fetters of logical thought and revel in long-forgotten freedom. " (Kris 1952:205).

Reprinted from The Psychoanalytic Review 56 (1969), 225-41.

But adults cannot resort to most forms of childhood humor except under extreme conditions of anxiety or during licentious occasions (such as those provided by stage performances or celebrations), for to talk nonsense or to act absurdly is to suggest a lack of maturity. Though everyone seems to need this kind of release from repression, it becomes increasingly difficult to obtain license as one grows older.

One of the elements of emotional maturity is the acceptance of restrictions upon one's pleasure-seeking (id) drives and the development of the ability to redirect the energies into secondary gratifications (sublimation). Herein resides our feeling of "lost freedom". Nevertheless, the demands of the id remain, modified as they are by other ego processes. They must find some secondary outlet. Wit, especially as an aggressive expression, is one of the most effective of these substitute gratifications. The word-play of wit is a development of childhood aggressive play activities, but there is a clear distinction in subtlety and ambiguity between childhood and adult comic expressions. The formal devices of wit are the same in childish and mature humor (puns, poetic devices, non sequiturs, balanced phrasing, etc.), but the expression of them is more complex in adult life, the aggressions more veiled, and the results more ambiguous. Wit thus functions as a channel back to childhood and serves as an aggressive form of expression which remains permissible because of the development of increasingly complex formal devices.*4 Jokes perform a defensive function, denying the reality principle for the moment in favor of an infantile word-play and "nonsense" world in which dangerous expressions of aggression can be projected into harmless situations, thereby causing the jokes to serve the pleasure principle. Jokes can function as a steam-valve in this way, allowing the defense of aggressive expression against something which is causing a threat (and thus creating anxiety) by regressing to childish expressions of wit.

Regression is relative, however, and seems to vary in direct relation to the amount of anxiety present. Certain expressions hark back further in our experience than usual and are a fairly accurate indication that abnormal anxieties are being felt which are, in fact, closer to infantile fears. To be sure, wit is by its very nature anxiety-producing. It asserts itself in an aggressive - often a contest - situation in which anxiety is a natural concomitant. Furthermore, in wit certain topics emerge which are otherwise taboo. However, under some circumstances, because of historical events in specific areas (for instance, war or depression), anxiety may become all-pervasive. In such cases, jokes arise to counterfeit the threatening situation, to cast it into harmless form, and thus to provide an anxiety release. The more threatening the situation, the more harmless and infantile the created world must become. Such periods provide the perfect breeding grounds not only for childish expressions of wit, but for these joke cycles which enable one to multiply one's ego gains by the number of witticisms which emerge because of the suggestive possibilities of form and subject.

Regression occurs because the childhood world was a more permissive one; if one assumes the mask of a child, one can get away with aggressive expressions otherwise unavailable to him in his adult role. The aggressor must insist that he is harmless in order to be able to get away with his attack. Where one's antagonist is especially powerful (therefore productive of the most intense anxieties in the contest situation), there is a natural tendency for the individual to regress totally to the childish stance in order to be able to fight back at all.*5

This regression is not simply a matter of defense, however. In childhood, the individual has achieved certain basic triumphs (such as the mastery of motor activity or language) to which he returns not only for defensive weapons, but also for the simple pleasure of the reenactment of these earlier victories. The regressive techniques bring about a feeling of safety in the already mastered infantile world. Thus conflict is asserted in the aggressive nature of a joke, yet denied in its regressive use of childish forms and techniques. Or, to put it in the form of an oxymoron, the joke becomes a harmless aggression - an aggression which hurts no one, but which provides a transitory gain for the ego of the joker.

The deceptive harmlessness of the joke is, of course, apparent in its nonactive aspect (i.e. the aggression is talked, not enacted). Even the spoken aggression may be further ameliorated by couching it in symbolic terms. The apparently nonsensical world in which the tree-climbing elephant exists, for instance, allows us to sidestep certain societal restrictions which would be imposed in more overt expressions of the themes and attitudes found in these jokes. The veil of nonsense is so opaque that the serious nature of the underlying rationale of the humor is effectively concealed. This is as it should be, or rather as it always is. The release, the safety-valve function of oral humor, would be less effective if one knew what he was saying or laughing at. This veiling from consciousness is one way of duping society into the casual acceptance of argument. As an escape from the pyschological pressures of the human condition, we must translate or transmute reality into an unrecognizable form. That these forms should be those first used by children simply indicates that under certain conditions we continue to fight the same battles as adults and with the same weapons.

The specific questions we raise now are: What is the nature of the reality for which the elephant jokes are a sanctioned means of combat and escape? What early anxieties have been retriggered which necessitate the reactivation of such childish forms of defense and release? In our attempt to cast light on the problem, we will first discuss the latent meanings disguised in this joke cycle and then attempt to show what caused them to arise when and where they did.

I

Like so many other joke cycles in American folklore, the elephant jokes contain a considerable amount of sexual content. However, in some of the jokes the content is latent and is probably not completely comprehended by those transmitting the jokes. In the elephant joke cycle, the elephant is the epitome of sexual power. His immensity (especially that of his phallus), and his alleged ability to procreate even under the most trying conditions are recurrent themes. The big, apparently clumsy, yet tremendously powerful and surprisingly adept elephant is in some ways a modern-day successor to the giant or ogre antagonist in folktales who poses a serious threat to the well-being of the hero. As Jack has to cut down the giant's stalk, and as Odysseus must put out the eye of Polyphemus, so the modern American has to emasculate his nemesis, the omnipotent elephant.

This suggests that there are at least two distinct types of elephant jokes. In one the animal is the intimate elephant with huge parts, capable of acting as a sexual aggressor (often with other animals). The sexual superiority is signaled not only by his large organ, but also by the ability to perform intercourse with impossible partners in impossible situations. The other type represents a defense against the superphallic elephant. In these one finds diverse techniques of keeping the elephant away or of castrating him. It should be noted that in the first type, it is the elephant who is the protagonist; the elephant is somewhere, has something, or is performing some act. In the second type the elephant is the antagonist or victim; someone does something to or for the elephant.

The associations of phallic grandeur with the elephant are considerably older than the present elephant joke cycle in American oral tradition. For example, in American Negro folklore, there is an epic toast which concerns a fight between lion and elephant. In the struggle the elephant is portrayed as being obviously sexually superior to the lion (Abrahams 1964:136-47). A widely current joke, which incidentally found its way into the first-draft version of Tennessee Williams' Cat on a Hot Tin Roof, tells of a man and his wife who take their young son to a zoo. They visit the elephant house, where the son notices that the bull elephant has an erection. The son asks his mother, "Mommy, what is that?" She quickly replies, "That's nothing, son", whereupon the father comments, "She's just spoiled." In other jokes, the human protagonist does not compare so favorably. A piece of folk poetry dating from the 1930's in northern California construction camps goes as follows:

I took my gal to the circus
The circus for to see
When she saw the elephant's trunk
She wouldn't go home with me.

The phallic reference is made abundantly clear by the next verse:

I took my gal to the ballgame
The ballgame for to see
When the umpire yelled, "Four balls"
She wouldn't go home with me.

The symbolic significance of the elephant's trunk is clear. It is the shape and mobility of the trunk which contributes a great deal to the image of the elephant. In a typical risqué cartoon, an elephant stands outside a tent beside which a car is parked. On the back of the car is a placard saying "Just Married". The elephant is shown inserting his trunk in-between the two flaps of the tent. The caption reads, "Great Heavens, Paul!"*6 The following representative elephant joke texts should serve to illustrate the phallic and the castrative aspects of the cycle.

II

First the elephant becomes intimate. He may appear in bed or in the bathtub.

1. How can you tell if there is an elephant in bed with you?
   He has buttons on his pajamas this big (with gesture spreading hands apart about a foot).
2. How do you know if an elephant is in the bathtub with you?
   By the faint smell of peanuts on his breath.

The true nature of the danger caused by the intimate elephant is made clear.

3. How do you know when an elephant's in bed with you?
   Nine months later you have a problem.

Elephantine anatomy is frequently depicted in sexual terms.

4. Why does an elephant have four feet?
   It's better than six inches.
5. Did you hear about the man who got a job in Africa circumcizing elephants?
   Well, the pay wasn't much, but the tips were tremendous. *7
6. Do you know how to make an elephant fly?
   You start with a zipper about 20 inches long.
7. Do you know why elephants have long trunks?
   So they can French (kiss) giraffes.

That the elephant is especially interested in amorous affairs is explicit.

8. How do elephants make love in the water?
   They take their trunks down.
9. How does the elephant find his tail in the dark?
   Delightful.

The alleged sexual prowess of the elephant is demonstrated in a variety of ways. It may be a comment on the size of his seminal discharge, or it may be more obliquely stated by a reference to the lengthy period of pregnancy, the duration presumably being a result of superior genital power.

10. What's big and gray and comes in quarts?
    An elephant. *8
11. How do you tell if a woman has been raped by an elephant?
    She's pregnant for two years.

Even a prostitute, symbolizing unlimited sexual capacity, can easily be impregnated by the elephant.

12. What do you get when you cross an elephant and a prostitute?
    A three-quarter ton pickup.

Perhaps the greatest tribute to the elephant's genital superiority is his apparent ability to indulge in intercourse with impossible sexual partners.

13. Why did the elephant marry the mosquito?
    Because he had to.

Not only can the elephant impregnate any animal, small or large, but he is able to execute difficult sexual aggressive attacks on his victims. In the early jokes, the elephant was depicted as climbing trees. As Freud (1917:162) noted long ago, flying or climbing in defiance of the law of gravity can be a symbolic form of erection. The symbolic interpretation is reinforced by the elephant's manifest motive in climbing the trees. Invariably he wishes to jump down on top of some unwary passing victim (e.g. mice, crocodiles, beavers, cheetahs, etc.) (for sample texts, see Abrahams 1963:99). In some elephant jokes, the sexual aggression directed against other animals is overt.

14. Why do elephants climb trees?
    To rape squirrels.
15. Why do elephants wear springs on their feet?
    So they can rape flying monkeys.
16. What is the most fearsome sound to a flying monkey?
    Boing, boing.

In some phallic elephant jokes, the elephant's physical abilities are contrasted with the weaknesses of humans. Whereas the elephant can do anything, the human can do nothing. In some cases, the human weakness is explicitly said to be sexual failure.

17. Can you get four elephants in a Volkswagen?
    Hell, no - it's damn near impossible to get a little pussy in one.
18. What is harder than getting a pregnant elephant in a Volkswagen?
    Getting an elephant pregnant in a Volkswagen.

It should also be noted that the elephant's superiority is not limited to the genital area. The elephant excels in all of the various body functions. An example is his anal power.

19. What the difference between a saloon and an elephant fart?
    One's a bar-room; the other is more of a BarOOOMM!
20. How can you tell an elephant has been using your bathroom?
    You can't flush.
21. How do you housebreak an elephant?
    You get fourteen copies of The New York Times - Sunday edition.

III

In all of the above examples, the elephant is giant animality unleashed. The elephant, in the Paul Bunyan tradition, does everything on a very large scale. This makes the second type of elephant joke, in which the mighty beast is humbled and humiliated, strikingly different. The elephant may well be a representation of the infantile view of the father figure in regard to his enourmous size, strength, sexual appetite and ability. Like the father, he is found in intimate bedroom and bathroom (both genital and anal) situations. But although he is familiar in the home, he is to be feared. His actions are interpreted in terms of violence and rape. He is like the giant in the world of folktales. And, as in the folktale, some way must be found for the smaller observer to usurp the place of the omnipotent elephant, to cut him down to size and rob him of his defeating powers.

There are several devices utilized to conquer the elephant. One, based upon the initial extraordinary phallic characteristics of the elephant, is castration. Sometimes the castration is symbolic, sometimes literal.

22. How do you keep an elephant from charging?
    Take away his credit card.
23. How do you keep an elephant from stampeding?
    Cut his 'tam peter off.
24. What did the elephant say when the alligator bit off his trunk?
    Very funny (nasalized).*9

A more elaborate way of eliminating the elephant is to hunt and capture him.

25. How do you catch an elephant?
    First you get a sign that says "No elehants allowed". Then a pair of binocu-
    lars, a milk bottle, and a pair of tweezers. You put up the sign that says
    "No elehants allowed", and all the elephants in the area gather around and
    laugh because elephants is spelled wrong. And then more elephants come
    and then more and more. They all tell their friends about this sign that's
    spelled wrong. Pretty soon you have a whole mob of laughing elephants, so
    you take the binoculars and turn 'em around the wrong way so that the ele-
    phants are real small and then you take the tweezers and pick 'em up and
    put 'em in the milk bottle.

In this text, there is evidence of a child opposing an adult. The elephant is the adult who knows how to spell; the hunter is the child who is laughed at by the elephant for being unable to spell. But the child-hunter only feigns ignorance in order to be able to trap the adult-elephant.*10 The fact that the elephant laughs at the apparent ineptness of the hunter in making a schoolboy spelling error and that the elephant tells his friends much as parents will their friends of their children's errors, sometimes in front of their children, makes the final revenge all the sweeter. The magical technique of reducing the elephant's size by look-ing through the "wrong" end of the binoculars is very clever. The idea that the child would like to look at life in a way which would reverse the relative size differential between himself and adults (i.e. to make them, especially his parents, small enough to be manipulated with tweezers) is an important one in the elephant joke cycle. The cycle provides a means of reversing reality so that the small becomes great, and the great becomes small. To reduce the great elephant in size is to bring about detumescence in the giant rival. This is perhaps more obvious in an alternative way of annihilating the elephant.

26. How do you kill a blue elephant?
    Shoot it with a blue elephant gun.
27. How do you kill a pink elephant?
    You grab it by the balls (or trunk) and squeeze like hell until it turns blue and then you kill it with a blue elephant gun.

The most drastic means of taking away the elephant's masculinity is to transform him into a female. Whereas at the beginning of the cycle the elephant wore tennis shoes which were usually too tight, causing wrinkles, later on he wore ballet slippers.*11 More and more, the elephant began to do effeminate things, such as painting his toenails or floating on his back (thereby assuming a passive or female position). Even though the pronoun referring to the elephant is masculine, the activities are definitely feminine. In some texts, the plural "their" is employed so that the gender could be conveniently ambiguous. In a few instances, feminine pronouns were used, which revealed that the elephant had changed sex completely.

28. Why do elephants paint their toenails red?
    To hide in cherry trees.
29. Have you ever seen an elephant in a cherry tree?
    See. It works, doesn't it? (In masculine versions, testicles rather than toenails are painted.)
30. Why did the elephant put straw on her head?
    She wanted to see if blondes had more fun.
31. How do you give an elephant a shower?
    All you need is a few girls, some cake, cookies, and perhaps a little tea.

In this text, the phallic elephant is completely humbled. Shorn of his supermasculinity, he is a bride-to-be. No longer the dominant male, he is a potential victim of other dominant males. Through castration and feminization, the elephant's genital superiority is eliminated. "He" becomes "she".

IV

Looking at the elephant cycle in terms of the family romance, one can see both facets of the standard ambivalence towards the father-figure. On the one hand, there is the fascination with and envy of his physical parts and powers; on the other hand, there is the Oedipal success story which requires that this archetypal rival be emasculated and his position of power usurped. As in fairy tales where the hero who is initially fascinated by the minutiae of the giant's intimate life must ultimately slay the giant, thereby asserting his hitherto untested masculinity, so also in the elephant jokes the narrator-joker must triumph over the elephant.

Ultimately, this triumph is motivated by the desire to magically usurp the power of authority and assert it toward the mother (or, more typically in fictions and real life, a mother-substitute). But the ambiguous attraction-rejection of the giant elephant signifies more than just a fictive fulfillment of the Oedipal wish. The powers of the elephant provide more than a threat; they also suggest a model, an ego ideal. As such, the elephant's actions represent fulfillment of sexual desire. The elephant's powers are to be emulated and usurped. His actions are described totally in id terms. The ambiguous interest in and fear of the elephant are conditioned by both the wish for the implementation of sexual desires and the fear of reprisal for doing so; i.e. the fear of castration. The giant-figure represents the possibility of the freeing of desires and the triumph over restraint through power. The elephant is, then, as much a wish-projection as an adversary, and this would account, at least in part, for the two types of elephant riddles.

To point out that the elephant joke mirrors, in its special way, the Oedipal strivings which are inherent in the Western family system is not to explain why, just at this time, such a topic and figure should be of interest to so large a segment of the population. Theoretically, these Oedipal pressures are continually present. Yet rarely are they expressed in such a broadly popular form, a form which has evoked considerable comment and interest. Perhaps there is something unique in the early sixties which has triggered a mass anxiety about authority figures of especially awesome sexual capacities.

Although society and the creative individuals within it are too complex to assign definitively any single cause or set of causes for a release mechanism of the sort represented by the elephant jokes, one may nevertheless attempt to suggest certain forces which might have been instrumental in triggering such a vital and widespread response. The intensity of the response indicates that the initiating force must be of correspondingly great psychic importance. One cannot help but notice in this regard that the rise of the elephant joke occurred simultaneously with the rise of the Negro in the Civil Rights movement. The two disparate cultural phenomena appear to be intimately related, and, in fact, one might say that the elephant is a reflection of the American Negro as the white sees him and that the political and social assertion by the Negro has caused certain primal fears to be reactivated.

At first glance, this may seem to be a radical hypothesis, but there are a number of parallels between the figures of the elephant and the white stereotype of the Negro. There is, first of all, the obvious association in the minds of many Americans of both the elephant and the Negro with the African jungle. To some, the Negro is envisaged as a recent descendant of a tree-dwelling wild animal, and this animal sensuality is the source of both attraction and fear. The elephant in the tree, as we have seen, is the same kind of attractive, yet repulsive, superpotent animal. Beyond this, however, the elephant as he appears in the cycle has many of the attributes of the Negro man in his most fascinating and feared form in the popular imagination. Both the male Negro and the elephant are pictured as having unusually large genitals and commensurate sexual capacity. Furthermore, part of the public image of them relates to great size, strength, and endurance.

This conception of Negro masculinity is a fiction at best, *12 but it nevertheless persists. Until the recent Negro revolution, however, the fear could be dissipated, not only by actual social subjugation but also through folk humor, e. g. the "Rastus and Liza" joke cycle in which the Negro, depicted as a lazy domestic animal, is unable to work or think. These means of reducing the fear are no longer as available, and the Negroes in uniting for their cause have produced a contrary image which is powerful, enigmatic, and occasionally vindictive (as in the Black Muslim movement). This supplanting image has crystallized the previously concealed but long-present sexual fascination and castration fear. The Negro is now felt as a threatening phallic force to be reckoned with. The defense against this threat is regressive and projective in that the feared object is controlled by recourse to essentially juvenile joking techniques and the casting of the Negro into the shape of the elephant.

Further evidence for the connection between the Negro and the elephant is provided by the manifest color content of many of the elephant jokes. Some of the earliest examples had to do with the elephant's color.

32. Do you know why elephants are gray?
    So you can tell them from bluebirds (redbirds, blackberries).

But then the elephant began to paint himself or his clothes various colors in order to disguise himself to avoid being seen or noticed.

33. Why do elephants wear green tennis shoes?
    To hide in the tall grass.

Does the elephant, like the Negro, hope to fit into the natural environment and not be noticed by a simple act of changing his color, as another fact of the public image of the Negro would suggest? The preoccupation with the elephant's color might then reflect the public's concern with the Negro as either "colored man" or "man of color". *13

This hypothetical association of Negro and elephant might seem implausible if the elephant joke were an isolated phenomenon, but it is not. It is part of a wider contemporary vogue for joking riddles, one important strand of which has been riddling descriptions consisting of enumerations of colors which refer directly to the Negro. The earliest of these color riddles ridiculed prominent Negro individuals.

34. What's black and catches flies?
    Willie Mays (Negro centerfielder of the San Francisco Giants).

Around the same time that the elephant jokes were becoming popular, riddles concerning Negroes were depersonalized and referred to the generic "nigger".

35. What do they call a Negro with a Ph. D. in Mississippi?
    Nigger.

Moreover, at the same time that the elephant began to fly, the Negro also took
to the air, and in the process he usurped the powers of the white comic strip
hero Superman.

36. What's black and has a red cape?
    Super Nigger.

Fear of the Negro came closer to the surface, and the thought that the Negro
might possibly resort to physical attack was expressed.

37. What's dangerous, lives in a tree, and is black?
    A crow with a machine gun.
38. What do they call a six-foot-four Negro with a machine gun in Mississippi?
    Sir.

It should now be clear that the concern with color and the explicit sexual content of the elephant jokes are not mutually exclusive. Instead, the presence of
both factors is explicable in terms of a Negro-elephant equation. Once again,
the association of color and sexuality is also found in other joking riddles with
specific reference to the Negro.

39. What's black and comes in a white box?
    Sammy Davis, Jr. *14
40. What is black and white and rolls in the grass?
    Integrated sex.

The white is not only awed by the supposed genital superiority of the Negro, he
fears for the retention of his women. *15

V

It is not easy to make sense of nonsense. However, the elephant joke cycle
exists as a cultural phenomenon at a specific point in time and space. The widespread and popular nature of these materials can be explained as an outlet for
the reenactment and control of Oedipal problems. But a purely psychological
analysis alone would not explain why the cycle arose precisely when it did. The
social-historical context must also be taken into account. The development of
the Negro freedom movement, causing anxiety even among those sympathetic
to the movement, would seem to be the catalytic agent producing such a regressive response. One must realize that there is no inconsistency in arguing
that the elephant may be both the adult sexual rival, as opposed to the child,
and the Negro sexual rival, as opposed to the white. Both rivals represent
power, in part sexual, which threatens and which therefore must be conquered.
It is easier to conquer in fantasy than in reality. If killing the elephant eliminates either the father or Negro or both, and if it accomplishes this harmless-
ly under cover of nonsense so that the killer need feel no guilt, then the function
and significance of elephant jokes are clear. *16 These jokes, like all expres-

sions of wit, are serious business.

NOTES

*1 For a sample of the considerable humor literature, see Kiell (1963:139-42).

*2 For reports of the elephant cycle, see Dundes (1963c), Abrahams (1963), Brunvand (1964), Barrick (1964a), Cray and Herzog (1967). Elephant jokes were widely diffused via the mass media; see Time Magazine, Elephants by the Trunk (August 2, 1963), 41; Beastly Riddles Are Big, Seventeen (August 1963), 228-29; Beatty (1963); Gilbert (1963). (Many of these are mentioned in Barrick (1964a.) There were a number of joke folios that emerged filled with these jokes - some authentic, some ersatz: The Elephant Book; a sequel, Elephants, Grapes & Pickles; Hans and Babcock (1963); Blake (1964).

*3 Freud's most extended statement of the psychology of wit is contained in his monograph Wit and Its Relation to the Unconscious, most recently translated as Jokes and Their Relation to the Unconscious. The most important works of his followers are found in Kiell (1963).

*4 Freud (1960) emphasized this element of formal control duping the super-ego through economy of means in his work cited above.

*5 For a discussion of the totality of regression in the state of submission in regard to the Negro slave in the United States, see Elkins (1959). For the way in which this suppression caused an effect on Negro folklore in the depiction of the hero in childish trickster form, see Abrahams (1964:65-69).

*6 Over Sixteen (New York: Elgart Publishing Company, 1951), 19.

*7 This is a variant of an old joke usually told about a nurse or nurse's aid working in a hospital. Legman (1928:59) cites a text in which a rabbi earns more than a priest "because he gets all the tips".

*8 This text was reported in Dundes (1963c:41). With few exceptions, all of the texts in this article were collected in the vicinities of Austin, Texas, and Berkeley, California. Some seem to be unique, though most were collected in both places and were in all likelihood equally popular throughout the United States There are few texts which emerged in our collecting experience or in print which are not susceptible to the analysis pattern suggested here.

*9 Abrahams (1963:100). The use of voice qualifiers in castration humor is common. For example, the use of a high-pitched falsetto occurs in the emphasized portions of the following punch lines: "Operator, I've been cut off!" "Hey, there's sharks in these waters. " "Watch out for the barbed wire fence!" "What barbed wire fence?" For an excellent account of castration humor, see Legman (1952).

*10 The "adult" status of the elephant is also revealed by the answer to the question "How do you talk to an elephant?" The answer - "Use big words" - reflects a child's-eye view of adult vocabulary, and in fact a child might well try to use "big words" when speaking to adults.

*11 We are indebted to John Greenway for pointing out that the introduction of the ballet slippers may have been a result of the reissue of Walt Disney's movie Fantasia around the time of the currency of this cycle.

*12 The attribution of greater sexual appetite and competence to an enemy appears to be a fairly general phenomenon. See Seidenberg (1952). For representative texts of white jokes about Negro sexuality, see Bennett (1964). For a literary reference in which Negro genital superiority is couched in elephantine imagery, see Steinbeck (1939).

*13 From the white's point of view, the absurdity of the elephant's trying to conceal his true nature and color by wearing human shoes of a certain color might be analogous to what some whites think is the rationale underlying the Negro's attempts to adopt certain status symbols of white culture and dress. But while the Negro might prefer not to be recognizable on the basis of color, he cannot possibly conceal his color, no matter what he wears or owns. As an elephant is indubitably an elephant no matter what color his sneakers or toenails are, so also the Negro's identity is unmistakable. The white stereotype of Negro values may, in this light, illuminate the text: "Why did the elephant sit on the marshmallow? Because he didn't want to fall in the cocoa." This could express the white conviction that the elephant (Negro) would prefer to sit precariously on the small white "safe" marshmallow rather than fall down to be immersed in the larger mass of brown cocoa. It is worth remarking that the wordplay on "color" in the elephant joke cycle, if the present Negro-elephant hypothesis is correct, is reminiscent of a type of punning wit commonly found in dreams. Further, the "grape-banana-plum" riddle cycle which followed hard on the heels of the elephant jokes was equally castratory and used color descriptions even more emphatically. For texts, see Barrick (1964a) passim.

*14 This text and several of the other racial color riddles cited here were reported in Abrahams (1963).

*15 As Mac E. Barrick (1964b) has pointed out recently, the successor to this type of "nigger" riddle is a whole series of narrative jokes utilizing, often ironically, the Southern stereotype of the Negro but with a point of view which is ambivalent in regard to the attitude toward the Negro.

*16 An interesting corroboration of our hypothesis comes from clinical data contributed by psychiatrist L. Bryce Boyer. He reports: "I one time had a patient in analysis who spent some interviews around the theme of racial problems, then found himself telling elephant jokes, then resumed the talk about racial problems. His own conflicts at that period dealt specifically with castration fears and fantasies of retribution against his father and authority figures.

He clearly equated Negroes and elephants with his father and specifically spoke of the Negro's alleged huge genitals and the elephant's trunk while also talking of childhood memories of seeing his father's penis, the size of which was most impressive to him" (from personal correspondence).

19

THE NUMBER THREE IN AMERICAN CULTURE

"Nothing is as difficult to see as the obvious. " Bronislaw Malinowski,
A Scientific Theory of Culture.

Ever since the publication of H. Usener's monograph in 1903, no one has questioned the importance of the number three in Greek and Roman culture. Subsequent investigations of classical literature, law, and medicine (Göbel, Goudy, Tavenner) have served only to confirm the pattern. More recent scholarship (Deonna, Dumézil) has demonstrated the existence of the pattern in most of Western civilization and has suggested it may be a characteristic of Indo-European culture. Some of the more convincing evidence is provided by mythology and more specifically, by the widespread occurrence of triads of deities. Typical examples would be the Babylonian Ea, Anu, and Enlil, and the Hindu Brahma, Vishnu, and Shiva. Also pertinent is the widespread distribution of single gods with three heads (Kirfel). However, relatively few of the numerous studies of the number three have concerned themselves with the "three-determinism" of contemporary thought.

In a valuable study which appeared polygenetically the same year as Usener's, Raimund Müller suggests that modern European culture is just as three-oriented as classical culture was. Unfortunately, because Müller's essay was published in a somewhat obscure graduate exercise program, it has had little influence. As for American culture in particular, only one of the studies made by classicists and Indo-Europeanists (Lease) and some of the latest of a long line of overtly Christian treatises seeking to reveal the presence of the Trinity in nature (e.g. Strand) have documented in any detail that the number three is of ritual importance in the United States.

One should realize that three is not a universal pattern number. There are several pattern numbers, each with its own distribution. The majority of American Indian cultures have four as their ritual or sacred number. Sometimes a member of Euro-American culture is surprised or amused at the American Indian's obvious cultural insistence upon fourfold repetition. Parsons (1916:596) remarked on the "obsessive character" of the Zuni use of four. Earlier, Buckland (1895:96) had mistakenly thought that all American Indians had four as their ritual number, but he was unaware of the ritual five among numerous tribes in western North America (Jacobs 1959a:224-28; Lowie 1925:578). The occurrence of five in South America and in China (Geil) suggests that the ritual use of five may be of considerable antiquity. Of course, American Indians are not particularly bothered by what appears to us as an exaggerated use of four of five rep-

Reprinted from Every Man His Way: Readings in Cultural Anthropology, ed.
Alan Dundes (Englewood Cliffs: Prentice-Hall, 1968), 401-24.

etitions, just as we are not irritated by our own equally persistent use of three-fold repetitions.

It should also be noted that three is not the only pattern number in American culture. In fact, there is clearly a plurality of pattern numbers - two, seven, and twelve are three obvious examples. Certainly, philosophical dualism is very much a part of American culture and individuals do dichotomize. Common polarities include: life/death, body/soul, and male/female. Indeed, although Lease (1919:72, n.2) suggests that the primary divisions of the human arm and leg, not to mention the finger, tend to support trichotomic thinking, the ana-tomical datum would appear to reinforce "two" rather than "three". There are two sexes, two ears, eyes, nostrils, arms, legs, and so forth. These univer-sally recognized pairs would help to explain why dualism is probably worldwide. Whether one uses such criteria as dual social organization (e.g. in moiety sys-tems) or some variation of a "self-other" or "us-them" dichotomy (e.g. as in exogamy), there seems little doubt that "two" is more widely distributed in the world than "three". In American culture one finds quite frequently that there are alternative classification schemes: one binary and one trinary. The present thesis is not that the number three is the only numerical native category in American culture, but rather that it is the predominant one.

The following general statements about the nature of trichotomy may be of interest. (1) Often three appears to be an absolute limit; there are three terms or three categories and no more. In folk speech one can give three cheers for someone, but not two or four. (And each cheer may consist of "Hip, Hip, Hooray.") The starter for a race will say "One, two, three, go." He will not count to two or four. (Cf. the three commands "On your mark, get set, go.) The alphabet is referred to as the ABC's and in the common folk simile, some-thing is as easy as ABC; one does not speak of learning his AB's or his ABCD's. (2) If there are more than three terms, the additional ones will not infrequently be defined primarily in terms of one of the three basic terms, usually one of the extremes. For example, in shirt sizes, one finds small, medium, and large. The size "extra-large" is certainly linguistically and very probably conceptually derived from "large", rather than possessing separate individual status. (3) One source of trichotomies consists of positions located in reference to some initial point. In golf one tries to shoot par for the course. He may, however, shoot "under" par or "over" par. In music, the point of reference may be "middle C", which serves, for example, as a midpoint between the base and treble clefs in addition to functioning as a point of reference from which to describe voice ranges (e.g. "two octaves above middle C"). (4) On the other hand, a third term may be the result of splitting a polarity. If A and B represent two extremes, then a trichotomy may be achieved by establishing their average, median, or mean as a midpoint. Or if "early" and "late" represented extremes in descri-bing arrivals and departures, then "on time" would presumably by the midpoint. Obviously, in some instances, it is difficult to say whether the midpoint or the extremes came first. (5) Another common means of trichotomy formation is the merging or combining of two terms such that one has A, B, and AB. In Robert's Rules of Order it is stated that "an amendment may be in any of the following forms: (a) to insert or add, (b) to strike out, or (c) to strike out and insert". In theory, any polarity can be converted to a trichotomy by this or the immediately preceding principle. Moreover, it is decidedly easier to move from two to three (cf. Usener 1903:323) than from three to two. The majority of the most common trichotomic schemes in American culture could not easily be put into a dichotomic mold. (6) The strength of the trichotomic tendency is indicated in part by its "repetition compulsion". In a considerable number of tripartite schemes, each of the three units in question may itself be divided into three parts. Each of these parts may in turn be broken down into three subdivisions and so on almost ad infinitum. (7) A final generalization concerns the special case of the triune or the three-in-one. In some trichotomies the three subdivisions are not separate and independent; instead they are part of a whole. The doctrine of the Trinity as opposed to a doctrine of tritheism illustrates this form of trichotomy.

We may now turn to specific examples of trichotomy in American culture. One of the very best sources for the study of native categories is folklore. Folklore, consisting as it does of native documents or autobiographical ethnography, is prime data for investigations of cognitive patterning. A number of scholarly studies have described the frequent occurrence of "three" in European folklore (e.g. Lehmann, Müller) and indeed the overwhelming consistency of trifold repition in both classical and modern European folklore led the distinguished Danish folklorist Axel Olrik to claim that the "law of three" was one of the fundamental epic laws governing the composition of folk narrative. There has also been a Christian-anthropological treatise (Seifert) that has sought to demonstrate threeness as a manifestation of the trinity in the myths of primitive peoples. This is questionable, but certainly in Euro-American folktales there are three brothers, three wishes, three magic objects, and often a three-day interval of waiting or fighting. In jokes, which are the modern equivalents of Märchen (fairy tales), there are commonly three principals: an Englishman, an Irishman, and a Scotchman; a minister, a priest, and a rabbi; or a blonde, a brunette, and a redhead. Structurally, there are usually three action sequences in such jokes. Three is equally popular in other genres of American folklore.

In American folksongs there are numerous examples of trebling and it is doubtful whether many singers are fully conscious of it. For example, in many songs the verse consists of a line which is repeated three times before being followed by a final line. Typical illustrations include: "John Brown's body lies a moulderin' in the grave...but his soul goes marching on"; "John Brown had a little Indian...one little Indian boy"; "Polly put the kettle on...we'll all have tea"; "Go tell Aunt Rhody (Nancy)...her old grey goose is dead"; "Lost my partner, what'll I do?...skip to my Lou, my darlin' "; etc. In other instances, a word or phrase is thrice repeated: "Row, row, row your boat", "Mary had a little lamb, little lamb, little lamb", "Do you know the muffin man, the muffin man, the muffin man?" "Did you ever see a lassie, a lassie, a lassie?" and such other favorites as "Buffalo gals, won't you come out tonight?" "Joshua fit the battle of Jericho", "Here we go round the mulberry bush", and "London Bridge is falling down", to list just a few.

The number three also figures prominently in American superstitions. Sometimes, it signifies luck: "Third time's a charm". Sometimes it is the opposite: "Three times a bridesmaid, never a bride", "Three on a match is bad luck", and "Going down for the third time" (i.e. drowning). Riddles as well as superstitions may reflect triadic form. The celebrated riddle of the Sphinx, which is very old and very widely distributed, is a particularly noteworthy example, especially if one considers that, in a way, the riddle constitutes a folk definition of man: "It first walks on four legs, then on two, then on three legs." In many versions the "morning, noon, and night" time trichotomy is used as a metaphor for the "three" ages of man, "Four legs in the morning, two legs at noon, three legs at night" - making the tripartite categorization even more explicit.

The pattern is also found in traditional games. In the popular parlor game of Tick-Tack-Toe, whose title itself is trinary, the object of the game is to get three x's or ciphers in a row. In card games, three of a kind or sequential runs of at least three cards may be important. In games such as "Hearts", where each individual passes cards to his neighbor, the number passed is three. The playing cards themselves are of interest. While there are four suits (possibly a reflection of a Chinese origin), there are but three face cards in American decks of cards. When it is realized that some European sets have four face cards, and further that the particular face cards in American culture are a King, Queen, and Jack, a secular trio of father, mother, and son, the three penchant becomes more apparent.

Threeness also occurs in team games or sports. In the "national pastime" threes abound. In baseball there are nine players; nine innings; three outs; three strikes; first, second, and third base; left, center, and right field; and often three umpires. Moreover, the fact that in professional baseball both batting and fielding averages are calculated to three places, pitching "earned run averages" (ERA) consist of three digits, and box scores commonly list "runs, hits, and errors" does tend to suggest a ternary pattern. While the patterning is not perfect (a walk is earned by four balls), three does seem to be the prevailing number. Batters are measured in part by the number of RBI's (runs batted in) and whether or not they hit over .300. (Is it just a coincidence that this particular percentage is singled out?)

Other sports in the United States reveal similar patterning. In football, the "line" consists of seven men (another magic number), but is divided into a left side, center, and right side in common parlance. The left and right sides consist of three slots: guard, tackle, and end. The backfield has four men, but only three linguistic slots: quarterback, halfback and fullback. (This is analogous to the front, side, and back yards of a house, in that four areas are labeled with just three basic designatory terms, and perhaps analogous also to the three instruments found in the normal form of the string quartet: violins, viola, and cello.) Obviously, there are other number patterns present in football. Ten yards is the immediate objective and there are four attempts (downs) permitted to attain this goal. However, a field goal is three points and a touchdown is six points.

In professional boxing, bouts take place in a "ring" which is surrounded by three strands of rope. Rounds consist of three minutes of fighting. A comparison of American and European practices once again reveals the American bias. Whereas fights in Great Britain and most of continental Europe are judged by the referee alone, in the United States the winner is determined by a referee and two judges, i.e. by three votes.

One could find many additional examples from other American sports, but perhaps most striking are the following points. In many instances, only the first three participants to finish a race receive official recognition. Similarly, in horseracing the three possibilities are win, place, and show. Noteworthy also is the fact that in many American games there is more than the binary possibility of winning or losing. The third alternative, that is, drawing or tying, allows the choices "win, lose, or draw", which is consistent with trichotomic patterning. Even the partisan cheers at athletic events often consist of three words, e. g. fight team fight, hold that line, get that ball.

Another form of spectacle, the circus, though not strictly speaking a game, provides a rather striking example of trichotomy. Besides the obvious difference between a one-ring show and a three-ring circus, the latter being an excellent example of the "three-in-one" type of trichotomy, among American circus performers there has historically been a burning desire to do things in triplicate. Specifically, there were attempts to "turn a triple somersault from a trapeze bar to a catcher's hands as a grand finale of the flying return act" and to "do a triple from a springboard" (E.C. May 1932:249). The goal, though culturally appealing, was extremely difficult physically and a host of would-be triplers actually broke their necks in attempting this feat (E.C. May 1932:255). The existence of trebling in circus acts and of the "three-in-one" tent show may serve to illustrate how a particular widespread pattern of culture can be manifested in a single aspect of culture, an aspect which might easily be overlooked.

Another revealing aspect of folk culture concerns naming conventions. Perhaps the trichotomy here is attributable in part to the theory and methodology of logical definition itself. In formal definitions, the trinary criteria are term, genus, and differentia. In any event, scientific names for plants and animals are often in trinomial form, giving genus, species, and variety. In American culture most individuals have three names, any of which may be converted into initials: John Fitzgerald Kennedy to JFK. Most formal documents have space for three names and individuals with only two names may be obliged to indicate "none" or n.m.i. (no middle initial) in the middle name slot. Significantly, it is the last or third name which is the principal identifier. The clumsiness of this system has led to the practice on many forms of requesting that the last name be given first. Organizations as well as individuals have three word names. Typical American organizations' titles include: American Anthropological Association (AAA), American Medical Association (AMA), and Ku Klux Klan (KKK). In some instances, the organization's title has more than three words, but there are still only three initials: Daughters of the American Revolution (DAR), Parents and Teachers Association (PTA), and Congress of Industrial Organizations (CIO). In addition to individuals and organizations, there are the names of projects: Tennessee Valley Authority (TVA), of chemical products: trinitrotoluene (TNT), and of tests: Thematic Apperception Test (TAT). The names of the three major television networks are: ABC, CBS, and NBC. In fact, often the set of three initials has virtually replaced the words for which they stand: COD, DNA, DOA, FBI, FOB, GOP, LSD, MGM, RIP, rpm, TKO, USO, and VIP. The item may be considered a local family expression such as FHB (family hold back), a command directing family members to refrain from taking too much food so that guests will have enough. However, most of the items are national in scope, as in the case of the common abbreviation for the whole country: USA. The preeminence of the three letter gestalt is also suggested by SOS, in which the Morse Code signals consist of three dots, three dashes, and three dots.

A final bit of folkloristic evidence for the existence of a trichotomic pattern in American culture is provided by folk speech. The model for America's rhetorical heritage includes such triple constructions as veni, vidi, vici (and it was surely no accident that all Gaul was divided into three parts) or liberté, égalité, fraternité. Small wonder that American political style favors: life, liberty, and the pursuit of happiness; a government of the people, by the people, and for the people. Political slogans likewise may consist of three words: I Like Ike; We Shall Overcome. But nonpolitical folk expressions are equally three-structured: beg, borrow, or steal; bell, book, and candle; blood, sweat, and tears; cool, calm, and collected; fat, dumb, and happy; hither, thither, and yon; hook, line, and sinker; hop, skip, and jump; lock, stock, and barrel; me, myself, and I; men, women, and children; ready, willing, and able; signed, sealed, and delivered; tall, dark, and handsome; Tom, Dick, and Harry; and wine, women, and song. Railroad crossing signs warn motorists to "stop, look, and listen". Avertising clichés manifest the same structure. A skin cream advertisement maintains: "she's lovely, she's engaged, she uses Pond's"; the breakfast cereal Rice Krispies is represented by "Snap, Crackle, and Pop". Commercial products such as SOS scouring pads and 3-in-1 Oil use three in their names, while others claim to have an essential three-initial ingredient (Shell gasoline has TCP) or to operate on three levels (such as fighting headaches three ways). Superman, a mass media folk hero for American children, is introduced in threes: "Faster than a speeding bullet, more powerful than a locomotive, able to leap tall buildings at a single bound. It's a bird! It's a plane! It's Superman!" Superman's own formula is "Up, up, and away".

Many American verbal rituals are in the same tradition. The various countdowns prior to the starting point of events may be in threes: ready, set, go; or ready, aim, fire. The auctioneering phrase - going once, going twice, sold; or going, going, gone - is an example. There is also the barker's cry: "Hurry, hurry, hurry", often followed by "Step right up". American judicial rituals also provide illustrations. The cry of "hearye" or "oyez" repeated three times is one, while the oath sworn by a witness is another. A witness is sworn by asking him to repeat "truth" three times, as he must do when he swears to "tell the truth, the whole truth, and nothing but the truth". Similarly, in wedding ritual, there is the promise to "love, honor, and obey".

There are many more examples from American folk speech. Some are in rhyme: "First is worst, second the same, but third is best of all the game." Some are not: "A minute in your mouth, an hour in your stomach, a lifetime on your hips"; or the Army credo, one version of which directs, "If it moves, salute it! If it doesn't move, pick it up! If you can't pick it up, paint it!" Even more interesting is the American tendency to build triple constructions from original single ones. Thus starting from "Those who can, do" one moves to add, "Those who can't, teach." In final form, one has "Those who can, do; those who can't, teach; and those who can't teach, teach teachers!" The same pattern is reflected in a popular American leave-taking formula: "be good". The second stage: "If you can't be good, be careful" is followed by the third: "If you can't be careful, have fun" (or "name it after me").

It is not just in American folklore that the trichotomic and trebling tendency is found. Almost every aspect of American culture is similarly three-patterned. One may examine food, clothing, education, social organization, religion, time, or any other aspect of American culture and one will find abundant examples of trichotomy. Yet, most Americans are unaware of the pervasiveness of this pattern. It might therefore be worthwhile to observe a small portion of this patterning.

Americans customarily eat three meals a day (at morning, noon, and night). One must remember that three meals a day is by no means a universal custom. Moreover, while the actual number of artifacts employed to move the food from a container to the mouth may vary with the type of meal and its formality, there are only three basic implements: knife, fork, and spoon. With respect to silverware, it is of interest that Emily Post, an authority on American etiquette, states that one of the important differences between place settings in formal and informal dining concerns the number of forks. On formal occasions, there should be no more than three forks (and three knives), whereas in informal dining, the three fork limit is absent. In many American homes the sets of china include three plate sizes: bread and butter, luncheon, and dinner. While the number of courses served at a meal is, like the number of eating implements, determined in part by the occasion and place, one might conceivably consider that dinners served in average restaurants consist of three parts: soup or appetizer; entree with vegetable or salad; and dessert with coffee. (One might define the segments of the continuum of a meal served in a restaurant on the basis of the number of times the waiter or waitress removes dishes or brings a new set of food items to the table.) In any event, while the number of courses is admittedly open to question, it is true that entrees are commonly divided on menus into meat, poultry, and fish. And it is equally true that patrons order their steak to be cooked: rate, medium, or well-done. The beverage choice may be "coffee, tea, or milk". If an alcoholic beverage were desired, the choice might be beer, wine, or whiskey. Noteworthy is one dessert commonly served in restaurants, Neapolitan ice cream with its three flavor layers: chocolate, strawberry, and vanilla.

Of theoretical interest is the fact that the smallest detail may reveal the same patterning present in larger aspects of culture. Such a detail is the cutting of sandwiches. While it is true that the cutting of sandwiches is almost always binary, the way in which sandwiches are cut in half may be significant. In restaurants sandwiches are usually halved with a diagonal cut so that the patron is presented with two triangular halves. At home, however, sandwiches are often cut to form two rectangles. The point is that when the sandwiches are cut into rectangles, there is no opposition to the basic binary division, but rather a reinforcement of this pattern. The rectangle has four sides which consist of two pairs of parallel lines, i.e. its length and its width. In contrast, when the sandwiches are cut into two triangular sections, the resultant three-sided figures represent trinary, not pure binary division. Note also that on the rarer occasions when sandwiches are divided into four rather than two sections, the same kind of 'restaurant-home' patterning prevails. In a restaurant the sandwich is normally divided by means of two diagonal cuts into four triangular sections:

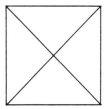

At home, the mother making smaller sandwich sections for her younger children is more likely to divide the . ····· h into four square sections:

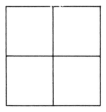

From this, one might be led to hypothesize a possible association of "two" with
informal occasions as opposed to the association of "three" with more formal
occasions. In any case, sandwiches, surely a very popular item on the American menu, consist of two bread covers and a "middle". Sometimes the "middle"
consists of three components, such as bacon, lettuce, and tomato (the BLT
sandwich). The popularity of the club sandwich or triple decker, in which three
slices of bread are used, is also worth noting.
    Clothing is as rewarding a subject as food for the study of cultural patterns.
As noted earlier, many articles of clothing come in three sizes: small, medium,
and large. Moreover, generally speaking, American clothing is worn in three
layers. Beneath the layer visible to one's fellows lie undergarments (e. g. underwear). For outside wear and for warmth, one may don such outergarments as
an overcoat. Thus with respect to any one part of the body, for example, the
feet, one might find socks, shoes, and overshoes. That this is a manifestation
of culture patterning is suggested by the fact that not all cultures prescribe
three layers of clothing. Socks and underwear are not universal. One is tempted to suggest that the body is divided into three basic parts for clothing purposes. In terms of standard indoor apparel, one ordinarily covers the feet, the
lower torso up to the waist, and the upper torso above the waist. In men's
clothing, for example, these three parts are dressed separately. Shoes and
socks are put on· after shorts and trousers. Undershirt and shirt clothe the
third unit of the body. Although stylistic features do vary, men's sport jackets
more often than not have three buttons down the front and often, though not always, there are three buttons sewn on the cuffs of the jacket. The usual number
of outside pockets on such jackets is three and in the upper one of these pockets,
one may place a handkerchief. The handkerchief may be folded into a triangle
so that one point protrudes or, in a fancy dress variant, the handkerchief may
be folded such that three points protrude.

The subject of folding is a most fascinating microcultural detail. It appears, for example, that a binary versus trinary distinction occurs with respect to folding letters. Personal or social letter paper should be folded once, thus forming two parts. In contrast, business letter paper is ordinarily folded twice, thus "dividing" one letter into three parts (Post 1960:503). Note that the two-part letter is informal and the three-part letter is formal, a distinction paralleling one made previously in connection with alternative ways of cutting sandwiches. (The association of tripartite division with formality is also manifested in the ritual folding of the American flag into triangles on ceremonial occasions.) The outside of the envelope provides further data. On the front of the envelope, one writes the address of the person to whom the letter is to be sent and this address is frequently divided into three parts. On the first of the three lines, one puts the addressee's name, usually preceded by one of three titles: Mr., Mrs., or Miss, e.g. Mr. Alan Dundes. The second line typically has a number, a street name, and the word street or its equivalent, e.g. 985 Regal Road. The third line consists of city, state, and ZIP code (or zone number), e.g. Berkeley, California 94708. The two versus three distinction occurs on the first line. The use of two names may indicate a close and personal relationship between the sender and addressee, while the use of three names or two names plus the middle initial very probably indicates that there is some social distance and a certain amount of formality in the relationship. (The most intimate relationship, that signaled by a reciprocal "first name" arrangement, is of course not feasible in written as opposed to spoken tradition.) The formalizing effect of the presence of a third party upon a previous two-party group is also relevant (Simmel). (Cf. the folk judgment: two's company, three's a crowd!)

Some examples of American material culture have already been discussed, but there are many more. Traffic lights are usually divided into three parts: red/stop, yellow/caution, and green/go. Superhighways commonly have three lanes (the middle one of which contributes to a metaphor for American political positions: left, right, and middle of the road). Freeway signs often list the next three exits. Standard gear shifts in automobiles have traditionally been divided into forward, neutral and reverse. While this might appear to be necessary, the further division of forward into first, second, and third gears is not. Even the modern automatic shift systems have a low gear and two drive positions. Some makes of cars come in three degrees of quality, although obviously the idea of first-rate, second-rate, and third-rate is disguised.

Moving away from automobiles, we may note some other examples of American technological culture. Until recently most record players and tape recorders had three speeds; there are three major types of motion picture film (8, 16, and 35 millimeter); stoves and window fans may have settings of low, medium, and high; toasters frequently have settings of light, medium, and dark; modern light bulbs have three settings for three degrees of brightness; and typewriters have single, double, and triple spacing. Cold drink vending machines usually offer three choices and one may make a choice by depositing a nickel, dime, or quarter. In slot machine gambling, the winning combination may be three of a kind, e.g. three lemons.

The pattern is also found in the telephone. On modern telephones, one finds that on the dials there are groups of three letters which correspond to one

finger slot. Moreover, the United States and Canada have recently been divided
into more than one hundred telephone areas, each of which is identified by a
three-digit area code. By means of this system, DDD (Direct Distance Dialing)
has been established. Other three-centered features include the three-digit
numbers for information (411) or repair (611), not to mention the standard basic
time unit of telephone calls: three minutes. While the telephone is not as obvious an example as the three-color American flag, it is influenced by the same
general culture pattern.

The American educational system reflects the pattern too, with its breakdown
into primary, secondary, and higher education. It is in primary or elementary
school that the three R's (Reading, 'Riting, and 'Rithmetic) are taught. Higher
education consists of three degrees: bachelor's, master's, and doctoral. In colleges where a credit system is employed, the usual number of credits needed
to be promoted is thirty, a multiple of three. Most college courses are worth
three credits and they ordinarily meet three times or three hours a week. The
college school year is divided into two semesters, Fall and Spring, plus a summer session. (A trimester scheme, in which the three school year units are
equal, is in effect at a few colleges.) Frequently, a "social organizational" distinction is made between freshmen and upperclassmen, with the latter consisting of three classes: sophomore, junior, and senior. (The alternative distinction of lower division versus upper division is in the binary cultural category
and provides an illustration of the dichotomy-trichotomy choice.) Interestingly
enough, this scheme parallels the professional rankings in which at least linguistically there is a distinction between "instructor" and the upper three ranks:
assistant professor, associate professor, and (full) professor. While at college,
a student may specialize in the humanities, the social sciences, or the natural
sciences. If he distinguishes himself, he may receive his bachelor's degree
cum laude, magna cum laude, or summa cum laude. In graduate schools, doctoral candidates may be examined in three major fields of specialization and
their thesis committees consist of at least three members. Even educational
philosophy and methodology is three-bound. One teaching technique consists of
"Preview, Teach, and Review", which keeps its tripartite form in an analogous
folk pedagogical principle: tell 'em what you're going to tell 'em; tell 'em; and
tell 'em what you told 'em.

American social organization, like American education, is under the influence
of the pattern. The continuum of the American population is divided into upper,
middle, and lower classes. These distinctions have even been further refined
so that the upper class yields upper upper, middle upper, and lower upper. In
the same way, American intellectual levels are high brow, middle brow, and
low brow. American government is divided into three branches: executive,
legislative, and judiciary. While the legislative branch is bicameral, it is of
interest that senators are elected for six year terms with a stagger system
such that only one third can be changed at one time. In terms of sociopolitical
geographical units, most Americans feel loyalty to their community, their
state, and their country.

Perhaps the best example of trinary social organization is found in the American military system, which consists of the Army, Navy, and Air Force. With
a supreme Secretary of Defense, one has a prime illustration of the division of

a unity into three parts, a secular parallel to the sacred Trinity. Each of the services has a system of rank based in part upon three. In the Navy, for example, the three initial grades are: Seaman Recruit (one stripe), Seaman Apprentice (two stripes), and Seaman (three stripes). The sequence of unrated men, that is, SR, SA, and SN, does not continue; instead a new sequence begins: Third Class Petty Officer (one chevron), Second Class Petty Officer (two chevrons), and First Class Petty Officer (three chevrons). Although there is a Chief Petty Officer grade, his uniform and status are quite different from PO3, PO2, and PO1, different enough so that the apparent binary split between "officers" and "men" is in fact trinary: officers, chiefs, and men. This trichotomy is even more obvious when the criteria of separate messing and berthing and the extension of privileges (e. g. the time of the expiration of liberty or shore leave) are taken into account. A threefold division of officers is less obvious (and there is, of course, a system of four stripes rather than three) but junior officers include: Ensigns, Lieutenants Junior Grade, and Lieutenants. Senior officers include Lieutenant Commanders, Commanders, and Captains. Flag officers include Rear, Vice, and Full Admirals.

Army social organization is similar, although triangular infantry organization was replaced in 1957 by a pentomic plan. However, historically, Army units have been based on a three-in-one breakdown (Lease 1919:67). A battalion consisted of three rifle companies, a rifle company of three rifle platoons, and a rifle platoon of three squads. A strong survival of triangular organization is found in the Boy Scouts, the American analog of primitive puberty initiation societies. The ranks include tenderfoot, second class, and first class scouts. Thereafter, the accumulation of merit badges and the satisfaction of various requirements permits a scout to attain the ranks of Star, Life, and Eagle Scout. An Eagle Scout may, upon the earning of additional merit badges, be awarded Eagle Palms: a Bronze Palm (5 badges), a Gold Palm (10 badges), or a Silver Palm (15 badges). The ritual use of three is also explicit in such items as: a triangular neckerchief; a Scout badge whose design is the fleur-de-lis; the Scout sign, a gesture whose most salient characteristic is three upstretched fingers; the Scout handclasp, accomplished by extending the left hand with the three middle fingers outstretched; and the Scout Oath, which consists of three parts.

Military material culture, so to speak, and military ritual demonstrate the identical pattern. Whether it be ship division into Forward, Amidships, and Aft or the color of anchor chain paint markings (to indicate how much chain is out) into red, white, and blue fifteen fathom lengths, the trichotomic principle prevails. Military music, that is to say, bugle calls, is based upon three notes, the triad. Noteworthy also is the use of fanfares on ritual or formal occasions. There are either three trumpets playing the tones of the triad in unison or playing three part harmony. Moreover, it may not be amiss to point out that in terms of bugle playing technique, the most frequently used method of increasing tonguing speed is known as triple-tonguing. Even more pertinent to the present inquiry is occurrence of triple meter. Ternary time is not common in primitive music, and thus its presence in Western and American music is all the more striking. Besides the glaring example of waltz time, there is the rhythm employed in military ritual drumming. For instance, one pattern is based upon a series of three beats.

This may be contrasted with typical ritual drumming patterns of American Indian culture in which the pattern number is most often four. One such is four beats with the first beat heavily accented. Note well that the concept of the triplet itself is quite a remarkable example of trichotomy. It is in essence the substitution of three notes in place of one. Although 3/8 does not equal 1/4, culturally sanctioned and conditioned aesthetics permit, if not encourage, the substitution of three eighth notes in place of one quarter note beat.

Nonmusical examples of military ritual include the sentry's challenge "Halt, who goes there?" "Advance and be recognized", and "Pass". At Officer's Candidate School (OCS) officer trainees during their three months sojourn (="ninety day wonders") learn of the three types of court martial: summary, special, and general. They may also learn that the final act of military funerals is the firing of three volleys. (One wonders if the act of an assassin in firing three shots at the President is purely fortuitous and one wonders further about the statement of the assassin of the assassin that he meant to fire three shots instead of one!) The twenty-one gun salute for the President appears to be a combination of two sacred numbers - twenty-one is thrice seven.

The occurrence of three-symbolism in American religion is almost too obvious to require mention. In American culture, three major faiths are distinguished: Catholicism, Protestantism, and Judaism. Judaism can be broken down into three types. Orthodox, Conservative, and Reform. Of course, the Old and the New Testaments provide numerous examples. Noah who had three sons sent the dove out of the three-storied ark three times. (See Lehmann 1914: 18; and Lease 1919:66 for other Old Testament examples.) Christian examples include the three Magi, Satan's three temptations of Christ, Peter's three denials of Christ, the three crucifixions at Calvary, the three Marys, the three nails, the three days intervening between the burial and the resurrection, and Christ's age of thirty-three. After the resurrection, Christ showed himself three times to his disciples (John 21:14) and asked Peter three times "Lovest thou me?" (John 21:17). Of course, the ultimate charter for belief in three is the concept of the Trinity, with its sacred confirmation of the notion of three-in-one. Christian culture includes the triptych, such mottoes as "faith, hope and charity", and a three-movement ritual gesture starting at the forehead to make the sign of the cross. As for American religions, one can see that the Mormons' reverence of the three Nephites is just as patterned as the addition of the concept of Purgatory in Catholicism to form a third alternative to the previously binary Heaven and Hell.

The nature of culture is such that if one finds a pattern in social organization and religion, one is likely to find that pattern manifested in time and language (or vice versa, of course). Whorf, in his celebrated analysis of the relation of thought and behavior to language, made special mention of the cultural relativ-

ity of time concepts. While his statement "The three-tense system of SAE
(Standard Average European) verbs colors all our thinking about time" (1964:
143) does lean perhaps a little too far in the direction of linguistic determinism, the keen insight is a valid one. It is of considerable historical interest
that Brinton made the following statement in 1894: "The two universal categories of the understanding (or modes of perception), Space and Time, invariably
present themselves in a threefold aspect: Time as the Past, the Present, the
Future, as expressed in the grammar of every language; Space, as Length,
Breadth, and Thickness; or, with reference to position, Above, Beneath, and
Here. " (1894:169); emphasis added). Brinton saw the relationship between
grammatical categories and concepts of time. His error lay in assuming the
universality of his own particular native categories. Certainly in American
culture, the continuum of time (and admittedly the concept of continuum is itself culturally relative) is segmented into past, present, and future. The day
may be divided binarily into night and day, but dawn and twilight provide middle
terms at the two junctures. Day is alo divided into morning, noon, and night.
Moreover, the twenty-four hour day is also divided into morning, noon, and night.
types of work, e. g. in hospitals, there are commonly three eight-hour work
shifts. Noteworthy also is the formal way of referring to a particular day. The
reference consists of three parts: month, day, and year, e. g. January 1, 1968,
or 1/1/68. The principal time indicators, the watch and the calendar, refer to
three units. The average watch has three hands: hour, minute, and second.
Calendars indicate day, month, and year. It is of interest that many calendars,
in addition to displaying the current month on any one page, also provide small
displays of the month immediately preceding and the month which is to follow.
This symbolizes a concern with both past and future while living in the present.

The past, present, and future trichotomy remains constant no matter what
the time unit is. Whether one is concerned with day, week, month, or year,
there is yesterday, today, and tomorrow. The limiting nature of three is demonstrated by the fact that if one wishes to refer to, let us say, days other than
those three, one must do so in reference to the two extremes, e. g. the day before yesterday, the day after tomorrow. There is no independent term available for measures outside of the basic three. In some instances, even dependent terms outside of the limiting three are lacking. Thus one can say last
night, tonight, and tomorrow night, but while one can refer easily to the night
before last, one cannot with equal idiomatic facility speak of the night after tomorrow night. With weeks, months, or years, one can employ "last, this, and
next", and thus weeks falling outside the extremes are the week before last
and the week after next. Curiously enough, the same type of structure found in
time applies to trinary linear kinship terminology. Ego has parents (=yester-
day) and he has children (=tomorrow). Linear relatives beyond these two extremes must be named in reference to one of the two extremes, e. g. grandparents or grandchildren. Moreover, in either direction, there is something
of a trinary terminological limit. Ego has parents, grandparents, and great-
grandparents, generational distinctions being signaled by a distinct prefix. Additional distinctions can be made only by successive repetition of the last prefix, e. g. great-great-grandparents. The same holds for ego's children, grandchildren, and great-grandchildren. Note also the incremental repetition of one

to three words in parent (1), grandparent (2), and great-grandparent (3). The
time-kinship parallel is also obvious in American values. In a scheme like past,
present, and future (or man, woman, and child), it is the third and last term
which is valued most. Americans are future-oriented and to the amazement of
their enemies, they tend to forget about the past. Similarly, they are child-
oriented and they tend to forget about their elders, banishing them to old age
homes or communities.

Still another time trichotomy stems from regarding noon as a midpoint. Time
is denoted in reference to noon inasmuch as A.M. and P.M. are before and after noon respectively. In the same fashion, historical time in American culture
is measured with respect to the birth of Christ. Years are either B.C. or A.D.
However, the initial points of reference are separate from the periods of "before" and "after", just as the present is in theory distinct from the past and the
future. Thus noon is neither A.M. nor P.M. Twelve o'clock is ambiguous and
one is required to say twelve midnight or twelve noon. It should be noted that
in Europe generally, an unambiguous four-digit time indicator system is employed. The practical advantages of a four-digit symbol such as 1530 over a
three-digit 3:30 are obvious - there are two three-thirties daily - and this is
probably why the American military has adopted the more efficient four-digit
system. Incidentally, a possible mathematical-logic analogue for the "before"
and "after" terms in reference to an initial point is provided by the usual ways
of relating one term to another. Either a equals b; a is less than b, or a is
greater than b. Distinctions such as a is slightly less than b or a is much less
than b are not culturally defined as relevant or significant. There are only the
three possibilities. Similarly we have three ways of relating man to nature,
man subjugated to nature (less than); man in nature (equal); and man over nature
(greater than); in interpersonal relations, an individual is inferior (or subordinate), equal, or superior (or superordinate) to another.

The discussion of time is in part a discussion of the terminology of time and
is thus a discussion of language. In any case, the very nature of the Sapir-Whorf
hypothesis would make one suspect that if trichotomy were a pattern of American culture, it would also be found in American English. However, the greater
part of Whorf's own consideration of English suggests that English has primarily
binary features. Whorf emphasizes that there are basically nouns and verbs
(1964:215), with the nouns of two sorts: individual nouns and mass nouns (1964:
140). Whorf also draws attention to the fundamental categorical distinction between singular and plural. All this leads him to see some of the linguistic correlates of the strong tradition of philosophical dualism in Western civilization
and he cites the example of the dichotomy of form and substance (1964:141).
(He might also have cited active/passive, mind/body, spirit/flesh, and many
other polarities.) While Whorf is undoubtedly correct in his fundamentally binary analysis, there are some trinary features besides the three-sense system
which he might have mentioned. The pronouns are first person, second person,
and third person. (The names of these distinctions are themselves part of the
pattern.) In modern English there are no more than three distinct forms of any
one pronoun, e.g. he, his, him. Third person nominative singular is divided
into he, she, and it, corresponding to the genders masculine, feminine, and
neuter. Hoijer's argument (1954:97) that this is strictly a grammatical survival

with no semantic correlate is somewhat beside the point, even assuming he is correct. Whether it is actually part of linguistic structure or whether it is simply part of what traditional grammarians say is linguistic structure, the fact remains that in our educational system, the distinction between the three genders is made. What members of a culture think about their language (i.e. folk linguistics) can influence other aspects of culture probably almost as much as the actual linguistic patterning. Linguists with their concern for the latter have tended to ignore folk linguistics, that is, folk analytical categories. Brown (1960:342) has put the matter well in her proposition that "many of the perceptions we derive from language do not arise from anything inherent in the structure of the language itself, but as the result of what we have been taught about it". That American grammarians analyze English sentences into actor/action/ goal or subject/predicate/object is important culturally, regardless of whether or not this is in fact an accurate delineation of English structure. Grammarians also distinguish simple, compound, and complex sentences. In punctuation rules, one finds three major medial marks: comma, semicolon, and colon, whose orthographic symbolism itself reflects trichotomic structuring (a, ab, and b). There are also three principal terminal marks: period, question mark, and exclamation point. The latter marks are allegedly indicators of the three major sentence types: declarative, interrogative, and exclamatory. In another instance of orthographic symbolism, one finds that ellipsis, an indefinite quantity, is signaled by the definite convention of using three periods or asterisks.

Of course, there are actual trinary structural features of English. One of the most important of these is the number of degrees employed with modifiers - specifically, the comparative and superlative. One might even go so far as to conjecture that it is the "good, better, best" paradigm, perhaps more than any other single factor, which has encouraged the concept formation of three classes or three types of merchandise sizes, quality, etc. In a recent study, Deonna has brilliantly pointed out (1954:415) that three is in part a semantic derivative of the superlative degree and cites the roots "ter", "tri", and "tre" as evidence. In French, for example, très is a superlative. (In English, one might think of terrific and tremendous. Moreover, etymologies of triumph - and trump in the game of bridge - might show that three was all-powerful, just as the origins of terminus, in the sense of limit and eternity - ternity is an obsolete form of trinity - in the sense of time without limit, or past plus present plus future, or as a synonym for the deity - who is tripartite - may stem from an archaic ur-three root.) In any event, Whorf's distinction between nouns and verbs notwithstanding, tripartition in English is an important structural feature. The division of time and history into threes would appear to be influenced by verb action tense (past, present, future), while the division of objects or object qualities into three would seem to be related to the degrees of comparison (correct, more correct, most correct). Whether the relationship of linguistic feature to other aspects of culture is causal or only correlative, the fact that there are trichotomies of verb tense, modifier degree, pronoun category, and gender tends to support the notion that patterning underlying a culture generally will be evident in language.

That trichotomy is a cognitive category in the sense that individuals tend to perceive in threes is suggested by the results of experiments in gestalt psychol-

ogy. Continua involving both sight and sound were segmented into groups of
three (Köhler 1959:83, 89). However, experiments such as the classic pioneer-
ing ones made by Wertheimer (1923) did not take the pattern number three into
account. Subjects did tend to see things in threes, but Wertheimer attributed
his results to such factors as organization (in terms of proximity) and the group-
ing of similar forms (such as three dots opposed to three circles). The results
might be more a matter of "three" gestalt, an explanation which would no doubt
have delighted Wertheimer. Subjects might, for example, see threes even in a
continuous line of dots. In any case, it is difficult to isolate such variables as
proximity and form similarity when three figures are used in the experiment.

This brings us to an important theoretical point and one of the primary purposes of the present paper. Thus far, an attempt has been made to show that
the pattern of trichotomy does in fact exist as a native category in Western
and, more specifically, American culture. What remains to be seen, however,
is how such a native category can unconsciously affect the formation of supposedly objective analytical categories. This is the really insidious part of cultural
patterning. No individual can escape his culture and its built-in cultural cognitive categories. Yet many individuals think they have escaped, and they claim
to have described the nature of objective reality in culture-free terms. But
often what scientists and scholars present as bona fide analytical categories
are in fact ethnocentric extensions of their own native categories. While a few
analysts specify that their trichotomic models are solely for heuristic purposes
(and certainly a tripartite scheme would have both mnemonic and aesthetic
value in American culture), many do not do so, and the reader is led to believe
that the trichotomic model comes from the data, not from the analyst. Having
identified a folk pattern of trichotomy in a variety of aspects of American culture, one is in an excellent position to perceive the arbitrary and culturally
determined nature of many of our accepted "objective" analytic schemes.

No doubt there will be those who will be offended by the implication that their
analytical categories are but folk or native categories in disguise. They may
claim that the analytical categories in question really do correspond to objective reality. (This would also be the argument of those defending the notion of
the Trinity.) Others, with a penchant for nit-picking, will be quick to point out
that some of the analytical schemes here presented have long been discarded.
The point is that all of the following analytical schemes did or do have some
standing in American culture. Not just Gaul, but the whole world is divided into
three parts. There is animal, vegetable, and mineral. (These and other categories are so deeply embedded in our culture that it may be difficult for some
to see their arbitrariness.) Yet is there an absolute difference between plant
and animal life or is there a continuum? Similar examples may be taken from
almost any discipline. Entomologists define insects as those members of the
phylum Arthropoda in which the body is divided into three parts: head, thorax,
and abdomen. The question is : are insects truly morphologically tripartite or
do we simply see them as tripartite? And what of the trichotomy explicit in the
metamorphic continuum of some insects into larva, pupa, and adult? Are the
three stages simply a reflection of the same cultural convention which suggests
that literature has a beginning, a middle, and an end or that plays commonly be
written in three acts?

At least we are consistent, for all the world is conceived and perceived in tripartite terms - by us. The continuum of states of matter is neatly divided into solid, liquid, and gas. The projection of this scheme to the entire earth results in distinguishing land (solid), sea (liquid), and air (gas). These in turn are subdivided. The air or atmosphere may be broken down into troposphere, stratosphere, and ionosphere, while the earth may be divided into three types of climate zones: frigid, temperate, and torrid. (Cf. the spacial-geographical divisions such as North, Central [or Middle], and South America or the East, the Middle West, and the West.) As the world is divided, so is man. The human ear is divided into the outer, middle, and inner ear, the brain into cerebrum, cerebellum, and medulla, the small intestine into the duodenum, the jejunum, and the ileum. Are these divisions any less arbitrary than the segmentation of human voice range continuum into soprano, mezzo-soprano, and alto (female), and tenor, baritone, and base (male)? But the issue is not just taxonomic or classificatory. When physicians prescribe dosages in threes, e.g. one pill every three hours or three pills a day, or when infants are given a three-in-one DPT (diphtheria toxoid, pertussis vaccine, and tetanus toxoid) shot or a series of three polio shots, the question is whether this is the most efficacious procedure, medically speaking, or not. Perhaps the ritual element is in fact an additional beneficial feature.

One can pick up an elementary textbook in any discipline and find numerous instances of three-determined thinking. It is really astonishing to realize that anthropologists, students of cultural conditioning, have been so culture-bound in their theoretical formulations. Among the numerous versions of a three stages of man theory (cf. Comte, Hegel, and Vico), one thinks of Morgan's savagery, barbarism (which is subdivided into Opening, Middle, and Closing periods), and civilization, and Frazer's stages of magic, religion, and science. Other obvious examples of tripartition include Van Gennep's classic analysis of rites of passage in which he distinguishes rites of separation, transition, and incorporation.

There is just as much three-conditioning evident in the other branches of anthropology. In physical anthropology, the traditional conventional number of races is three: Caucasoid, Mongoloid, and Negroid, although the inadequacy of the classification is well known. Similarly, European peoples are divided into northern, central, and southern, that is, Nordic, Alpine, and Mediterranean. In the study of body measurement and typology, tripartition is also found. (The folk system of measuring females in terms of bust, waist, and hips is in the same pattern.) In craniology, for example, the measurements of the various craniometric indices fall invariably into one of three categories (cf. Comas 1960:406-12). Archaeology is even more three-ridden. The three-age system of Stone, Bronze, and Iron is still in vogue (Heizer), but more important are the subdivisions of time periods. Ages are divided into three. Thus the Stone Age is commonly divided into Old, Middle, and New, i.e. Paleolithic, Mesolithic, and Neolithic. The Paleolithic can then be subdivided into Lower, Middle, and Upper Paleolithic. The Upper Paleolithic can then be broken down into Aurignacian, Solutrean, Magdalenian. If this weren't enough evidence to indicate that archaeologists are culture-bound, one should consult V. Gordon Childe's argument that tripartition is a necessary means of establishing chronological sequences in archaeology (1956:66) and that this is true, not because of any Hegelian metaphysics or trinitarian mysticism, but because of the very nature of the material to be seriated. The question is, of course, whether the method of tripartition is really dictated by the nature of the material or is it rather dictated by the nature of the culture of the archaeologist? If human history is a continuum, then the segmentation of a portion of that continuum into ages, stages, or levels is arbitrary.

Anthropology is typical insofar as the three-patterning of its scholarship is concerned. It would be easy to cite hundreds of examples from other disciplines. Yet anthropologists do not seem to have been aware of the pattern. Whorf, one of the pioneers in the study of the cultural conditioning of thought pattern, failed to see the influence of tripartition on his own work. His coinage of the three-word phrase "Standard Average European" is an example. His decision to compare three isolates of English - "clean", "with", "ramrod" - with three isolates from Shawnee would be another. (Note also his three-part figure in which he shows how one Hopi word equals three English words and how one English word equals three Eskimo words.) Another indication that anthropologists are not aware of their cultural propensity for tripartition is found in Edward Hall's The Silent Language. Hall, in collaboration with George L. Trager, developed an elaborate tripartite scheme which distinguished what was termed formal, informal, and technical levels. However, Hall, an expert on the implicit assumptions of various cultures, claimed that Americans had a bipolar way of analyzing data and that "The ease with which Americans tend to polarize their thoughts about events may make it difficult for them to embrace an approach which employs three categories rather than two". (1959:66).

Having demonstrated that the number three is a folk category in American culture, a folk category which has made inroads into the various analytic categories of academic disciplines, it remains to be seen what the meaning, if any, of the category is. It is one thing to describe a cultural category; it is another to speculate about its origin and meaning. Does the category stem from the family group of father, mother, and child? Is it a reflection of the divine nature of the universe as defined by trinitarian Christian doctrine? A Whorfian would no doubt place language rather than social organization or religion at the source. Thus a Whorfian might claim that the tense system, the first, second, third person distinctions, and the "good, better, best" paradigm were the roots of the pattern. A Freudian would argue along different lines (Glenn). Freud suggested that the number three was a masculine symbol, the phallus cum testiculis.*1 This is most interesting in the light of Freud's own work: e.g. Three Contributions to the Theory of Sex, or the id, ego, superego classification. Incidentally, the standard kinship notation employed by anthropologists would tend to support Freud's view. The triangle represents a male while a circle represents a female. However, the convention of three as a masculine symbol is more probably a manifestation of the traditional symbolism of Western civilization than a cause or origin of trichotomy. Only if one were to argue that male as opposed to female thought was trichotomized and that male thought was a compensatory activity for not being able to give birth to children as females do could one make a case for a most hypothetical origin theory. The only child a man produces is a brainchild. His intellectual project serves as his "baby". His products bear his stamp, the number three, the mark of masculinity. Since the majority of Western constructs and classification schemes have been devised by men rather than women, this could account for the preoccupation with three.*2 This type of explanation would also make clear why aspects of American culture which are exclusively masculine, e. g. the military, the Boy Scouts, baseball, are especially three-ridden. (Note also that the Christian Trinity is all masculine. This would be further evidence that three is male creativity denying or replacing female creativity.) However, like most psychological explanations, this one is highly speculative. One must conclude that it is difficult if not impossible to state with any degree of certainty what the ultimate origins of trichotomy might be.

One thing is certain though, and that is that trichotomy is a pattern of American culture. Whether it is related to masculinity or male mental creativity or not, it is, and will probably continue to be, an important cognitive category in American (and Old World) culture. As for how individuals learn about the pattern, there are probably many sources. Three dimensions of space, the three tenses of time, and the good-better-best paradigm all exert some influence. But an American three-year-old has already been exposed to the category in folkloristic form, perhaps before he realizes the space, time, and linguistic features. For are there not three men in a tub? three bags of Baa Baa Black Sheep's wool? three little kittens who lost their mittens? three little pigs? Is not the third item called for by Old King Cole his fiddlers three? Is there an American child who has not heard the story of the three bears? This latter story is a narrative listing of trichotomies in which the mediating third term is invariably "just right". (Note that the third term is associated with the child bear rather than the mother and father bears.) The child is conditioned by his folklore to expect three and his culture does not disappoint him. Language, social organization, religion, and almost all other aspects of American culture confirm the pattern.

Trichotomy exists but it is not part of the nature of nature. It is part of the nature of culture. At this point, if anyone is sceptical about there being a three-pattern in American culture, let him give at least three good reasons why.

NOTES

*1 Freud was by no means the first to suggest that the number three might be related to phallic symbolism. See, for example, Inman (1868:76, n.1, 89). As a matter of fact, the folk had also interpreted the number three in phallic terms long before Freud. For an example from modern Greek folklore, see Wachsmuth (1864:80, n.24). Since anthropologists frequently "discover" data which is already known (to the people in the culture under study), they can understand how a modern student of symbols could "discover" an interpretation which was in some sense already known to the people who use these symbols.

*2 One small bit of personal biographical data does support this thesis. The author first began to jot down examples of "threes" while awaiting the arrival of his third child. However, it was not until some time after the child's birth

that it occurred to the author that his mentally straining to produce examples
of threes might be a curious idiosyncratic form of intellectual couvade!

20

THINKING AHEAD: A FOLKLORISTIC REFLECTION OF
THE FUTURE ORIENTATION IN AMERICAN WORLDVIEW

The study of worldview has intrigued anthropologists for some time. Malinowski's statement (1922:517) is typical: "What interests me really in the study of
the native is his outlook on things, his Weltanschauung... Every human culture
gives its members a definite vision of the world..." Robert Redfield, perhaps
the one anthropologist most interested in the subject, defined worldview as "the
way a people characteristically look outward upon the universe" (1953:85). More
recently, Geertz has stated that a people's worldview is "their picture of the
way things, in sheer actuality are, their concept of nature, of self, and of society" (in Dundes 1968:303). Generally, it is assumed that worldview, in the
sense of a cognitive set by means of which people perceive, consciously or unconsciously, relationships between self, others, cosmos, and the day-to-day
living of life, is patterned (Kluckhohn 1949:358; Redfield 1953:86).

Part of the problem in analyzing worldview structure stems from the fact that
worldview is often implicit rather than explicit. It is unlikely that informants
are any more consciously aware of their worldview (cf. Foster 1966:387) than
they are of the grammatical principles which underlie the language they speak.
Nevertheless, worldview, like grammar, can through rigorous ethnographic
description become subject to conscious thought. But how then can the would-be
student get at the task of describing worldview?

If one holds a holistic concept of culture and if one accepts the notion of the
all-pervasiveness of worldview within a given culture, then in theory one could
begin anywhere, with any bit of cultural material, in the search for worldview.
One could find clues to worldview in kinship data, grammar, child rearing details, agricultural techniques or any one of a thousand bits and pieces of culture.
Each anthropologist could thus logically begin a study of worldview from the
data with which he is most familiar. However, there are some very good
reasons for electing to utilize folklore as source material for the study of worldview.

Reprinted from Anthropological Quarterly 42 (1969), 53-72. This paper was
originally prepared for the symposium "World Views: Their Nature and Their
Role in Culture" held at Burg Wartenstein, the European Conference Center of
the Wenner-Gren Foundation for Anthropological Research, in August, 1968.
The author wishes to express his gratitude to Lita Osmundsen, Director of Research of the Foundation, to Professor Will Jones of Pomona College, organizer
of the symposium, and to all the other participants for their constructive criticisms.

To the extent that folklore constitutes an autobiographical ethnography of a
people, it provides an outsider, e.g. the visiting ethnographer, with a view of
the culture from the inside-out rather than from the outside-in. Not only is folklore a people's own description of themselves and hence possibly less subject
to the influence of the ethnographic reporter's unavoidable ethnocentric bias
than other kinds of data, but it is frequently the case that in folklore implicit
worldview principles and themes are made explicit (cf. Kluckhohn 1949:359).
Unfortunately, the great potential of folkloristic data for studies of worldview
is less often realized than recognized by anthropologists. Melville Jacobs in
his important study of Clackamas Chinook myths and tales, The Content and
Style of an Oral Literature, devotes a whole chapter to worldview but alas the
chapter consists of only five pages. Occasionally genres other than myth, for
example, proverbs (cf. Raymond 1954; Shimkin and Sanjuan 1953) have been
utilized for the extrapolation of worldview. Probably one of the most interesting studies made thus far is that made by a Hungarian folklorist which revealed
that one individual tale-teller's personal worldview was remarkably similar to
the worldview expressed in the folktales collected from that individual (Erdész
1961). But despite these and other studies (e.g. Forde 1954), it would appear
that folklore as source material for the serious study of worldview has yet to
be tapped.

As a test case for the feasibility of using folklore for worldview analysis, I
have selected one aspect of American worldview, or at least one distinctive
feature said to be an attribute of American worldview, namely, the futuristic
orientation, to see whether or not there is any folkloristic data manifesting
this alleged attribute. If folklore does in fact provide a concrete form in which
implicit worldview is often made explicit, and if American worldview includes
a future orientation, then one would expect to find that orientation expressed in
American folklore.

There is one apparent problem in using American folklore as source material
and that is the fact that so much of that folklore is patently derived from European tradition. Certainly one could find without difficulty cognate forms of many
American proverbs in England and other old world cultures. Yet what is really
most important in the present context is a proverb's occurrence and specifically
its frequency of occurrence in the United States. In a way the critical issue is
whether or not it is possible to distinguish "American worldview" from "Anglo-
American" or "English" or even "Western European worldview". It is the inevitable vexing question of where or how the would-be analyst should make his
arbitrary "cuts". The task of distinguishing multi-cultural relativism, cultural
relativism, sub-cultural relativism, and perhaps ultimately individual relativism is a terribly challenging and frustrating one. Are there elements of American worldview distinct from Western European worldview? Are there elements
of American Negro worldview distinct from general American worldview? I
suggest that though there are common elements, i.e. similarities, in the worldviews of related peoples, there are also important differences. Sometimes the
differences may entail degree rather than kind. Thus, for example, one might
find future orientation in Europe but not always in as intensified a form as in
the United States. Similarly, one might find past orientation in the United States,
but not to the extent that one can find it in tradition-bound areas of Europe. In

a number of rather striking instances, it is precisely the slight but definite
changes introduced in American versions of European folkloristic items which
seem to signal crucial differences in general American and European worldviews.

That Americans are future-oriented has been noted by a number of observers
(e. g. Williams 1952:405; Florence Kluckhohn 1953:349), but rarely is any detailed evidence cited. A representative statement is made by Florence Kluckhohn when she writes: "Americans, more than most people of the world, place
emphasis upon the future - a future which we anticipate to be 'bigger and better' "
(1953:349). One of the relatively few attempts to document this future-orientation was made by Evon Z. Vogt in his study of a Texas community. A chapter
entitled "Living in the Future" begins: "To look forward to the future, to forget
or even reject the past, and to regard the present only as a step along the road
to the future, is a cherished value in American culture and a conspicuous feature of life on the frontier. This future-time orientation and associated value
emphases on 'progress', 'optimism', and 'success' have had a profound influence on the settlement and development of Homestead". (1955:93). Nevertheless, his data (most of which is in the form of verbatim statements taken from
the appropriate sections of high school student autobiographies, the sections
dealing with career expectations - hardly a random sample!) is from just one
community. While it is tempting to generalize about American worldview on the
basis of informants from a single community, it is obviously sounder methodologically speaking to utilize data which is representative of a wider sampling
of the American people. Of course, Vogt may be assuming (and quite rightly in
my opinion) that general American values and worldview are manifested in the
statement elicited from his Texas informants. The point is that documentation
for the assertion that Americans in general are future-oriented is not offered.

In American folklore there is plenty of relevant evidence and this evidence is
for the most part not regional. Rather the proverbs, folk metaphors, and other
traditional linguistic clichés and formulas are found throughout the United
States. It should also be noted that a future-orientation in American folk speech
does not exist in a cultural vacuum. The penchant for regarding the future may
well be correlated with a tendency to denigrate or ignore the past. Furthermore,
the attitudinal contrast between past and future in American worldview is in turn
part of a larger, more comprehensive paradigm. If one were to delineate a
portion of this worldview paradigm, one might well include the following associated dichotomies:

Past	-	Future
Before	-	After
Backward	-	Forward
Behind	-	Ahead
Beginning	-	End
Old	-	New
Traditional	-	Original
Parent	-	Child

However, the principal aim of the present essay is to examine the tendency of

Americans to look, think, and plan ahead as it is expressed in folklore (especially folk speech).

Americans look into the future in part because they are end oriented. "The ends justify the means." "All's fair in love and war." Beginnings and origins are not so important in a future oriented society. It is the end which counts. "Tall oaks from little acorns grow." Whether the end is catching worms or saving stitches, one's actions are directed towards such future ends. "The early bird catches the worm." "A stitch in time saves nine." The positive attitude towards ends is revealed by such phrases as to be the "end" or the "living end" or to be "endsville" or to refer to something as the "be and end all" though there may well be anxiety about "making ends meet". Obviously, the great concern with the "happy ending" in popular films and novels is another example.

Americans invariably want "something to look forward to". They have been so conditioned since earliest childhood. One of the most recurrent questions directed to young children from parents, teachers, and other adults it: "What do you want to be when you grow up?" Children thus learn to be curious about "what's in store" for them. When they join such organizations as "Future Farmers of America" or "Future Homemakers of America", they are attempting to keep "the end in sight" which they are encouraged to believe is a good thing. They soon discover that the question "where am I now?" is not nearly as pressing as "where will I be 'x' years from now?" (even though in 'x' years the identical question will be repeated). They invariably "hope for the best" and dream that some day their "ship will come in" or that some day their "prince will come" as it is stated in one form of the ideal of romantic love, in this case in a song from the movie Snow White. Actually, many folksongs aid in the enculturation process, e. g. the various verses of "She'll be comin' around the mountain when she comes". The same is true of popular songs: "There's gonna be a great day." Children in secondary schools evaluate their peers, not so much in terms of present status as in terms of future promise. Consider the category "most likely to succeed", among others. In this future oriented context, it is certainly no accident and it is certainly appropriate that pregnant American women refer to themselves as "expecting"!

A striking example of future-oriented worldview is found in American greeting and leave-taking rituals. While to be sure there are present oriented formal greetings: "How do you do?" and "How are you?", these are purely rhetorical questions. Informal greetings, in contrast, may involve genuine requests for information. (It is noteworthy in any case that most American greetings are phrased in question form perhaps suggesting the possibility of change in state or status.) While there are past-oriented informal greetings, e. g. "How have you been?" the most common are future-oriented: "How are things going?" "What's up?" "What's new?" "What's happening?" "What's the latest?" "What's with you?" When one is asked "How are things going?" one is being requested for a prediction as to the direction of change. Are things going well, better than yesterday, and are they going to be even better tomorrow? The common greeting "What's new (with you)?" emphasizes the tremendous concern with novelty. Americans thirst for the new and for "news". Yet the news must be new. "There is nothing deader than yesterday's news (paper)." Novelty must always be just around the corner, in the future. Once it is introduced, it is no longer new or news. It is the <u>anticipation</u> of the new, the constant taking and retaking of political polls to try to predict the direction of news which appeals to most Americans. Novelty itself "wears off fast". The future becomes present and is shunted immediately and ignominiously into the category of past. Even in the greeting context, one often hears "So what else is new?" as a means of signalling that one has already heard a piece of news. A possible historical factor which may have encouraged the positive attitude towards what is new is, quite obviously, the emigration pattern from Europe and elsewhere to the United States. People cut past ties with the Old World to come live in the New World. (Interesting is Tillich's insight [1966:66] that whereas Europe is endangered by the curse of the past, America is endangered by going ahead without looking back.)

In leavetaking formulas, there is similarly an overt reference to a future action. "See you later", "See you around", "Be seeing you", "See you", "You all come back and see us", "We really must get together one of these days", etc. One can, of course, simply say "good-bye", but the fact is that one normally does make a reference to future activity: "Good-bye, enjoy your lunch", or "Good-bye, have a good time at the party" etc., or there is a request for future action, "Say hello to ___ for me (when you see him)". (It is true, of course, that similar "I'll be seeing you" formulas occur in European languages, e.g. German, French, and Spanish. However, one is tempted to distinguish semantically between "until we meet again" which, after all, could be never and a positive assertion promising a definite future meeting "I'll see you later".)

Before continuing with future-reflecting folklore per se, it might be well to consider briefly the related folkloristic repudiation of the past. If "thinking ahead" is good, then "looking back" is bad! The various folkloristic responses to present and past mistakes will illustrate the point: "Don't worry about it"; "Everybody makes mistakes"; "Nobody's perfect"; "Let bygones be bygones"; "Never mind about that"; "No use crying over spilled milk"; "That's water over the dam"; "It doesn't make a particle of difference"; "Let it go"; "I don't give a damn"; "To hell with it"; "Don't bother with it"; "Don't mention it"; "No regrets"; "I'll overlook it this once"; "Don't let it happen again"; "Oh that's all right"; "Forgive and forget"; "Forget it"; etc. One finds a similar philosophy displayed in some superstitions. There is danger in turning towards the past. For example, it is supposed to be bad luck for a person to retrace his steps once he has set out to do something. The implication is clearly that one must go forward, never backward. One thinks also of the idea that "lightning never strikes twice". Literally interpreted, this is a superstition about the supposed characteristics of lightning. However, metaphorically interpreted, the phrase suggests the non-repetitive nature of history. It affirms novelty and emphatically denies that the future will conform to the pattern of past events. Even if one has been successful in the past, one is expected to point towards the future. One risks the displeasure of his peers if he "rests on his laurels". It is not necessarily that "History is bunk", but rather the idea that one cannot change the past. Thus there is no point in being a "Monday morning quarterback" (and commenting critically on events which took place on the football field the preceding Saturday or Sunday). For Americans, only the future is subject to change. Americans thus accept the past fatalistically (as opposed to past-oriented societies who accept the future fatalistically!). "That's the way the ball bounces [cookie crumbles]" etc.

The favoring of future over past also has correlates in the penchant for new rather than old, and for child rather than parent. It is the new generation which counts. Politicians depend upon slogans like "New Deal" or "New Frontier". American manufacturers invariably replace their products (laundry soaps, toothpastes, cigarettes, television sets, etc.) with new improved versions, which are presumably intended to make consumers dissatisfied with last year's "obsolete" model. It is the "new faces" in acting; it is the newcomer, the new-lyweds, the tenderfoot, and the freshman who attract the greatest interest. There are awards for the "rookie of the year". There are few for the second year man. He is already "old hat", an accepted part of the present and past. (Cf. "Sophomore slumps" among college students.) Nobody wants to be an "old fogy", "old fashioned", or "behind the times" (cf. also the somewhat unflatter-ing associations attached to such stereotype characters as the LOL [Little old lady] and the "Dirty old man"). Instead, one wants to be avant garde, "ahead of his time", part of the "wave of the future". The idea is if one looks (thinks, plans) ahead, he can get ahead. "Where there's a will, there's a way."

It is not only the past which is sacrificed to the future; it is also the present. Sometimes it is an unpleasant present which is denied in favor of a reference to a brighter future. "Better luck next time"; "Tomorrow's another day". In ad-dition, there is the proverbial cry of baseball fans backing a loser: "Wait til next year." Yet the "wait and see" philosophy may offer hope in the more im-mediate future for "The ballgame's never over until the last man is out", "Where there's life, there's hope". But it is not just the unpleasant present which is denied. Americans are so future oriented that they are discontent even with pleasant presents. For the present reality no matter how good it is can never be as good as what the future might be. Other peoples on the face of the earth might be discontent with the present but for a different reason i.e. perhaps for them the present represents a departure (deemed unfortunate) from the more perfect past. With Americans and their belief in efficiency, evolution, progress, perfectability, etc., "the best is yet to come". Whatever one has, one hears, "You ain't seen nothin' yet" or "If you think this is ___ wait until you see ___". The same kind of sentiment is expressed in the American military slogan: "We have not yet begun to fight". (Other future oriented military phrases include: "Don't fire until you see the whites of their eyes" and "I shall return".) Never-theless, in American culture, one never does catch up with the carrot on a stick in front of the donkey; one never does reach the "pot of gold at the end of the rainbow". (Now there is a compact folkloristic expression of American world-view!)

The present is but "preparation" for the future, a future which never comes: "Tomorrow never comes". (cf. the Boy Scout motto "Be Prepared" and the no-tion of "Prep" schools). Consider the educational cursus honorum. Middle class Americans try to do well in high school, not because they really enjoy high school but because they want to be admitted into college. They then try to do well in college, not because of college per se, but because they want to get into medical school, law school, graduate school, etc. There is always the next dip-loma, a still better meal ticket, until the final reward (cf. "went to his reward" as a folk circumlocution for dying), a place in heaven, when presumably the deferred reward is deferred no longer.

It should be noted that it is not just pleasure alone which fills the future. Futurism is not necessarily associated with optimism. An example of futurism plus pessimism would be reflected in the idea of "putting something aside for a rainy day". Thus it is not just pleasure which may be postponed; pain may also be put off into some future realm. Pain in America includes paying cash or being unable to purchase a desired item because of an insufficiency of cash on hand. This pain is postponed by means of the installment plan: buy now; pay later. Indeed, the whole "credit" way of life is based upon future payment for present actions. But whether one buys now and pays later or pays now to receive later - as in medical insurance, life insurance, and retirement plans, the same future orientation pervades the philosophy. In life insurance, for example, according to most plans, one receives (or one's heirs or beneficiaries receive) only after life has ceased. This is why some Americans often "look forward" to the prospective demise of a "loved one" (!) as an effective means of obtaining wealth, thus fulfilling an American ideal of "getting rich quick". Even when some Americans buy antiques which are ostensibly objects belonging to the past, the underlying motivation is frequently the hope that the items purchased will increase in value. "Just think how much this will be worth x years from now" and "how much it will bring on the open market".

Certainly, the future orientation permeates American business theory and method. It is glaringly apparent in advertising. "There's a Ford in your future" would be one obvious example. It is not enough merely to "keep up with the Jones", although that at least would eliminate the possibility of falling behind or being passed by. Rather one is urged to "be the first on your block" to purchase a particular item. Whether it is a matter of "How to win friends and influence people" or "30 days to a more powerful vocabulary" or the standard pictorial drama of "before"(=past or perhaps present) and "after" (=future), the pattern of perfectability or improvement in the immediate or even distant future is a recurrent one. Perhaps the most blatant example of futurism in American business concerns the announcement of only so many more "shopping days left until Christmas". When Christmas finally does come, it is frequently an anticlimax. It would appear that it is build-up and the anticipation of the future which tickles the American esthetic palate. The present picture is never as glamorous or as thrilling as the "previews of coming attractions" led us to believe what was "coming soon at your neighborhood theater" would be. At concert and at pricefight, the audience is inevitably informed about what is coming and more often than not the promise of the "next" presentation succeeds in making the present evening pale by comparison.

Nowhere is the future-orientation and the emphasis upon build-up more clearly displayed than in the punchline joke. Here is an admirable example of how folklore encapsulates worldview and more specifically how the structure of folklore delineates in microcosm the structure of worldview. In most American jokes, the whole joke is told for the sake of the final line. So much of our art (and sex) esthetic depends upon achieving a climax (cf. Lee in Dundes 1968:341). It is the final response to the joke which provides an index to the success or failure of the joke-teller. The structure of the joke reflects the whole cultural propensity to build towards a bigger and better end, in this case a punchline which provokes or evokes loud laughter. (Even the sequence of jokes in a joke-telling session may illustrate this tendency as one joke is followed by another, which is told by someone other than the first joketeller with the conscious or unconscious competitive hope that the second joke's punchline will be more climactic than the punchline of the first.) Americans also prefer that the joke be new or at least one that they have not heard before.

All this is in sharp contrast to the oral literature of past rather than future oriented peoples. Among most past oriented peoples, it is the past, it is the known which is valued. It is more likely that beginnings (e.g. creation myths) rather than ends (e.g. punchlines) matter. American Indian audiences already know the tale's plot and they enjoy the entire episode, not just the final punchline. One might speculate that one possible reason for the paucity of punchline jokes among American Indians - at least the less acculturated ones - is that punchline jokes would not appeal to a people without a future-climax building worldview.

There are also specific types or genres within American joke-lore which seem to reflect the future orientation. One thinks of the cross-breed riddle: "What do you get when you cross a ___ with a ___?" (e.g. a hoot owl with a nanny goat: a hootenanny). Here it is clear that the end desired dictated the particular means used (cf. Abrahams and Hickerson 1964). Perhaps the ultimate in end-directed American folklore is a group of riddles in which the riddler offers his audience the answer and asks them for the question, e.g. the answer is 9W, what is the question? ("Is it true, Herr Maestro Wagner, that you spell your name with a 'V'?") In this light, the extremely popular joke cycle which consists of what are called "shaggy dog stories" may be seen as a metacultural parody of future-oriented worldview. The shaggy dog story consists of a long, often a very long buildup to what is usually regarded as a disappointing punchline - it frequently depends upon a pun or a perverted proverb (cf. Brunvand 1963). The audience's reaction is usually that the poor punchline was not worth the long buildup. One is reminded of the phrase "to win the fur-lined bathtub" or the "solid gold chamber pot" which are used ironically on the occasion of a remarkable action by someone else. In both cases, the reward is less than was expected or deserved. If the shaggy dog story builds expectations and then denies them, it may be said to be playing upon the future-oriented, goal-directed worldview of most Americans. On the other hand, the specific fact that the great effort expended upon the buildup of the joke did not result in an appropriate pay-off punchline may well be a realistic appraisal of the fallacy of living for the future, inasmuch as the "future-becoming-present" is, as we have noted, almost always something less than the long anticipatory period had prepared us for. When one finally gets to the punchline, the "end" of the joke, it just wasn't worth it. In shaggy dog stories, the "end" does not justify the means! Of course, the frustration of expectations in jokes is comic; in life it may be tragic!

Having found some indications of future-oriented worldview in American folklore, one is tempted to undertake studies comparing the worldviews of two or more cultures. There have been few enough attempts to describe single worldview systems and consequently the literature on comparative worldview is, to put it mildly, very sparse. The opportunity for investigating comparative worldview in the present essay arises because most of the cultures of the world have, or at least had, a past-oriented rather than future-oriented worldview (cf. Heil-broner 1959:18-21). Americans have reworked many old world cultural elements and predictably enough, the American versions of customs with European cognates reveal the unmistakable influence of future orientation. For example, in the celebration of All Souls Day in Europe, respect is paid to the dead, that is, to the ancestors, to the past. (The same is true of All Saints Day inasmuch as saints are part of the past.) In the United States, the Halloween festival has been converted to a celebration for children, not parents. Though remains of departed spirits survive in the form of ghosts and other creatures, memorial visits to the graves of ancestors have been replaced by parents giving treats to children who threaten to play pranks on them. In accordance with a futuristic-optimistic view, the child - who represents the future - is bribed to be good. The emphasis is upon the child, the future, rather than upon the deceased ancestors, the past.

A similar past-future comparison is afforded by birthday rituals. In Norwegian tradition (and presumably in the traditions of other past-oriented cultures), a child who reaches the age of seven celebrates the seventh year just passed. In other words, the child and his family take pride in what has been accomplished. But in American tradition, a child who is seven years old celebrates his arrival into a new status, the next year. Frequently, there are eight candles or eight spanks - the spanks possibly marking one more than the number of years since the original spank administered by the obstetrician. The eighth candle or spank is explicitly "one for good measure" or "one to grow on", a clear push towards the future. (An alternative custom involves a pinch instead of a spank with the accompanying verbal formula: "A pinch to grow an inch".) Note also that American children when questioned about their age will often not say, "I'm seven", but rather "I'm seven and a half" or "I'm seven going on eight" or even "I'll be eight in January" which is a clearcut refusal to accept the past and present coupled with a definite penchant for looking ahead.

There is a partial contradiction in children wanting to be older. They want to be older because they anxiously await the future and the future for them as individuals involves their becoming older. On the other hand, there is a point at which an individual is no longer "young" and "full of promise". The "new" or "younger" generation suddenly becomes the "older generation". The moment a man becomes a father, he becomes his child's "old man". Naturally, a member of the older generation is a part of the present or status quo at best or a part of the past at worst. Such a generation is destined to be forgotten, to be replaced by a new generation, new breed, etc. The critical point in American culture is not clear and obviously it could vary somewhat in individual cases. Possibly it is around age 30 ("Don't trust anyone over thirty"), a multiple of the American ritual number three (Dundes 1968:401-24). Up to thirty, one is a comer, a good prospect, someone on the make. After thirty, one has joined the Establishment. The vagueness of critical age criterion lies in the vagueness of "middle age". When in American culture does a young man become middle aged? In any event, it is certain that the older one becomes, the less future he has! Since American culture is future-oriented and since individuals are frequently measured in terms of potential and possible future productivity, there is much more interest in young people than in middle aged or old people. It is difficult to grow old in

a youth-oriented culture and individuals may dye their hair or refuse to admit
their age in an attempt to "pass" for a more youthful version of themselves.
With less to look forward to before entering their "second childhood", there
may develop a tendency to look back to the "good old days". "When you and I
were young, Maggie". In a future-oriented, child-oriented society, one can
understand why parents live for or perhaps more aptly live through their children. Thus as an individual's own future begins to diminish and his prospects
dim, he shifts his aspirations to the future of his children or grandchildren.

In contrast, one finds that in past-oriented societies individuals are measured
in terms of age and how much past experience they have. The older they are,
the wiser they are thought to be and the more respect they deserve. Children
take pride in their parents' achievements and boast of their ancestors. (In
American culture, in contrast, it is the parents who boast of their children's
accomplishments while children may actually consider it to be a disadvantage
to be the child of a famous father.) It is easy to see, furthermore, that residence
patterns are related to worldview. In a past oriented worldview, young people
must move in with one set of parents. One continues to live in with one's past.
A new element, that is, a bride (or groom) is absorbed into the previous (=past)
pattern. In contrast, in future-oriented worldview one finds neolocal residence.
Newlyweds want to make their own future away from the "dead hand of the past".
In fact there is even resistance to the idea of the past - in the form of in-laws
moving eventually to the young people's household.

In addition to Halloween and birthday ritual, one may profitably examine divination theory for an instructive differentiation between past and future oriented
worldview. In a past oriented culture (e. g. most of the cultures in Africa), divination is defined largely as determining past causes of present states. Thus a
diviner may be asked to discover why a given person has become ill or why there
is a drought. In contrast, in American culture, divination techniques normally
concern predicting the future, e. g. ascertaining what the sex of an unborn child
will be or the identity of one's future mate. Thus diviners in African (and other
past oriented) societies seek past origins, that which has caused the present.
In future oriented American society, diviners are used primarily to predict
what the future will be or bring, that is, what the present will become, not what
has caused the present. This does not mean that there are no references to the
future in a past oriented society. The point is rather that in such a society the
future is determined by events in the past. Accordingly in folklore, all the proph-
ecies of a child's future greatness or a hero's future death are all set in the past.
Often the predictions are made even before the child is born. The future is totally controlled by the past. In one sense - from the perspective of a future oriented society - such individuals really had no future at all. Similarly, in modern
American culture, the minority who depend upon astrology and daily horoscopes
are undoubtedly more past than future oriented. They may desire to know their
future (a goal consistent with the dominant American worldview), but they assume that its course has already been determined by past events, e. g. by the
sign of the Zodiac under which they were born. True future orientation, allied
as it is in American culture to individualism, rugged individualism, and to
achieved rather than ascribed status is more typically associated with the notion of making one's own future rather than passively playing out the part pre-

scribed by a predetermined procrustean pattern established in the past.

An individual is expected to have a hand in creating his own future. One admires a "man who knows where he's going" especially if he looks like he's "going far" and if he looks like he's "getting somewhere" while one may disdain a man with "no future", a "man who doesn't know where his next meal is coming from". Consider the common insult technique in American folklore of directing the future action of an enemy. I am going to tell him "where to get off"; "to go jump in the lake"; "What he can do with his ....." More important, Americans judge one another, not on the basis of what an individual is, but on the basis of what he will do or become. Evaluation and decision making is very different in past and future oriented societies. In a past-oriented society, one acts and judges others in accordance with the presumed wishes of one's ancestors, that is, according to a paradigm of the past. In a future-oriented society, one acts in accordance with how one thinks one's parents or more probably one's peers (or one's children) will judge or react to the planned action. A principal worry is "What will the neighbors say?" Proposals are often couched in such language as "what would you say to the idea of ....." or "what do you say we go to ....." Typical negative judgments express the same futurity: "I don't think he'll ever get the hang of it"; "... ever set the world on fire"; "...ever get off the ground"; "... ever amount to much". Healthy scepticism is signalled by: "That remains to be seen"; "That'll be the day"; "That I'd like to see"; "I'll believe it when I see it". Even outright warnings intended to dissuade someone from a particular action are cast in terms of future consequences: "You'll be singing a different tune"; "You're going to get yours"; "You'll never get away with it"; "Some day you're going to get it" (it being "come-upance"). Americans wonder and worry about how people and events will "turn out". Hopefully, bad things will "come out in the wash" leaving a bright future!

The significance of the future orientation in American worldview as revealed in American folklore is relevant, I feel, to both teaching and research. In educational philosophy, the past versus future orientations are critical. In past oriented educational systems, students are expected to know (typically via verbatim memorization) the "classics" of the past. So it is that if the future must conform to the patterns of the past, then students must record in their notebooks and minds exactly what their professors tell them (cf. Adams in Dundes 1968: 507). Many past-oriented professors still insist on the memorization of facts with rote learning right up until the final examination which consists of a full regurgitation presented for inspection. The technique was designed to make the young old, to bring the past into the present and to guarantee its continuation in the future. In future oriented educational philosophy, students are taught to critically question the past in order to build a new and different future. From this perspective, students are no longer sponges to soak up the alleged, infallible wisdom of the professor. The emphasis is upon change, not the changeless; upon the new, not the old; upon originality, not conformity to tradition; upon relativity, not upon absolutes; upon the future, not the past!

The implications of a future oriented worldview for research are no less important than those for teaching. It is once again the contrast of future and past oriented cultures. A past oriented culture, say in terms of acculturation theory, is likely to conceive its future in terms of its past. Thus the Ghost Dance and other nativistic movements like the cargo cults invariably consist of future projections involving glorified reinstatements of the past. Similarly in research, scholars in a past oriented society would be intent upon demonstrating how well present and future events "prove" the validity of one or more authorities of the past. But scholars in a future oriented culture would be likely to evaluate the past in terms of the future. Thus they might anxiously peruse the works of the past looking for hints of precursors indicating future trends. The point is that methodologically they would probably start with the particular trend and then go back to the past to find prefigurations of it. This is why scholars in a future oriented society write the conclusions of their papers first! They are end, not beginning oriented. With the "end in sight", they begin the search through past studies to find the means to their end, that is, the data to support their conclusions. Even the ritual formula of the scientific method which demands that a hypothesis be tested reflects the futuristic bias. In theory, one proposes a "new" hypothesis which one tests (or which one asks colleagues to test) in future experiments. But in practice isn't the hypothesis really a tentative conclusion in disguise? It is analogous to writing the introduction to a paper only after the conclusion is written, an introduction in which one pretends to test various assumptions. This is perfectly understandable in the light of end or future oriented worldview. Where one is going is more important than where one has been.

The basic philosophy of induction or "reading back" from empirical data like folklore to "prior" organizing principles like worldview is end-oriented. One begins with the known and the known is the end or consequence. One searches for causes to explain effects. The association of inductive reasoning with future-orientation is also indicated by the nuances of the word "induce" meaning to bring forward or bring about as in "inducing a hypnotic state". In contrast, the logic of deduction entails working from given (past) premises to projected conclusions. As in inductive reasoning, one begins with the known, but in this case the known is the beginning, not the end. Deductive reasoning is therefore beginning oriented rather than end oriented. It is true that deduction is nominally concerned with delineating future events, but the future in a deductive system is totally controlled by the past premises, usually assumed without question. It is analogous to the closed future dictated by past oriented astrological data previously mentioned. The past orientation of deduction is also signalled by its additional meanings of tracing derivations or descents. In any case, whether induction or deduction is employed, the passionate concern with "prediction" in science overrides all. One does not have science, it is sometimes said, unless one can predict, that is, unless one can foretell the future accurately! It is surely no accident that a future-oriented society worships prediction.

One of the most fascinating offshoots of scientific prediction is science fiction. Here again is an opportunity to compare past and future oriented societies. In past oriented societies, the principal projections of interpersonal relations such as parent-child or sibling struggles are placed in the past, the far distant past. The normal expressions of fantasy is found in the form or genre of myths. In contrast, in future-oriented societies such as ours, there seems to be a tendency for the myths of the past to diminish in force but this is accompanied by a tendency to project the nuclear and conjugal family traumas into the far distant future by means of a science fiction setting. Thus the modern monsters are creatures found in space or produced by mad scientists of other worlds. They differ only slightly from the traditional chimerical monsters of the past. One of the critical differences is the matter of the time setting: future as opposed to past.

The fact that I began this essay with my conclusion: American folklore <u>will</u> reflect the future orientation in American worldview, <u>will</u> hopefully not offend anyone. I trust by such a beginning I did not raise expectations which were not fulfilled! As I have noted above, the technique of beginning with the end in sight and then writing or rewriting an introduction to match the conclusion is well known in academic circles even though it may not always be readily admitted. I can only say in conclusion that I hope that <u>future</u> research will confirm the present analysis. Time will tell!

BIBLIOGRAPHY

Aarne, Antti
1913   Leitfaden der Vergleichenden Märchenforschung (= Folklore Fellows
       Communications 13) (Hamina).
1928   Märchentypen (= FF Communications 74) (Helsinki).
Abbot, A. E.
1962   The Number Three: Its Occult Significance in Human Life (London:
       Emerson Press).
Abraham, Karl
1948a Selected Papers on Psycho-analysis (= The Psycho-Analytical Library
       13) (London: Hogarth).
1948b "Contributions to the Theory of the Anal Character", in Selected Papers
       of Karl Abraham (London).
Abrahams, Roger D.
1962   "Playing the Dozens", JAF 75, 209-20.
1963   "The Bigger They Are, The Harder They Fall", Tennessee Folklore Bulle-
       tin 29, 94-102.
1964   Deep Down in the Jungle... Negro Narrative Folklore from the Streets
       of Philadelphia (Hatboro, Pennsylvania: Folklore Associates).
Abrahams, Roger D., and Joseph C. Hickerson
1964   "Cross-fertilization Riddles", Western Folklore 23, 253-57.
Adams, Don
1960   "The Monkey and the Fish: Cultural Pitfalls of an Educational Adviser",
       International Development Review 2, 22-24. Reprinted in Dundes (1968).
Anderson, Flavia
1953   The Ancient Secret (London).
Anderson, George K.
1965   The Legend of the Wandering Jew (Providence, R. I.: Brown University
       Press).
Anonymous
1912   "Skatologische Inschriften", Anthropophyteia 9, 503-10.
Arewa, E. Ojo, and Alan Dundes
1964   "Proverbs and the Ethnography of Speaking Folklore", American
       Anthropologist 66.6 (2), 70-85. Reprinted in this volume.
Armstrong, Robert Plant
1959   "Content Analysis in Folkloristics", in Ithiel de Sola Pool (ed.), Trends
       in Content Analysis (Urbana, Ill.).
Atherton, John
1957   "Threes", The New Yorker 33 (March, 2), 103.

Austin, William M. (ed.)
  1960 Report on the Ninth Annual Round Table Meeting on Linguistics and
        Language Studies: Anthropology and African Studies (= Georgetown
        University Monograph Series on Languages and Linguistics 11) (Wash-
        ington, D.C., Georgetown University Press).
Bach, Adolf
  1960 Deutsche Volkskunde (Heidelberg).
Baillie, John
  1950 The Belief in Progress (1950).
Barnes, Harry Elmer
  1965 An Intellectual and Cultural History of the Western World, 3rd rev.
        ed. (New York).
Barnouw, Victor
  1955 "A Psychological Interpretation of a Chippewa Origin Legend", JAF
        68, 73-85; 211-23; 341-55.
Barrick, Mac E.
  1964a "The Shaggy Elephant Riddle", Southern Folklore Quarterly 28 (1964),
         266-90.
  1964b "You Can Tell a Joke with Vigah If It's About a Niggah", Keystone Folk-
         lore Quarterly 9, 166-68.
Bascom, William R.
  1942 "The Principle of Seniority in the Social Structure of the Yoruba",
        American Anthropologist 44, 37-46.
  1949 "Literary Style in Yoruba Riddles", JAF 62, 1-16.
  1953a "Folklore and Anthropology", JAF 66, 283-90.
  1953b Drums of the Yoruba of Nigeria (= Ethnic Folkways Library, Album
         P 441) (New York: Folkways Record and Service Corp.).
  1954 "Four Functions of Folklore", JAF 67, 333-49.
  1955 "Verbal Art", JAF 68, 245-52.
  1965 "The Forms of Folklore: Prose Narratives", JAF 78, 3-20.
Baumgarten, Franziska
  1952 "A Proverb Test for Attitude Measurement", Personnel Psychology 5,
        249-61.
Bayard, Samuel
  1953 "The Materials of Folklore", JAF 66, 1-17.
Beatty, Jerome, Jr.
  1963 "Tradewinds", Saturday Review (August 3), 7.
Beckwith, Martha Warren
  1931 Folklore in America: Its Scope and Method (Poughkeepsie: The Folklore
        Foundation).
Bédier, Joseph
  1945 The Romance of Tristan and Iseult (New York: Doubleday Anchor).
Bell, F.L.S.
  1931 "The Place of Food in the Social Life of Central Polynesia", Oceania
        2, 117-35.
Benedict, Ruth
  1931 "Folklore", Encyclopaedia of the Social Sciences, 6 (New York: Mac-
        Millan), 288-93.

1935   Zuni Mythology (= Columbia University Contributions to Anthropology 21).

Bennett, D. J.
1964   "The Psychological Meaning of Anti-Negro Jokes", Fact 1.2, 53-59.

Berkeley-Hill, Owen
1921   "The Anal-erotic Factor in the Religion, Philosophy and Character of the Hindus", International Journal of Psycho-Analysis 2, 306-38.

Bettelheim, Bruno
1955   Symbolic Wounds (London: Thames and Hudson).

Bidney, David
1953   Theoretical Anthropology (New York).

Blake, Robert
1964   101 Elephant Jokes (New York: Pyramid Books).

Bloomfield, Maurice
1923   "Joseph and Potiphar in Hindu Fiction", Transactions and Proceedings of the American Philological Association 54, 141-67.

Blumensohn, Jules
1933   "The Fast among North American Indians", American Anthropologist 35, 451-69.

Boas, Franz
1895   Indianische Sagen von der nord-pacifischen Küste Amerikas (Berlin).
1910a   Kwakiutl Tales (= Columbia University Contributions to Anthropology 2).
1910b   "Psychological Problems in Anthropology", American Journal of Psychology 21, 371-84.
1916   Tsimshian Mythology (=31st Annual Report of the Bureau of American Ethnology) (Washington, Government Printing Office).
1940   Race, Language and Culture (New York: MacMillan).

Bødker, Laurits
1965   Folk Literature (Germanic) (= International Dictionary of Regional European Ethnology and Folklore, II) (Copenhagen).

Boehm, Felix
1930   "The Femininity-complex in men", International Journal of Psycho-Analysis 11, 444-69.

Bogoras, Waldemar
1913   Chuckchee Mythology (= Jesup North Pacific Expedition Publications 8).

Bonaparte, Marie
1946   "The Legend of the Unfathomable Waters", American Imago 4, 20-31.

Bonser, Wilfred and T. A. Stephens
1930   Proverb Literature: A Bibliography of Works Relating to Proverbs (London).

Bourke, John G.
1891   Scatalogic Rites of All Nations (Washington: W. H. Lowdermilk).

Brauer, Jerald C. (ed.)
1966   The Future of Religions (New York: Harper and Row).

Brewster, Paul G.
1953   American Nonsinging Games (Norman).

Brinton, Daniel G.
  1868 The Myths of the New World: A Treatise on the Symbolism and Myth-
        ology of the Red Race of America (New York: Leypoldt and Holt).
  1894 "The Origin of Sacred Numbers", American Anthropologist 7, 168-73.
Brough, J.
  1959 "The Tripartite Ideology of the Indo-Europeans: An Experiment in
        Method", Bulletin of the School of Oriental and African Studies 22,
        69-95.
Brown, Dora Worral
  1960 "Does Language Structure Influence Thought?", ETC: A Review of
        General Semantics 17, 339-45.
Brown, Norman O.
  1959 Life against Death (New York: Random House).
Brunvand, Jean
  1960 "More Non-Oral Riddles", Western Folklore 19, 132-33.
  1963 "A Classification for Shaggy Dog Stories", JAF 76, 42-68.
  1964 "Have you Heard the Elephant (Joke)?", Western Folklore 23, 198-99.
  1968 The Study of American Folklore: An Introduction (New York: W. W.
        Norton).
Buckland, A. W.
  1895 "Four, as a Sacred Number", Journal of the Anthropological Institute
        25, 96-102.
Burk, Caroline Frear
  1900 "The Collecting Instinct", Pedagogical Seminary 7, 179-207.
Bury, J. B.
  1955 The Idea of Progress: An Inquiry into its Origin and Growth (New York).
Caillois, Roger
  1961 Man, Play, and Games, translated by Meyer Barash (New York).
Caldwell, James R.
  1945 "A Tale Actualized in a Game", JAF 58, 50.
Campbell, Joseph
  1956 The Hero with a Thousand Faces (New York: Meridian).
Carvalho Neto, Paulo de
  1956a Concepto de Folklore (Montevideo: Editorial Livraria Monteiro Lobato).
  1956b Folklore y psicoanalisis (Buenos Aires: Editorial Pisque).
  1962 La Investigación Folklorica (Fases y Técnicas) (Quito: Editorial Uni-
        versitaria).
Chao, Yuen Ren
  1959 "How Chinese Logic Operates", Anthropological Linguistics 1, 1-8.
Child, Francis James
  1962 The English and Scottish Popular Ballads, 5 vols. (New York: Cooper
        Square Publishers).
Childe, V. Gordon
  1956 Piecing together the Past (New York: Frederick A. Praeger).
Christiansen, Reidar Th.
  1953 "Knut Liestøl in memoriam", Norveg 3, 1-16.
  1958 "Myth, Metaphor, and Simile", in T. A. Sebeok (ed.), Myth: A Sym-
        posium (Bloomington, Ind.).

1962 European Folklore in America (= Studia Norvegica 12) (Oslo: Universitetsforlaget).

Clift, J. G. N.
1909 "Fasting", Journal of the British Archaeological Association 15, 157-70.

Cloud, Henry Roe
1916 "From Wigwam to Pulpit", Southern Workman 45, 400-406.

Comas, Juan
1960 Manual of Physical Anthropology (Springfield: Charles C. Thomas).

Count, Earl W.
1952 "The Earth-diver and the Rival-twins: a Clue to Time Correlation in North-Eurasiatic and North American Mythology", in Tax (1952).

Cox, George W.
1881 An Introduction to the Science of Comparative Mythology and Folklore (London).

Craigie, W. A.
1898 "Evald Tang Kristensen, A Danish Folklorist", Folk-Lore, 194-224.

Crane, T. F.
1888 "The Diffusion of Popular Tales", JAF 1, 8-15.

Crawley, E. S.
1897 "The Origin and Development of Number Symbolism", Popular Science Monthly 51, 524-34.

Cray, Ed and Marilyn Eisenberg Herzog
1967 "The Absurd Elephant: A Recent Riddle Fad", Western Folklore 26, 27-36.

Davidson, Levette Jay
1951 A Guide to American Folklore (Denver: University of Denver Press).

Dégh, Linda
1968a "The Hook", Indiana Folklore 1, 92-100.
1968b "The Runaway Grandmother", Indiana Folklore 1, 68-77.

Deonna, W.
1954 "Trois, superlatif absolu", L'Antiquité Classique 23, 403-28.

Dessauer, Renata
1928 Das Zersingen. Ein Beitrag zur Psychologie des deutschen Volksliedes (= Germanische Studien 61) (Berlin).

Devereux, George
1951 "Cultural and Characterological Traits of the Mohave Related to the Anal Stage of Psychosexual Development", Psychoanalytic Quarterly 20, 398-422.

Doren, Charles van
1967 The Idea of Progress (New York).

Dorson, Richard M.
1950 "Folklore and Fake Lore", American Mercury 70 (March), 335-43.
1951 "Folklore Studies in the United States Today", Folklore 62, 353-66.
1955 "The Eclipse of Solar Mythology", JAF 68, 393-416.
1957 "Standards for Collecting and Publishing American Folktales", JAF 70, 53-57.
1959a American Folklore (Chicago: University of Chicago Press).
1959b "A Theory for American Folklore", JAF 72, 197-215.

1963a "The American Folklore Scene, 1963", Folklore 74, 433-49.

1963b "Current Folklore Theories", Current Anthropology 4, 93-112.

1964 Buying the Wind (Chicago: University of Chicago Press).

Dragomanov, Mixailo Petrovic

1961 Notes on the Slavic Religio-ethical Legends: The Dualistic Creation of the World (= Russian and East European Series 23) (Bloomington: Indiana University Publications).

Drake, Carlos C.

1967 "Jung and his Critics", JAF 80, 321-33.

Drake, Samuel Adams

1900 The Myths and Fables of To-Day (Boston).

Dumézil, Georges

1958 L'idéologie tripartite des Indo-Européens (Brussels: Collection Latomus).

Dundes, Alan

1961 "Brown County Superstitions", Midwest Folklore 11, 25-56.

1962a "From Etic to Emic Units in the Structural Study of Folktales", JAF 75, 95-105. Reprinted in this volume.

1962b "On the Psychology of Collecting Folklore", Tennessee Folklore Society Bulletin 28, 65-74. Reprinted in this volume.

1962c "Re: Joyce - No in at the Womb", Modern Fiction Studies 8.2 (Summer), 137-47.

1962d "The Binary Structure of 'Unsuccessful Repetition' in Lithuanian Folk Tales", Western Folklore 21, 165-74.

1962e "Trends in Content Analysis: A Review Article", Midwest Folklore 12, 37.

1962f "The Father, the Son, and the Holy Grail", Literature and Psychology 12, 101-12. Reprinted in this volume.

1962g "Earth-Diver: Creation of the Mythopoeic Male", American Anthropologist 64, 1032-51. Reprinted in this volume.

1962h "The Folklore of Wishing Wells", American Imago 19, 27-34.

1963a "Advertising and Folklore", New York Folklore Quarterly 19, 143-51.

1963b "Structural Typology of North American Indian Folktales", Southwestern Journal of Anthropology 19, 121-30. Reprinted in this volume.

1963c "The Elephant Joking Question", Tennessee Folklore Society Bulletin 29, 40-42.

1964a "Robert Lee J. Vance. American Folklore Surveyor of the 1890's", Western Folklore 23, 27-34.

1964b "Texture, Text, and Context", Southern Folklore Quarterly 28, 251-65.

1964c The Morphology of North American Indian Folktales (= Folklore Fellows Communications 195) (Helsinki).

1965a "The Study of Folklore in Literature and Culture: Identification and Interpretation", JAF 78, 136-52. Reprinted in this volume.

1965b Review of Julius E. Heuscher, A Psychiatric Study of Fairy Tales, in JAF 78, 370-71.

1966a "Metafolklore and Oral Literary Criticism", The Monist 50, 505-16. Reprinted in this volume.

1966b "The American Concept of Folklore", Journal of the Folklore Institute 3, 226-49. Reprinted in this volume.

1968a "Introduction to the Second Edition", in Vladimir Propp, Morphology of the Folktale (Austin, Texas).

1968b "Thinking Ahead: A Folkloristic Reflection of the Future Orientation in American Worldview", Anthropological Quarterly 42, 53-72. Reprinted in this volume.

1969 "The Devolutionary Premise in Folklore Theory", Journal of the Folklore Institute 6, 5-19. Reprinted in this volume.

Dundes, Alan (ed.)

1965 The Study of Folklore (Englewood Cliffs, N.J.: Prentice-Hall).

1968 Every Man his Way: Readings in Cultural Anthropology (Englewood Cliffs: Prentice-Hall).

Durost, Walter Nelson

1932 Children's Collecting Activity Related to Social Factors (Teachers College, Columbia University Contributions to Education 535) (New York).

Eikel, Fred, Jr.

1946 "An Aggie Vocabulary of Slang", American Speech 21, 29-36.

Eisler, Michael Joseph

1921 "A Man's Unconscious Phantasy of Pregnancy in the Guise of Traumatic Hysteria: A Clinical Contribution to Anal Erotism", International Journal of Psycho-Analysis 2, 255-86.

The Elephant Book (Los Angeles: Price, Stern, Sloan, 1963).

Elephants, Grapes & Pickles (Los Angeles: Price, Stern, Sloan, 1964).

Elkins, Stanley M.

1959 Slavery (Chicago: University of Chicago Press; New York: Grosset and Dunlap paper reprint).

Elmore, Clyde M. and Donald R. Gorham

1957 "Measuring the Impairment of the Abstracting Function with the Proverb Test", Journal of Clinical Psychology 13, 263-66.

Elwin, Verrier

1949 Myths of Middle India (Madras: Oxford University Press).

1954 Tribal Myths of Orissa (Bombay: Oxford University Press).

Erben, Karel Jaromir

1857 "O dvojici a o trojici v bájeslovī slovanskem" [About the Number two and the Number Three in Slavic Mythology], Časopis Musea Královstvī Českého 31, 268-86; 390-415.

Erdész, Sándor

1961 "The World Conception of Lajos Ami, Storyteller", Acta Ethnographica 10, 327-44.

Farnsworth, William Oliver

1913 Uncle and Nephew in the Old French Chansons de geste (NewYork: Columbia University Press).

Fenichel, Otto

1938 "The Drive to Amass Wealth", Psychoanalytic Quarterly 7, 69-95.

1953 "The Scoptophilic Instinct and Identification", in The Collected Papers of Otto Fenichel, first series (New York).

1954 "Trophy and Triumph", in The Collected Papers of Otto Fenichel, second series (New York).

Ferenczi, Sandor

1950 Further Contributions to the Theory and Technique of Psycho-analysis (= International Psycho-Analytical Library 11) (London: Hogarth).

1956a "The Ontogenesis of the Interest in Money", Sex in Psychoanalysis (New York: Dover).

1956b Sex in Psycho-analysis (New York: Dover).

Firth, Raymond

1926 "Proverbs in Native Life, with Special Reference to those of the Maori", Folk-Lore 37, 134-53, 245-70.

Fischer, Heinrich

1909 "Abortspruch aus Rumänien", Anthropophyteia 6, 439.

Fischer, J. L.

1960 "Sequence and Structure in Folktales", in Wallace (1960).

1963 "The Sociopsychological Analysis of Folktales", Current Anthropology 4, 235-95.

Fiske, John

1873 Myths and Myth-Makers: Old Tales and Superstitions Interpreted by Comparative Mythology (Boston: James R. Osgood).

Forde, Daryll

1954 African Worlds: Studies in the Cosmological Ideas and Social Values of African Peoples (London: Oxford University Press).

Foster, George M.

1966 "World View in Tzintzuntzan: Re-examination of a Concept", in Summa Anthropologica, en homenaje a Roberto J. Weitlaner (Mexico, D. F.: Instituto Nacional de Anthropología e Historia).

Frazer, James G.

1927 The Devil's Advocate: A Plea for Superstition (London).

1935 Creation and Evolution in Primitive Cosmogonies (London:Macmillan).

1951 The Golden Bough, abridged edition (New York).

Freud, Sigmund

1900 "The Interpretation of Dreams", in Freud (1938).

1913 "Totem and Taboo", in Freud (1938).

1917 A General Introduction to Psycho-analysis (New York: Permabooks, 1953).

1938a The Basic Writings of Sigmund Freud (New York: Modern Library).

1938b "Three Contributions to the Theory of Sex", in Freud (1938a).

1949a Collected Papers 2 (London: Hogarth).

1949b Collected Papers 3 (London: Hogarth).

1949c "Character and Anal Erotism", Collected Papers, vol. 2 (London).

1957 The Future of an Illusion, trans. by W. D. Robson-Scott (Garden City: Doubleday Anchor Books).

1958 Civilization and its Discontents, translated from the German by Joan Riviere (Garden City).

1960 Jokes and their Relation to the Unconscious, translated by James Strachey (London).

Freud, Sigmund and D. E. Oppenheim

1958 Dreams in Folklore (New York: International Universities Press).

Fromm, Erich

1951 The Forgotten Language (New York: Grove Press).

Gaidoz, H.

1885 "Folklore in the United States", Mélusine 2, 530-38.

Geertz, Clifford
1957 "Ethos, World-view and the Analysis of Sacred Symbols", Antioch Review 17, 421-37. Reprinted in Dundes (1968).

Geil, William Edgar
1926 The Sacred 5 of China (Boston and New York: Houghton and Mifflin).

Georges, Robert A. and Alan Dundes
1963 "Toward a Structural Definition of the Riddle", JAF 76, 111-18.

Gerould, Gordon Hall
1957 The Ballad of Tradition (New York).

Gilbert, Eugene
1963 "Elephants Lead the Herd of Teener Jokes", AP Newsfeature (November, 14).

Ginsberg, Morris
1963 The Idea of Progress: A Revaluation (London).

Ginzberg, Louis
1925 The Legends of the Jews, vol. 1 (Philadelphia: Jewish Publication Society of America).

Glade, Dieter
1966 "Zum Anderson'schen Gesetz der Selbstberichtigung", Fabula 8, 224-36.

Glenn, Jules
1965 "Sensory Determinants of the Symbol Three", Journal of the American Psychoanalytic Association 13, 422-34.

Göbel, Fritz
1935 Formen und Formeln der epischen Dreiheit in der griechisden Dichtung (Stuttgart: W. Kohlhammer).

Goja, Hermann
1920 "Das Zersingen der Volkslieder. Ein Beitrag zur Psychologie der Volksdichtung", Imago 6, 132-242.
1964 "The Alteration of Folksongs by Frequent Singing: A Contribution to the Psychology of Folk Poetry", in Sidney Axelrad and Warner Münsterberger (eds.), The Psychoanalytic Study of Society (New York), III, 111-70.

Goldhizer, Ignaz
1876 Der Mythus bei den Hebräern und seine geschichtliche Entwickelung (Leipzig).

Goldstein, Kenneth S.
1964 A Guide for Field Workers in Folklore (Hatboro, Pennsylvania: Folklore Associates).

Gomme, Alice Bertha
1964 The Traditional Games of England, Scotland, and Ireland (New York).

Gorham, Donald R.
1956 "Use of the Proverbs Test for Differentiating Schizophrenics from Normals", Journal of Consulting Psychology 20, 435-40.

Gossen, Gary H.
1964 "A Version of the Potawatomi Coon-Wolf Cycle: A Traditional Projection Screen for Acculturative Stress", in Search: Selected Studies by Undergraduate Honors Students at the University of Kansas 4 (Spring), 8-14.

Goudy, Henry
1910   Trichotomy in Roman Law (Oxford: Clarendon Press).
Griffin, William J.
1959   "The TFS Bulletin and Other Folklore Serials in the United States: A
Preliminary Survey", Tennessee Folklore Society Bulletin 25, 91-96.
Groot, Adriaan D. de
1965   Saint Nicholas: A Psychoanalytic Study of his History and Myth (The
Hague: Mouton).
Guirand, Felix
1959   "Assyro-Babylonian Mythology", in Larousse Encyclopedia of Mythology (New York: Prometheus Press).
Günther, R. F.
1912   "Worauf beruht die Vorherrschaft der Drei im Menschen?", Nord und
Süd 142, 313-25.
Hain, Mathilde
1951   Sprichwort und Volkssprache: Eine volkskundliche-soziologische Dorf-
untersuchung (= Giessener Beiträge zur deutsche Philologie 95) (Gies-
sen).
Hall, Edward T.
1959   The Silent Language (New York: Fawcett Publications).
Hall, G. Stanley
1891   "Children's Collections", Pedagogical Seminary 1, 234-37.
Halliday, W. R.
1913   Greek Divination (London).
Hallowell, A. Irving
1938   "Freudian Symbolism in the Dream of a Salteaux Indian", Man 38,
47-48.
1947   "Myth, Culture, and Personality", American Anthropologist 49, 544-
56.
Halpert, Violetta
1950   "Folk Cures from Indiana", Hoosier Folklore 9, 1-12.
Hand, Wayland D.
1943   "North American Folklore Societies", JAF 59, 477-94.
1946   "North American Folklore Societies: A Supplement", JAF 59, 477-94.
1960   "American Folklore After Seventy Years: Survey and Prospect", JAF
73, 1-11.
1965   "Status of European and American Legend Study", Current Anthropology 6, 439-46.
Hans, Marcie and Lynn Babcock
1963   There's an Elephant in My Sandwich (New York: Citadel Press).
Harrison, Barbara
1963   "Dundes Continued", American Anthropologist 65, 921-22.
Hartland, Edwin Sydney
1890   The Science of Fairy Tales (London).
1895   "The Forbidden Chamber", Folk-Lore Journal 3, 39.
1896   The Legend of Perseus (London).
Haywood, Charles
1961   A Bibliography of North American Folklore and Folksong, 2 vols.,
2nd ed. (New York: Dover).

Heilbroner, Robert L.
1959 The Future as History (New York: Harper and Row).
Heizer, Robert F.
1962 "The Background of Thomsen's Three-age System", Technology and Culture 3, 259-66.
Herskovits, Melville J.
1930 "Kru Proverbs", JAF 43, 225-93.
1946 "Folklore after a Hundred Years: a Problem in Redefinition", JAF 59, 89-100.
1950 "The Hypothetical Situation: A Technique of Field Research", Southwestern Journal of Anthropology 6, 32-40.
Herskovits, Melville J. and Frances S.
1958 Dahomean Narrative (Evanston, Ill.).
Herzog, George
1936 Jabo Proverbs from Liberia (London: Oxford University Press).
1945 "Drum-signalling in a West African Tribe", Word 1, 217-38.
Hickerson, Joseph C., and Alan Dundes
1962 "Mother Goose Vice Verse", JAF 75, 249-59.
Hocart, A. M.
1948 "Fasting", in Encyclopaedia of the Social Sciences, ed. by Edwin R.A. Seligman (New York: Macmillan), vol. 5, 144.
Hockett, Charles F.
1958 A Course in Modern Linguistics (New York).
Hodgen, Margaret T.
1936 The Doctrine of Survivals: A Chapter in the History of Scientific Method in the Study of Man (London).
Hoijer, Harry
1954 Language in Culture (Chicago: University of Chicago Press).
Holmes, Urban T.Jr. and Sister M.Amelia Klenke
1959 Chrétien, Troyes and the Grail (Chapel Hill).
Honti, Hans
1939 "Märchenmorphologie und Märchentypologie", Folk-Liv 3, 307-18.
Huckel, Helen
1953 "Vicarious Creativity", Psychoanalysis 2.2, 44-50.
Hultkrantz, Åke
1950 General Ethnological Concepts (= International Dictionary of Regional European Ethnology and Folklore (Copenhagen).
Hyatt, Harry M.
1935 "Folk-Lore from Adams County Illinois", Memoirs of the Alma Egan Hyatt Foundation (New York).
Hymes, Dell
1962 "The Ethnography of Speaking", in Thomas Gladwin and W.C. Sturtevant (eds.), Anthropology and Human Behavior (Washington: Anthropological Society of Washington), 13-53.
Inman, Thomas
1868 Ancient Faiths Embodied in Ancient Names (London).
Isaac-Edersheim, E.
1941 "Der ewige Jude", Internationale Zeitschrift für Psychoanalyse 26, 286-315.

Jacobs, Joseph
 1894 "The Problem of Diffusion: Rejoinders", Folk-Lore 5, 129-46.
Jacobs, Melville
 1959a The Content and Style of an Oral Literature (Chicago: University of
   Chicago Press).
 1959b "Folklore", The Anthropology of Franz Boas (= Memoir 89 of the
   American Anthropological Association) (San Francisco: Howard Chand-
   ler), 119-38.
 1959c Review of V. Propp, Morphology of the Folktale, in JAF 72, 195-96.
 1960 The People are Coming Soon (Seattle: University of Washington Press).
 1964 "Oral Literature", Pattern in Cultural Anthropology (Homewood, Ill.:
   Dorsey Press), 319-45.
Jakobson, Roman
 1939 "Franz Boas' Approach to Language", International Journal of American
   Linguistics 10, 188-95.
Jakobson, Roman, and P. Bogatyrev
 1929 "Die Folklore als besondere Form des Schaffens", in Donum Natalicium
   Schrijnen: Verzameling van Opstellen door Oud-leerlingen en Bevriende
   Vakgenooten opgedragen aan Mgr. Prof. Dr. Jos. Schrijnen (Nijmegen-
   Utrecht: Dekker), 900-13.
Jakobson, Roman and Morris Halle
 1956 Fundamentals of Language (The Hague: Mouton).
Jimenez, A.
 1960 Picardía Mexicana (Mexico City, Libro Mex).
Jones, Ernest
 1950 Papers on Psycho-Analysis, 5th ed. (London).
 1951a Essays in Applied Psycho-analysis, 2 (= International Psycho-Analytical
   Library 41) (London: Hogarth).
 1951b "The Psychology of Religion", in Jones (1951a).
 1951c "Psycho-Analysis and the Christian Religion", in Jones (1951a).
 1951d "A Psycho-Analytic Study of the Holy Ghost Concept", in Jones (1951a).
 1951e "Mother-Right and the Sexual Ignorance of Savages", in Jones (1951a).
 1951f "Psycho-Analysis and Anthropology", in Jones (1951a).
 1957 "How to Tell your Friends from Geniuses", Saturday Review 40
   (August, 10), 9-10, 39-40.
 1961 "Anal-erotic Character Traits", in Papers on Psycho-analysis
   (Boston: Beacon Press), 413-37.
Jung, Carl Gustav
 1916 Psychology of the Unconscious (New York: Moffat, Yard and Co.).
 1958 Psyche and Symbol (Garden City).
Jung, Carl G. and Carl Kerenyi
 1963 Essays on a Science of Mythology (New York).
Kaplan, Bert
 1962 "Psychological Themes in Zuni Mythology and Zuni TAT's", The
   Psychoanalytic Study of Society 2, 255-62.
Kardiner, Abram
 1939 The Individual and his Society (New York: Columbia University Press).
 1945 The Psychological Frontiers of Society (New York: Columbia University
   Press).
Karpman, Ben D.
 1948 "Corprophilia: A Collective Review", Psychoanalytic Review 35, 243-72.

Kiefer, Emma Emily
1947 Albert Wesselski and Recent Folktale Theories (= Indiana University Publications, Folklore Series 3) (Bloomington).
Kiell, Norman
1963 Psychoanalysis, Psychology and Literature: A Bibliography (Madison: University of Wisconsin Press).
Kimmerle, Marjorie M.
1947 "A Method of Collecting and Classifying Folk Sayings", Western Folklore 6, 351-66.
Kirfel, Willibald
1948 Die dreiköpfige Gottheit (Bonn: Ferd. Dümmlers Verlag).
Klein, Melanie
1960 The Psycho-Analysis of Children (New York: Grove Press).
Kluckhohn, Clyde
1949 "The Philosophy of the Navaho Indians", in Northrop (1949).
1953 "Universal Categories of Culture", in Kroeber (1953).
1959 "Recurrent Themes in Myths and Mythmaking", Proceedings of the American Academy of Arts and Sciences 88, 268-79.
Kluckhohn, Clyde, Henry A. Murray, and David M. Schneider (eds.)
1953 Personality in Nature, Society and Culture 2 (New York: Alfred A. Knopf).
Kluckhohn, Florence Rockwood
1953 "Dominant and Variant Value Orientations", in Kluckhohn et al. (1953).
Köhler, Wolfgang
1959 Gestalt Psychology (New York: Mentor Books).
Köngas, Elli Kaija
1960 "The Earth-Diver (Th A. 812)", Ethnohistory 7, 151-80.
Kramer, Samuel Noah
1959 History Begins at Sumer (New York).
Krappe, Alexander H.
1930 The Science of Folklore (New York: The Dial Press).
Kris, Ernst
1952 Psychoanalytic Explorations in Art (New York: International Universities Press).
Kroeber, A. L. (ed.)
1953 Anthropology Today (Chicago: University of Chicago Press).
Krohn, Kaarle
1926 Die Folkloristische Arbeitsmethode (= Instituttet for Sammenlignende Kulturforskning, series B, 5) (Oslo).
Kubie, Lawrence S.
1937 "The Fantasy of Dirt", Psychoanalytic Quarterly 6, 388-425.
Kuusi, Matti
1957 Parömiologische Betrachtungen (= Folklore Fellows Communications 172) (Helsinki).
1966 "Ein Vorschlag für die Terminologie der parömiologischen Strukturanalyse", Proverbium 5, 97-104.
Lado, Robert
1957 Linguistics across Cultures (Ann Arbor).

Lang, Andrew
   1899   Myth, Ritual and Religion, vol. 1 (London: Longmans, Green, and Co.).
Laoye, H. H.
   1954   "Yoruba Drums", Nigeria 45, 4-13.
La Sorsa, S.
   1963   "Il numero tre nella medicina popolare", Annali di Medicina Navale
          68:171-74.
Leach, MacEdward
   1962   "Problems of Collecting Oral Literature", Publications of the Modern
          Language Association 77, 335-430.
Leach, Maria
   1949- The Standard Dictionary of Folklore, Mythology and Legend, 2 vols.
   50   (New York: Funk and Wagnalls Company).
Lease, Emory B.
   1919   "The Number Three, Mysterious, Mystic, Magic", Classical Phil-
          ology 14, 56-73.
Lee, Dorothy
   1950   "Codifications of Reality: Lineal and Nonlineal", Psychosomatic
          Medicine 12, 89-97. Reprinted in Dundes (1968), 329-43.
Legman, G.
   1952   "Rationale of the Dirty Joke", Neurotica 9 (Winter), 49-64.
   1964   The Horn Book: Studies in Erotic Folklore and Bibliography (New Hyde
          Park, N. Y.: University Books).
Legros, Elisée
   1962   Sur les noms et les tendances du folklore (= Collection d'études publiée
          par le Musée de la vie wallonne 1) (Liège).
Lehmann, Alfred
   1914   Dreiheit und dreifache Wiederholung im deutschen Volksmärchen
          (Leipzig: Robert Noske).
Leisure, Harold Laurence
   1940   "American Legends in the Making", Southern Literary Messenger 2,
          331-34.
Lessa, William A.
   1961   Tales from Ulithi Atoll: A Comparative Study in Oceanic Folklore
          (University of California Publications Folklore Studies 13) (Berkeley
          and Los Angeles: University of California Press).
Lévi-Strauss, Claude
   1958   "The Structural Study of Myth", in Sebeok (1958).
   1960a "The Problems of Invariance in Anthropology", Diogenes 3 (Fall), 22.
   1960b "L'analyse morphologique de contes russes", International Journal of
          Slavic Linguistics and Poetics 3, 122-49.
   1963   Structural Anthropology (New York: Basic Books).
Lévy-Bruhl, Lucien
   1936   Primitives and the Supernatural, trans. Lilian A. Clare (London).
Lindner, Robert (ed.)
   1953   Explorations in Psychoanalysis (New York: Julian Press).

Littleton, C. Scott
1967 "Toward a Genetic Model for the Analysis of Ideology: the Indo-European Case", Western Folklore 26, 37-47.

Locke, Frederick W.
1960 The Quest for the Holy Grail (= Stanford Studies in Language and Literature 21).

Lombroso, Cesare
1895 The Man of Genius (London: Walter Scott).

Loomis, Roger Sherman
1927 Celtic Myth and Arthurian Romance (New York).

Lord, Albert B.
1960 The Singer of Tales (Cambridge, Mass.: Harvard University Press).

Lovejoy, Arthur O.
1957 The Great Chain of Being (Cambridge, Mass.).

Lovejoy, Arthur O. and George Boas
1935 Primitivism and Related Ideas in Antiquity (Baltimore).

Lowie, Robert H.
1908 "The Test-Theme in North American Mythology", JAF 21, 109.
1925 "Five as a Mystic Number", American Anthropologist 27, 578.

Lukas, Franz
1894 "Das Ei als kosmogonische Vorstellung", Zeitschrift des Vereins für Volkskunde 4, 227-43.

MacCulloch, J. A.
1951 "Fasting (Introductory and Non-Christian)", in Hasting's Encyclopaedia of Religion and Ethics (New York: Charles Scribner), vol. 5, 759.

Malinowski, Bronislaw
1922 Argonauts of the Western Pacific (New York: E. P. Dutton).
1935 Coral Gardens and their Magic II (New York: American Book Company).
1954 Magic, Science and Religion (Garden City: Doubleday).

Mallery, Garrick
1888 "Manners and Meals", American Anthropologist 1, 193-207.

Mann, John
1958 "The Folktale as a Reflector of Individual and Social Structure", unpublished doctoral dissertation (Columbia University).

Maranda, Elli-Kaija Köngäs
1963 "The Concept of Folklore", Midwest Folklore 13, 69-88.

Martin, György and Ernö Pesovár
1961 "A Structural Analysis of the Hungarian Folk Dance (A Methodological Sketch)", Acta Ethnographica 10, 1-40.

Maspero, G.
1915 Popular Stories of Ancient Egypt, translated by C. H. W. Johns (New York).

Matthews, Washington
1902 "Myths of Gestation and Parturition", American Anthropologist 4, 737-42.

May, Earl Chapin
1932 The Circus from Rome to Ringling (New York: Duffield and Green).

McClelland, David C. and G. A. Friedman
1952 "A Cross-cultural Study of the Relationship between Child-training

Practices and Achievement Motivation Appearing in Folk Tales", in Swanson et al. (1952).

McMillan, Douglas J.
1964 "A Survey of Theories Concerning the Oral Transmission of the Traditional Ballad", Southern Folklore Quarterly 28, 299-309.

Mead, Margaret and Martha Wolfenstein (eds.)
1955 Childhood in Contemporary Cultures (Chicago: University of Chicago Press).

Messenger, John C., Jr.
1959 "The Role of Proverbs in a Nigerian Judicial System", Southwestern Journal of Anthropology 15, 64-73.

Miller, Robert J.
1952 "Situation and Sequence in the Study of Folklore", JAF 65, 29-48.

Milner, G. B.
1969a "What Is a Proverb?", New Society 332 (6 Febr), 199-202.
1969b "Quadripartite Structures", Proverbium 14, 379-83.
1969c "De l'armature des locutions proverbales: Essai de taxonomie sémantique", L'Homme 9, 49-70.

Mitra, Sarat Chandra
1901 "Riddles Current in Bihar", Journal of the Asiatic Society of Bengal 70.3, 33-58.

Moedano, N., Gabriel
1963 "El folklore como disciplina antropológica", Tlatoani 17, 37-50.

Moll, Otto E.
1958 Sprichwörter-bibliographie (Frankfurt).

Morgan, Lewis H.
1876 "Ethnical Periods", Proceedings of the American Association for the Advancement of Science 24, 266-74.

Morote Best, Efraín
1950 Elementos de Folklore (Definición, Contenido, Procedimiento) (Cuzco, Peru: Universidad Nacional del Cuzco).

Müller, Raimund
1903 "Die Zahl 3 in Sage, Dichtung, und Kunst", in XXX Jahresbericht der K. K. Staats-Oberrealschule in Teschen am Schlusse des Schuljahres 1902-1903 (Teschen: K. und K. Hofbuchdruckerei Karl Prochaska), 1-23.

Nadel, S. F.
1937 "A Field Experiment in Racial Psychology", British Journal of Psychology 28, 195-211.

Nathhorst, Bertel
1968 "Genre, Form and Structure in Oral Tradition", Temenos 3, 128-35.

Nettl, Bruno
1962 An Introduction to Folk Music in the United States, 2nd ed. (Detroit: Wayne State University Press).

Neumann, Siegfried
1966 "Zur Terminologie der parömiologischen Struktur-analyse", Proverbium 6, 130.

Newell, William Wells
1888a "On the Field and Work of a Journal of American Folk-Lore", JAF 1, 1-7.

1888b "Notes and Queries", JAF 1, 79-81.
1888c "Folk-Lore and Mythology", JAF 1, 163.
1888d "Gypsy Lore Society", JAF 1, 235.
1890 "The Study of Folklore", Transactions of the New York Academy of Sciences 9, 134-36.
1895 "Folk-lore Studies and Folk-lore Societies", JAF 8, 231-42.
1898 Review of R. E. Dennett, Notes on the Folk-Lore of the Fjort, in JAF 11, 302-04.
1963 Games and Songs of American Children (New York).
Northrop, F. S. C.
1949 Ideological Differences and World Order (New Haven: Yale University Press).
Olrik, Axel
1909 "Epische Gesetze der Volksdichtung", Zeitschrift für deutsches Altertum 51, 1-12.
1965 "Epic Laws of Folk Narrative", in Dundes (1965). = Translation of Olrik (1909).
Opie, Iona and Peter (ed.)
1951 Oxford Dictionary of Nursery Rhymes (Oxford).
Orlansky, Harold
1949 "Infant Care and Personality", Psychological Bulletin 46, 1-48.
Ortutay, Gyula
1959 "Principles of Oral Transmission in Folk Culture", Acta Ethnographica 8, 175-221.
The Oxford Dictionary of English Proverbs, 2nd ed. (Oxford, 1948).
Paine, Levi Leonard
1901 The Ethnic Trinities and their Relations to the Christian Trinity (Boston and New York: Houghton, Mifflin).
Parsons, Elsie Clews
1916 "The Favorite Number of the Zuni", Scientific Monthly 3, 596-600.
Patai, Raphael, Francis Lee Utley, and Dov Noy (eds.)
1960 Studies in Biblical and Jewish Folklore (= American Folklore Society Memoir 51) (Bloomington: Indiana University Press).
Pearce, T. M.
1954- "Tracing a New Mexican Folk Play", New Mexico Folklore Record 9,
55 20-22.
Penzer, Norman M.
1923 The Ocean of Story: Being C. H. Tawney's Translation of Somadeva's Kathā Sarit Sāgara II, 120-121, III, 109-110 (London).
Petsch, Robert
1899 Neue Beiträge zur Kenntnis des Volksrätsels, in Palaestra 4 (Berlin).
Pike, Kenneth L.
1954- Language in Relation to a Unified Theory of the Structure of Human
60 Behavior, 3 parts (Glendale, California: Summer Institute of Linguistics).
Posinsky, S. H.
1957 "The Problem of Yurok Anality", American Imago 14, 3-31.
Post, Emily
1960 Etiquette 10th ed. (New York: Funk and Wagnalls).

Pound, Louise
1952 "The Scholarly Study of Folklore", Western Folklore 11, 100-108.
Prescott, Joseph
1952 "Notes on Joyce's Ulysses", Modern Language Quarterly 13, 149.
Propp, Vladimir
1958 Morphology of the Folktale (= Indiana University Research Center in
Anthropology, Folklore, and Linguistics Publication 10), edited by
Svatava Pirkova-Jakobson. Also issued as part III of IJAL 24.4 and as
volume 9 of the Bibliographical and Special Series of the American
Folklore Society.
Puckett, Newbell N.
1926 Folk Beliefs of the Southern Negro (Chapel Hill).
Pudney, John
1954 The Smallest Room (London: Michael Joseph).
Radin, Paul
1914 "Religion of the North American Indians", Journal of American Folklore 36, 335-73.
1956 The Trickster (New York: Philosophical Library).
Raglan, Lord
1956 The Hero (New York: Vintage).
1957 "Reply to Bascom", JAF 70, 359-60.
Ramos, Arthur
1958 Estudos de Folk-Lore: Definiçã e Limites, Teorias de Interpretaçāo,
2nd ed. (Rio de Janeiro: Livraria-Editôra do Casa do Estudante do
Brasil).
Rank, Otto
1912 "Die Symbolschichtung im Wecktraum und ihre Wiederkehr im Mythi-
schen Denken", Jahrbuch für psychoanalytische Forschungen 4, 51-115.
1922 Psychoanalytische Beiträge zur Mythenforschung 2 (Leipzig: Interna-
tionaler Psychoanalytischer Verlag).
1959 The Myth of the Birth of the Hero and Other Writings, ed. by Philips
Freund (New York: Vintage).
Rank Otto, and Hanns Sachs
1916 The Significance of Psychoanalysis for the Mental Sciences (= Nervous
and Mental Disease Monograph Series 23) (New York).
Raymond, Joseph
1954 "Attitudes and Cultural Patterns in Spanish Proverbs", The Americas
11, 57-77.
Read, Allen Walker
1935 Lexical Evidence from Folk Epigraphy in Western North America
(Paris, privately printed).
Redfield, Robert
1952 "The Primitive World View", Proceedings of the American Philosophical Society 96, 30-36.
1953 "Primitive World View and Civilization", in The Primitive World and
its Transformations (Ithaca: Cornell University Press).
1959 "Anthropological Understanding of Man", Anthropological Quarterly
32, 3-21.

Redlich, E. Basil
  1939 Form Criticism: Its Value and Limitations (London).
Reik, Theodor
  1915 "Gold und Kot", Internationale Zeitschrift für Psychoanalyse 3, 183.
Reynolds, Reginald
  1943 Cleanliness and Godliness (London: George Allen and Unwin).
Richmond, W. Edson (ed.)
  1957 Studies in Folklore (Bloomington: Indiana University Press).
Richmond, W. Edson, and Elva van Winkle
  1958 "Is there a Doctor in the House?", Indiana History Bulletin 35, 115-35.
Rigby, Douglas and Elizabeth
  1944 Lock, Stock and Barrel: The Story of Collecting (Philadelphia, New
        York, London).
Roberts, John M., Brian Sutton Smith, and Adam Kendon
  1963 "Strategy in Games and Folk Tales", Journal of Social Psychology 61,
        185-99.
Róheim, Géza
  1921 "Primitive Man and Environment", International Journal of Psycho-
        Analysis 2, 157-78.
  1922 "Psycho-analysis and the Folk-tale", International Journal of Psycho-
        Analysis 3, 180-86.
  1923 "Heiliges Geld in Melanesien", Internationale Zeitschrift für Psycho-
        analyse 9, 384-401.
  1926 "Die wilde Jagd", Imago 12, 465-77.
  1934 "The Evolution of Culture", International Journal of Psychoanalysis
        15, 394.
  1940 "Society and the Individual", Psychoanalytic Quarterly 9, 526-45.
  1941 "Myth and Folk-tale", American Imago 2, 266-79.
  1943 The Origin and Function of Culture (= Nervous and Mental Disease
        Monograph Series 69) (New York).
  1952 The Gates of the Dream (New York: International Universities Press).
  1953a "Fairy Tale and Dream", The Psychoanalytic Study of the Child 8,
        394-403.
  1953b "Dame Holle: Dream and Folk Tale", in Lindner (1953).
Röhrich, Lutz
  1966 Sage (Stuttgart: J. B. Metzlersche Verlagsbuchhandlung).
Rooth, Anna Birgitta
  1957 "The Creation Myths of the North American Indians", Anthropos 52,
        497-508.
Sagarin, Edward
  1962 The Anatomy of Dirty Words (New York: Lyle Stuart).
Saville, Marshall H.
  1920 The Goldsmith's Art in Ancient Mexico. Indian Notes and Monographs
        (New York: Heye Foundation).
Scheffler, John D.
  1936 "The Idea of Decline in Literature and the Fine Arts in Eighteenth-
        Century England", Modern Philology 34, 155-78.

Schutte, William M.
1957   Joyce and Shakespeare: A Study in the Meaning of Ulysses (New Haven).
Schwartz, Emanuel K.
1956   "A Psychoanalytic Study of the Fairy Tale", American Journal of
       Psychotherapy 10, 740-62.
Schwarzbaum, Haim
1960   "Jewish and Moslem Sources of a Falasha Creation Myth", in Patai
       et al. (1960).
Scott, Charles T.
1965   Persian and Arabic Riddles: A Language-Centered Approach to Genre
       Definition (= Publications of the Research Center in Anthropology,
       Folklore, and Linguistics, Indiana University 39) (Baltimore).
1969   "Some Approaches to the Study of the Riddle", in Bagby Atwood and
       Archibald A. Hill (eds.), Studies in Language, Literature, and Culture
       of the Middle Ages and Later (Austin, Texas), 110-27.
Sebeok, Thomas A.
1953   "The Structure and Content of Cheremis Charms, Part I", Anthropos
       48, 369-88.
1959   "Folksong Viewed as Code and Message", Anthropos 54, 141-53.
Sebeok, Thomas A. (ed.)
1958   Myth: A Symposium (Bloomington: Indiana University Press).
Seeger, Charles
1962   "Who Owns Folklore? - A Rejoinder", Western Folklore 21, 93-101.
Seidenberg, Robert
1952   "The Sexual Basis of Social Prejudice", Psychoanalytic Review 39,
       90-95.
Seifert, Josef Leo
1954   Sinndeutung des Mythos: Die Trinität in den Mythen der Urvolker (Wien,
       München: Verlag Herold).
Shimkin, D. B., and Pedro Sanjuan
1953   "Culture and World View: A Method of Analysis Applied to Rural Rus-
       sia", American Anthropologist 55, 329-48.
Silberer, Herbert
1925   "A Pregnancy Phantasy in a Man", Psychoanalytic Review 12, 377-96.
Simmel, Georg
1902   "The Number of Members as Determining the Sociological Form of the
       Group", American Journal of Sociology 8, 1-46, 158-96.
Skinner, Alanson
1927   "The Mascoutens or Prairie Potawatomi Indians, Part III, Mythology
       and Folklore", Bulletin of the Public Museum of the City of Milwaukee
       6.3 (January).
Smith, W. Robertson
1957   The Religion of the Semites (New York: Meridian Books).
Sneller, Anne Gertrude
1964   "Growing Up", NYFQ 20.2 (June), 89-90.
Sokolov, Y. M.
1950   Russian Folklore, transl. Catherine Ruth Smith (New York).
Spence, Lewis
1921   An Introduction to Mythology (New York: Farrar & Rinehart).

1947   Myth and Ritual in Dance, Game, and Rhyme (London).
Spencer, Katherine
  1947   Reflection of Social Life in the Navaho Origin Myth (= University of New Mexico Publications in Anthropology 3).
Spiro, Melford E.
  1967   Burmese Supernaturalism (Englewood Cliffs, N.J.: Prentice-Hall).
Steinbeck, John
  1939   The Grapes of Wrath (New York: Modern Library).
Tax, Sol, et al. (eds.)
  1953   An Appraisal of Anthropology Today (Chicago: University of Chicago Press).
Tax, Sol (ed.)
  1952   Selected Papers of the 19th International Congress of Americanists (Chicago: University of Chicago Press).
Steiner, Rudolf
  1929   The Interpretation of Fairy Tales (New York).
Stekel, Wilhelm
  1959   Patterns of Psychosexual Infantilism (New York: Grove Press).
Strand, T. A
  1958   Tri-ism: The Theory of the Trinity in Nature, Man and his Works (New York: Exposition Press).
Sutton-Smith, Brian
  1959   "A Formal Analysis of Game Meaning", Western Folklore 18, 13-24.
Swanson, G.E., T.M. Newcomb, and E.L. Hartley (eds.)
  1952   Readings in Social Psychology (New York: Holt).
Szentpal, Olga
  1958   "Versuch einer Formanalyse der Ungarischen Volkstanze", Acta Ethnographica 7, 257-334.
Tavenner, Eugene
  1916   "Three as a Magic Number in Latin Literature", Transactions of the American Philological Association 47, 117-43.
Taylor, Archer
  1938   "Problems in the Study of Riddles", Southern Folklore Quarterly 2, 1-9.
  1943   "The Riddle", California Folklore Quarterly 2, 129-47.
  1951a English Riddles from Oral Tradition (Berkeley and Los Angeles: University of California Press).
  1951b Review of Waldemar Liungman, Sveriges Samtliga Folksagor: Ord Och Bild in Western Folklore 10, 185-86.
  1952   "Riddles", in Frank C. Brown Collection of North Carolina Folklore (Durham).
  1959   Review of V. Propp, Morphology of the Folktale, in The Slavic and East European Journal 17, 187-89.
  1962   The Proverb (Hatboro, Pennsylvania).
Taylor, Archer, and Bartlett Jere Whiting
  1958   A Dictionary of American Proverbs and Proverbial Phrases 1820-1880 (Cambridge).
Thompson, Stith
  1919   European Tales Among the North American Indians: A Study in the

Migration of Folk-Tales (= Colorado College Publication, Language Series II, 34), 319–471.

1929 Tales of the North American Indians (Cambridge: Harvard University Press).

1938 "American Folklore after Fifty Years", JAF 51, 1-9.

1946 The Folktale (New York: The Dryden Press).

1955- Motif-Index of Folk-Literature, 6 vols. , 2nd ed. (Bloomington: Indiana
58 University Press).

1958 "Myths and Folktales", in Myth: A Symposium (Bloomington).

1961 The Types of the Folktale, 2nd revision (= FF Communications 184) (Helsinki: Suomalainen Tiedeakatemia).

Thornton, Weldon

1964 "An Allusion List for James Joyce's Ulysses, Part 2, 'Nestor'", James Joyce Quarterly 1.2 (Winter), 3.

Tillich, Paul

1966 "The Decline and the Validity of the Idea of Progress", in Brauer (1966).

Tindall, W.Y.

1950 James Joyce: His Way of Interpreting the Modern World (New York).

Tupper, Frederick Jr.

1910 The Riddles of the Exeter Book (Boston).

Turner, Lorenzo D

1960 "The Role of Folklore in the Life of the Yoruba of Southwestern Nigeria", in Austin (1960), 45-56.

Tylor, Edward B.

1958 The Origins of Culture (= Primitive Culture, Part I) (New York).

Usener, H.

1903 "Dreiheit", Rheinisches Museum für Philologie 58, 1-47; 161-208; 321-62.

Utley, Francis Lee

1961 "Folk Literature: An Operational Definition", JAF 74, 193-206.

1965 Lincoln wasn't there or Lord Raglan's Hero, supplement to The CEA Critic 22.9, 1-33.

Vance, Robert Lee J.

1893 "Folk-Lore Study in America", Popular Science Monthly 43, 586-98.

Varagnac, André

1965 "Les causes de la décadence du folklore dans les pays industriels", in Georgios A. Megas (ed.), IV International Congress for Folk-Narrative Research in Athens: Lectures and Reports (Athens), 600-05.

Vega, Carlos

1960 La Ciencia del Folklore (Buenos Aires: Editorial Nova).

Voegelin, C.F., and Z.S. Harris

1947 "The Scope of Linguistics", American Anthropologist 49, 588-600.

1952 "Training in Anthropological Linguistics", American Anthropologist 54, 324-25.

Voget, Fred W.

1967 "Progress, Science, History and Evolution in Eighteenth- and Nineteenth-Century Anthropology", Journal of the History of the Behavioral Sciences 3, 132-55.

Vogt, Evon Z.
1955   Modern Homesteaders: The Life of a Twentieth-Century Frontier
       Community (Cambridge: Harvard University Press).
Wachsmuth, Curt
1864   Das alte Griechenland im neuen (Bonn).
Waite, A.E.
1933   The Holy Grail: Its Legends and Symbolism (London).
Von Waldheim, Dr.
1909   "Breslauer Locus-Inschriften", Anthropophyteia 6, 433-35.
Wallace, Anthony F.C. (ed.)
1960   Men and Cultures (Philadelphia).
Waugh, Butler
1966   "Structural Analysis in Literature and Folklore", Western Folklore
       25, 153-64.
Webster's New World Dictionary of the American Language, College Edition
(Cleveland and New York, 1960).
Wertheimer, Max
1923   "Untersuchungen zur Lehre von der Gestalt", Psychologische Forsch-
       ung 4, 301-50.
Westermarck, Edward
1907   "The Principles of Fasting", Folk-Lore 18, 391-422.
1922   The History of Human Marriage 5, vol 2 (New York: The Allerton Book
       Company).
1930   Wit and Wisdom in Morocco: A Study of Native Proverbs (London).
Weston, Jessie L.
1901   The Legend of Sir Lancelot du Lac (London).
1957   From Ritual to Romance (New York: Doubleday Anchor).
Wheeler-Voegelin, Erminie
1949   "Earth Diver", in Standard Dictionary of Folklore, Mythology and
       Legend, vol. 1, ed. by Maria Leach (New York: Funk and Wagnalls).
Wheeler-Voegelin, Erminie and Remedios W. Moore
1957   "The Emergence Myth in Native North America", in Richmond (1957).
White, Newman I.
1952   "The Frank C. Brown Collection: Its History, Nature, and Growth", in
       The Frank C. Brown Collection of North Carolina Folklore (Durham),
       vol. 1, 12-28.
White, William A.
1923   "Psychoanalysis and Vocational Guidance", Psychoanalytic Review 10,
       254-55.
Whiting, B.J.
1932   "The Nature of the Proverb", Harvard University Studies and Notes in
       Philology and Literature 14, 273-307.
1952   "Proverbs and Proverbial Sayings: Introduction", in The Frank C.
       Brown Collection of North Carolina Folklore (Durham, North Carolina).
Whitney, Lois
1924   "English Primitivistic Theories of Epic Origins", Modern Philology
       21, 337-78.
Whorf, Benjamin L.
1964   Language, Thought and Reality (Cambridge, Mass.: MIT Press).

Wilbur, George B. and Warner Münsterberger (eds.)
  1951 Psychoanalysis and Culture (New York: International Universities Press).
Wildhaber, Robert
  1965 "A Bibliographical Introduction to American Folklore", New York Folklore Quarterly 21, 259-302.
Wilgus, Donald K.
  1959 Anglo-American Folksong Scholarship Since 1898 (New Brunswick: Rutgers University Press).
Williams, Robin, M., Jr.
  1952 American Society: A Sociological Interpretation (New York: Alfred A. Knopf).
Witty, Paul A. and Harvey C. Lehman
  1930 "Further Studies of Children's Interest in Collecting", Journal of Educational Psychology 21, 112-27.
Wolfenstein, Martha
  1954 Children's Humor (Glencoe).
  1955 " 'Jack and the Beanstalk': An American Version", in Mead and Wolfenstein (1955).
Worthington, Mabel P.
  1956 "Irish Folk Songs in Joyce's Ulysses", Publications of the Modern Language Association 71.3 (June), 321-39.
Wright, Lawrence
  1960 Clean and Decent (New York: Viking Press).
Wycoco (Moore), Remedios
  1951 "The Types of North-American Indian Tales", unpublished doctoral dissertation (Indiana University).